MW01491867

Negotiation for Procurement and Supply Chain Professionals

Third Edition

Negotiation for Procurement and Supply Chain Professionals

Jonathan O'Brien

Publisher's note

Every possible effort has been made to ensure that the information contained in this book is accurate at the time of going to press, and the publishers and author cannot accept responsibility for any errors or omissions, however caused. No responsibility for loss or damage occasioned to any person acting, or refraining from action, as a result of the material in this publication can be accepted by the editor, the publishers or the author.

First published in Great Britain and the United States in 2013 by Kogan Page Limited as *Negotiation for Purchasing Professionals*
Second edition (*as Negotiation for Procurement Professionals*) 2016
Third edition 2020

Apart from any fair dealing for the purposes of research or private study, or criticism or review, as permitted under the Copyright, Designs and Patents Act 1988, this publication may only be reproduced, stored or transmitted, in any form or by any means, with the prior permission in writing of the publishers, or in the case of reprographic reproduction in accordance with the terms and licences issued by the CLA. Enquiries concerning reproduction outside these terms should be sent to the publishers at the undermentioned addresses:

2nd Floor, 45 Gee Street   122W 27th Street   4737/23 Ansari Road
London EC1V 3RS   New York, NY 10001   Daryaganj
United Kingdom   USA   New Delhi 110002
www.koganpage.com   India

© Jonathan O'Brien 2013, 2016 and 2020

The right of Jonathan O'Brien to be identified as the author of this work has been asserted by him in accordance with the Copyright, Designs and Patents Act 1988.

ISBNs
Hardback   978 1 78966 260 3
Paperback   978 1 78966 258 0
Ebook   978 1 78966 259 7

British Library Cataloguing-in-Publication Data

A CIP record for this book is available from the British Library.

Library of Congress Control Number

2020936072

Typeset by Hong Kong FIVE Workshop
Print production managed by Jellyfish
Printed and bound by CPI Group (UK) Ltd, Croydon CR0 4YY

For Elaine, Emily and Hugh

*Dedicated to the memory of Dave Smith to
whom I am very grateful; who encouraged me to write and
helped me to clarify and structure many of
the complex topics in this and my other books.
A clever man who was always generous with his time
to help others learn and understand things.
You are missed.*

CONTENTS

LIST OF FIGURES

LIST OF TABLES

PREFACE

This award-winning, practical book is for anyone who buys and wants to negotiate more effectively with suppliers. It is a book that provides a proven negotiation process together with 100 winning tactics and techniques to help build repertoire. It also provides real guidance about how to plan and execute negotiations so as to gain greater confidence and secure the best outcomes.

When it comes to negotiation there is often an imbalance between seller and buyer, with the seller having an advantage. An internet search will reveal tens of thousands of books out there about negotiation in one form or another. The problem, however, is that almost all of them are aimed at the seller. Add to this the fact that those in sales roles typically receive more training than buyers and are better resourced, both of which mean they are better able to plan how they will negotiate with you – so the game is not stacked in the buyer's favour. This book seeks to address this imbalance.

Negotiation is often treated as a discrete activity, distinct from the other activities of the procurement or supply chain functions as if it is something different that buyers or supply chain professionals 'go and do' from time to time. But negotiation is part of each and every interaction with a supplier and should be regarded as such, suggesting anyone who interfaces with a supplier requires some degree of negotiation capability.

Good negotiators are made not born, and that means that anyone can become good at negotiation. To the uninitiated the art of negotiation may appear a specialist skill, and despite the plethora of material and training out there, the route to acquiring this skill is often difficult to grasp. This is because negotiation, as a skill, has many layers. All of these need to be understood, considered and used in concert in order for a negotiator to be truly in control. Much of the established theory on negotiation considers only part of what is needed to be effective, perhaps focusing on negotiation tactics for the event itself or the psychological theory that sits behind negotiation. This may be useful for a seasoned negotiator with experience doing it for real, but for those setting out to learn negotiation it can be hard to know where to start and what to do. This book seeks to address this.

Developing negotiation capability requires an understanding and command of negotiation theory and process, brought to life through the deployment of proven tactics and techniques creating what is often referred to as 'negotiation style', which may be unique to an individual. The ability to adapt this negotiation style to suit the negotiation is crucial, and so self-awareness and self-management are also highly important. This book provides a step-by-step approach that empowers buyers and supply chain professionals, puts them in control of a negotiation and enables them to understand and maximize their position based upon the proven Red Sheet® methodology.

This book is aimed specifically at the buying community and those who work with and manage supply chains, and is suitable for virtually anyone at any level. It provides background and structure to understand negotiation theory and it outlines a deep range of winning tactics and techniques. It can help execute critical multimillion-dollar team-based negotiations. It can help the buyer who has a single supplier meeting to prepare, or it can help a supply chain professional secure increased effectiveness and reduce risk. It can help you buy a car or get a better deal on something you want. It can even help your love life (more on that later). If you buy things or mangage supply chains, you need to read this book.

I am interested to learn of your experiences of negotiation and using the approaches outlined in this book. Please feel free to e-mail me at jonathan@jonathanobrien.co.uk and share.

ACKNOWLEDGEMENTS

This is the third edition of the second of the four titles I have written. It is part of the purchasing and procurement trilogy that also includes *Category Management in Purchasing* along with *Supplier Relationship Management*, both also published by Kogan Page. These three titles are designed to work together to provide those in procurement and supply chain functions with the complete toolkit to achieve great results from the supply base.

In this book I wanted to provide something that could really make a difference to how people buy and manage suppliers and supply chains. However, the challenge with negotiation is that, while a good planning process is essential, there will always be the dynamic of the interaction that can bring all sorts of pressures and demands for instant responses on an individual and it is only by understanding what is being played out and having a good repertoire of responses to hand that the individual will then retain the advantage. Writing a book that could bring practical help here was hugely challenging and is somewhat akin to attempting to use words to describe how you ride a bicycle.

I need to thank many people for their contributions to this book. Thanks to Dr Alan Ebbens for burning the midnight oil to do huge amounts of research, for helping me make sense of the psychology around personality and for help to develop the COW SOAP ACE model which I think was first conceived in a hot tub, helped along with a glass of red wine. Thanks to Professor John Potter of John Potter Global who has more than your everyday experience of negotiation but rather has worked with police and security teams the world over to secure release of hostages or resolve security disputes. John freely shared his rich insights and experience and provided much guidance as well as some interesting stories that help properly contextualize what you will find in some of these pages.

Thanks to Dave Smith, who sadly we lost in 2019. It was Dave who encouraged me to start writing these books. Dave was one of the original co-creators of Red Sheet and had a remarkable intellect and ability to bring structure and clarity to complex topics. This he did for many of the things I have developed over the years including some of the concepts in this book, especially the power section, which was conceived as we worked together in Sri Lanka. Thank you – you are greatly missed, Dave.

Thanks to Lisa Barton for throwing in some winning techniques including the mobile phone example. Thanks to Lili Thomas for her help to research NLP, work which subsequently led me to become an NLP Master Practitioner. Thanks to Mark Hubbard for original input on game theory, the flow chart idea and Table 8.5. Thanks to all those who helped to read 'that wot I wrote' to correct all the spelling and grammar misdemeanours I truly believed weren't there when I read it through, namely: Julie Houghton, Angela Garwood and my wife Elaine. Despite this I think my proficiency with the semi-colon has developed further since the first book; I finally feel I've got the little thing under control. Thanks also to the various commissioning editors at Kogan Page for believing in me and for the support during the writing process. Thanks to all the companies and individuals I have worked with as that collective experience has largely shaped my understanding and helped me write this book.

I need to thank those on the team back in 2005 who helped develop the original groundbreaking Red Sheet negotiation approach which has gone on to become what it is today, namely Mark Hubbard, Craig Johnstone, Dave Smith and Philip Usherwood.

The biggest thank you is once more to my family, who gracefully accept without complaint a husband and dad in 'book-writing mode' for extended periods of time. Finally, thank you to you for buying this book. I hope it equips you with something worthwhile and invaluable that will help you in all your future negotiations.

Thank you to the Association of Purchasing and Supply Chain (CESA) of HEC School of Management in Paris for awarding this book (1st edition) as Specially Commended and shortlisting it for the ACA-Bruel Prize in 2013.

Most of the models and concepts in this book are new and original work; many are groundbreaking. I have made every effort to properly research, reference and duly credit all work of others; however, there are some terms and concepts that appear to simply be out in the public domain with no attribution so I apologize if any credit to the originator has been missed.

The Red Sheet methodology given in the Appendix with examples referred to in this book is copyright Positive Purchasing Ltd. It is available as a digital collaborative planning app with resources and a full e-learning library via redsheetonline.com. More details and how to subscribe can be found at www.redsheetnegotiation.com.

ABOUT THE AUTHOR

Jonathan O'Brien is CEO and owner of the international procurement consultancy and training provider, Positive Purchasing Ltd (www.positivepurchasing.com). Jonathan has over 30 years' experience working in procurement. He has worked all over the world to help global organizations transform their procurement capability through training, education and working directly with practitioners and executive teams to drive in the adoption of negotiation, category management, supplier relationship management and other strategic procurement methodologies.

Jonathan is an electronics engineer who moved into procurement. His career in engineering soon shifted into supplier quality assurance, and it was the hundreds of supplier audits undertaken involving detailed examination of business practice and process that provided a sound understanding of how organizations work, and thus began the process of working with companies to help them improve. A move to a senior buying role in a large utility company shifted the focus to the commercial aspects of procurement and this career path culminated in a global category director role for an airline business. Jonathan moved to an internal consultant role and helped lead a series of major organizational change programmes. A subsequent move into consultancy, initially with a large global strategic procurement consultancy and later with his own business, provided Jonathan with the opportunity to work with some of the biggest and best-known companies in the world to help improve procurement capability, gaining a rich experience along the way.

Jonathan holds an MBA from Plymouth University Business School, a Diploma in Marketing and an HNC in Electronics, is a Member of the Chartered Institute of Purchasing (MCIPS), an NLP Master Practitioner and a former registered Lead Assessor of quality management systems.

Jonathan and his team at Positive Purchasing Ltd have developed and created the Red Sheet® negotiation tool that has become the way many individuals and corporations plan and deliver negotiation. It was the world's first negotiation planning tool developed solely for procurement teams and incorporating game theory principles.

Jonathan has published four titles so far with fourteen editions across these and continues to write. His work has been translated around the world. He is also an accomplished broadcaster and artist and lives with his family in Plymouth, UK.

You can e-mail Jonathan at jonathan@jonathanobrien.co.uk.

Introduction

This is a practical book for anyone who buys or manages supply chains. As the chapters unfold so too will a detailed and structured approach to plan and execute the biggest or most important of negotiations. However, striking a multimillion-dollar deal or buying a nuclear submarine may not be an everyday occurrence for most of us. Sometimes we just need to get the right price for something we're buying, ensure we can get what we need from the producer or even figure out how to concede to the demands of our kids without giving too much. This book provides a range of approaches that will help here too.

The book is based around the proven Red Sheet® methodology, a process used the world over to underpin negotiations. It also provides deep insight into what negotiation is and how we can develop personal approaches that will enable us to become highly effective negotiators.

To get the most from this book it is important to do three things: first, read it in its entirety to understand the full end-to-end approach in case you end up having to buy that nuclear submarine at some point; second, decide what to leave out and pick out the bits that will help you with the everyday negotiations; and third, develop your style and build your repertoire. Just like you have your own personality, quirks and things you do or say when you want to show others how you feel, you also need your own negotiation personality or 'negotionality', and this may be something that changes according to the situation.

This book will provide a winning negotiation methodology along with some suggestions, tactics and techniques, but ultimately only you can decide and shape your negotiation style. As Zartman and Berman (1982) suggest, 'good negotiators are made, not born', and you can be as good as your heart desires.

A strategic procurement trilogy

This book is intended to work alongside two further books I have written on key strategic procurement methodologies. Together, these three books have been written as a collection, each designed to enhance, complement and integrate with the frameworks and approaches of negotiation planning and strategic procurement approaches, specifically category management and Supplier Relationship Management (SRM). Indeed, many of the tools you will find in these other two texts can also be found within these pages, applied slightly differently to help structure our negotiation for success. These three separate methodologies are in fact the core strategic approaches necessary for modern, best practice strategic procurement and to be effective need to work in concert with each other. Therefore, this book has been written so as to be used together with *Category Management in Purchasing* and *Supplier Relationship Management* (both also published by Kogan Page). Where a tool has already been expanded in one of these other works it is not repeated again in this book but referenced at a high level. It is recommended all three publications are used together to provide the complete strategic procurement approach.

---

25 pathway questions

This book is organized so as to explore all aspects of negotiation in the most logical way possible. It seeks to provide answers and practical steps for 25 key or 'pathway' questions. If you can answer all of these questions with confidence then you're in great shape. However, for many organizations these are difficult questions that represent the gap between aspiration and reality. They also help reveal the pathway to move towards making effective category management a reality. This book will help to not only form answers to these questions but to develop real actions that enable the firm to progress and realize great value from a quality category management deployment.

Negotiation pathway questions

1 What is negotiation and why do we need to be good at it?

2 What things prevent us from being good negotiators and what things can help us?

3 In what ways do sellers gain an advantage over us in a negotiation and what can I do to counter this?

4 How can I plan for a negotiation? What process do I follow?

5 I need to negotiate something – where do I start?

6   What are the different types of negotiation and how do I decide which one to adopt?

7   How should I determine my ideal negotiation outcomes?

8   How can I ensure a single aligned and united approach amongst everyone on my side who has an interest in the negotiation?

9   If I negotiate across cultures when do I need to adapt my negotiation approach in order to be successful and how exactly can I do this?

10   How do my individual personality traits (and those of others who will negotiate with me) help or hinder a specific negotiation?

11   What behaviours, style and demeanor will help me succeed at negotiating?

12   How can I know my opponent and how best to interact with each individual in order to put myself in the strongest position possible?

13   What power do I hold relative to my opponent?

14   How do I increase my negotiation power position and/or undermine that of my opponent?

15   What is the underlying 'game' my opponent is playing and how do I change the game to my advantage?

16   How do I determine the specific points or requirements to negotiate?

17   How can I manage and stay in control of trades and concessions?

18   What is the best way to manage the meeting or negotiation event?

19   What tactics and techniques will help me be successful?

20   How can I stay in control of my body language and read that of my opponent?

21   How can I tune into what is hidden 'behind the words' of my opponent and how can I manage what I say and how I say it to be most effective?

22   How do I ensure what we agreed during the negotiation is followed through and realized?

23   How do I negotiate effectively with multiple opponents or when I am not face-to-face with my opponent?

24   What must organizations do to improve negotiation capability overall?

25   What can I do to develop my skills to become really good at negotiation?

Introducing negotiation

01

This chapter introduces and defines negotiation and explores types of negotiation and how negotiation works. It considers the link between negotiation and our personality and the need for self-awareness and perhaps compensation for certain personal traits. It also considers how personality needs to be supported by process and repertoire for negotiation to be effective.

Pathway questions addressed in this chapter

1 What is negotiation and why do we need to be good at it?

2 What things prevent us from being good negotiators and what things can help us?

6 What are the different types of negotiation and how do I decide which one to adopt?

We've evolved to negotiate

It's true that good negotiators are made not born, but it's also true that some people seem to have a natural instinct for negotiation. Zartman and Berman (1982) suggest that those who are good at negotiation possess certain characteristics; they are patient and self-assured while having the ingenuity to find winning solutions and the stamina to reach a conclusion. They also suggest good negotiators act with integrity. It is easy to believe that negotiation is a pursuit reserved for a select few who fit the profile, and then perhaps who have some sort of specialist training. This is not the case, and anyone can become a great negotiator, although it is true to say our natural-born personality influences our negotiation ability. However, as we will see, self-awareness and personal adaption can overcome this.

Karrass (1996) states 'in life you don't get what you deserve, you get what you negotiate'. This may, as some including Hansen (2010) argue, be a somewhat adversarial view of negotiation, especially in the context of purchasing negotiation. However, the fact remains that we are able to better our position if we know how to convince others to let us have more than we might otherwise get. Negotiation is in fact something we all do to a greater or lesser extent in our daily lives, although we may not realize it. It is something we learn early on and it is linked closely to our survival instincts and how we have evolved and continue to do so. We naturally want the best we can get for ourselves and then for those close to us. This goal isn't static but rather one that continues to grow. Once we reach one goal, we look for the next and so on. The human tendency is to continually seek to maximize our position. In his groundbreaking 'hierarchy of needs' work, Maslow (1943) describes the individual needs we have as humans and the sequence in which they need to be satisfied before we can realize new needs and therefore grow or develop (see Figure 1.1). In the developed world we have long since evolved to satisfy our basic needs. I am confident in the knowledge that I won't need to go out hunting for food for my evening meal tonight. The

Figure 1.1   An interpretation of Maslow's hierarchy of needs

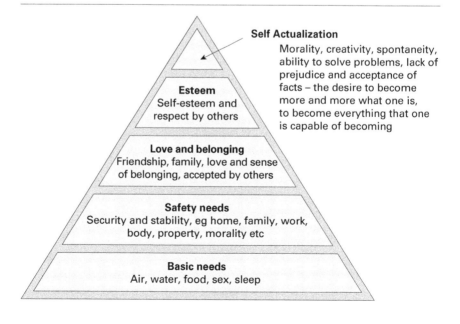

most that will be required will be a trip to the supermarket and after that the refrigerator. However, as the human race is compelled to scramble up the pyramid, from a variety of starting points, it is negotiation that is a key enabler in helping us do this. If you want to see this in action watch how children learn early on to push for what they want. I don't recall ever teaching my children any negotiation tactics but my daughter knew precisely the right time to ambush me with a question like, 'Dad... will you increase my pocket money?' having first checked to see I was in a good mood. She knew that posing the question while doing the 'big saucer eyes' routine would help, and she would even have a series of justifications prepared in the event I said no. These might include 'Everyone else at school is getting more'. Further interrogation by me here would reveal a very low sample size, but then a proposed trade would emerge, this time with benefit to me: 'if you give me a raise I can start taking responsibility for buying my clothes and that means you won't need to take me shopping and wait around in girls shops', and so on.

Negotiation is not a specialist capability, but rather a life skill and one that we all need and develop to a greater or lesser extent. When used in a business context this skill can be readily developed with the use of a good, structured process to plan how we approach the negotiation.

Defining negotiation

Negotiation is the process by which two or more parties confer or interact to reach consensus or agreement. It is an activity with a start, middle and end; a means by which we can move from one place to another and a way for the parties to deal with their differences or reach a resolution to a problem.

It may be formal or informal, face-to-face or without any direct human interaction, a short single event or an ongoing series of interactions. There are many scenarios where negotiation is needed and used; here are some:

- buyer and seller attempting to agree mutually acceptable price, terms and basis for the purchase;
- a supply chain professional working with multiple players in a supply chain to drive improvement or realize CSR objectives;
- a discussion with our kids about what time they need to be home;
- nations at war attempting to reach a peaceful settlement;

- securing the safe release of a hostage;
- an online e-auction;
- the management of a factory attempting to agree new terms and conditions with the workers, perhaps negotiating collectively with a worker's union;
- negotiation by proxy.

Negotiations often take place between individuals, but can also be between groups, with each group acting collectively on behalf of its members or for a company or entity. Sometimes more than two parties may be involved. Tri-partite and multi-partite negotiations are where three or more parties may need to reach a single consensus or agreement. Such negotiations are highly complex and require careful management.

Negotiation involves conferring and some sort of exchange between the parties. A traditional approach, and one that is still insisted upon in many cultures, demands that this happens face-to-face. Salespeople prefer face-to-face interactions where possible because building a relationship, instilling trust and getting the other party to like you are vital enablers to closing a deal. We are social animals and respond more favourably when the other person is opposite us. Face-to-face interaction also increases the opportunity to 'read' the other party and so experienced negotiators will also prefer personal engagements. However, this is not always possible and practical. A face-to-face meeting with a hostage taker is unlikely, so too may be an interaction with a potential new supplier located halfway around the world, and during an e-auction the buyer clearly seeks to prevent any direct contact. Furthermore, our acceptance and comfort with new communication technology is also changing attitudes to negotiation. Increasingly, negotiations are being conducted by phone, webconference, videoconference, e-auction, Skype, e-mail, LinkedIn, online messaging and text. These forms of technology offer a new and alternative approach to negotiation and one that takes away some of the pressure of the situation to perform in front of our opponent, allowing inexperienced negotiators to fare better, provided they learn some basic skills. They do, however, introduce a series of new challenges and we will explore these later.

Claim or create value

Negotiations fall into one of two types according to where the potential value in a negotiation will come from. Luecke (2003) describes these as distributive and integrative, in other words negotiations that either claim value or seek to create value.

Claim value

Here parties negotiate and compete over the distribution of a finite amount of value. This is like dividing a pie (see Figure 1.2); the pie is only so big and what one party claims the other has to give up. 'Claiming' negotiations by their nature are competitive, with the aim of each party to secure the most value. Agreement centres around the portion of the pie parties compete over.

Figure 1.2   The value pie – claiming or creating value

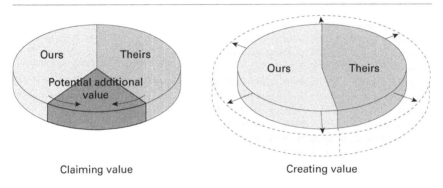

Claiming value   Creating value

Create value

Parties cooperate with the aim of achieving the maximum value between them. Here the objective is to try and grow the pie, giving benefit to both slice-holders. Reaching agreement is based around balance in the effort and energy each party is prepared to contribute to secure the return of the benefits to both parties. If this is unbalanced then there may not be agreement. Negotiators who create value by definition have more value available and so are more likely to achieve a favourable outcome.

The win/win illusion

Negotiation is all about getting a win/win! Well, no, not necessarily. However, the concept of the win/win has been the subject of many negotiation books suggesting this is the only way. It is not, it is just one. In addition to the win/

win there may also be a **WIN**/win, where, although both parties have reached an agreement, the outcome is more balanced in the favour of one party who has secured a much bigger win. There could even be a win/lose where there is still agreement, but reluctant agreement on the part of the losing party, perhaps because they have no choice or perhaps they have been duped in some way, and may not even realize it at the time of agreement. The win/win, **WIN**/win, and win/lose all involve agreement between the parties. In the case of a lose/lose there is no agreement, typically where both parties have walked away. Figure 1.3 shows the different combinations and the nature of the agreement in each case.

Figure 1.3   Different forms of agreement in a negotiation

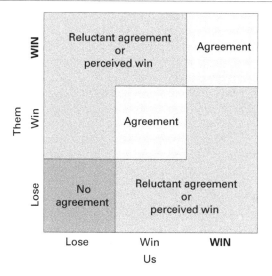

The straight win/win fits entirely with negotiations that seek to 'create' value between the parties. In a collaborative, perhaps long-term relationship this is entirely appropriate. For a negotiation that seeks to 'claim' value, a less balanced result may be possible and even appropriate. However, in this case, when one side realizes they have been disadvantaged, they are unlikely to be happy with the outcome and this could even mar any future dealings. Yet to be in this position the disadvantaged party must have agreed to it. While agreement may have been made reluctantly, for example, if there was no alternative, such agreement might also follow poor negotiation. Good negotiation therefore means recognizing agreement is, most often, a choice, not an obligation.

Another reason for agreement to be unbalanced is that the party may have been duped or fooled into agreement. If I sold my car for a good price, but failed to mention the significant engine problem, what the other party thought was a win/win would soon turn out to be a win/lose. Some may be happy to dupe the other party in this way, especially if they can't be tracked down later, but the ethics of such a practice require careful thought, as does the nature of any future relationship needed. At the outset the disadvantaged party in this win/lose scenario would have perceived the result as a win/win. This is called a perceived win and is a key factor in securing agreement in a negotiation. Perceived wins are not limited to scenarios where one party gets duped. For example, if a big retailer, already squeezing margins with their supply base, tells a supplier 'if you want to continue as our supplier you must support an in-store promotion by supplying product below cost', the supplier could refuse (lose/lose), or the supplier could reluctantly agree. This could be viewed as a win/lose, **WIN**/win, or even a win/win, especially if the supplier took the view that the loss is a small price to pay to secure future business. The win in a negotiation is therefore subjective based upon our perception of the deal we have done. If we believe we have achieved a good result then we believe we have a win. The win is also relative to our position and our perception of our position. For this reason creating the illusion of a win with the other party is a powerful tactic and the basis of many sales approaches the world over. Haggling hard with a street-seller in Tunisia for a wooden African mask and securing it for one tenth of the original price might seem an incredible result when compared to our usual understanding of discounting. Chances are we overpaid but just don't know it and are unlikely to ever know, so remaining blissfully ignorant and happy with our purchase until we try and take it onto the plane home and find it exceeds the cabin baggage limits.

Effective negotiation is therefore about pursuing a win/win if we are to create value, but if we are claiming value it is about securing agreement that maximizes our win and that might involve working to create an illusion of a win/win, even though the actual result may really be more in our favour. Similarly it is important to be on our guard against believing we have secured a favourable win, but actually have not, and to remember that agreement is a choice that should be exercised carefully. It is equally important to guard against acting out of fairness for our opponent when it is not appropriate. More on that shortly.

Starting out

The first step in any negotiation is to be certain the negotiation can take place and has a chance of succeeding.

No ZoMA, no hope of a result

For a negotiation to be successful then it must be possible for all parties to reach some sort of agreement. Say I decide to sell my car and advertise it for sale at £7,000, having first researched its value and determined this would be the highest price I could expect to realize given the car's age and condition. My confidence might initially lead me to believe I may just obtain this price and convince someone to buy it, while being ready to lower my expectations, especially if time went by and there was no interest. However, my minimum selling price would be £6,000, because below this I would be better part-exchanging the vehicle at a garage as this carries less risk. I might therefore intend to sell my car for a price somewhere between £6,000 and £7,000 and clearly the higher the better. A buyer who shows an interest in my car might have a budget of £6,000, but could go to £6,500 if he saw something that was really good. Say the buyer searches for cars advertised in the price range between £5,000 and £7,000, confident in his ability to negotiate down anything that is outside his budget. Therefore, the area of overlap between each party's acceptable range is between £6,000 and £6,500.

Lewicki, Minton and Saunders (1999) described this as the 'Zone of Potential Agreement' or ZoPA. However, this term seems to fall short, as in a negotiation we not only need a potential agreement, but an actual agreement where both parties will definitely settle on a single position that is mutually acceptable and beneficial. Therefore a more appropriate term for the range where deals acceptable to both parties are made is the 'Zone of Mutual Agreement' or ZoMA (see Figure 1.4) as it more accurately describes what needs to exist for a negotiation to be successful.

As in the example above there is a ZoMA. However, if I had decided I would not go below £7,000 and the buyer is not prepared to go a penny above £6,000, then there is no ZoMA so there can be no agreement. Both parties would at some point walk away. The reality at the outset of many negotiations is that we don't know for certain if there is a ZoMA. Experience, knowledge and research will help inform us here but even so we are unlikely to understand the boundaries of the ZoMA. Doing that is part of both the negotiation pre-planning and execution process and a good negotiator will use all sorts of tactics to attempt to flush out where our boundaries lie and hide theirs. However, ultimately, if we are certain there can be no ZoMA, there is little point negotiating.

Figure 1.4   The ZoMA (Zone of Mutual Agreement)

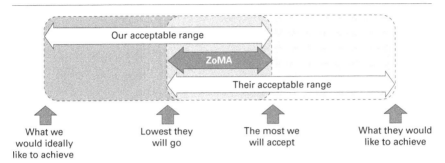

Getting them to the table

Having a ZoMA, reaching agreement and the ability to implement what was agreed are the success factors in negotiation. However, success factors are meaningless unless both sides want to negotiate. For a negotiation to take place there must be two or more parties and all parties must need or want to engage and therefore must want to reach an agreement. If one party doesn't want to engage or is happy with the status quo there is no basis for them to negotiate. This can be a major problem, as it doesn't matter how good we are at negotiating, if we can't get the other side to the table then there will be no negotiation. Kolb and Williams (2001) suggest three approaches here that can help:

- *Offer incentives.* Sell the potential benefits the other party could gain if they engage. Here it is important not to give away any negotiation position, but rather talk of general outcomes. For example, when a car salesman engages with a customer viewing the open-top car on the forecourt who says she is 'just looking for the moment', he won't offer a price or start talking terms; instead he will try and spark a conversation about the delights of driving such a car on a sunny day with the wind in your hair and heads turning as you pass. 'Just looking' might then become 'tell me more'.

- *Quantify the cost of doing nothing.* In the case of the car salesman this might be: 'I'm not expecting this car to be here for long; we've already had lots of interest'.

- *Enlist allies to help back our cause.* If the customer viewed the car together with a friend, a good car salesman would work on extolling the virtues to both individuals, even though one wasn't a potential buyer, but knowing that creating an ally in the friend could help the sale.

There must be some means of interacting and conducting the negotiation such as a face-to-face meeting, teleconference or online exchange. Sometimes negotiation can just happen without it being planned. Perhaps an ongoing e-mail exchange with a supplier about a potential piece of work can develop into an exchange about price and terms and then subsequent agreement to proceed. Gently transitioning into a negotiation with the other party can give us an advantage, as they may not have prepared in the same way they would have done if we had signalled our intentions beforehand. However, it can also work against us. If we invite the other party to a meeting to discuss something and then start negotiating, they may feel ambushed and, if smart, will apologize for misunderstanding our intentions for the meeting and ask to reconvene when they have had a chance to prepare properly. It is therefore important to understand when an exchange with another party becomes a negotiation and decide if we are sufficiently prepared to proceed. If not, don't be afraid to buy time. Having said this, 'not coming to the table' can also be a powerful negotiation tactic designed to signal to the other that no movement from the stated position is possible. This is because when a party agrees to come to the table, that party is also signalling that they are ready to make concessions. Therefore if an opponent is declining to engage consider if this genuinely indicates they will not move, or perhaps there is no ZoMA. Otherwise this may just be a tactic to compel us to accept their position. Figure 1.5 shows these prerequisites along with the success factors for a negotiation.

Figure 1.5   Negotiation prerequisites and success factors

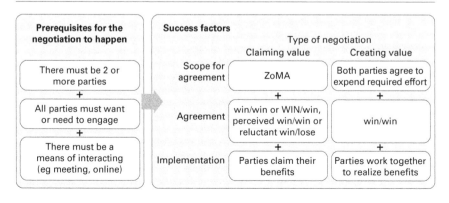

The enemy within

If we want to get good at negotiation what are we up against here? Human nature: specifically ours, our personalities and the experiences that have shaped us and make us who we are. Negotiation is a game and it is important to remember that; there are many forces or dynamics that come from deep within us, many of which we may be unaware of but which emerge when we play the negotiation game. The same is true within our opponent. Psychology can help us make sense of what happens in our mind before, during and after a negotiation and there is a series of forces that can change or have a profound impact on a negotiation, either positively or detrimentally. If we can understand these forces and what drives us, and what might be driving the other party, then we can use this emotional competence to assume better control of how the game is played, which is why I have placed this section right at the front of this book. There are five forces that make up the enemy within and that we need to understand and manage if we want to become proficient negotiators: our need to win, our fear of failure, our bias towards self-belief, the power of relationships, and our need to trust.

Our need to win

In negotiation terms this is possibly the single most powerful force within us and one that can drive an individual to be relentless and uncompromising in pursuit of his or her goal, often at the expense of others. Franken and Brown (1995) suggest that a need to win comes from a deep-rooted fear that the world is essentially hostile and so the only way to survive is to win. This means that people who feel the need to win do this by taking what they can rather than attempting to reach a goal through mastery and work. As a consequence people with a strong need to win tend to be more forceful and aggressive in the pursuit of their goal. While this can be useful in certain negotiations where a win/lose or even a WIN/win is needed it can be damaging if we need a long-term mutually beneficial outcome, ie the one that must be built through mastery and work. The need to win is part of our personality (and one we will come back to later when we explore negotiation preparation) and here there are some apparent differences between sales and procurement people. Typically, those who are drawn to selling or account management roles have an inherent need to win. They are more often than not highly competitive, highly motivated individuals who are happy to be paid based upon the results they achieve. In contrast, the need to win is much less common across those in procurement and supply chain roles. Therefore if we fail to appreciate the 'need to win' dynamic then our personalities will place purchasing and supply chain at a disadvantage to salespeople. More importantly we need the ability to adapt our personality for any given negotiation and have robust ways of dealing with highly competitive counterparts. Later we will explore practical steps that do just this.

Fear of failure

Distinct from 'the need to win', the fear of failure is another powerful dynamic in negotiations that can work positively or negatively. It is our fear of failure that can motivate us to reach a high level of performance. Indeed, performers will often claim it is their fear of failing that motivates them to strive for perfection in stage or screen performances, believing their future may become uncertain if they fail. However, fear of failure can also prevent us reaching our goal by acting as a threat to our ability and making us hold back.

Conroy, Willow and Metzler (2002) suggest there are five consequences of failure that can do this. They are the fear of:

- experiencing shame and embarrassment;
- devaluing our self-esteem or self-estimate;
- making our future uncertain;
- losing social influence;
- upsetting important others.

In the context of a negotiation, being driven to reach a goal because we don't want to fail is a good thing to an extent, and for certain negotiation scenarios. However, our negotiation performance will be impaired and restricted if we perceive that the process may cause us embarrassment, or we are uncomfortable with upsetting the other party, or we perceive our actions could threaten our future career in some way. Furthermore, if a tough negotiation results in the other party simply saying 'no' and continuing to maintain this position it can be disheartening and create a sense of failure. These are personal consequences; therefore the fear of failure in a negotiation context is driven by personal factors rather than the fear of failing to achieve a negotiation target. Conroy, Willow and Metzler (2002) also suggest a strong link between the degree to which we fear failure and our personalities. Those with a propensity to anxiety, pessimism or who have low self-esteem have a greater fear of failure. Managing this within a negotiation requires us to understand our personalities and be capable of compensating where needed. Individuals with low self-esteem will need to work harder in order to be bold when negotiating. Our competence here is also relevant; in other words, if we believe we are capable, we can overcome any fear of failure our personalities might naturally instil in us. Therefore to negotiate effectively we not only need to understand who we are, but we also need to have confidence in our abilities. We will return to 'personality' as a core success factor for negotiators later.

Bias in self-belief

This is about the degree to which we may over- or underestimate our reactions or how we believe we will behave in a given situation. For example, the punchy kid who thinks he is invincible may actively court getting into a fight because he believes he is stronger, smarter and better than he actually is and is certain he will win.

In a negotiation context, if we have an overly high estimation of our abilities related to our actual abilities we might believe we can achieve a great result with little planning or preparation. This is something I can relate to from my first procurement role. Then, in my young and reckless days, my misguided confidence made me certain that I merely needed to turn up to an important negotiation with a chemical supplier. Leading up to the event, I pictured myself sitting in the room in full control of the negotiation, driving towards a spectacular result with the supplier conceding to my every demand. I pictured myself reporting the success to my boss following the event and being congratulated on a great result. It didn't go well, largely due to my complete lack of preparation in the face of a very informed and experienced supplier. I ended up looking like an amateur and this was baggage I subsequently carried in all future dealings with that supplier.

Wells and Sweeney (1986) call this 'bias in self-assessment' and suggest this bias is, just like 'fear of failure', linked to our self-esteem. If we have high self-esteem then we believe in ourselves and can be over-confident in our abilities. Similarly, if we lack self-esteem we will tend to underestimate our abilities. Experience can help temper this effect; the punchy kid will only let himself get so many bloody noses before his experiences change his actions. Once again we see a strong link between our personalities, our self-esteem and how we perform in a negotiation.

As a footnote here, in the days leading up to the event, the art of picturing yourself in the situation and delivering a strong performance is a very powerful mental conditioning technique and one commonly used by performers.

It is especially good if you have low self-esteem and seems to subconsciously prepare us for success. If you picture yourself succeeding you probably will. Likewise if you picture yourself failing this is exactly what you are programming your subconscious to do. Of course using this technique should not, as in my case above, be a substitute for good planning and preparation.

The power of relationships

We are sociable creatures. Relationships and what other people think of us are important to a greater or lesser extent depending, once again, on our personality. Relationships can introduce powerful ties and senses of obligation to the other party. They can also act as a powerful driver in influencing our actions.

In a negotiation our relationship with the other party cannot be ignored if we are to be effective. If we have a close relationship with the other party, either due to personal factors or from a history of collaborative business dealings, then our approach to the negotiation will be within the context of maintaining this relationship as being of paramount importance. Risking upset in the other party would tend to be avoided and the negotiations might typically be based around mutual benefit (or a win/win) and proceedings might have a high degree of trust-based agreements. In certain cultures this is the only way negotiations take place (we will explore this more later). However, in Western culture, if there is no relationship a different set of dynamics can emerge. Pushing hard to get an agreement, upsetting the other party and seeking an outcome that may not be mutually beneficial might not faze a seasoned negotiator given the right opportunity. As an example, it is these dynamics that emerge during an online e-auction where there is no relationship, just a remote engagement via an online portal.

For this reason, suppliers will put great effort into attempting to build relationships. If they can make us like them, have us believe the relationship is paramount or they can create some sense of obligation then it makes it more difficult to take a hard line with them during a negotiation. When a used car salesman uses a line like 'we're not going to fall out over a few hundred dollars are we' in the context of finalizing the purchase price for a car, the salesman is attempting to instil a sense that there is a relationship, ie a position from which we can 'fall out' and therefore making it difficult to avoid compromise. Building a strong relationship is not necessarily a bad thing; indeed in many business scenarios it is exactly what is needed, but it is something we must be alert to, in control of and understand the boundaries.

Our need to trust

Our need to trust is an important and often underestimated component of human interaction and is both an enabler of our actions and a key to interpersonal relationships in various settings. McKnight, Cummings and Chervany (1995) suggest trust embodies three elements:

- *The potential negative consequences*. When there is risk, uncertainty or if negative consequences are possible, successful interaction requires trust.

- *Dependence*. Dependency doesn't necessarily need to involve trust; however, trust does involve dependence on another party. Astley and Zajac (1991) suggest that dependency on another party also places them in a situational position of power. Therefore when someone trusts they are effectively giving power to the other party through dependency.

- *Feelings of security*. If we are anxious or fearful, we may not trust the other party but we may be willing to depend upon them, especially if we have little alternative. This is an emotional response and the more we trust, the more secure we feel.

The need to trust can be mitigated to a degree by reducing dependency on the other party and the power they hold. We will explore this in more detail later; however, the need to trust remains a powerful component in a negotiation and cannot be ignored. Things can change post-agreement and contracts can be breached, leaving the prospect of compromise or a bloody legal battle. Trust is inescapable.

If we can convince the other party to trust us then we have increased our power. I witnessed an exchange between a frustrated passenger on the London Underground and a senior member of staff who was trying to help. There was a line closure and the passenger was attempting to find an alternative route to get somewhere in a hurry. The member of staff provided some advice and suggested a different way to get there. The passenger rejected it and argued it wouldn't work and she wouldn't get to her destination on time. The staff member gently put his right hand on her arm and said, 'trust me I've been doing this job for 34 years now I know what I'm talking about'. The woman paused, her entire body seemed to relax a little and she looked the official in the eyes and said, 'OK, then I'll try it', thanked the man and hurried off. Clearly that line was enough to create an immediate sense of trust. However, I'm willing to bet if I'd later tracked down the woman and shown her a photo of the member of staff then asked, 'do you trust this man?' she would say no. Trust in the context of a negotiation is often little more than an illusion created by one party and it is this tactic that has been used by salespeople for centuries.

Trust is also linked to the culture we are in or negotiating with. In Western culture trust is rarely considered a significant factor, despite it actually being highly relevant to what drives us at a subconscious level. However, in Eastern and Middle Eastern cultures trust is usually a pre-requisite to a successful negotiation. Here, without a relationship of trust, the negotiation will rarely begin let alone succeed.

Fairness and reciprocity

Finally, we are also up against our natural tendency for fairness and reciprocity towards our opponent. This is possibly one of the most powerful destructive forces that comes to bear in a negotiation if we are not aware of it, yet it can also work in our advantage to influence the other. Cialdini (2007) describes what he terms the 'rule of reciprocation' as the human tendency to repay or reciprocate when a gift is given. This gift might be a physical object; however, it could also be a kind deed or act of generosity. If someone extends help or support, we might feel the need to 'repay' this with some flowers. If we get invited to someone's party, we feel the need to invite them. If someone gives us a birthday present, we feel the need reciprocate for their birthday, and so on. When we reciprocate, we also tend to quantify the size of the gift made to us and reciprocate in equal measure with a sense of obligation remaining in us until every part of the perceived debt to the other that we create in our mind is repaid. Reciprocity works throughout our lives, even down to someone giving us a smile triggering an automatic smile back.

In negotiation, reciprocity comes into play in the way parties make concessions and trades and our sense of fairness towards conducting dealings according to a 'something for something' principle. 'Something for something' trades on the fact that humans are programmed to reciprocate. It is a technique we use to our advantage to ask for something in return from our opponent as a response to their demands. However, it can work against us as we can also be caught up in our own internal sense of obligation and even guilt to reciprocate when the other offers a concession. Suppliers are quick to capitalize on this and create a 'win/win illusion' with the suggestion that we must both give in equal measure to end up at a point of mutual agreement, often halfway between our respective positions (indeed the tactic

'Split the Difference' trades on this dynamic). In a Value Creation scenario where true 'win/win' is appropriate, this sort of reciprocation may be well placed; however, as we have already seen, most negotiations are more WIN/win in pursuit of Value Claiming and so suppliers will seek to construct a negotiation range that compels us to exchange trades towards the centre, each reciprocating in equal measure to get there. The rule of reciprocity can make us feel like we have negotiated well, but we may have simply been guided to the intended end position by a clever supplier.

Reciprocity in negotiation changes with culture and whilst the human tendency to reciprocate is universal, those who we feel obliged to the most change with culture.

Reciprocity, and specifically the sense of need or guilt that it can trigger in us that might compel us to concede unnecessarily, can be averted by learning to become more aware of our feelings of obligation and exercising choice about when we reciprocate. It can also be dealt with by letting go of any preconceptions that trades must be given in equal measure – there is no basis for this; instead decide according to the situation.

Developing capability

It is difficult to describe exactly how to be good at negotiation. There is a good reason for this because negotiation requires a mix of skills and knowledge together with many things that happen at a subconscious level; we need to know 'what' needs to happen to be successful (declarative knowledge) and 'how' to negotiate (procedural knowledge). When I taught my son to ride a bicycle for the first time, I began by describing what he needed to do but mastery only came when he learnt how this worked in practice. Describing what things to do to balance or why pedalling faster when things wobble makes little sense until it is experienced for real.

Knowing 'what' to do

Declarative knowledge is about understanding the concept of negotiation and knowing what to do. This is about planning and having a robust process or roadmap to follow, developed according to what has been found to be effective.

There are few good processes to aid negotiation planning out there, with most of the wisdom in this area concentrating more on tactics and techniques. However, effective negotiation does require an effective planning process. Experienced negotiators may appear to just instinctively know what to do without reference to any process; however, they will still be working through a series of discrete steps learnt through experience.

Negotiation is often viewed as a specialist art; a skill that is difficult to acquire. This is not the case and this misconception comes from the way negotiation is often taught and how people try to learn it. Effective negotiation skills cannot be developed by learning tactics and techniques alone but instead starts by learning a process and framework to deploy them at the right time for the right reasons.

A significant part of this book is built around the process to follow for effective negotiation using the 'Red Sheet' methodology. This is a proven process that sits at the heart of good negotiation. It acts like a roadmap that helps to navigate a steady course through the complexities of negotiation, and provide for the things that can catch us out, to secure a favourable agreement. Irrespective of what process is used it should provide for the following:

- the sequence of steps to follow end-to-end;
- pre-planning and data gathering;
- a means to assess our position relative to the other person's;
- event planning and tactics;
- negotiation strategy;
- anticipating the other's position and responses;
- personality, behaviours and styles needed;
- identifying alternatives;
- post-negotiation review.

Knowing 'how' to do it

The analogy of getting good at negotiating as similar to becoming proficient at cycling is very powerful. As I have already said, it is impossible to describe or read a book about how to ride a bicycle and all the things that happen in our heads that mean we can do it. However, there is more, and once we have mastery of the bicycle we then learn specific responses to each of the different hazards and situations or unexpected events when we cycle from one place to another. Again much of this is without conscious thought but we develop a repertoire of manoeuvres and responses that we call on as we go. Negotiation is just like this. Declarative knowledge is about understanding the concept of negotiation and knowing what to do. This is about planning and having a robust process or roadmap to follow, developed according to what has been found to be effective.

Procedural knowledge is knowing how to negotiate and comes from our unconscious memory of how to do things. This is about developing our capability so we know how to respond given a specific situation that we may not be able to fully plan or anticipate. This know-how becomes our personal negotiation repertoire and forms a critical part of our capability in this area. It comes, in part, from personal experience and by doing it for real but it is also developed by learning to use proven tactics and techniques, many of which are included later in this book.

Personality, process and repertoire

As we have seen, the 'enemy within' can work against us, so effective negotiation requires us to understand our personalities, specifically those traits that might be counterproductive, and moderate these using self-management. We must be alert to the power of relationships and trust; both required at some point but when misplaced can trip us up. A process or roadmap is essential to ensure our planning covers all aspects and we are able to navigate through the negotiation and finally, our negotiation capability is developed by learning and being able to recall and use a range of tactics, techniques and approaches for each and every situation. Effective negotiation is therefore about personality, process and repertoire, and that is the subject of the rest of this book.

Countering the seller's advantage

This chapter explores the differences between sellers and buyers and why procurement and supply chain professionals seem to be at a disadvantage in the face of a seller. It considers how process, personality and repertoire of the seller accentuate this disparity and it begins to explore the negotiation approaches the purchasing community need in response.

Pathway questions addressed in this chapter

3 In what ways do sellers gain an advantage over us in a negotiation and what can I do to counter this?

Surely procurement and supply chain people are exceptional negotiators?

If you work in procurement or supply chain there seems to be an expectation among the rest of the business and the world in general that you must therefore be a brilliant, well-trained negotiator capable of pitching up to any supplier and getting a result that would be out of reach for anyone else. This is just like when the IT guy arrives to fix your PC; because they work in IT others often assume they know everything there could ever be to know about computers, networks and even how to get past level five on the game you're playing at home. The reality (in both cases) is often quite different.

I can recall in my early career having a strong feeling of inadequacy as I was being called upon to carry out a series of supplier negotiations but without any training or reference of what 'good' looks like. Overall I felt like I was bluffing it but felt I might disadvantage myself if I shared my concerns. Looking back, I learnt much from those early experiences, but I just didn't realize it at the time.

As we have seen in Chapter 1, if we feel we might fail then in certain cases this can sub-optimize negotiation performance. It is therefore essential that procurement and supply chain professionals are able to plan and execute negotiations with confidence. Getting to this point is not a big leap but to gain this confidence we must be comfortable not only with our own negotiation abilities but also with our ability to deploy these in the face of a well-planned and expertly executed negotiation where the supplier seems to have a dominant position. However, for the purchaser, things are not necessarily balanced from the outset. Sales teams are regarded as a critical driver of overall business performance and so they are typically highly capable and well-resourced in order to maximize sales performance. So if we are to deliver effective negotiations with confidence, we must first understand what, or more specifically who, we are up against, the ways they attempt to gain advantage and how we can counter these.

Good negotiation is about process, personality and repertoire. This is true for both parties, so we not only need to consider our own competence and alignment in these three areas but also that of the supplier. As Sun Tzu (6th century BC) stated:

> If you know your enemies and know yourself, you will not be imperilled in a hundred battles.

While it can be counterproductive to regard suppliers as enemies, the business world can learn much from military strategies and the fact that Sun Tzu's *The Art of War* is still in print over two-and-a-half thousand years later suggests he was onto something. For that reason the rest of this chapter will consider how sellers have the advantage in terms of process, personality and repertoire and how we can begin to counter this advantage.

The process behind the salesperson

Negotiation is the process by which two or more parties confer or interact to reach consensus or agreement. Within procurement and the supply chain, negotiation is only one component of good strategic sourcing and supply chain management. Ideally it is aligned with, and informed by, everything else the function is doing. However, within sales there is less of a distinction between negotiation and selling. Webster (1968) defines selling as 'achieving a common understanding through communication' which is remarkably similar to how we define negotiation. The process of sales and negotiation is one and the same for much of what the seller does; where one stops and the other starts is often indistinct. This is the case if we are engaging with a new supplier, considering extending business with an existing supplier or just managing a relationship with a particular supplier. So in considering the 'process' that salespeople apply in order to be effective at negotiation we need to consider the 'process' of selling. These include the step-by-step methodologies used to guide the seller towards a sale, enabling systems and the capability of the seller.

Their methodology to sell to you

For most businesses, sales effectiveness is not left to chance and few organizations will rely on the prowess of key individuals alone. Instead the approach is systematic, following a process that has been proven to work and one that is implemented with a discipline across the entire sales function. There are many well-regarded sales processes out there to guide the salesperson through the various stages of engaging with a customer and winning them over. Spiro, Stanton and Rich (2007) describe a complete approach to the management of a sales force including a step-by-step process. This is often called the 'sales funnel' (Figure 2.1) and represents how a large number of initial sales contacts are managed through the sales process to arrive at a much smaller number of sales, with many initial prospects falling away throughout for various reasons as a natural consequence of the sales process. Individual stages of the sales funnel process might be managed by different parts of the organization. Prospecting or handling an initial contact, perhaps following a call, interaction, website enquiry, exhibition meeting or similar response to some form of marketing activity might be carried out by a specific team who would then 'qualify' these initial contacts where interest exists. Qualification leads to 'sales leads' that are individuals or organizations with both the interest and potential authority to purchase a product or service.

At this stage an experienced salesperson might take the lead and engage with the buyer to understand specific needs and attempt to match what is on offer with the needs of the buyer. This is where sales skills come to the fore to create a 'qualified prospect', one where the individual or organization has

Figure 2.1 The sales funnel (adapted from Spiro, Stanton and Rich 2007)

moved from being interested to expressing a need for the goods or services. This is a critical stage in the process, requiring skill and agility in the seller to adapt, express and emphasize key attributes of their offer in such a way that the buyer perceives it to be the right solution. Perhaps you've known someone described affectionately as 'able to sell snow to the Eskimos', which if possible would require great skills to accomplish as well as a big ice box to carry samples. Such skills combine both listening and careful use of language, but crucially include a high degree of adaptability of approach. Therefore, while we are moving through a step-by-step sales process there are many layers within the overall approach required for effective selling. It is also worth noting that at the point within the process where the seller is attempting to establish the buyer's needs, if the buyer is unable to precisely articulate the requirements for the potential purchase then the seller is effectively being handed power by the buyer and the freedom to help define the buyer's requirements for him or her. This is a common mistake made by procurement and supply chain practitioners who can be seduced by the supplier's apparent helpfulness, perhaps believing such discussions exist outside of any negotiation and are therefore exploratory and harmless. This is not the case. I will come back to this in later chapters.

Qualifying prospects also involves the seller further establishing the ability and likelihood of the individual or organization to buy as well as any obstacles or risks that must be understood. Sales resources are expensive and precious so efforts are carefully focused. Approaches here vary from one organization to another but the process of qualification involves forming a view based upon a number of factors. Sellers will therefore typically seek to establish information around:

- budget availability;
- authority to act;
- alignment with wider organizational direction, needs and directives (and thus likelihood of the sale to succeed);
- who stands to gain or lose the most;
- who is an ally who could help smooth the sale;
- who might sabotage this;
- who is, and is there approval from, the 'economic buyer' (the individual who will ultimately make the decision and/or holds the budget)?

With a qualified prospect, a firm proposal can follow which the seller will hope to then move into a final phase of negotiation, closing and the transacting the deal.

For the buyer, the stages of selling are likely to be largely invisible; for the seller their actions will be based upon systematically moving through these stages. Negotiation is called out within this sales process as a single step towards the end. While this might reflect the timing of a meeting or interaction that is convened for this purpose, the process of negotiation actually starts right back at the stage when a lead is first qualified, when the seller seriously engages with the buyer. Good salespeople don't just turn up and ask you what you want; instead they work to build a relationship and win your trust from the outset. As the seller works to understand the needs of the buyer and qualify the prospect, the foundations for success are being laid down. This happens the world over and in certain cultures initial relationship building is a prerequisite to any meaningful discussions taking place. Trust is even more essential and the earlier the seller can establish some sort of trust the greater the likelihood of achieving the sale. To see this in action, consider how sellers have turned to using social media and social networking. Here smart sellers spotted the opportunity for referrals via networks of 'people who know people' to create almost instant trust. In fact the networking expert Jan Vermeiren (Vermeiren and Verdonck, 2011) suggests that a referral from a trusted colleague leads to an 80 per cent chance of a sale.

While selling processes, such as those described above, provide the stages to progress, there are other more subtle games at play as the seller systematically attempts to move the customer towards a sale, building trust and relationship along the way. The AIDA (Attention, Interest, Desire, Action) model, commonly attributed to advertising sales pioneer E St Elmo Lewis (1903), describes the underlying selling process:

A – **Attention**: get the attention of the customer

I – **Interest**: get the customer interested by demonstrating advantages and benefits over features and attributes

D – **Desire**: convince the customer they want and desire the product or service and that it will fulfil their needs

A – **Action**: close the sale; get the customer to buy!

We can expect our engagement with the seller to be part of a broader managed sales process and within this the seller will seek to build a relationship, win trust and create desire and a compelling reason for us to engage and to negotiate towards a sale. The seller will be focusing their resources and effort based upon their assessment of likelihood and ability for the sale to succeed which will require them to gather information along the way.

There is a final dynamic here that provides advantage to the seller and that is internal business alignment and the way the seller is organized. While the salesperson will be facing off against us and our organization, sitting behind him or her will be an organization that is fully aligned with the sales process, providing the necessary support where needed. For example, discussions between the seller's operational or development functions and prospective buyers outside of the sales process, or without the knowledge of the salesperson, would be rare. It would be even more rare for such functions to give the buyer vital intelligence that might help the buyer negotiate a good deal. In fact this would be viewed as disloyal and inappropriate.

The dynamic is very different for the purchaser. If we look behind the buyer who is facing off to the supplier we are unlikely to see such an aligned and supportive wider organization. Here the buyer is, in fact, often fighting the rest of the organization in order to maintain the necessary position with the supplier. Departments outside of the procurement or supply chain functions often claim the right to freely engage directly and build relationships with suppliers, with intervention by procurement or supply chain in these relationships viewed as undermining status. The problem here is that people across organizations don't receive training in how to engage with suppliers and how to be alert to the game at play so fail to see the impact of sharing what might seem to be a harmless bit of information with a supplier.

Suppliers know this so will freely use a 'divide and conquer' approach to not only secure support for their cause but to gain vital intelligence.

Systems they use

Selling processes need to be enabled. At the heart of modern selling is a good Customer Relationship Management (CRM) system, almost certainly electronic – either web-based (such as SalesForce.com (archived at https://perma.cc/6QSV-NVTX)) or sitting on a corporate server accessed by the sales team. A CRM system is a means by which a supplier will capture and share within their sales team knowledge of your business and details of each and every engagement they have with you and the rest of your business. CRM systems help to coordinate and align the supplier's efforts to stage-manage specific engagements and communication activities so they are attempting to proactively move you through the various steps towards a successful sale. It is not by chance that the account manager remembers the names of your children or where you went on vacation last year, or that they call you exactly at the date you said you would be ready for a discussion. Instead, a good salesperson will record such detail in their CRM system for retrieval later when they next meet you or to prompt a specific action with you. The development of the relationship with the buyer is usually stage-managed with salespeople having direct and real-time interaction with the CRM system.

Sales team capability

Any approach that can help win customers and clinch sales is big business. An online search will reveal a plethora of training, winning ways, books, experts, tips and techniques, aimed specifically at enabling the sales community. In contrast, those in procurement and supply chain do not enjoy such a rich depth of similar help and support and this is evidenced in several ways. For example, there are more than three times the number of sales-related publications versus those aimed at the procurement and supply chain communities, and only a fraction focus on strategic procurement or how good supply chain management can bring competitive advantage. For negotiation alone there are over 20,000 books that touch on the subject in some way but most are written from a sales perspective. Indeed, only a few hundred of these consider negotiation with suppliers and only a handful are specifically aimed at those in procurement or supply chain functions. There is a similar imbalance for investment in training and development for those in sales and marketing teams when compared to purchasing teams. The US Bureau of Labor places this disparity at ten to one with salespeople receiving ten times more training than the average procurement or supply chain practitioner. This places the buyer at quite a disadvantage from the outset. Furthermore, personal development for salespeople is not confined to selling or negotiating skills but often extends into other areas that can help facilitate relationship and trust building. This might include coaching in specific aspects of psychology, body language and use of specific language techniques such as NLP (Neuro-Linguistic Programming). Few buyers receive such training but arguably if they did it would help improve negotiation capability. The result here is that we can expect to be facing off against a highly capable seller that is better resourced, is better supported and has received much more training.

The sales personality

If good negotiators are made not born, what about salespeople? If negotiation and selling are intertwined, does this mean that good sellers are made not born also? Well, perhaps and to answer this it is necessary to consider the typical salesperson's personality. The established literature on the subject seems to consistently suggest four traits that are regarded as important in a salesperson. These are the ability to build relationships, individual motivation, knowledge and empathy.

People who build relationships with you

Salespeople need to be good at relationships. Saxe and Weitz (1982) suggest that customer-oriented selling requires relationships to be nurtured, which they define as a desire to help customers assess their needs and purchases as well as avoiding deception, manipulation and pressure. In contrast, Dichter (1964) describes a somewhat different approach, suggesting a good salesperson needs to perfect the ability to make superficial relationships, in other words he or she must be a chameleon according to the circumstances. Weitz, Sujan and Sujan (1986) go one step further and suggest that effective selling requires adaptive behaviour so that the salesperson has sufficient emotional intelligence to know how to behave in a given situation and to be aware of, and able to control and modify, his or her self-presentation in different situations and contexts. A good salesperson will therefore know just how to handle him- or herself, instinctively adapting the style of interaction to be-have in a way that makes people in any situation like them. As we saw in Chapter 1 this plays right to the heart of a basic human need – the need to be liked, to not want to upset others – a need so powerful it can significantly influence our actions in response. Relationship building is a key factor in recruiting salespeople but not one that can be empirically evaluated. Instead, recruiters will often talk of attributes such as 'instant like' of an individual. You will undoubtedly know such individuals, people who, in any given situation, can make people like them early on.

The highly motivated sales team

Salespeople are often highly motivated individuals, happy to participate in reward structures where a percentage of their personal income is dependent upon their performance. Weitz, Sujan and Sujan (1986) cite motivation as a key enabler for sellers and suggest this includes the degree of physical effort put into the sale or negotiation and how long the seller is prepared to keep going to clinch the sale. They also suggest the seller is able to exercise choice in terms of what to focus on and the best approach to use to be successful. This means the salesperson is going to be hungry and determined to win. The outward signs of this behaviour include:

- persistence to drive towards an outcome;
- establishing allies in your organization who can influence their cause;
- finding ways to get airtime with you... and so build the relationship;
- going to great lengths to close the sale... doing whatever is necessary.

Sales team knowledge

While not a personality trait, knowledge is a key factor in selling. Clearly any good salesperson needs to have a good knowledge of the product or service being sold (Saxe and Weitz, 1982). However, there is more here. Weitz, Sujan and Sujan (1986) suggest a clear link between knowledge and performance and propose that effective selling requires knowledge beyond products (or services) and procedural aspects of the sale, but is also linked to the knowledge of the customer's values and beliefs. As we have seen, a good salesperson will seek to build a relationship, but to gain an advantage in doing this he or she will also attempt to gain knowledge of who you are, perhaps through research. These days, no good salesperson will turn up for a meeting or negotiation without first having put your name into Google, LinkedIn or Facebook.

The empathic salesperson

Empathy is the ability of the seller to understand and share the feelings of the buyer and is widely regarded by practitioners and scholars as an important element of effective selling. Von Bergen and Shealy (1982) described empathy as 'a vital part of the process of identifying and satisfying customer needs'.

McBane (1995) suggests empathy in the context of selling has three components:

1 **The ability to adopt the viewpoint of the buyer.** To do this the seller must have both a knowledge of people and how they behave in various situations as well as the ability to perceive how the buyer might feel picking up on various visual, spoken and sensory cues (Deutsch and Madle, 1975). It is for this reason that salespeople often receive coaching in understanding the body language of others and how to read the position of the buyer by listening for clues masked behind what is actually said. By adopting the viewpoint of the buyer, the seller is then able to better anticipate their reactions, recognize their needs and adapt the sales approach accordingly, thus increasing the chances of a favourable outcome.

2 **Concern shown for the feelings and welfare of the buyer.** This is the ability to sense the feelings of the other person but without actually experiencing their emotions and triggering an altruistic response directed towards helping them. While 'how can I help?' might be something a seller would say, empathy means the seller has a genuine desire to help when he or she senses help is needed. This in turn develops relationship and builds trust.

3 **Emotional contagion.** This is where our emotions are induced by the emotions of others and where the observer has an emotional experience parallel to the person's actual emotions. For example, if a person sees another's joy they will experience joy themselves, like an infant's smile making the parent happy. If the buyer gets positively excited about a potential deal, the seller will share the same emotion. However, there is a flip side here too. Strong emotional contagion means that when the observer is seeing suffering or negative emotions it induces a similar negative emotion, perhaps leading the observer to vent his or her own

frustration rather than inducing helping behaviour, reducing the observer's ability to respond and communicate effectively (Miller *et al*, 1988; Stiff *et al*, 1988). Within a selling context, negative emotional contagion impedes the seller and interferes with the seller's ability to make adjustments to the buyer's concerns. Good salespeople can suddenly find themselves searching for a suitable response in the face of a buyer who appears genuinely angry or distressed. It is this dynamic that sits behind the often effective negotiation tactic of acting like 'you're hurting me' and creating a display of apparent suffering at being beaten down or offended as this reduces the other party's ability to respond robustly. The very same technique is used by plumbers all over the world who, it seems, learn early the sharp intake of breath and shaking of the head at what you thought was a reasonable request.

So are salespeople made not born? It is true that certain individuals seem to naturally have the right personality traits for selling roles. Indeed, Sullivan (1953) suggests that empathy, for example, is a trait that we are born with. However, the general view suggests that empathy develops through continuous practice and social experience (Mead, 1934). So it would seem it is possible for a salesperson to learn to be empathic. Furthermore, an intelligent and willing individual who is suitably incentivized will soon find ways to build relationships, develop personal motivation and amass the knowledge required to be effective. So salespeople are generally 'made'. However, it seems organizations direct significant effort and resources into 'making them' at a level that is disproportionate to the buyers they interface with.

The salesperson's repertoire

Repertoire is the collection of approaches, tactics and techniques that the salesperson has available to him or her, and the way these are used to shape, guide or control the sales interaction or negotiation towards a favourable outcome. Repertoire is unique to the individual and is learnt and developed over time through observing and studying selling and negotiation, by experimentation and trying different approaches and by adopting those that are found to help. The purpose of repertoire of the salesperson within an interaction with a buyer is to deploy tactics and countermeasures at the right moment that will reduce the number of possible alternatives the buyer has and to create a compelling reason for the buyer to act.

Repertoire provides a means of control, and the ability of the salesperson to shape the interaction is possibly one of the critical factors that determine the effectiveness of the salesperson. Bolton and Bolton (1984) link this shaping behaviour closely to assertiveness. The more assertive the salesperson, the better they are able to shape and control, and, most likely, the more developed their repertoire. McBane (1995) also establishes an inter-relationship with the personality of the salesperson and his or her ability to shape in this way, specifically with respect to empathy. An empathic salesperson is more likely to be able to select the right response from his or her repertoire to guide the buyer towards a sale or a favourable negotiation outcome if he or she can adopt the viewpoint of the buyer and show concern for the feelings of the buyer. However, McBane (1995) also suggests this ability is reduced where the buyer is showing negative emotion.

Repertoire is therefore a crucial enabler for any salesperson, providing the right ammunition at the right moments within a negotiation process. Selecting what to use when comes with experience.

I once asked a good friend of mine who sold cars for a living what he did to convert a prospective buyer who was 'just looking' into someone who bought a car. He described a series of tactics within his repertoire that he would draw on according to what was happening, but he would only do this once he believed the customer was genuinely interested and able to buy a vehicle. If a couple or family were viewing he would start describing ways the vehicle would enhance their family's lifestyle so the family would begin to picture themselves in the vehicle, taking it on family days out. Sometimes he might attempt to suggest some degree of scarcity or need to act quickly by using phrases such as 'I've had lots of interest in this car' or 'there's still time to take advantage of the special deal on this vehicle' and at the point when he had the customer on the verge of making a decision he would simply say 'shall we do this then?' and start producing paperwork. It was rare anyone would resist. These tactics my friend learnt over the years by experimentation and by asking and watching others. He simply then made them his own.

The disadvantaged buyer

We can conclude that good salespeople are made not born, but organizations put significant resources into making them! As a buyer we are likely to be up against a well-trained negotiator systematically working through a proven and well-organized sales process. The salesperson is likely to have received much more training than us including training in sales and the softer skills that help facilitate the sale and will most likely be a highly personable individual who somehow manages to make us like and trust him or her. Depending upon their experience salespeople could have an extensive repertoire of tactics, many of which we may be unaware are being deployed.

For many procurement and supply chain professionals a supplier negotiation, or even just a supplier meeting, is often just another meeting within an already busy schedule that limits the time and space to plan well. The supplier's sales teams on the other hand are often well-resourced, with a good, aligned support team and their day job is getting your sale so they have the headroom to invest time and effort in planning a winning approach.

A good salesperson will attempt to gather as much intelligence as possible about you, your organization and your position to help plan their approach. Suppliers may well leverage relationships they have established across the business in order to gather information.

All in all, the buyer appears significantly disadvantaged in the face of a supplier negotiation. The reasons for this are historic in most organizations but the situation is not all that bad. In fact, purchasers have more power than is often realized and it is entirely possible to counter the seller's advantage and create your own advantage.

Seizing the advantage

Remember good negotiation is about process, personality and repertoire. Equipped with a sound knowledge of the process salespeople use, it is possible for purchasers to understand the game they find themselves in and, by adopting an alternative process that is proven to work, it is possible to play it to an advantage. We can establish better control over how our entire organization interfaces with a supplier so at every touch point our stakeholders are 'on message' to deliver only information to a supplier that will aid our negotiation preparation, thus preventing the supplier from gaining useful intelligence from our own people, often without them realizing the implications of what they share.

If we are aware of the personality traits that form part of the salesperson's make-up, and our own personal traits and potential weaknesses, we can ensure that relationships are built on our terms. Awareness can also help us avoid falling into the 'trust trap' and better manage what we say and our body language. We can even learn to capitalize on chinks in the salesperson's armour, perhaps by displays of apparent suffering within a negotiation to disarm the seller. We can learn the supplier's repertoire and recognize specific tactics and what they are designed to do, and build our own repertoire to counter these and establish our own advantage.

If we can begin to do all these things then we can seize the advantage in a negotiation through process, personality and repertoire. The rest of this book helps provide the roadmap to follow, starting with process in the next chapter.

Red Sheet – 03
a winning process
for negotiation

This chapter aims to outline a proven process for planning, executing and reviewing negotiations. It introduces the Red Sheet® methodology that provides the framework for the rest of this book and identifies the enabling factors that are needed together with the negotiation process in order to be effective at negotiation.

Pathway questions addressed in this chapter:

4   How can I plan for a negotiation? What process do I follow?

A process-based approach

Good negotiation needs a good process – a structure that combines all the things we need to do to be effective, provides direction for the timing and sequencing of these activities and is repeatable. Contrary to how many negotiators appear to operate, leaving things to 'being good in the room' is not enough and certainly not transparent or manageable from an organizational viewpoint. Good negotiators follow some sort of methodology or approach for what they do. Sometimes this may be undefined and learnt through experience but nevertheless they are repeating steps that have been found to work. Across the vast sea of negotiation literature there is precious little in terms of process and what exists is often difficult to adopt in practice. Instead most of the published works concentrate on tactics, techniques and principles of successful negotiation, leaving the reader to work out how it all fits together in real-life negotiation situations. This is perhaps one of the reasons why negotiation can often be regarded as a special skill and why those new to negotiation might describe feeling as if they don't really know what they are doing.

Process gives confidence, alignment and common ways of working across a team. It increases capability by establishing a repeatable approach in the minds of the users. It shifts the reliance away from personality and repertoire alone but utilizes the power of planning together with available intelligence to develop winning approaches and secure results. For those in procurement or supply chain functions, following a proven negotiation process is even more important than for our sales counterparts and helps the buyer gain some advantage over a well-trained seller.

Introducing Red Sheet

The Red Sheet is a negotiation planning tool that provides the structure and process for effective negotiation. It is a process that has been proven to work well and is used the world over, by many large corporations. Indeed, in some it is mandated for negotiations above a certain value. The original Red Sheet was developed uniquely for the procurement community in response to the lack of planning approaches in this sector, and has since been further developed, and is used universally, for all types of negotiation.

Red Sheet, as the name suggests, started life a large sheet of red paper (Figure 3.1). It is a tool containing the entire end-to-end stages of negotiation planning and execution in a poster form designed to promote collaboration. The poster was designed to be placed on a wall or a table to allow a team to crowd around and work through the process together. The physical poster-based Red Sheet, along with the family of physical Red Sheets in different sizes and complexity, continues to be the way many organizations like to work to maximize group-based interaction and planning. However, the Red Sheet methodology is now deployed in many forms including electronically online.

The Red Sheet structure and sequence is described throughout the rest of this book and defines the proven process that sits behind highly effective negotiations and is provided in full in the Appendix. In addition the methodology helps both individuals and organizations to be effective at negotiation in many different ways, specifically it:

Figure 3.1   Using Red Sheet

- promotes collaboration and alignment in the face of the supplier;
- helps rebalance the disparity between the salesperson's training and experience and that of the buyer;
- removes the reliance on an individual's need to use tactics and theatre during the event;
- provides a roadmap to help steer through the negotiation event itself with confidence;
- integrates the negotiation activity with the wider procurement function activities, ensuring intelligence and insight gained elsewhere is fully utilized.

Negotiation STEP by STEP

If you want to take someone with severe fear of flying on an aeroplane you're unlikely to get them onboard by just taking them to the plane among the throng of regular passengers and the stresses of a modern airport. Instead, achieving this goal might require a series of small steps. First you might get them familiar with the idea of taking a flight, then a trip to the

Figure 3.2 The overarching STEP framework that underpins negotiation planning

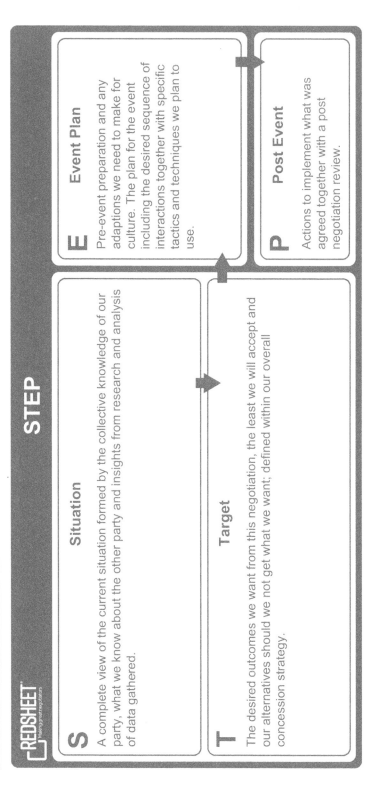

REDSHEET
Making great negotiations

STEP

S **Situation**

A complete view of the current situation formed by the collective knowledge of our party, what we know about the other party and insights from research and analysis of data gathered.

T **Target**

The desired outcomes we want from this negotiation, the least we will accept and our alternatives should we not get what we want; defined within our overall concession strategy.

E **Event Plan**

Pre-event preparation and any adaptions we need to make for culture. The plan for the event including the desired sequence of interactions together with specific tactics and techniques we plan to use.

P **Post Event**

Actions to implement what was agreed together with a post negotiation review.

airport to see the planes and people coming and going. If this went well then next you might book a seat on a flight you're prepared not to take and attempt to take the person through security and to the gate. Finally you might persuade them to walk onto the plane and take their seat, encouraging and supporting them all the way.

To get someone to do something they don't want to do means taking it one step at a time. It is the same for negotiation. If we set out trying to go from our starting position to your most desired outcome in one step we are unlikely to win cooperation from the other party. Instead we need to work through a series of steps towards our end goal. The skill comes in the way we take these steps.

Negotiation as a series of steps is a crucial mindset for negotiators. This step-by-step concept is so important that the entire Red Sheet methodology has been structured within an overarching STEP framework: Situation, Target, Event Plan and Post-Event (Figure 3.2). This is not simply a happy coincidence and handy reminder, but is also a powerful action-based planning approach based upon the established STP framework (Situation, Target, Proposal). Across the STEP framework within Red Sheet are 15 smaller steps that comprise the full end-to-end negotiation planning, execution and review process and the majority of the remainder of this book will work through each of these in turn, starting by exploring each of the four overarching STEP sections.

STEP One – Situation

The first STEP is 'Situation' and contains a further eight smaller steps within Red Sheet (Figure 3.3). It is impossible to determine the outcome we want from a negotiation if we don't appreciate our current position. Furthermore, if we start negotiating without this any outcome is likely to be sub-optimal as we will almost certainly lack knowledge of the strengths or weaknesses of our position and will have failed to anticipate how the other party might attempt to gain an advantage.

'Situation' ensures a methodical approach to negotiation planning that necessitates full research and analysis in order to establish a clear view of the current situation. This lays the groundwork for our negotiation planning. It helps to establish the context and objectives for this negotiation; identify those who need to be involved and consulted; determine any cultural differences or factors we need to attend to; and consider the personality match of our team to the negotiation in question, as well as everything we know about the other party's anticipated team line-up. This section is also about

Figure 3.3 The Situation STEP within Red Sheet

1. BACKGROUND

Background and context of the negotiation, including a timeline.

2. OBJECTIVES

Value objectives, relationship objectives and ideal outcomes for the negotiation.

3. STAKEHOLDERS

Stakeholder map, RACI assessment and engagement plan.

4. CULTURE

Assessment of cultural factors using key cultural indicators.

5A. NEGOTIONALITY®

Our team line up Portfolio Analysis and negotionality assessment.

Negotionality Assessment

6A. OPPONENT

Their team and event intelligence.

7A. POWER

Factors giving each party power and knowledge of position.

Example

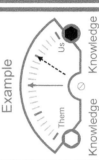

Us

Them

Knowledge   Knowledge

8A. GAME

Game being played now.

establishing what negotiation power we hold and what the other party holds and more importantly whether this is understood. Finally this section uses Game Theory to help analyse and shape the negotiation. When combined, the outputs from each of these steps provides a complete picture of our position as we approach the negotiation and forms the basis for determining outcomes and setting targets.

STEP Two – Target and negotiation strategy

STEP Two is 'Target and negotiation strategy' and contains six steps (Figure 3.4). The first four are a continuation from the 'Situation' stage where we are beginning to set targets and ways forward for the negotiation in response to specific areas of our current position. Here the specific target outcomes for this negotiation are defined together with a plan for our behaviour in the negotiation (in response to our understanding of personality make-up for our team) along with plans to maximize power. The individual points we wish to negotiate (our 'negotiables'), matched against those we anticipate the other party has, along with concession strategy are identified.

Failure to set targets and plan for concessions is one of the main reasons for failure or for achieving less favourable negotiation outcomes. The problem here is one of human nature and our tendency to jump straight to a solution and 'doing something' rather than thinking about where we want to be. The other issue here is one of self-bias (see Chapter 1) and an over-confident belief in our ability to secure a good result in the negotiation, thus diminishing the importance of planning in our minds. There is one other factor here that makes the concession planning very important and that is, as we saw in Chapter 2, salespeople are typically better trained and re-sourced than the procurement community so are likely to be more adept at leveraging a succession of concessions from us. Targets and a well-considered plan for concessions dilute the seller's advantage and help place the purchaser in control. Target setting and concession planning are therefore critical elements in the negotiation planning process.

STEP Three – Event Plan

STEP Three is the 'Event Plan' and contains three steps (Figure 3.5). Initially we must consider how the results of the Culture section from STEP One affect the way we need to behave and act during the event. The second is

Figure 3.4 The Target and negotiation strategy STEP within Red Sheet

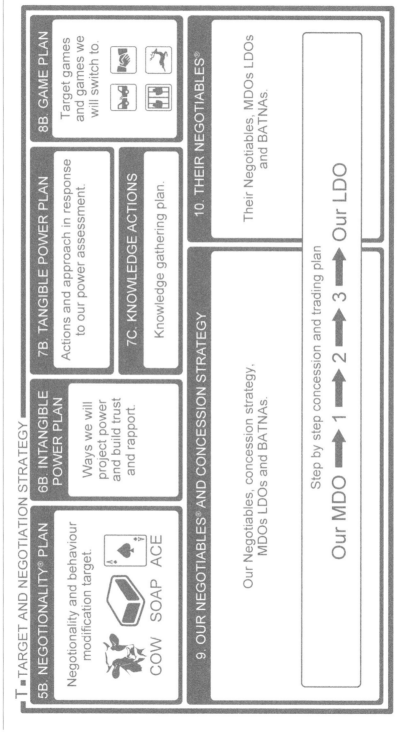

T – TARGET AND NEGOTIATION STRATEGY

5B. NEGOTIONALITY® PLAN

Negotionality and behaviour modification target.

COW   SOAP   ACE

6B. INTANGIBLE POWER PLAN

Ways we will project power and build trust and rapport.

7B. TANGIBLE POWER PLAN

Actions and approach in response to our power assessment.

7C. KNOWLEDGE ACTIONS

Knowledge gathering plan.

8B. GAME PLAN

Target games and games we will switch to.

9. OUR NEGOTIABLES® AND CONCESSION STRATEGY

Our Negotiables, concession strategy, MDOs LDOs and BATNAs.

Step by step concession and trading plan

Our MDO → 1 → 2 → 3 → Our LDO

10. THEIR NEGOTIABLES®

Their Negotiables, MDOs LDOs and BATNAs.

about the preparations for the event including event logistics and communications and the third is the plan for the negotiation event itself. This shouldn't be left to chance. Here we consider planning the things we can do to be in control of the event as much as we are able including considering room layout (where we can) and what we will do at the start of the meeting. We also establish a preferred agenda for the negotiation. It is difficult to hold steadfast to an agenda or plan for how we want the negotiation to run in the face of the other party who will most likely have their own agenda; however, our agenda helps us maintain some direction as the negotiation ebbs and flows around us. It also helps us plan specific tactics and techniques we might deploy as things unfold.

Figure 3.5   The Event Plan STEP within Red Sheet

STEP Four – Post-Event

STEP Four is the 'Post-Event' review and contains two final steps (Figure 3.6); the first being any post-event actions that are required. Once the negotiation is complete any agreement is worthless unless it is implemented. A plan and supporting actions to turn what was agreed into reality is required; there may also be things that we need to take forward to a subsequent negotiation with the other party so these must be captured.

The final step within Red Sheet is about reviewing outcomes and capturing learnings. Getting good at negotiation is about learning by experience. A highly effective, but often neglected, post-negotiation event step is to review how the negotiation went, to capture the key learnings and share knowledge with others internally. Doing this well requires those involved to make a conscious effort to review each negotiation once complete.

Figure 3.6   The Post-event STEP within Red Sheet

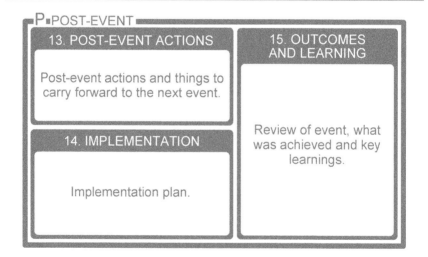

Using the Red Sheet

The Red Sheet is provided in full, section by section, in the Appendix and summarized in Figure 3.7. As we have learnt, good negotiation is about process, personality and repertoire. The full 15-step approach within Red Sheet represents the proven process that allows procurement and supply chain professionals to plan, execute and review their negotiations and, if well deployed, will increase the likelihood of a favourable negotiation outcome.

The Red Sheet process is a thorough and detailed planning approach and one that assumes a degree of internal collaboration. All the steps are essential where the negotiation involves an area of spend that is significant in some way; for example, in terms of total spend, importance to the business, complexity, risk, need for innovation or future potential. Here a team-based approach will almost certainly be essential. This is because any significant spend areas will attract the interest and demand the involvement of key stakeholders, the same stakeholders the supplier will work hard to develop relationships with which, if not aligned with us, could work against us. However, there are many other negotiation scenarios for less significant spend items but which still require a robust process; for example, a buyer having a one-to-one meeting with a supplier to discuss a routine area of supply. Following the full 15 steps of the Red Sheet approach could prove to be overly cumbersome and unnecessary for these everyday negotiations. Instead it is enough to apply only those steps or tactics that will help secure the right result. Good negotiation requires adaptability and the skill to apply negotiation principles to any scenario, drawing on suitable tactics and techniques to help. This comes from learning negotiation in its entirety and then learning what to leave out. This book will therefore concentrate on the full Red Sheet process. Figure 3.8 gives a possible simpler pathway through Red Sheet, following only the essential steps needed for effective negotiation in one-on-one or non-complex scenarios.

A collaborative approach

While everyday, non-complex negotiations might be planned and conducted by a procurement or supply chain professional alone, with little or even no need for interaction or consultation with the wider business, negotiations for areas of spend that are significant or complex require collaboration. Collaboration not only helps ensure that the needs and wants of all concerned are, where possible, met but it establishes alignment and a united front facing off to a supplier both before, during and after a negotiation event. Such collaboration doesn't just happen by chance. In fact, achieving a level of constructive collaboration requires intense and sustained energy because it is about convincing people to get involved in what we're doing, rather than the many other things they would otherwise be doing, and then about keeping them there. In practice this involves forming a team, creating a mini-project with a series of planning workshops where those involved plan and possibly even participate in the negotiation event itself. The ability of the procurement or supply chain practitioners to lead and marshal this

Figure 3.7 The full 15-step Red Sheet process

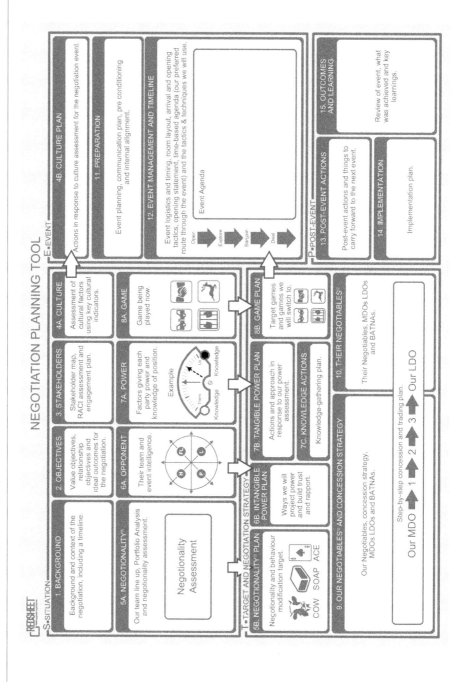

NEGOTIATION PLANNING TOOL

REDSHEET

S-SITUATION

1. BACKGROUND
Background and context of the negotiation, including a timeline.

2. OBJECTIVES
Value objectives, relationship objectives and ideal outcomes for the negotiation.

3. STAKEHOLDERS
Stakeholder map, RACI assessment and engagement plan.

4A. CULTURE
Assessment of cultural factors using key cultural indicators.

4B. CULTURE PLAN
Actions in response to culture assessment for the negotiation event.

E-EVENT

11. PREPARATION
Event planning, communication plan, pre conditioning and internal alignment.

12. EVENT MANAGEMENT AND TIMELINE
Event logistics and timing, room layout, arrival and opening tactics, opening statement, time-based agenda (our preferred route through the event) and the tactics & techniques we will use.

Event Agenda

Orien
Explore
Bargain
Deal

15. OUTCOMES AND LEARNING
Review of event, what was achieved and key learnings.

5A. NEGOTIABILITY
Our team line up, Portfolio Analysis and negotionality assessment.

Negotionality Assessment

6A. OPPONENT
Their team and event intelligence.

7A. POWER
Factors giving each party power and knowledge of position.

Example
Knowledge
Team Us
Knowledge
Knowledge

8A. GAME
Game being played now.

P-POST-EVENT

13. POST-EVENT ACTIONS
Post-event actions and things to carry forward to the next event.

14. IMPLEMENTATION
Implementation plan.

T-TARGET AND NEGOTIATION STRATEGY

5B. NEGOTIONALITY: PLAN
Negotionality and behaviour modification target.

COW SOAP ACE

6B. INTANGIBLE POWER PLAN
Ways we will project power and build trust and rapport.

7B. TANGIBLE POWER PLAN
Actions and approach in response to our power assessment.

7C. KNOWLEDGE ACTIONS
Knowledge-gathering plan.

8B. GAME PLAN
Target games and games we will switch to.

9. OUR NEGOTIABLES' AND CONCESSION STRATEGY
Our Negotiables, concession strategy, MDOs LDOs and BATNAs.

Our MDO 1 2 3 Our LDO
Step-by-step concession and trading plan.

10. THEIR NEGOTIABLES'
Their Negotiables, MDOs LDOs and BATNAs.

Figure 3.8 The abbreviated Red Sheet process (simple negotiations)

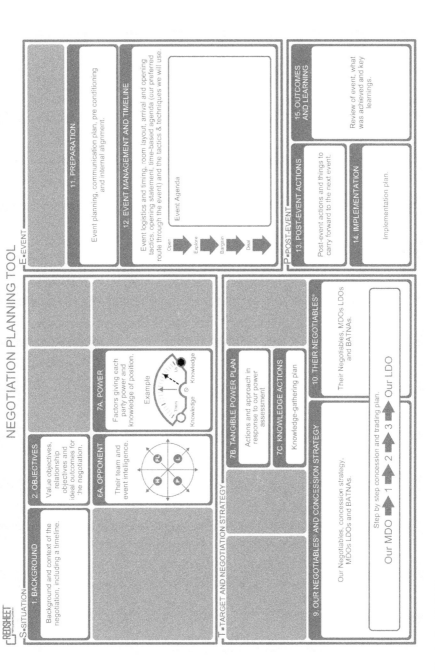

© Positive Purchasing Ltd 2013

collaboration is key to ensuring benefits are fully realized. Those within procurement or supply chain functions, however, may lack the experience and capability needed here, as the required skill set is not that of a traditional procurement or supply chain practitioner and so development may well be needed in these areas:

- establishing and managing a team;
- conflict resolution skills;
- coaching skills;
- leadership skills;
- facilitation skills;
- project management skills.

Getting started

To use the Red Sheet methodology, work through each of the sections in turn. Within this book the sections are laid out in sequence as the chapters unfold, allowing practitioners to follow and apply the process. Each section is explained in detail along with supporting reference information, tactics and techniques. The full Red Sheet is given in the Appendix.

Red Sheet is a sequential methodology and each of the 15 sections guide, practitioners and teams but is also a templates to be completed along the way. When the first 12 'pre-event' sections are complete the result is a powerful plan for the negotiation event. Red Sheet is a tool to encourage collaborative working where a team approach is appropriate so sections should be worked together with those who need to be involved or who will be part of the negotiation process. Thought and time from a group of people to work through the various sections produces a precious and powerful thing. The power lies in the fact that those involved will now have alignment of thinking and will hold in their heads a plan for how the negotiation will run and their role to support this. At this point the complete Red Sheet becomes merely a record of the discussions and insights gained along the way with the real output and benefit now in the minds of those concerned. Of course not all negotiations are big events requiring a full team, so for simple, everyday one-on-one-type negotiations the same mental preparation comes from working through those Red Sheet sections that are relevant (see Figure 3.8).

Planning the negotiation

04

This chapter explores how to get started with planning a negotiation. It begins by considering 'why' we are negotiating in the first place and then 'how' we might proceed considering both the value and relationship objective. Stakeholder involvement is examined and finally this chapter outlines how a timeline can help support negotiation planning.

Pathway questions addressed in this chapter

4 How can I plan for a negotiation? What process do I follow?

5 I need to negotiate something – where do I start?

6 What are the different types of negotiation and how do I decide which one to adopt?

7 How should I determine my ideal negotiation outcomes?

8 How can I ensure a single aligned and united approach amongst everyone on my side who has an interest in the negotiation?

13 What power do I hold relative to my opponent?

23 Are all negotiations the same or are there situations where I need a different approach?

Red Sheet steps covered in this chapter

1 and 2

Background

The first step in our negotiation planning is to understand what it is we are going to plan for, the type of negotiation this is and the supporting short- to medium-term activities needed. Red Sheet step 1 (Background) and step 2 (Objectives) provide the structure here and an example of a completed step 1 and 2 is given in Figure 4.1. Where a negotiation team is involved this may be the first time the team comes together and so working this step with the team will help with scoping and alignment. Completing this step (as for all other steps within the Red Sheet methodology) isn't simply a case of filling in the boxes; instead it requires careful thought and, where a team is involved, discussion, debate and agreement. The next few sections explain what needs to be considered in order to contextualize and plan for the negotiation we are going to conduct and complete steps 1 and 2.

Why negotiate?

The starting point in preparing for any negotiation is to be clear about the negotiation we are about to prepare for. That is not such a crazy statement as a small amount of time invested here can make a dramatic difference to our preparation. Such clarity is essential for team-based negotiations if everyone is to be aligned. The starting point is therefore to answer three questions: what, with whom and why are we negotiating?

Who are we negotiating with?

The company or entity we are negotiating with and around which we will tailor our negotiation approach. It is possible the decision maker may not be the party we engage with. For example, if I buy a house I might never meet the seller but instead negotiate with the agent or realtor, empowered perhaps to make certain concessions. But it is the seller who ultimately makes the decision. In this case negotiation planning would then need to be tailored to both negotiator and decision maker.

What are we negotiating?

Define the scope for the negotiation. This might seem obvious at first but take a moment to be clear about this. For example, if you are buying an item of production line equipment then needless to say this will be the focus for the negotiation. But what about future spares? What about delivery, installation, maintenance and even future disposal? Are you buying just one

Figure 4.1 Red Sheet step 1 – Background (worked example)

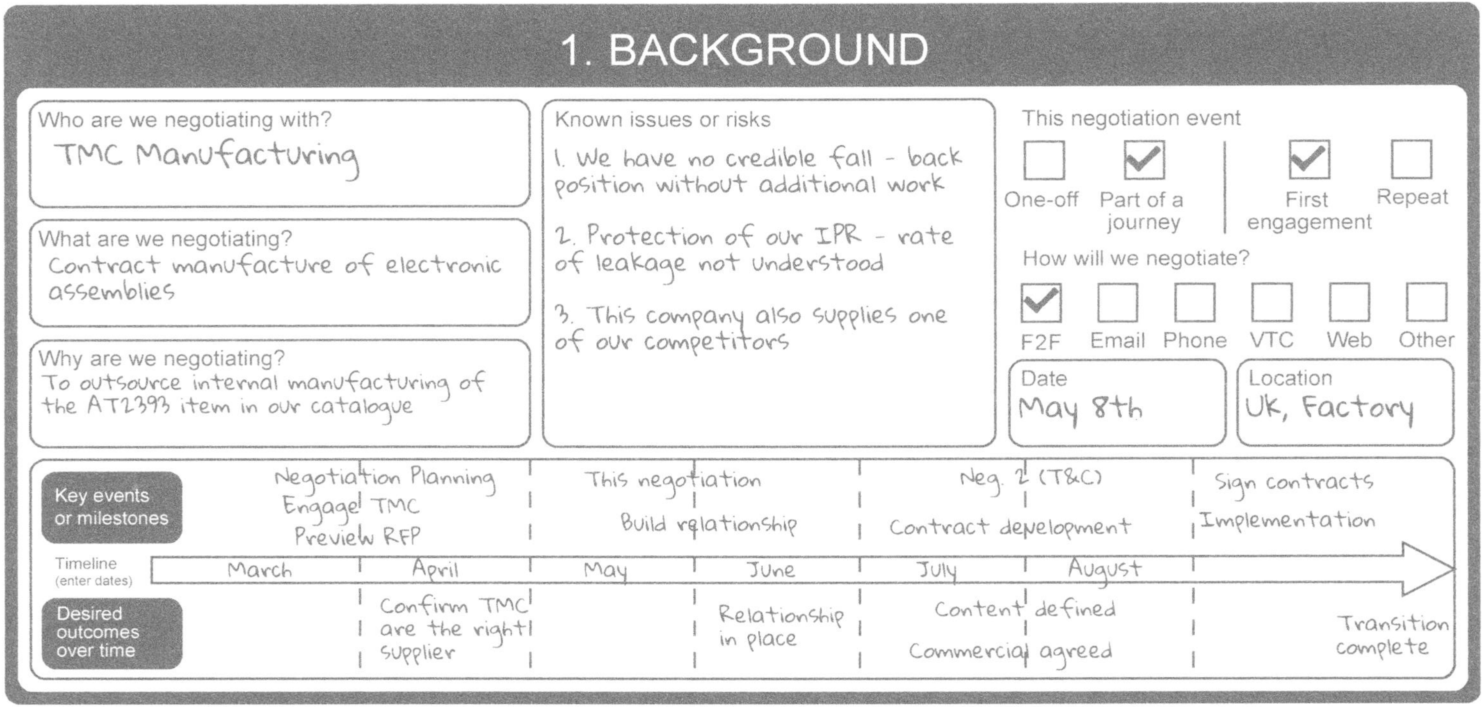

1. BACKGROUND

Who are we negotiating with?
TMC Manufacturing

What are we negotiating?
Contract manufacture of electronic assemblies

Why are we negotiating?
To outsource internal manufacturing of the AT1293 item in our catalogue

Known issues or risks
1. We have no credible fall – back position without additional work
2. Protection of our IPR – rate of leakage not understood
3. This company also supplies one of our competitors

This negotiation event

One-off ☐ | Part of a ☑ journey | First ☑ | Repeat ☐
engagement

How will we negotiate?
F2F ☑ | Phone ☐ | VTC ☐ | Web ☐ | Other ☐
Email ☐

Date
May 8th

Location
UK, Factory

Key events or milestones	Negotiation Planning Engage TMC Preview RFP		This negotiation Build relationship		Neg 2 (T&C) Contract development	Sign contracts Implementation	
Timeline (enter dates)	March	April	May	June	July	August	
Desired outcomes over time		Confirm TMC are the right supplier		Relationship in place	Content defined Commercial agreed		Transition complete

piece of equipment or is this part of a bigger programme of investment that might give you more leverage?

Consider how this negotiation relates to the total cost of ownership and what value beyond the primary acquisition might be needed from this supplier now and in future. Consider what is included and what is not. Consider also if we are negotiating around what gets supplied directly to us or what happens back up the supply chain. Use brainstorming if a team is involved, and then an informed choice regarding the scope of the negotiation is possible, which should then be summarized in a simple statement.

Why are we negotiating?

This is the most important question to answer early on and is about considering what outcomes are hoped for by negotiating. Planning and executing a negotiation takes time, effort and energy so it is good to be certain the investment is worthwhile. For example, setting out to negotiate to reduce the amount of tax we need to pay tends to be a waste of time, but securing a deferral or special terms less so. Sometimes we may have no choice but to negotiate; however, where we do have choice it is important to be certain the effort is worth the potential benefit. Perhaps the level of benefit is near certain or perhaps highly speculative but in any case check: there should be a conscious decision as to whether it is worth investing the time and energy in negotiating.

There are other reasons to choose not to negotiate. Sometimes maintaining a relationship is paramount and so negotiating might be detrimental. In such cases the right approach may well be to simply accept what the other party is proposing: an approach that underpins many happy marriages.

Agile negotiation planning

Every negotiation is different, and there are many different ways we can approach a negotiation. Depending upon the situation some approaches will be more effective than others – one size does not fit all. Agility is key to negotiation success coupled with the capability to select and deploy the right approach for a given situation. How we plan and indeed what to plan for must be determined according to the situation, the nature of the negotiation we are about to do, how it fits with the longer term and what we want to achieve. Agility in negotiation planning begins by considering these different factors as we move through steps 1 and 2 and shaping our approach accordingly.

Identifying known issues or risks

At the outset of our planning it is good to identify any known issues or risks we face when going into this negotiation. This step can easily be missed, but could be crucially important in shaping our approach to the negotiation or having the right alternatives in place early on. Things to consider here might include:

- risk or consequences if we don't secure a certain outcome;
- risk of default on what is agreed during a negotiation (eg based upon past experience of the individuals concerned);
- risk of unethical behaviour by our opponent;
- known weaknesses on our part or internal issues around our capability to negotiate effectively;
- any other factors that could prevent us working towards or securing a good outcome.

Understanding the journey

There are occasions where a single interaction and negotiation event is all that is required to reach a satisfactory outcome and conclude a transaction, such as an eBay purchase or buying a house. Here interactions with the seller or the seller's agent are limited to those needed in order to conclude the sale and fulfil contractual obligations and perhaps some niceties to make this go smoothly; for example, a house seller might leave instructions for operating the boiler and details of when the rubbish/trash gets collected. Any relationship beyond this would be unlikely, unnecessary and possibly inappropriate. These are true one-off arm's-length commercial transactions and typical of a value-claiming approach.

However, for value-creating negotiations where we anticipate an ongoing relationship, our negotiation will most likely be one of many interactions over time. It is this big-picture perspective that helps select the most appropriate approach for this negotiation and the most suitable tactics, balancing the drive for immediate benefits against the long-term relationship and future interactions. Genuine value-creation negotiations should therefore be considered as part of a bigger journey with short-term targets shaped by the long-term aims. Therefore, as we begin our negotiation planning it is important for us to map the journey we intent to travel on. Doing this presents us with a series of opportunities:

- *What we can't get today we can try for tomorrow.* Getting everything we want from a single negotiation is rarely possible as compromise gets in the way. However, a longer-term perspective provides the opportunity to secure benefits a step at a time, working towards a longer-term objective.

- *Seize the moment.* Timing is everything and there may well be a good or bad time to push for certain outcomes and leave others alone.

- *Capitalize on the value of the relationship.* If both parties recognize the relationship has value, in other words both want to remain in it, then it means compromise for the sake of the relationship is possible and this is a source of leverage.

- *Leave a footprint.* Each time we negotiate as part of a longer-term journey we take a step toward our long-term goals. However, suppliers love to find ways to increase prices and will seek ways to reposition things previously agreed. This becomes more difficult for the supplier if we leave a footprint, in other words we firm up individual points of agreement. Here the use of master, framework or preferred agreements with suppliers helps. Such agreements typically define how the relationship works and the agreed pricing and terms for individual transactions. These don't need to be contractual so long as they don't commit to levels of business but do serve to crystallize points of agreement.

Therefore, at the outset, determine if this is a one-off negotiation or part of a longer-term journey. Table 4.1 shows the characteristics of each. Determine this with the supplier's anticipated value objective in mind. If we believe we need a value-creating approach and we think we are on a long-term journey but the other side has a different plan we may end up weakening our position and conceding for the sake of a relationship we don't have. Judging this accurately requires a good understanding of the relationship we have and being clear about how it needs to develop, if at all.

First vs repeat engagement

Judging the relationship requires some sort of reference point. If this is a repeat negotiation, then our previous experience of the relationship is a good barometer for the future. However, if this is our first engagement with the supplier then the relationship is not yet formed. The value or potential value of the relationship has not yet been established so this has little standing or influence and is not yet a source of leverage. The dynamics at the first engagement are therefore very different:

Table 4.1 Characteristics of a one-off negotiation vs negotiation as part of a journey

Factor	One-off Negotiation	Negotiation as Part of a Journey
Relationship	• none or superficial in order to gain an advantage over the other party or conduct business in a pleasant way	• ongoing relationship, perhaps long-term • importance and value of relationship depends upon long-term needs • personal relationships and trust also play a part
Negotiation objectives	• most I can get	• achieve long-term objectives • maintain relationship needed to do this • maximize current position, balanced with long-term aims
Alternatives (if desired outcomes not achieved)	• walk away	• work on other forms of value • come back and attempt to secure required outcome during future negotiations
Remedies (if other party lets you down or even dupes you)	• legal recourse • never go back • put it down to experience and move on	• attempt to discuss and agree a mutually beneficial solution • leverage the obligations both parties have to the relationship to remedy the problem • ultimately, review the appropriateness of the long-term relationship and be prepared to move away

- There will be no or little trust established between parties.
- Parties will have little direct knowledge of the other and so will be 'sizing each other up'.
- If we don't know our opponents, it is easy for them to play different characters or adopt styles and tactics designed to unsettle us.
- The seller may well focus on forced relationship development and attempt to make us like them to help secure a result.

- First engagements should be handled cautiously, allowing only the type of relationship that fits with our goals to begin to be developed.

How will we negotiate?

Another consideration at the outset is how we will negotiation and the basics about the negotiation event itself – the date, location and method (eg face-to-face meeting, video or web conference, phone, or will this happen over time using e-mail, a web event or other means?). This might seem an obvious step but it is important so we can map out our planned negotiation activities over time and also so we can plan for the way the negotiation will be conducted. For example, a single face-to-face event negotiation requires a completely different plan, approach and skill set to one that might play out over time by e-mail with some calls or web conferences along the way. In Chapter 15 we will explore how to be successful for remote negotiations.

To negotiation and beyond! Building a negotiation timeline

As for any achievement of significance, good planning plays a pivotal role in a successful outcome, and when more than one individual needs to be involved those concerned must work in concert to achieve this. A raft of literature and approaches on planning exist out there, and most individuals working in a business role will have had some sort of exposure to such techniques so I will only briefly touch on this subject, with further reading recommended where needed. The point is that, for a negotiation, as for any other important activity, a plan is needed. If you, or your organization, have adopted a specific planning approach that is familiar and known to you, then you should use this, but whatever you do keep it simple.

In its crudest form planning is about determining the individual activities, and their sequencing, required to reach the desired outcome. However, in the case of a government of a significant world country attempting to negotiate peace between two warring nations, a single meeting is unlikely to be enough and the list of activities would be overwhelming. Once again reaching our goal is about taking small steps and determining a series of smaller achievements or milestones along the way. Therefore, negotiation planning is about determining the individual milestones and supporting activities required to reach the desired outcome either for a single event or across multiple events to achieve wider outcomes (as defined by the long-term relationship objectives). A simple Gantt chart approach is all that is needed here; however, in line with the overriding principles of Red Sheet, the development of the plan should be done collaboratively so the stakeholders who need to be involved, or who will be part of the actual negotiation event, fully appreciate and agree the programme of activities and their role to support the process. An example is shown in Figure 4.1.

Determining negotiation objectives

The next early step in our negotiation planning is to determine our objectives for the negotiation. Red Sheet step 2 (Objectives) provides the structure here and an example of a completed step 2 is given in Figure 4.2.

We cannot begin to plan effectively if we do not know, or are unclear about, what we are trying achieve. We could wait until all our planning is complete, and that might seem more logical, but good targets are not a one-time thing; rather, they evolve and are refined throughout the planning process. For this reason, it is essential to begin to determine our objectives for the negotiation early on. We must decide if we are setting out to 'claim' or 'create' value (our value objective) and the overall aims and intent for the relationship, if any. We also need some idea of the sort of outcomes we are seeking from the negotiation. Those involved will almost certainly have some sort of idea here – after all, why would we be contemplating a negotiation otherwise? Target setting therefore begins by getting our team and key stakeholders to articulate what they believe we want to get from the negotiation. Discussing and refining these will help us arrive at a set of objectives understood by all on our side which wc will use to drive our negotiation. It is likely that there will be different needs and expectations, so discussion will help secure alignment and agreement and honing targets to arrive at a succinct list of target outcomes. These should then be used to shape the rest of our negotiation planning.

Remember, a good target is one where everyone is clear what good looks like and where you know when you get there. Acronyms such as SMART (make them Specific, Measurable, Attainable, Relevant and Timely) can help sometimes, but can hold us back if we want to express a general aim such as to improve a relationship. The point here is shaking out a shortlist of the agreed target outcomes for this negotiation, and once defined, coming back to them and further building them as we continue our planning process.

Figure 4.2   Red Sheet step 2 – Objectives (worked example)

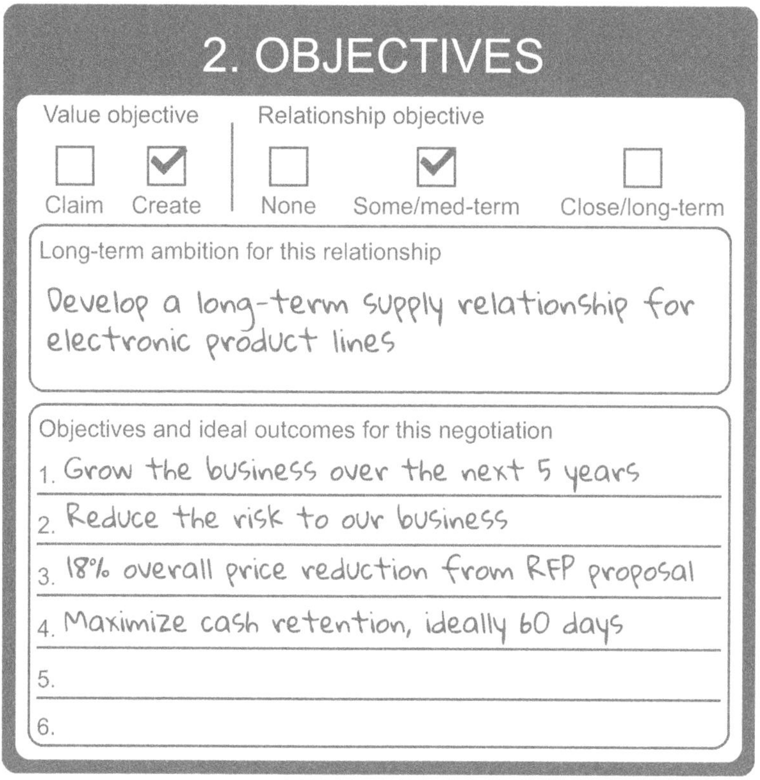

2. OBJECTIVES

Value objective | Relationship objective

☐ Claim   ☑ Create | ☐ None   ☑ Some/med-term   ☐ Close/long-term

Long-term ambition for this relationship

Develop a long-term supply relationship for electronic product lines

Objectives and ideal outcomes for this negotiation

1. *Grow the business over the next 5 years*
2. *Reduce the risk to our business*
3. *18% overall price reduction from RFP proposal*
4. *Maximize cash retention, ideally 60 days*
5.
6.

The value objective

Negotiation isn't just something confined to business situations; it is a skill for life! It is something we all get involved in to a greater or lesser extent throughout our daily interactions, whether we realize it or not.

As we saw in Chapter 1 there are fundamentally two types of negotiation: those that seek to claim value, often as a 'one-off' and 'distributive' interaction determining how the distribution of a fixed amount is split; and those that seek to create value, perhaps as part of a longer-term relationship that seeks to increase the available value to all parties. The value objective shapes every aspect of negotiation planning and execution so it is important to establish this clearly at the outset.

Negotiation is part of much of our everyday lives and there are different types of negotiation, each having different value objectives. Table 4.2 lists these and in every case there is a clear link between the value objective and the anticipated future relationship or sustainability of the arrangements between the parties. Where a relationship is needed or arrangements between parties must remain sustainable for both then only a value-creation approach will ensure this. If there is no need or desire for any sort of relationship beyond the immediate interaction, negotiation tends to default to value claiming.

Where the future is ignored in favour of value claiming the results can, in some instances, be catastrophic with wayward children or warring nations. A footnote here is the relevance of perception. Experienced negotiators

Table 4.2   Different types of negotiation

Types	Examples	Claiming or Creating Value?
Employment	• new employee • asking for a raise • negotiating a promotion • negotiating exit terms	**It depends** – companies (and in particular rigid HR policies and procedures) often drive a value-claiming approach, especially for low-grade employees. Here workers might be regarded more as a commodity that is acquired. However, for more senior or highly skilled employees approaches shift more towards creating value. Asking a new partner to join a law firm would almost certainly be approached on a creating value basis with negotiations focusing on securing a motivated individual who will add value to the firm rather than securing at the least acceptable salary. There is a strong link between initial motivation and 'value creation' negotiation in employee negotiations.
Parenting	• staying out late • getting something they want • homework • behaviour modification	**Value creation** – parent/child negotiations are almost always attempting to create value as both parties will have an eye to the bigger picture and end game; parents want to stay in control and raise good kids and children seek to shift the boundaries more in their favour. Claiming value negotiations tend to have short-lived success and lead to rebellion at some point.

Table 4.2   *continued*

Types	Examples	Claiming or Creating Value?
Settlement	• personal injury or loss following some negligence eg workplace accident, hospital error • your bank makes an error and freezes your account causing personal disruption	**Value claiming** – settlement negotiations are usually the end stage within some sort of dispute so an ongoing relationship tends to be unlikely. For this reason the game here is about maximizing your position and outcome and that's why lawyers make a lot of money from personal injury claims. There are exceptions – loved ones who have lost someone due to a hospital error might elect not to sue but insist on a review of arrangements to prevent it happening again or measures to help others in similar situations. These exceptions and using a value-creating approach are however driven by personal beliefs and philosophies with the driver being some sort of act for the greater good.
Collective Bodies	• trade unions acting on behalf of a workforce • class action; lawyers acting on behalf of many people against one company or institution	**It depends** – a class action led by a lawyer against a big pharmaceutical company on behalf of many individuals affected by unexpected side effects from a drug will most likely seek to claim value as no ongoing relationship is needed. However, in the case of a trade union it depends upon the power and opportunity the trade union has or chooses to use. In the UK during the 1970s, trade unions across the manufacturing sector amassed huge power, with value-claiming negotiations being commonplace. These approaches would be unsustainable and unpopular in many sectors today so a more balanced, 'value-creation' approach tends to prevail.

Table 4.2 *continued*

Types	Examples	Claiming or Creating Value?
Countries	• peace or terms of surrender • agreeing borders • access to resources • trade terms • immigration policies	**Value creating** – history is littered with examples of countries who have attempted to claim value from another and there are many war memorials to prove it, not to mention a world full of country-level tensions against specific others in some regions. At a country level the only negotiation that can ever deliver sustainable results is one that creates value for both parties; any disparity, whether real or perceived, tends to create tensions.
Security	• hostage release • diffusing terrorist threats or action • preventing a suicide bomber from completing his or her mission	**Value claiming** – while politicians often say 'we don't negotiate with terrorists', behind-the-scenes negotiations with criminals are commonplace. Security negotiations are fundamentally about claiming value, eg securing the safe release of the hostage and the future wellbeing of the kidnappers is irrelevant. If you are certain you can send in a SWAT team without the hostages being hurt then claiming value here might be the right approach. However, most hostage negotiators will tell you this scenario is rarely recommended. Instead winning negotiation approaches try, where possible, to create the perception of creating value and going some way to meeting the demands of the bad guys. Real concessions that help the bad guys might need to be made but they are typically done in a managed way to maintain the illusion of creating value, while maintaining an underlying claiming-value objective.

Table 4.2   *continued*

Types	Examples	Claiming or Creating Value?
Relationships	• getting married • friendships • relations	**Value creating** – life is a negotiation and if you consider the essence of any close relationship and the daily interactions we have, love, longevity and happiness depend upon a long-term value-creating approach. Most people can think of someone who 'claims value' in relationships and how this works against them.
Commercial	• buying something • selling something • individual to individual • business to individual • business to business	**It depends** – both value-claiming and value-creation approaches are appropriate and used depending upon the circumstances and the required relationship or longevity of arrangements between parties.

might attempt to claim value while apparently seeking to create value, knowing that the illusion of value creation is more likely to trigger reciprocation by the other party. For example, consider a hostage situation where police have established communication with a kidnapper. The conversation might go along the lines of:

Police: 'Tell us what you want.'
Kidnapper: 'I want firearms.'
Police: 'There are some things I can't do, but I can give you food. Do you need some food, if so I will arrange for whatever food you need?'
Kidnapper: 'Yes.'

This is a classic exchange for police managing a security situation. The negotiation might appear to be creating value by giving something to the kidnappers to help their position; however, the gesture is not what it seems as concealed within the container the food is delivered in will be a listening device allowing police to listen to the kidnappers' conversation. The illusion of creating value was simply a tactic.

The perception of 'creating value' can also be born out of a relationship and as we saw in Chapter 1 relationships are powerful things. If someone makes us like them and attempts to suggest there is some sort of relationship, our human tendency is to reciprocate, which is just what the salesperson wants us to do; hence salespeople put so much effort into relationship building.

Why most sellers want to create value

The supplier's value objective, and hence how they will approach the negotiation, will differ. If there is potential for repeat business or some sort of ongoing relationship the supplier will almost always seek a value-creation approach and attempt to forge the conditions for up-selling beyond the immediate engagement. That said, there is a world of difference between a multibillion-dollar negotiation with a strategic partner supplier with whom we have a shared destiny and high mutual dependence and an individual purchase of a can of Coca-Cola. For the strategic partner both parties would most likely recognize what is at stake and what could be gained. Undoubtedly each party would put significant resources into building and maintaining a strong value-creation-based relationship. For our Coca-Cola purchase most people won't have a direct relationship with the Coca-Cola Company; however, we only need to check their mission statement to realize they want some sort of relationship with us, and the rest of the world also. This apparent value-creation approach is of course a product of them seeking to create long-term consumer relationships with their brand. As a happy coincidence, at the time of writing, the Coca-Cola mission statement even included the objective 'to create value and make a difference'.

Winning a customer for the first time is hard work and involves winning trust. Convincing a customer to buy a second or third time is much easier because the trust has already been won and the sales effort is reduced. This is the heart of brand theory and selling and why building relationships, whether directly or via a brand, is a primary objective of sellers. In the majority of selling scenarios the supplier will therefore apparently adopt value-creation approaches, both real and by creating a perception in order to win us over.

In contrast, value-claiming approaches by suppliers do exist but only where there is no need or desire to have any sort of ongoing relationship with us, for example, selling a house or some real estate, selling something on eBay, or the guy who turns up on the doorstep offering to re-surface your drive today for cash but whose phone number seems to be not in service when you later call to complain of problems.

Value claiming and value creation can also exist together side by side within a negotiation. For example, if a supplier provides a range of services, some may be critical and necessitate a relationship-based value-creation approach while others may be less so and freely available elsewhere with minimal impact of switching. In such cases suppliers typically seek to bundle offerings together and attempt to project a value-creation approach for the entire offering based upon dependency. However, by unbundling it is possible to negotiate on a value-claiming basis for the elements where we have choice and adopt a value-creation approach where the area of supply is critical. This is a fundamental tactic to gain leverage as it creates a competitive tension with the supplier for the generic elements but there is also risk by diluting the overall volume of business with the supplier so the critical area of supply becomes less attractive to them. Where value claiming is used alongside value creation the risks much be considered. Furthermore, bundling, providing it is on our terms, can give us further leverage against the critical area of supply.

The value objective is specific to the single negotiation we are planning and our preparation starts by determining our own value objective and making our best guess regarding that of the other party. The supplier's value objective is identifiable by research but also by considering the effort they are putting into building a longer-term relationship and the potential (as they would see it) for repeat business. This is summarized in Figure 4.3 where the different supplier responses to these variables are given. This shows how the supplier will either seek to claim value (perhaps while creating the illusion of value creation) or genuinely attempt to create value either directly with us or via branding.

Screwing the other party

The true Win/Win belongs to value-creating negotiations. Most value-claiming negotiations typically generate a WIN/win outcome, although the party with the lesser win may not fully appreciate this, or even a win/lose depending upon the choices buyer or seller make, degree of power and influence of the 'claiming party'. There is a point when a win/lose negotiation could be regarded as inappropriate, unfair, unethical or even illegal and where this point lies is a personal choice. However, in my experience, if you try to screw the other party by treating them unfairly or cheating them, your action will come back to haunt you at some point. I once interviewed a very successful key account manager with a large global company and managed to get him to talk candidly about how he engaged with buyers. He said,

Figure 4.3 Determining the supplier's value objectives

	Illusion	Creation
Lots	**'I'm doing you a favour'** Relationship as a power tactic, giving the illusion of value creation to hide a value-claiming approach *except* where a strong pre-existing relationship exists, and here the favour may be genuine. This then shifts to value creation for the sake of the relationship.	**'Together we are better'** True, long-term value-creation approach by the supplier with an eye to developing the relationship with you and increasing business and potentially unlocking synergic benefits.
	Claiming	**Branding**
Little	**'I'm only interested in maximizing my position'** Pure value claiming. Supplier will use all power available to secure the best outcome for them.	**'Buy what I'm offering'** Supplier wants you to buy and keep buying their product or service without the need for them to have a direct relationship with you. Branding and perception used to drive value creation and win trust.

Supplier's effort to build relationship (vertical axis)

None   Lots

Potential for repeat business

'Behind the friendly persona is someone who will never trust you [the buyer] and if you screw me, I'll get you back, maybe not straight away but in the future, when you need something like a delivery schedule shortened or help in a crisis. I'll always get my own back.' Therefore if we set out to do extreme value claiming to the detriment of the other party, be clear about the longer-term implications. It is possible to claim value in an ethical way with boundaries. If you do find yourself needing to use hard value-claiming approaches then it helps to make the other party like you; after all if someone likes you it is harder for them to get upset with you. This is a classic tactic used by used car salesmen when they know the car the little old lady is buying is unlikely to make it to the end of the road when she drives it away: but 'he was such a nice man'!

Relationship objectives

The value objective relates to the single negotiation we are planning. The relationship objectives look longer term and are the specific aims, aspirations and intent for where we want the relationship to go, if anywhere.

Relationships with suppliers are a double-edged sword. On the one hand they drive commitment, obligation, stability, security of supply and potentially benefits such as innovation and collaborative working. However, relationships can also dilute the benefits of competitive tension (when suppliers need to compete to win or retain business), compromise leverage and make it difficult to switch away. There are many scenarios where building a long-term relationship with a supplier is the right approach to minimize risk and maximize value; however, often a relationship beyond the commercial transaction is simply not needed, despite what the supplier might suggest.

Relationship objectives must be set on our terms and based around how important or critical the supplier is to us and not influenced by the degree to which the supplier wants a relationship or personal obligation to individuals. Don't be fooled when a supplier says, 'for the sake of our good relationship' or 'we're partners, right?'

Remember relationships are synonymous with value-creating negotiations so if we believe we need a value-creation negotiation then this suggests there is a wider relationship to some extent. Where this is the case there are two types of relationship with suppliers: relationships we have deliberately set out to cultivate and relationships we have ended up in. Relationship objectives should be set or reset in each case and in the case of the latter this serves to re-validate the appropriateness of the relationship or may possibly suggest the relationship serves no or little purpose moving forward.

Understanding and managing relationships with suppliers is explored in my book *Supplier Relationship Management* (also published by Kogan Page). Essentially the core principle of effective supplier relationship management is to precisely focus what energy and resources are available only on those suppliers who can make the most difference to our business. Factors that determine which suppliers are important enough to require a close, long-term supplier relationship include:

- current importance including high spend or high volumes driving business dependency;
- risk to our business (if there are supply difficulties or risk to our brand);
- market difficulty and complexity making switching difficult or impossible;
- future importance and potential including access to innovation;
- alignment of the supplier's plans with our goals.

If one or more of these points apply to a supplier then some form of relationship may be needed and so our long-term ambition for the relationship should be determined. This could take many forms but might include factors such as:

- increased business – increased scope of supply/volumes;

- collaboration – collaboration on joint improvement projects or initiative to create innovation, reduce cost or drive efficiency improvements;
- forward/backward integration – for the supplier to take over parts of our business or even merger or acquisition;
- becoming a priority customer – to secure improved assurance of supply so we have priority over their other customers if there are supply issues.

The supplier's perspective

In order to determine the relationship we need with a supplier, we must understand how the supplier views us, and get beyond any superficial relationship building by them. There is little point deciding to pursue a close, long-term collaborative relationship with a supplier if their relationship with us exists only to secure a short-term win. Understanding their preference for a relationship also helps determine their value objective. Here we use the supplier preferencing tool (in Figure 4.4, adapted from Steele and Court, 1996). This is a core tool used in Category Management and SRM to help buyers to understand how the supplier might view their account with us and also used by suppliers' sales teams to prioritize how best to direct their efforts.

Supplier preferencing considers two variables based on how we think the supplier sees our account with them today: how 'attractive' our account is to them and our spend on the account relative to the supplier's overall sales. For negotiation planning it helps to consider this dimension more in terms of 'their dependency on us'.

Attractiveness includes all the factors that might make a supplier interested in maintaining or growing their position as a supplier to us including:

- high volumes or high spend;
- our brand kudos;
- payment terms and payment on time;
- profit margin;
- ease of servicing the account;
- alignment of our business with their future;
- match of geographical operating locations;
- they like working with us.

Figure 4.4   Supplier preferencing tool (adapted from Steele & Court, 1996)

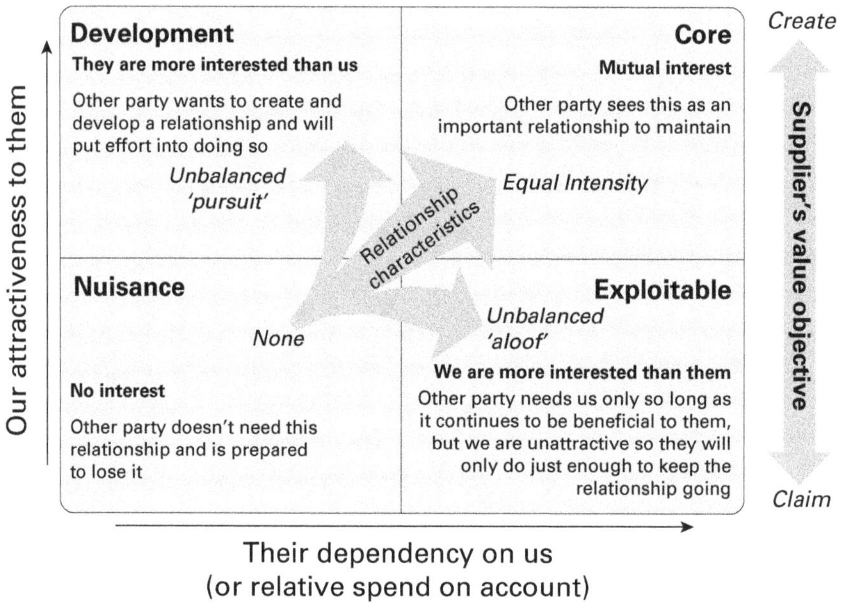

The factors that make an account attractive to the supplier also provide sources of power in a negotiation and the value to the supplier is frequently underestimated. For example, a buyer might focus on price and terms alone but the value to the supplier of associating their business with our brand could be significant, even if they don't mention it. Furthermore, giving authority to publicize the fact that we are their customer may be an easy concession to give that could be traded for benefit elsewhere. Attractiveness is a judgement, determined by putting our self in the place of the supplier and considering how our company might rate given the factors listed above. There may also be some tangible signs evident during interactions with the supplier such as their attentiveness to the relationship, whether or not their best people are put in charge of our account and how they might describe their business with us to others, eg as a 'showcase account'.

'Their dependency on us' includes all the factors that make our relationship important to them and the degree to which they need us, including the degree of spend with them relative to their overall turnover, and the impact or risk if they lost our business. If there is a high dependency on us, then the supplier's preference is to the right side of the matrix.

We can establish 'dependency' by asking the supplier, checking their annual accounts or considering if there are any other factors that make our business important to them.

To use the supplier preferencing tool, consider both axes and determine which quadrant the supplier would most likely place the account in. From here determine how the supplier is likely to approach the relationship, their likely value objective and then determine the implications:

- **Development.** The supplier views this as a relationship to grow and develop. They will put their best people on the job and negotiations will use value-creation approaches.

- **Core.** The supplier is seeking to maintain their position. If they see us as core then it is likely there is an established relationship here already, probably two-way, and the supplier will work to ensure this continues long-term. Their most experienced people will be appointed to look after the account and negotiations will tend to use value creation.

- **Nuisance.** Here we are unattractive to the supplier and there is no dependency. The supplier will be uninterested and this may well be apparent in interactions with them. They will use hard value-claiming approaches in any negotiation and these may even be high risk on their part as they will not be afraid to lose the business.

- **Exploitable.** Here we are unattractive to the supplier but they still want us at present. The supplier will do just enough to keep us where they want us so long as it continues to benefit them. Any apparent relationship building with the supplier will most likely be superficial and negotiation approaches will be moderate value-claiming but will avoid pushing too far.

With this insight we can check the assessment of the supplier's relationship and value objectives matches our relationship and value objectives. If it does not, then we should check assumptions and revaluate as needed. Use value-creating approaches if a relationship is needed and providing supplier preferencing suggests the supplier sees the account as 'development' or 'core'. However, if the supplier potentially regards the account as 'nuisance' or 'exploitable' then this suggests we should either revisit our relationship and value objectives or alternatively refocus the negotiation initially on increasing attractiveness to the supplier in order to bring about a shift in how they view the account.

Using Day One analysis to determine value and relationship objectives

Day One Analysis is a key tool used in Category Management and Supplier Relationship Management, so called because it is one of the first tools that can be used to give insight into what leverage or opportunities might exist. Similarly it is a useful tool to help negotiation planning when sourcing goods and services and can help us determine the value and relationship objectives that would be most compatible with our negotiation. Figure 4.5 gives the *Day One Analysis* tool with a summary of possible negotiation responses for each quadrant. Day one analysis is used by plotting on the matrix the categories, areas of spend or individual products we are setting out to negotiate according to the number of suppliers in a particular marketplace that could supply the category or item (ignoring any constraints we impose that limit this), against the number of buyers. The axes for Day One analysis need to be understood clearly. They are not sliding scales. There may be either one supplier or buyer or more than one supplier or buyer, but there is no middle ground. Day One analysis is best worked in a group,

Figure 4.5   Day One analysis to support negotiation planning

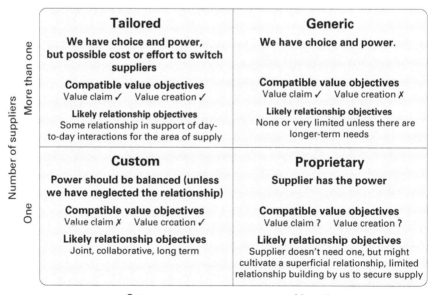

as use of the tool will typically spark discussions regarding differences in outcomes or positioning, depending on how people view the goods or services we are attempting to negotiate. This discussion is good and differences will often reveal insights into what is happening. Potential approaches for our negotiation for each quadrant are as follows:

- *Generic* (many suppliers, many buyers)
  In this quadrant we have the greatest choice and ability to switch; so we have the power. For a single negotiation we are unlikely to need a relationship with the supplier ongoing unless there are wider or more long-term needs outside this. The supplier's mindset is about beating the competition, so *value claiming* is normally the most suitable approach.

- *Tailored* (many suppliers, one buyer)
  Here the products and services are made uniquely for the organization. Anything that is branded or made to a unique, business-owned specification or drawing fits here. The supplier's focus is on selling its process and capability and because of this we may need some sort of relationship with the supplier, perhaps to facilitate day-to-day interactions between companies that support the tailored goods/services. As there is more than one supplier, we hold the power here too, so in theory it is possible to switch suppliers to gain the best value. However, switching may not be straightforward as in the generic quadrant and there may be issues around transition or acquainting the new supplier with specific requirements and manufacturing/service provision process. Depending upon the circumstances we could chose a *value claiming* negotiation approach, but equally we may benefit from a degree of *value creation* as well or instead.

- *Custom* (only one supplier and only one buyer)
  As the name suggests, this quadrant features the things that are custom-made for us only by only one supplier. Either the supplier or us may have a unique process or patented component and the arrangement is such that it can only be made by/sold to the other party. Here we will undoubtedly need a strong, collaborative and perhaps long-term relationship with the supplier. Moreover, the supplier may have accumulated certain know-how regarding the manufacture/service provision, increasing our dependency on them. The balance of power between us and the supplier would therefore most likely be shared assuming we have managed the relationship well. *Value claiming* negotiation approaches would be entirely inappropriate and here *value creation* would typically yield the best outcomes.

- *Proprietary* (one supplier, many buyers)

    This is where suppliers want you to be, as it gives them the power and a degree of control. They are very clever and will work to identify ways in which you can only come to them for their products. There are many ways suppliers do this including:

    - branding;

    - differentiation – making a product or service unique in some way;

    - added value – additional products or services added in with the aim to create real or the perception of much more value for money;

    - convincing a design team to specify make and part number on a drawing or specification;

    - bundling different generic or tailored products and services together to create a unique bundled offering.

In *Proprietary* the supplier does not need a relationship with us, but may cultivate a superficial relationship to shore up their position. There is little point in us attempting to build a collaborative relationship with the supplier; however, there is benefit in building a similar superficial relationship that seeks to make and keep us attractive to the supplier, which can help secure the best terms given the constraints. In terms of value objectives we have little power to drive *value claiming* and *value creation* could end up a one-way street on our part, yet both approaches are valid and work to a degree providing the constraints are kept in mind.

Actually doing it

Red Sheet step 1 – Background

Purpose of this step

The template for Step 1 can be found in the Appendix. Step 1 is concerned with identifying the background to the negotiation, the type of negotiation we are planning to conduct and how we will negotiate, and the timeline for planning. Figure 4.1 gives a worked example.

Completing this step

1   Identify who we are negotiating with, what we are negotiating and why we are negotiating and complete the first three boxes.

---

2 Identify and note any know issues or risks with this negotiation or not realizing a certain outcome.

3 Identify the type of negotiation this is, either one-off or part of a journey and whether this is the first engagement or a repeat negotiation, and tick the relevant boxes.

4 Determine how we will negotiate and whether face-to-face, by e-mail, phone etc. Tick the relevant boxes.

5 If the date and location (where relevant) for this negotiation event are known, note them here.

Develop a time-bound plan for the activities leading up to this negotiation and potentially any further events in the future.

Involving stakeholders

Step 3 of Red Sheet is concerned with the identification, categorization and engagement with the relevant stakeholders who should be involved or who can help secure success. Figure 4.6 gives an example.

Across an organization there may be a number of individuals who have a role to play here. Many of these will be obvious, as they will have a direct interest in the negotiation outcome: individuals who hold budgets or have specific needs from the supplier, but some will be less obvious. In the context of supplier negotiation planning stakeholders might include individuals or groups who:

- are users of the goods or service being negotiated;
- are responsible or accountable for the area of supply or the final products/ service it feeds;
- might benefit (or lose out) from a particular negotiated outcome;
- have information or knowledge that could give us strength or power in a negotiation (eg product alternatives, market understanding, future plans);
- have existing relationships or dealings with the supplier.

If we do not understand and engage with our stakeholders, we risk seeking the wrong outcomes, approaching a negotiation unprepared, or being mis-aligned. Furthermore, across an organization it is quite typical for there to be multiple points of contact and interface with any key supplier supporting

Figure 4.6   Red Sheet step 2 – Stakeholders (worked example)

3. STAKEHOLDERS

Who	R	A	C	I	Action required?
Peter Williams	✓				Make part of the team
Ho Ken		✓			Engage with him
Sam Morton			✓		Gather input
Natalie Norton			✓		Gather input
Saki Kamigawa				✓	
Julie David				✓	
Graham Lloyd				✓	Regular
Jerome Protier				✓	updates
Anna Gribble				✓	

service or supply fulfilment. Smart suppliers will use this to great advantage and establish multiple relationships to help shore up their position within a company. If all our stakeholders are not behind us, our negotiation position could be undermined by the supplier receiving different messages or using established relationships for intelligence gathering. Therefore at the outset a simple stakeholder map helps to identify who we need to engage with and provide the starting point to get them on board and aligned as appropriate.

Start by identifying and listing all the stakeholders or possible stakeholders as per the list above. The RACI model (Responsible, Accountable, Consult, Inform) is used to classify stakeholders according to how we need to engage with them (Figure 4.7). For the negotiation in question ask, 'Who in our organization is responsible for this area, who is accountable, who needs to be consulted here, and who needs to be kept informed?' Once mapped, the RACI status determines the nature of stakeholder engagement;

for example, a stakeholder who is 'responsible' for an area of supply might need to be part of our negotiation team while someone who is labelled as 'consult' may need nothing more than a meeting to gather information or insight.

Figure 4.7 The RACI model

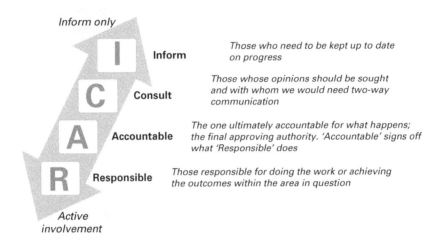

Finally, determine the actions needed in order to engage stakeholders. The required actions will vary according to their RACI classification and could range from a simple e-mail notification to inviting them to participate in a series of pre-negotiation planning meetings or even to be part of the nego-tiation team.

Actually doing it

Red Sheet step 3 – Stakeholders

Purpose of this step

Step 3 is concerned with the identification and classification of key stakeholders and with determining the actions needed in order to engage with them. Figure 4.6 gives an example and the template can be found in the Appendix.

Completing this step

1   Identify all the key stakeholders or groups of stakeholders for the negotiation and list them.

2   For each, determine their RACI classification according to their role and remit within the organization.

3   For each determine and plan the action required to engage with them.

Negotiating across cultures

05

This chapter aims to show why negotiation planning must consider and plan for any cultural differences between parties. The nature of cultural differences is explored and a model for categorizing cultural differences is provided. Finally, ways to adapt negotiation approaches are provided at country or region level.

Pathway questions addressed in this chapter

9   If I negotiate across cultures when do I need to adapt my negotiation approach in order to be successful and how exactly can I do this?

18   What is the best way to manage the meeting or negotiation event?

21   How can I manage what I say and how I say it to be most effective? How can I gain further advantage by tuning into what is hidden 'behind the words' of my opponent?

23   Are all negotiations the same or are there situations where I need a different approach?

Red Sheet steps covered in this chapter

4A and 4B

Defining culture

Culture is the ways of thinking and doing things that, in a society, are passed on from one generation to another, and includes language, norms and values and collectively creates a pattern of human behaviour. Culture is not biologically inherited but who we are is determined largely from environmental influences. It is established cumulatively through generations and holds societies together, providing the template for new generations to follow. No culture belongs to an individual but is shaped by groups over time; changes in culture therefore happen very slowly. The nature of a culture is determined over time by many factors including:

- climatic conditions;
- historical heritage;
- belief systems;
- the power of thought;
- socialization;
- information circulation;
- principles and moral values.

Culture is expressed at an individual level in customary ways of behaving and interacting in everyday life, religious beliefs and observance, moral standards and the way life is organized, especially family life. Outside of the individual, culture is expressed in the language, food, art, political, social, religious and economic structures that shape social interaction and the way the provision of basic human needs including food, shelter and safety is organized.

Cultures differ from region to region and country to country but can also differ within a country; for example, in Italy there are distinct cultural differences between north and south. Individual and unique cultures can exist where there is any established group who socialize and interact over time. Therefore organizations often have their own culture shaped over time by the values, beliefs and policies of the business, manifested in the way the organization is managed and how it interacts with employees, customers and partners. Organizational cultures tend to be strong where there are low rates of churn, where people are made to feel valued and important and where effort is put into defining the culture and expected behaviour. In large Japanese firms it is common for employees to dedicate their entire working life to one company with the company investing heavily in the development of each and every person. Each day might begin with workers coming together for exercise and to sing the company song; a daily mantra to corporate values embraced by the organizational family.

There are many commentaries on how the world is becoming a smaller place and talk of a 'global community' as if there is some end-game where everything melds into one, just as the English language now dominates global communications. It is true that more people are on the move, choosing to live and work in new parts of the world. Diversity is all around us and positively encouraged, and our universities have been doing a fine job of educating those business leaders of tomorrow sent from overseas to acquire a Western education, although this trend is now changing as many more countries match this with their own education capability. Communication, video and web teleconferencing mean global organizations are no longer collections of separate business units spread over the globe, so today, if you work for a global organization, you can expect to need to work with your counterparts in other countries on a daily basis.

The internet and much of modern music, film and communication largely appear on the face of it to transcend culture, somehow bringing the world together into some sort of new unified global culture defined by information. However, Hofstede *et al* (2010) argue this is an illusion and that it is important to differentiate that while 'the software of the machines may be globalized the software of the mind is not'. An increase in available information does not increase human capacity to absorb this information nor can it change value systems as these roots go deep. New communities settling on foreign soil 'fit in' and establish bridging techniques while preserving who they are or establish micro-territories that co-exist alongside the predominant culture. International students 'fit in' to our culture temporarily, but don't lose theirs. Communities and organizations put measures in place to ensure diversity based upon cultural awareness and accommodation is realized in all walks of life. If groups of people shape culture over time then one culture cannot readily merge into another just because people communicate and move around more. Instead, our shrinking world actually means we understand and respect each other's cultural differences a bit more, we are more open to new experiences and our social skills toolkit is better equipped. Despite advancement in cultural awareness on a worldwide level, individual cultures remain, as do the differences between them, and this has implications for negotiation planning and execution.

Determining culture

Cultural differences in negotiation

When a Chinese businessman says 'let's have tea first' the American counterpart may become frustrated at such a reluctance to get down to business. A German may see relationship building as an unnecessary delay and a sign of weakness, yet in the Middle East pressure to get straight to the business in hand without knowing the other would simply be avoided. Cohen (1997) suggests that equating culture with national character is an outdated and unhelpful concept. It doesn't always follow that Arabs will haggle and Russians will drive a very hard bargain. Nevertheless there are differences and negotiations can fail if these differences are not understood. Brett (2001) suggests that 'culture is often the culprit when negotiations across borders fail' and continues to state that familiar negotiation concepts such as 'power', 'interests' and 'priorities' take on different meanings in different cultures and therefore drive different negotiation strategies and different patterns of interaction. Hofstede *et al* (2010) suggest 'intercultural negotiations demand an insight into the range of cultural values to be expected among partners from other countries and compared against the negotiators' own culturally determined values'.

In order to negotiate effectively globally we need a means to understand the culture of the other party and how it differs from our own culture. This knowledge then shapes our entire negotiation process and determines how we plan to engage and interact, including:

- event planning;
- timing;
- meeting and greeting;
- room configuration;
- use of language;
- degree of confrontation;
- tactics;
- sources of power.

It is difficult to precisely categorize any culture, as there are no certain rules; cultures change over time and even differ within geographical boundaries. The only true way to fully understand a culture is to be immersed in it for an extended period of time. This is not entirely practical for negotiation planning and so to help establish culture-specific reference points for those countries we might negotiate with, we can turn to a significant wealth of research in this area.

Possibly the most useful body of established knowledge in this area comes from two researchers, Geert Hofstede and Shalom H Schwartz, who independently studied international cultures, identified a series of cultural measures and conducted global research projects to determine country-level classifications against these. In addition, further insight comes from the GLOBE (Global Leadership and Organizational Behaviour Effectiveness) project founded by Robert J House in 1993 and *The World Values Survey* (www.worldvaluessurvey.org (archived at https://perma.cc/L6YX-ZX6B)) provides a wealth of freely available cultural analysis based upon extensive country-level research. Many cultural indicators are available to better understand specific cultures. Of these, four are particularly relevant for effective negotiation:

- individualistic vs collective;
- authoritative vs egalitarian;
- short-term vs long-term;
- monochronic vs polychronic.

Individualistic vs collective

Hofstede (1980) describes an 'individualistic' measure of a country culture. He describes individualism as 'The degree to which the members of a society or group focus on and look after themselves and immediate family only'. The opposite is a 'collective' society, which means individuals are part of strong cohesive groups where the welfare and success of the collective or extended family is most important. Characteristics of an individualistic society include personal choice, equality and freedom with the focus being realizing personal success and building personal status and wealth. Allegiance to a group is a choice so long as it works for the individual and rights are defined and protected by law and contract. In Western society this is a cultural trait most will understand; however, things are very different in collective cultures where individuals are part of a group, perhaps an extended family, tribe, clan, caste, company and it is this membership that defines the individual. Consequently individuals acquire significant duties and obligations to the group where long-term allegiance is a given. Country cultures tend to be polarized towards one or the other. Table 5.1 gives the key characteristics of each.

This can be seen in action when individuals introduce themselves. In an individualistic culture someone might say, 'I'm Steve and I'm a school teacher.' However, in a collective culture we might hear, 'I'm Haruko Anzu and I am with the most excellent Toyota Company in Aichi where I have responsibilities for the procurement of engine components.' In an individualistic society the identity of the individual is defined by his achievement as an individual, perhaps even without the need to mention the name of the school where Steve teaches. The group the individual is part of defines identities in collective cultures, in this case the employer.

Collective cultures are founded upon interpersonal relationships and personal obligations. Status within the group or society counts for everything and so preserving 'face' is of the utmost importance. Therefore all actions will be carefully considered beforehand to ensure they will not cause any sort of humiliation or will not cause someone, including oneself, to become less highly respected.

Highly individualistic cultures can be found in North America, Australia, South Africa and most of northern Europe. Highly collective cultures include large parts of eastern Asia and South America. Effective negotiation across geographical borders requires an understanding of how we, and our opponent, are polarized so adaptations can be made. A negotiator used to an individualistic culture negotiating with a collective opponent will need to establish a strong rapport before business is possible. Once a relationship is in place discussions can proceed in a style that always seeks to preserve face with the other. If trust and respect are won and the proposed outcome is good for the collective then the deal will be done. Formalizing the agreement with a contract might be expected procedure; however, a collective culture seeks personal commitment over any contract. If an individualistic negotiator builds a genuine relationship based upon honour and trust, the deal will take care of itself; however, if such a relationship is not in place they could be shown no or little mercy. Table 5.1 also gives the implications for negotiating with individualistic and collective cultures.

Attitudes towards authority

As George Orwell wrote: 'All animals are equal but some are more equal than others.' The question here is to what degree do the other animals, or the society in question, accept this. In Scandinavian countries and some other north European countries status and position tend to need to be earned, perhaps by ability, experience or sheer hard work. Here, while authority is respected, it is also socially acceptable for someone in authority

Table 5.1 Individualistic vs collective cultures

Characteristic	Individualistic	Collective
What defines culture	• individual personality and self-expression • personal choice and equality • freedom and mobility – part of a company, social group or other collective body so long as it suits the individual • entrepreneurship and personal success • independence of the individual	• family, extended family, tribe, clan, caste • duties to the group • long-term allegiance and loyalty to the group • group success and achievement by partnership and cooperation • interdependence of the individual through social obligation
History, customs and traditions	• influence practice if individuals choose to preserve them en masse • easily abandoned if no longer seen as relevant	• all defining • determine the way things are done • preserved at all cost
What defines the individual	• chosen vocation and individual expression • tangible signs of success	• the group the individual is part of
What is important	• preserving and building individual status, wealth and position • loyalty and support for and of those who are close and matter	• welfare and success of the group • face – saving face of self and others, avoiding any sort of disgrace
Rights, obligations and duties of individuals	• defined and protected by law and contract • conflict or breach resolved by legal action	• defined by custom and practice, group values, norms and past favour • conflict or breach resolved by conciliation or referring to the group for consensus on action to take
Individual failure or wrongdoing	• triggers personal guilt • little tolerance for non-achievement – limits prospects and can cause removal from office	• triggers shame in front of the group • disapproval is a powerful sanction

Table 5.1 *continued*

Characteristic	Individualistic	Collective
What is rewarded	• individual achievements	• class or status of the individual • long-term dedication to the group
Transactions	• can be anonymous and at arm's length	• must be personal

Implications for negotiation

Characteristic	Individualistic	Collective
Individual drivers and motivators	• results • personal success • winning and goal achievement • self-interest	• relationship • group or company success • welfare of the group or collective • collective interest • face – saving face of self and others, avoiding any sort of disgrace • preserving and building the relationship at all costs • how they appear to others
Interactions between parties	• statements or requests may be bold, without reservation • timing and sequence as per agenda or pre-prepared plan or in response to how negotiation is proceeding • human contact a necessity to do business	• will only state a position if certain it will not cause embarrassment • will 'make a move' only when time is judged to be right, usually preceded by detailed probing to be certain the circumstances and timing are right • business interactions a consequence of human contact
Most prevalent approaches and tactics to a negotiation	• tend to be more 'value claiming' – determining the split of a fixed resources or 'dividing the pie' • leverage comes from a good BATNA	• tend to be more 'value creating' – integrative and assume the amount of resources available for distribution is not necessarily fixed – 'growing the pie' • leverage comes from status and relationship
Fairness standards	• precedent, contract or law • social ideology	• determined by the group

to be challenged if they are not thought to be doing a good job. The cultural mindset is that everyone is equal and status, power and wealth are available to those who work for it; politicians need to be elected and promotions are based on 'what' you know. Those in position are expected to continually demonstrate why they are worthy of their post. As the world tried to start hauling itself out of recession in 2012, many leaders of large corporates in some countries, the UK being one, started to come under repeated attack for their high remuneration. The right of the public at large to question authority was freely assumed and reinforced by the media, so much so that it began to attract governmental intervention. Schwartz (1994) and Schwartz *et al* (2012) call this 'egalitarian' and describe a cultural orientation where abuse of market or political power is not tolerated and those who are less powerful are supported.

The opposite of egalitarian is an authoritative society and examples would include China and large parts of both South America and Africa. Hofstede (1980) described this as how 'hierarchical' a culture is and the extent to which the majority of people in a society or group (ie workers in an organization, members of a group or family) accept, endorse and desire authority and expect power to be distributed unequally. In an authoritative society status may be given by birth or given as a reward for longstanding commitment. It may also be given if we have the right relationships with the right people. Here it is not 'what' you know but 'who' you know.

The key point here is those without status will willingly accept their place as part of the order of things and never seek to challenge. In an authoritative society members are cautious not to overstep what remit they have. It is common in business for nearly all decision making to reside at the top of the organization. This means that when negotiating with authoritative cultures it may be impossible for our opponent to make any sort of decision during the meeting; instead the matter will need to be referred to someone more senior, perhaps after the event. Further changes or concessions may well be requested thus extending and complicating the negotiation process. There is no avoiding this; it is the way things are done. However, the more senior the opponent the less of an issue this becomes and when a decision is made and agreement is reached it will not change with or without formal contract. Table 5.2 outlines the differences between the two polarizations.

Short- vs long-term

Short-termism has been cited as a central cause of the global financial crisis that hit towards the end of the first decade of this century (Blair, 2011).

Table 5.2   Authoritative vs egalitarian cultures

Characteristic	Authoritarian	Egalitarian
Hierarchy and authority	• authority is accepted and unquestioned, hierarchy is unchallenged, roles are ascribed • assigned, often inherited or by birth • tribal elder, father or company boss have authority	• everyone is equal • status is earned or acquired • defined by job role, title or office • those in authority are often open to scrutiny, challenge and question
Decision making	• strictly by those in position • common for decisions to have to be referred to the head of a business	• degrees of empowerment, perhaps even full empowerment
	Implications for negotiation	
Implications for negotiation	• decisions unlikely to be made during a negotiation, they will need to be referred to someone else • status counts for everything so they will expect you to be of equal status • when an agreement is given it will not change	• tendency to push for closure during the event • risk of agreement made without contract by an individual being unsupported by the wider organization later

Lenders relaxed rules and lent more and more against the apparent value in rising house prices. Borrowing increased as people refinanced and took advantage of the cash that was being made available; in the United States mortgage debt increased by 180 per cent. As the bubble was put 'at risk' in 2006, excessive debt and leverage, and the consequences of poor regulation across global financial institutions eventually took its toll. House prices fell, borrowers defaulted and financial institutions that were considered too big to fall, fell and the bubble burst, drenching us all in the consequences.

The tendency with short-term thinking is to unduly discount outcomes that occur far in the future and focus only on the here and now. Investors are too impatient for potential big benefit long-term returns and instead plump for short-term wins, often overvaluing them by doing so. The same investors that look after the long-term interests of our pension funds are motivated and rewarded based upon current year performance. An 18–24-month tenure for a global corporate CEO in North America is not uncommon; just long enough to sell the family silver and claim a hefty bonus for doing so, leaving the successor to figure out where next year's value will come from. If that isn't enough, the democratic process means politicians need not look beyond their term of office. Of course many do, especially those who revere the responsibility their office provides, but not all and some may even set the scene for a future crisis if re-election looks unlikely. Our appetite for the here and now is fuelled by new technology; today we can have what we want when we want it. Music, movies, information and a complete social summary of everything our friends and family have done in the last few hours are now just a click away.

Short-termism is not a global phenomenon, but rather a cultural trait that belongs to certain countries, largely those in the West. In fact long-termism is alive and well and residing (for the foreseeable future at least) in countries like China, Japan, Taiwan and Hong Kong. In a long-term society things are very different; members will think about long-term outcomes over the short-term goals when making decisions and will avoid actions that could cause shame later. Much of this long-term orientation comes from the philosophy of Confucius who emphasized personal and governmental morality, correctness of social relationships, family loyalty, justice and sincerity, all matters requiring individuals to play the long game and teachings that underpin much of Eastern culture. Long-termism drives persistence in all things as well as prudence in financial matters. Relationships and the status of individuals take on a heightened importance to ensure the cultural philosophy is preserved.

Long-termism also drives how government works and acts. While those in office might not always be democratically elected, political strategies tend to look very long-term indeed, focusing on making the right provision for future generations. China, for example, continues to invest in global infrastructure outside China for security and benefit that will take many decades to yield a return; motorways in Sri Lanka are being built to better connect producers and vast swathes of agricultural land in Africa to guarantee future food capacity. Table 5.3 gives the characteristics of both polarizations.

Approaches to negotiation need to be positioned to resonate with the cultural time horizon of the opponents. A short-termist negotiator attempting to secure a result from a long-term partner will fail if the proposed solution conflicts with longer-term objectives of the individual, company or wider society – or worse, might cause loss of face. Furthermore, because the partner is looking long-term there is unlikely to be a strong imperative to

Table 5.3   Short-term vs long-term cultural differences

Characteristic	Short-term	Long-term
Characteristics	• 'here and now' – outcomes that happen in the future are discounted • 'need it now' – appetite for fast returns and immediate satisfaction of need • measures and results drive decisions • transactions are arm's-length, failure to deliver is an accepted risk mitigated by contract	• decisions and actions primarily driven by impact or outcomes into the future • avoid anything that might cause loss of face • financial prudence • persistence in everything • transactions are relationship centric, failure to deliver would cause loss of face
Attitude to investing time, money or effort	• short-term horizon, even if less favourable • long-term investments avoided thus widespread underinvestment in such projects • personal incentives and reward for those managing investment funds based only on current performance	• long-term for the benefit of future generations • individuals motivated and rewarded by the sense of benefiting the society
Status and career	• elected or appointed • succession of career positions viewed favourably	• inherited or awarded because individual recognized as a key contributor to long-term success • 'job for life' not uncommon
Implications for negotiation		
Implications for negotiations	• successful outcomes will be judged by hard measures, eg price, time, specification • deal more likely to be viewed in isolation	• proposed deal must resonate with longer-term aims and objectives to be accepted • deal is one of many steps on a journey

close the deal promptly; in fact rushing to closure would be viewed as un-necessarily risky as it would prevent sufficient time to ensure the agreement is right long-term and will cause no loss of face. Negotiations therefore can be protracted and take many engagements before a conclusion is reached. All of these factors must be built into negotiation planning.

It's no time for the Hopi Indians

The Hopi Indians are a tribe of Native American people who live on the Hopi reservation on a plateau in north-eastern Arizona. The Hopi are a peaceful people who are descendants from ancient cultures, numbering around 7,000 in total today. They are a federally recognized tribe and speak their own Hopi language. The Hopi dictionary gives the meaning of Hopi as 'behaving one, one who is mannered, civilized, peaceable, polite, who adheres to the Hopi way'. To be Hopi is to strive towards a state of total reverence, respect and to be at peace with all things.

The traditional Hopi dictionary, however, has no word for 'time', and until recently, time was not part of Hopi lives. It seems incredible not to be able to describe time as we would but this was the reality for the Hopi peo-ple. When a Hopi Indian described an event in time he or she would do so by indicating the physical distance from them; an event in the distant past was like an object a long way in the distance behind them. The Hopi lan-guage also had no real tense so events were described by how long they lasted (using a physical indication of length) and its nature (eg will happen, has happened, is predicted to happen, is ongoing, happens regularly etc). The verbs the Hopi used here were also based upon physical space and movement: for example, something that was ongoing was described as 'spin-ning' and would be accompanied by a physical hand gesture to indicate this.

There was no word for time because there did not need to be. The Hopi saw their world as a series of interactions and collective activities that fol-lowed the pattern of the sun, moon and seasons. Segmenting intervals be-yond this by the divisions of a clock face served no purpose. Intervals of time were irrelevant because time was seen as abundant in Hopi culture, like a road that stretches off into the distance, and when there is all the time in the world there is little need to measure it. Instead what served purpose – and continue to – are relationships, honouring traditions and following the Hopi way.

This mindset is completely at odds with many, but not all, Western atti-tudes to time where our entire lives and environments are driven by time. Imagining a world without intervals of time is as difficult as grasping the concept of infinity. For many of us time dictates the entire pattern of our lives; it is relentless and unforgiving, providing little respite. Wasting time is often the greatest loss imaginable because we will never get that time back. Time is money, time is precious, time is something to be apportioned carefully so our time here can be used to the full. However, these differing attitudes to time can also help understand cultural differences.

Monochronic vs polychronic

Opposing attitudes to time around the world do not come from individual choices but are culturally and personality driven with personality arguably being heavily influenced by culture. While there are many factors that characterize the different aspects and values of a given culture, the one over-arching characteristic where all the individual cultural indicators seem to converge is the way individuals in a culture view time and how daily life is organized relative to time. In cultures where relationships and the good of the group are paramount, where authority is never challenged and the long-term implications are considered, individuals generally tend to have an attitude to time closer to the Hopi Indians. Just as time stretches out into the distance, so do relationships and the long-term bond with the group or family and the importance of human interaction over everything else and so this perspective defines the culture. In individualistic societies where authority must be earned and is open to challenge, and short-term results matter most, the culture tends to be the opposite – more time-bound.

The American anthropologist and cross-cultural researcher Edward T Hall (1990) characterized individual cultures by the degree of involvement people tend to have with each other. He combined this concept together with the opposing attitudes to time under the terms monochronic and poly-chronic cultures (see Table 5.4). Monochronic and polychronic are not measures of cultural polarizations, but rather are traits which form the visible indicators that help us understand culture. There is a clear correlation between attitudes to time and the other key cultural indicators, making this trait the prime indicator that forms the basis for our negotiation planning.

Hall (1990b) states that 'Monochronic is a characteristic of low-involvement peoples, who compartmentalize time; they schedule one thing at a time and become disorientated if they have to deal with too many things at once.' In a monochronic society time is viewed like a filmstrip running through a projector with activities compiled in sequence like scenes one after another. Across the wealth of time management books and courses out there, all provide guidance or a methodology that is based upon improving the way available time is apportioned and managed, with the goal always to free up

Table 5.4 Monochronic vs polychronic traits

Characteristic	Monochronic	Polychronic
Relationship with other cultural indicators	• tend to be individualistic • tend to be egalitarian • tend to be short-termist	• tend to be collective • tend to be authoritarian • tend to be long-termist
Tangible signs	• promptness, timekeeping, and schedule management • 'one thing at a time' and concentrate on the job in hand • schedule changes avoided and frowned upon • concern not to disturb others, privacy important • projects managed to strict deadlines • will get frustrated if kept waiting in a doctor's waiting room • routine and regularity provides security • respect for private property; unlikely to borrow or lend • short-term relationships apart from immediate family and those who are close	• timekeeping less important • will do many tasks at once 'like jugglers', doing just one thing is not stimulating enough – therefore in meetings polychrons will prefer to have other things on the go like checking e-mail or doodling • schedules flexible... won't hesitate to reschedule • interruptions commonplace • projects will be broken into parts • will find something to do when sitting in a doctor's waiting room • avoidance of regularity • will freely lend and borrow • long-term relationships and human interaction paramount • will switch between activities during the day

Implications for negotiations

Characteristic	Monochronic	Polychronic
Executing the negotiation	• focus on one thing at a time • pay attention to start and finish times • use an agenda and structure the meeting • seek a series of individual agreements to secure overall agreement • use direct language	• take longer • relationship based • decisions made at top of company • must be matched against long-term horizons • must save face • indirect, high context language, lying OK if it saves face

new time for more fun activities. Relationship building, leadership 'availability', time to work on projects and even family time are often reduced to activities that happen within discrete, allocated blocks of time. The engine of technology is focused on gadgets and apps that will save time. For monochronic individuals, or 'monochrons', promptness and timekeeping become ever more important as lateness and overruns threaten the next scene of our movie. Similarly the completion of individual tasks cannot be jeopardized by distraction or diversion, driving a 'one thing at a time' mindset with little tolerance for interruption.

Monochronism is visible in the way people and groups act and organize themselves. Watch-watching, timekeeping and schedule slavery might be the obvious signs, but there are more. In the United Kingdom it would be considered rude to walk up to two individuals deep in conversation and join in and even if you were important enough to do so the interruption would almost certainly be accompanied with an 'excuse me'. But this sort of conversational etiquette does not exist the world over. Once, while in a meeting with a Middle Eastern businessman, I was somewhat taken aback when one of his junior staff burst into his office and started talking in Arabic, cutting me off in mid-sentence. I waited for the intruder to be berated for the interruption, or at least an apology, but neither happened. In fact similar interruptions continued throughout the meeting together with phone calls and other happenings. At one stage three new people had entered the room, all appearing to have different conversations in Arabic while my host part-engaged with them, part-talked on the phone and every now and again would switch to English and part-continue our conversation. This, I learnt, was entirely normal in that country and culture so I resolved to learn Arabic so next time I could join in.

Multiple conversations and many different things happening at once are characteristics of a polychronic culture. Hall (1990a) identified this characteristic and states that 'polychronic people, possibly because they are so much involved with each other, tend to keep several operations going at once, like jugglers'. Individuals have evolved with this capability, a skill that eludes monochrons, and so exposure to polychronic environments can be like being placed inside a whirlwind and might even trigger a stress reaction as it will feel as if things are not getting done. This skill exists today in polychronic societies and with polychronic individuals, or polychrons, because relationships are paramount and all human interaction is much more important than that task in hand or any boundaries of time. Task achievement and realizing results are not the end-game but natural products of the right relationship. Whereas for monochrons it is task accomplishment that is most important and human interaction is simply an enabler to this.

Monochronic and polychronic polarization exists at country and cultural level. North America, most of northern Europe, Russia, Australia and New Zealand are predominantly monochronic, although the first-nation populations that reside in these territories remain polychronic. Southern Europe, Africa, most of Asia and most of South America are predominantly polychronic. There is a correlation with climate; where the sun shines more, time matters less. It is tempting at this point of realization to stop writing and emigrate; however, there is a further layer that brings hope for monochrons. Chronicity is a trait and, while influenced by the predominant country culture, works at an organizational and individual level too. It is possible to have a polychronic monochron where certain individuals from monochronic societies exhibit polychronic tendencies. Women, for example, might follow the same attitudes for timekeeping as the monochronic society they live in demands but often have a far greater capacity for multi-tasking than the male monochrons and can therefore fit more easily into a polychronic environment culture. It doesn't however follow that female monochrons necessarily make better negotiators in polychronic cultures as the advantage may well be offset by the culture having a high masculinity index (Hofstede, 1980), ie it lacks gender equality.

Retired monochrons might also complain of too much time on their hands and this tends to drive different behaviours, as they don't face the same time crunch others around them do. So monochronic and polychronic traits exist at a country and culture level but these traits will vary within a country too. (Table 5.6 gives a list by country.) Understanding our negotiation partner starts by understanding the predominant orientation of their culture but must also consider the individual or individuals with whom we will engage.

When monochronic and polychronic come together then there is potential for misunderstanding, abrasion and offence. However the biggest risk is simply failure to get any traction. A polychron will resist engaging without a relationship; a monochron will get frustrated at lack of progress towards a goal and will feel out of control if things appear to be drifting along without any plan. Hall (1990a) suggests that in these circumstances 'much of the difficult they experience can be overcome by the proper structuring of space', ie the way the individual relates to time. If a Western negotiator is meeting with an Eastern partner, success comes from abandoning the mindset of a negotiation 'event' and achievement of time-bound outcomes, and instead comes from concentrating on building a relationship at their pace with some aims in mind that we will get to 'when the time is right'. This is a complete shift in mindset away from time being the driver to the relationship and so the measure is no longer results but quality of relationship. In Western culture business relationships are often kept at 'arm's length'; you might send a Christmas or season's greetings card at the end of the year but you're unlikely to call them up at the weekend and suggest you go have a beer together. Relationships are more networks of acquaintances. In Eastern culture business relationships are more real and more personal so any relationship must be built on the foundations of honesty, integrity, respect and honour, and this takes time. It also means more time on a sofa in comfortable surroundings than in an office. The most fruitful cross-culture relationships tend to be the real ones that build over the long term and last. The caveat here is: this approach is valid where we don't hold all the leverage but yet we need to 'win' an outcome. In contrast, if a monochron has the power, then the polychronic effect can be lessened by reducing involvement and using screening to filter out obstacles in advance.

Chronicity is the primary indicator for a given culture so this should be assessed first when planning a negotiation. A more detailed evaluation can then be carried out using the remaining cultural indicators as needed. The Red Sheet negotiation methodology is built on this concept.

CASE STUDY – NEGOTIATING WITH FIRST NATION PEOPLE

First Nation people are the indigenous, aboriginal or native population of a country that existed and developed their territories pre-colonization. There are an estimated 220–350 million people worldwide (Bodley, 2015). In Australia the indigenous peoples account for around 3.3 per cent of the population, most of which are Aboriginal Australians. In North America there are more than 80 million, with Native Americans or Alaska Natives accounting for 2 per cent in the US population, and in Canada there are 634 (www.afn.ca) (archived at https://perma.cc/E4RH-W8X5) First Nation communities including the Inuit peoples south of the Artic Circle together and the Métis, accounting for 5 per cent of the total population. First Nation people can be found the world over.

History is littered with accounts of battles where explorers and colonists threatened the sovereignty of First Nation people and drove them from their land to gain access to the resources upon which their cultures depended. These accounts are further troubled by a history of persecution or treating First Nation people as lesser citizens, something that continues to this day in some places. Many of the countries that we now look to uphold human rights and good moral practice harbour these histories yet common across these same countries is modern legislation and practice that seeks to protect these people and actively re-balance their place in society. This includes, for example, The United Nations Declaration on the Rights of Indigenous Peoples, which sets out the policies and rights member states must establish and includes provision for diversity in employment, appointment of suppliers, protection of culture, preservation of language, access to health, education and natural resources.

First Nation people have their own culture and to this day strive to preserve this within the wider country cultures they exist within. In doing so it can create competing systems between western imposed norms and traditional group norms. The various legislation here generally seeks to address this and prevent actions from impacting First Nation people but also seeks to ensure the rights of these people are accommodated.

Today, in the US, Canada and Australia, First Nation people occupy and enjoy the rights to designated territories. There are many scenarios where there are impacts to land of the indigenous people such as for construction of dams, pipelines or for mining. Within the protection of these people, companies seeking to embark on such projects must engage in consultation to assess the impact, preserve and accommodate the rights of the First Nation people and give comfort to the government.

North State Hydro

One such example was a large utility company that wanted to construct a dam and hydro generation plant upstream of a First Nation reserve. The company, and I'll call them North State Hydro (NSH), determined that the project would impact the land, fishing points and hunting grounds across several First Nation communities downstream of the dam. NSH attempted to engage in consultation with the First Nation communities with a view to offering what NSH considered was a very attractive deal to compensate the communities. Negotiators were dispatched to make the deal happen but failed very quickly. Initially attempts to push for any sort of meeting where an offer could be proposed were thwarted by the fact that there appeared to be no single individual or point of contact who could act on behalf of the people. Negotiators then worked to 'pick off' people and communities one by one as would be typical western cultural practice, yet attempts to conclude any sort of transaction were resisted heavily. Where the company pushed for a meeting to offer or discuss a deal the response would be

▶

'come up and have tea with us every month and we will talk.' Across the various communities individuals resisted any sort of deal and would simply say, 'We've been here since time immemorial and we're here to stay.'

After a year of trying to secure an agreement, it was clear things were not working. The resistance by the First Nation people was difficult to understand but it was there, manifested by passive resistance to change or things easily changing or the peoples continually wanting something different and fuelled by the legal system that existed to protect and help them. NSH had made no progress.

Securing agreement between a monochronic and polychronic culture

It took NSH 20 years of work with multiple communities within each nation and many more families within each community to bring about an agreement. Progress only began to be made with a shift of focus away from trying to conclude a transaction towards developing a relationship. Over time they learnt that the communities didn't care about making an agreement but rather the long-term relationship for all communities. They learnt that individuals would resist any sort of deal for individuals without collective agreement and that saving face within the community and neighbouring communities was paramount – anything that prevented or threatened this would drive paralysis compounded with an anxiety about committing.

NSH shifted the focus towards building a new type of 'relationship agreement' with each community and one that resonated with all communities. They worked to identify each source of conflict or concern and what group or individual had the authority to make an agreement and then worked to define how the relationship would work over time to appease these. Contrary to how we might view agreement in western culture, here the relationship agreements became paramount, with primacy over the agreed contract and terms of the deal. What we might understand as ongoing contract management actions for a long-term deal became ongoing relationship meetings to maintain the agreed relationship. Hostilities continued but diminished over time, giving way to a base level of trust which provided the basis to work with the people and construct the new dam. Eventually, the monochronic culture of NSH and the country it existed in had found a way to broker a long-term agreement with multiple polychronic peoples. The relationship between the two continues to work effectively to this day.

Cultural differences

Once there is a broad understanding of a culture gained by considering polarization against the four key indicators above, good negotiation planning requires attending to some specific cultural differences. These include, but are not limited to: what is said, what is not said but indicated in other ways, and cultural protocols.

Cultural protocols

Cultures each have their own protocols about how things are done. Ignorance here can cost dear if we are trying to establish rapport. Protocols reflect cultural orientations. In an authoritative and hierarchical culture, how individuals with status are recognized tends to be important. If we negotiate with a group of Chinese people, the order they enter the room and where each individual sits follows strict protocol. The need to use both hands when presenting a business card in most of Asia is well understood, but less well known is the importance of never handing something over with your left hand in parts of the Middle East. There are societies where it is inappropriate to address a woman in a group or to shake hands with her. Despite what we uphold today as fundamental in our culture, gender equality does not yet transcend all cultural boundaries. Once again, prior research is essential here so as to avoid offence and ease the rapport building.

Lost in translation

Negotiation is the process by which two or more parties confer or interact to reach consensus or agreement and so language and communication are integral to this. However, with cultural differences come differences in how we communicate and the way language is used. Szalay (1981) suggests that in order to understand the differences we must make a distinction between what is said (ie the message itself or content) and the way it is being communicated (ie the way the message is conveyed, the words or even gestures used). It may seem entirely reasonable in a negotiation to assume that the words the other party speaks precisely and fully communicate a particular position, response or request. This is an incorrect assumption and one that accounts for failure to reach the desired outcome in many cross-cultural negotiations. There are several problems here:

- Our understanding of what we hear someone say is shaped by our own experiences and the way we see the world – our frame of reference. If we have a similar frame of reference to the next person then communication based upon the words spoken will be effective; if we do not then meaning may be misunderstood. I will return to this later.

- Frame of reference is largely determined by culture, with different cultural experiences producing different interpretations not shown in conventional dictionaries (Szalay, 1981).

- Cultural traits such as preserving face determine the degree to which a culture is reserved in what is actually said.

The culture trait indicator that is most useful here is the degree to which a culture is individualistic or collective, as this polarization appears to determine certain ways in which the culture will communicate and use language (see Table 5.5). There are five key differences to consider when negotiating: preserving face, directness, context, embellishment and lying.

Preserving face

Remember Steve, our schoolteacher in an individualistic society? If Steve was asked if he liked the school he teaches at, it would not be out of place socially for his reply to be 'not really, the children are badly behaved'. In fact this may even trigger empathy for Steve's troubled vocation. However, in a collective culture, founded upon interpersonal relationships, personal obligations and preserving 'face', such a response would be unthinkable. To speak of the group or employer with any sort of negativity would be disgraceful and dishonourable and would be avoided at all cost. In fact the personal sense of risk of bringing any sort of shame upon the group is so strong that individuals in collective cultures will go to great lengths to ensure their words could not be misunderstood.

Directness

In an individualistic culture direct language is often normal practice. A German or Dutch individual who found something wrong with his car following a service would not be reserved about taking his car back to the garage and saying something like, 'There is a problem with the service you have carried out on my car; I am dissatisfied with the service I have received.' Again in a collective culture this directness would be unthinkable, as it would bring shame on the individuals at the garage who had caused the problem. Here, if the car was returned at all, the language would be much more indirect and words would be chosen carefully so as to not cause any loss of face.

Context

Collective cultures use 'high-context' communication, which means it is not just what is said, but there is also a deeper layer of parallel communication that accompanies the words comprising implication, gestures and the use of body language. 'Yes' might mean 'yes', but it might also mean 'no'. I learnt this early on from training groups across Asia who would sit up straight and appear to pay complete attention to everything. If I asked a simple check question like, 'can you see my writing on the flip chart OK?' the group would nod in unison and say yes. Groups would never answer in the negative. However, with practice I learnt to read the signs. When delegates started conferring and looking for clarification in the notes of their neighbour that told me something hadn't been understood.

Embellishment

Collective cultures will colour and embellish sentences with additional words used to reinforce respect and protect face. For example, remember our Toyota worker Anzu, who introduced herself by saying something like, 'I am with the most excellent Toyota Company.' This is not only to reinforce and restate allegiance, but to ensure there is no chance of anything spoken being misunderstood and causing shame.

Lying

In an individualistic culture lying tends to be considered socially unacceptable, although not uncommon. Individuals found to be lying are viewed in a poor light and tend not to be trusted from that point on. However, in a collective society, telling the truth is secondary to saving face and so lying is often entirely appropriate.

The expected norms for human interaction and communication therefore shift with culture; sometimes it is subtle, sometimes profound. Failure to understand the differences and adapt accordingly means a failure to communicate effectively and will impede relationship development if that is the aim. Table 5.5 gives the key differences in communication for individualistic and collective cultures.

Table 5.5   Communication characteristics of individualistic and collective cultures

Characteristic	Individualistic	Collective
Message delivery	• direct • low context • forthright • 'tell it as it is' – words used precisely and fully describe the position or request • use of gestures and body language often low	• indirect • high context • reserved • meaning hidden behind the words used in implication, gesture, body language and colouration (additional words added to preserve face of others, avoid disgrace and respect hierarchy) • use of gestures and body language often high
Truth	• a social imperative; lying is socially unacceptable • lying will damage a relationship and is dealt with by exposing the individual's lies	• secondary to preserving face – better to lie than cause even the slightest hint of disgrace
Saliency	• while words are usually chosen carefully, they can be retracted and corrected – saying the wrong thing occasionally, within reason, has little consequence	• what is said will be analysed, scrutinized for hidden meaning and taken to heart • saying the wrong thing, and causing disgrace, has severe implications and does not get forgotten
Conflict and confrontation	• conflict accepted as a necessary part of reaching consensus • confrontation direct and face-to-face	• influence preferred • reluctance to confront directly and if at all face-to-face confrontation will be avoided

A big thumbs-up! But not for everyone

It is not just what is said that differs with culture, but also the gestures and actions that accompany human interaction. There are four areas to consider here:

Gestures to reinforce what is spoken

People in most of northern and eastern Europe and the Far East tend to use few gestures while speaking. While in most of southern Europe, South America and the Middle East speech is often accompanied by a stream of expressive gestures that somehow seem to illustrate and reinforce the point. Individuals from expressive cultures can get quite animated when something important is at stake, a spectacle we can observe at airports when people are complaining; sometimes it's almost possible to tell someone's nationality by the degree of arm waving.

Gestures that have their own meaning

There are also the gestures that don't accompany speech but are used in everyday life by societies the world over. The problem is they can mean different things to each. While departing from an airport in the Middle East the gentlemen operating the luggage scanner at the entrance to the airport helped me by lifting my heavy suitcase off the belt. Not knowing the Arabic for 'thank you' I gave him the thumbs-up sign. It was the only thing that came to mind at the time but, as it turned out, the gesture that means 'good job' or 'you're number one' across whole swathes of our planet has a very different meaning in the Middle East. It is in fact a gesture I strongly advise against using with security guards in Middle Eastern airports. I also advise against using any gesture unless you are certain of its local meaning.

Body language

Aspects of body language change with culture. However, Pease and Pease (2004) suggest that the general signals and meanings are the same the world over. What do change are expectations for eye contact, personal space, how you sit and what you do with your hands. I will cover body language again later in this book.

Gaining commitment

Committing to a course of action might be entirely normal for many cultures, but not all. Some collective cultures can be more reserved about commitment and will resist pressure to commit in order to remove any risk of bringing shame. In Egypt and parts of the Middle East securing a 'yes' can be quite a challenge; instead the response might be 'Insha'Allah', meaning God willing. When what was agreed fails to materialize there are two typical responses: 'Bokra' (meaning tomorrow, as if to try once more) or 'Malesh' (meaning forget it or never mind). This is how business is done, or not done, in many instances.

The subtle differences in acceptable gestures and actions among cultures could form the basis for an entire volume of books and then would not necessarily be correct. Prior research is therefore essential for international negotiations.

Culture, bribery and corruption

Corruption is alive and well! In Western business, corruption appears infrequently as transparency, accountability and following correct procedure typically drive practice. It is also socially unacceptable; however, it is a misconception to assume the rest of the world operates in the same way. There are two ways corruption can affect a negotiation: the negotiator might be disadvantaged by corruption (eg another party or outcome is favoured due to corrupt practices); or the negotiator might be offered some personal incentive to force a certain outcome. Corruption can appear in many forms:

- the unethical use of authority for personal gain;
- the rules of engagement or criteria for success change or are deliberately vague or applied differently;
- bribery, extortion or embezzlement;
- winning contracts according to who knows whom.

Corruption tends to be more prevalent in bureaucratic and authoritative cultures. If people accept authority without challenge then status carries more weight than correct procedure, leaving the opportunity for those in office to be influenced.

It is important not to let corruption take us by surprise; it is easy for a good person to inadvertently wind up in what appears to be a friendly situation one minute and then have somehow ended up with an envelope stuffed full of used bank notes. Those who corrupt are adept at taking people past a point of no return so they are then personally obliged. The overriding advice here is not to enter into any sort of corruption or bribery and reject it outright. If you negotiate across cultures then it is important to have your responses prepared for if and when you encounter corruption. Things to do include:

1 Research in advance:
 - the likelihood and nature of corruption in a given territory;
 - any wider organizational or corporate policies;
 - any procedure or guidelines for dealing with corruption;
 - the in-country legal position on corruption.

2 Consider what opportunity the other party might have within proceedings to make any sort of advance or suggestion of a bribe. Remove opportunities if possible, eg set up meetings in public places or meeting rooms with CCTV.

3 Watch for the signs. Bribes are rarely offered cold; instead the other party will attempt to establish if you are open to such a suggestion. Watch for questions around your personal circumstances, especially financial, or questions such as 'is there a way we can make this easy for you?' or 'why don't you let us help you out here?' If this happens, respond by bringing the focus firmly back to the business outcomes you are seeking, eg 'the only way you can help me is to reach agreement on the business in hand'.

4 Plan in advance what you will say and do if you end up in a potentially compromising position and at what point you will walk away. It helps to have prepared a form of words in your mind, perhaps: 'I'm uncomfortable with where this is going so I'm going to stop things there.'

5 Report what happened as quickly as you can within your organization.

Having provided this guidance, there are circumstances where entering into the practice of bribery or corruption is viewed as necessary by an organization and even appropriate. Practices that might appear unthinkable to one culture are the way things get done to another. I cannot provide any guidance on whether this is appropriate or not and this is very much a personal decision. However, if this is a method that needs to form part of a negotiation process it should not be done in isolation but as part of an approach that is sanctioned and agreed by the business, even if not made common knowledge.

Adapting for culture

The fact that the Chinese do business in a very different way to those in the West is widely understood, yet such differences don't appear to have prevented this nation from engaging with the rest of the world to become one of the most productive and fast-growing economies on the planet. So are they really that different or have they just figured out how to adapt their approach and accommodate Western ways in pursuit of their goal? I once asked this very question to a highly experienced negotiator who had been a Senior Vice-President of a global banking institution and had vast experience of international negotiation, striking multimillion-dollar deals across the world. His reply was simple: 'if you have something they want, they will get it just fine'. This is an important point to understand because we are led to believe that success is only possible if we adapt our approach across cultures. It is clear that adapting the approach in response to cultural differences helps things along as the likelihood for misunderstanding, offence and failure to make progress is reduced. Parties will find ways to bridge cultural differences when they really want to, but when they have something we want, or the balance of power might not rest with us, it becomes essential.

Tailoring the negotiation approach

In order to maximize the effectiveness of an international negotiation and secure the outcomes needed the approach needs to be tailored to the culture. There are three steps here (Figure 5.1): determining culture, understanding differences, and planning.

1 Determine culture

Determine the predominant nature of the culture to be negotiated with by considering the four cultural trait indicators. Table 5.6 provides a country-by-country list based upon an adaptation and interpretation of the most prominent research in this area. This table however comes with a health warning. This, or indeed any other such list, should be used as a guide only. It is impossible to stereotype or quantify any culture or people and there is never a definitive assessment for each trait as there are degrees. Regions, countries, districts and companies might exhibit these to a greater or lesser extent. Furthermore, as the body of research in this area is incomplete, historic or conflicting, a degree of interpretation has been applied here.

2 Understand differences

Determine the key cultural differences that need to be taken account of within a negotiation:

Figure 5.1   Steps for cultural adaptation

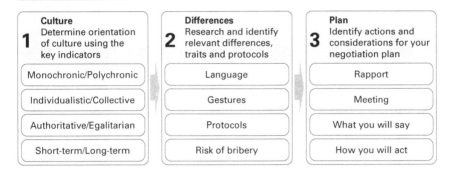

- *Language.* Consider how language is used and whether this is a high- or low-context society.
- *Gestures.* Understand the degree to which this culture uses gestures and, crucially, understand if there are certain things to do or not do.
- *Protocols.* Research the society, business and meeting protocols that are expected or normal practice.
- *Risk of bribery.* Determine if there is a real risk of bribery and how it might manifest itself.

Understanding differences requires research and this can be accomplished in many ways:

- *Desk-based research.* Kuperard publish a complete range of 'Culture Smart' books and there are many free web-based resources out there including www.kwintessential.co.uk (archived at https://perma.cc/SHQ8-PTY6).
- *Talk to those who have been there before.* In a global business, the chances are there are people in the organization who have done this or have experience of the culture. Talk to them; 15 minutes talking with someone who has done it before is often more valuable than all the books combined.
- *Feel your way.* While prior research is recommended here a culture is only truly understood once immersed in it. Irrespective of what you have researched it is good to 'feel your way'. Watch what others do, listen to

Table 5.6 Combined country-by-country cultural indicators

Region	Country	Monochronic/ Polychronic	Individualistic/ Collective	Authoritative/ Egalitarian	Short-/ Long-term
Africa	Algeria	polychronic	collective	authoritative	short-term
	Egypt	monochronic	intermediate	authoritative	short-term
	Ghana	polychronic	collective	authoritative	short-term
	Kenya	polychronic	collective	intermediate	short-term
	Libya	polychronic	intermediate	authoritative	short-term
	Nigeria	polychronic	collective	authoritative	short-term
	Sierra Leone	polychronic	collective	authoritative	short-term
	South Africa	monochronic	both	both	medium-term
	Zambia	polychronic	collective	intermediate	short-term
	Zimbabwe	polychronic	collective	authoritative	short-term
Americas	Argentina	polychronic	intermediate	intermediate	short-term
	Brazil	polychronic	intermediate	authoritative	medium-term
	Canada	monochronic	individualistic	egalitarian	short-term
	Chile	polychronic	collective	intermediate	short-term
	Colombia	polychronic	collective	intermediate	short-term
	Costa Rica	polychronic	collective	intermediate	short-term
	Ecuador	polychronic	collective	authoritative	medium-term
	El Salvador	polychronic	collective	intermediate	short-term
	Jamaica	polychronic	intermediate	intermediate	short-term
	Mexico	monochronic	collective	authoritative	short-term
	Panama	polychronic	collective	authoritative	short-term
	Peru	polychronic	collective	authoritative	short-term
	United States	monochronic (some polychronic)	individualistic	egalitarian (mostly)	short-term

Region	Country	Monochronic/ Polychronic	Individualistic/ Collective	Authoritative/ Egalitarian	Short-/ Long-term
Asia	China	polychronic (can appear monochronic)	collective	authoritative	long-term
	Hong Kong	polychronic	collective	both	long-term
	India	polychronic	intermediate	authoritative	medium-term
	Indonesia	polychronic	collective	authoritative	medium-term
	Iran	polychronic	intermediate	intermediate	short-term
	Iraq	polychronic	intermediate	authoritative	short-term
	Israel	monochronic	intermediate	egalitarian	short-term
	Japan	polychronic	collective	authoritative	long-term
	Kuwait	polychronic	intermediate	authoritative	short-term
	Malaysia	polychronic	collective	authoritative	medium-term
	Pakistan	polychronic	collective	intermediate	short-term
	Philippines	polychronic	collective	authoritative	short-term
	Saudi Arabia	polychronic	intermediate	authoritative	medium-term
	South Korea	monochronic	collective	intermediate	medium-term
	Taiwan	polychronic	collective	intermediate	long-term
	Thailand	polychronic	collective	intermediate	medium-term
	Turkey	polychronic	both	both	short-term
	United Arab Emirates	polychronic	intermediate	authoritative	medium-term
Australasia	Australia	monochronic	individualistic	egalitarian	short-term
	New Zealand	monochronic	individualistic	egalitarian	short-term

Table 5.6 *continued*

Region	Country	Monochronic/ Polychronic	Individualistic/ Collective	Authoritative/ Egalitarian	Short-/ Long-term
Europe	Austria	monochronic	intermediate	egalitarian	long-term
	Belgium	monochronic	individualistic	intermediate	short-term
	Croatia	monochronic	individualistic	egalitarian	short-term
	Denmark	monochronic	individualistic	egalitarian	medium-term
	Finland	monochronic	individualistic	egalitarian	medium-term
	France	monochronic (with polychronic)	individualistic	intermediate	short-term
	Germany	monochronic	individualistic	intermediate	long-term
	Greece	polychronic	both	intermediate	short-term
	Hungary	monochronic	intermediate	intermediate	short-term
	Iceland	monochronic	individualistic	egalitarian	short-term
	Ireland	monochronic	individualistic	egalitarian	short-term
	Italy	monochronic (and polychronic)	individualistic	both	short-term
	Netherlands	monochronic	individualistic	intermediate	medium-term
	Norway	monochronic	individualistic	egalitarian	medium-term
	Poland	monochronic	intermediate	intermediate	short-term
	Portugal	polychronic	collective	intermediate	short-term
	Russia	polychronic (and monochronic)	both	authoritative	short-term
	Spain	polychronic (and monochronic)	intermediate	intermediate	short-term
	Sweden	monochronic	individualistic	egalitarian	medium-term
	Switzerland	monochronic	individualistic	intermediate	medium-term
	United Kingdom	monochronic	individualistic	egalitarian	short-term

Use for guidance – use only as you make your own assessment. Adapted with interpretation and built upon the work of Hofstede, G *et al* (1980 and 2010), Schwartz, SH *et al* (2012), University of Iowa and the World Values Survey:

how they communicate and what is said and unsaid and hold back a bit while you orientate yourself. Often it is possible to simply ask what is expected of you. I have never met anyone who was offended by my asking what I should do.

3 Plan

Equipped with an understanding of culture and differences, develop a personal plan for how to engage. This 'culture plan' cannot exist in isolation but must be woven into the wider negotiation planning that unfolds through this book and the Red Sheet methodology. The plan should cover four specific areas:

- *Building rapport.* If negotiating with a collective polychronic culture, then developing a relationship is the main part of the process and should be planned in advance. Perhaps the first engagement is social and on neutral territory, perhaps dinner and conversation about family and common interests. Remember a relationship is not something that is simply switched on but builds over time with effort and integrity so planning to develop rapport is about planning a method of engagement rather than an activity or event.

- *Plan the meeting.* Plan all aspects of any meeting including where you will meet, how you will greet the other (eg presentation of business cards, giving of gifts), how you will enter the room and where people will sit, all in accordance with any expected protocols for this culture.

- *Tailoring what you say.* If you are from a culture where low-context direct language is the norm and your negotiation is with a high-context culture then you need to plan to adapt your communication style. Listen more to what is said and what might be implied, avoid any words that criticize or expose failings that might cause loss of face, reinforce your respect for the other by embellishment and use questioning that allows them to always answer in the positive and doesn't require a yes/no response. For example, in China asking a closed question such as 'will you agree to this proposal?' will not be received well as yes/no responses are disliked. It is likely the response might be 'yes' but to indicate only the question has been heard or an obtuse alternative response. Instead, asking open-ended questions is likely to be more successful: 'how do you feel about this proposal?'. If you don't get an answer the first time then repeat the question until you do; the Chinese admire relentlessness (Graham and Lam, 2003).

- *Tailoring what you do.* We have already explored how gestures and body language change with culture. With this knowledge you should plan for how you will adapt what you do so you can be empathic and are not caught off guard by the unexpected. It is also important to be ready for what they will do. An emotional outburst with lots of arm waving can be quite intimidating to a negotiator from a reserved culture if not prepared for it. Be clear about what gestures to avoid. Don't give the thumbs-up sign in the Middle East or the 'OK' sign in Brazil. Match your gestures and body language as appropriate. Mirroring the other party can be beneficial as it is a powerful form of empathy, eg they sit up straight, you do the same; they keep eye contact, you return it; but it is not necessary to start waving your arms about just because the other party does this. That said, in negotiations when I have chosen to make an outburst and be more animated than my culture would otherwise suggest, it seems to have helped and even increased respect by a notch or two. The important thing here is to choose your style and how much theatre you feel is helpful, and beyond that feel your way through.

Actually doing it

Red Sheet steps 4A and 4B – Culture

Purpose of these steps

Step 4A is concerned with assessing our culture and that of the other party and step 4B is concerned with summarizing the insights gained into a plan for tailoring the negotiation approach to take account of cultural factors. Figure 5.2 provides examples and the template can be found in the Appendix.

Completing step 4A

1 Determine and list our country culture (or prevailing culture) and the predominant country culture of the other party (either based upon location or where the negotiation team originate from, whichever is likely to shape proceedings more).

---

2   Determine the cultural indicators for both parties (using Table 5.6 for reference). Include any relevant notes regarding the assessment.

Completing step 4B

1   Determine and note the plan to build rapport.

2   Determine how the meeting must run, noting any cultural protocols that must be provided for.

3   Determine and list any specific things to say or not to say and any specific ways to act or gestures to be avoided.

Figure 5.2 Red Sheet steps 4A and 4B – Culture and culture plan (worked example)

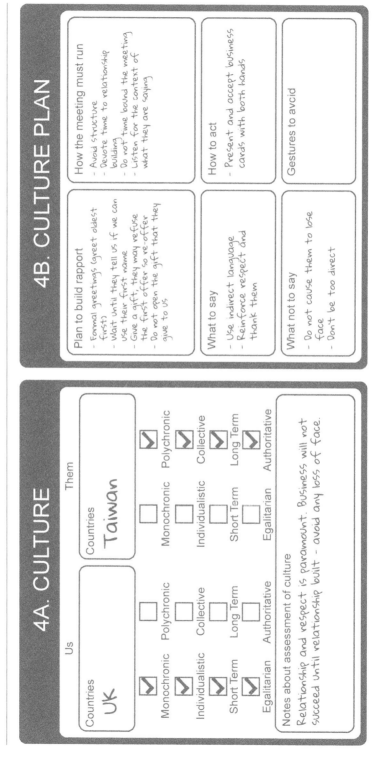

4A. CULTURE

Us

Countries
UK

- ☑ Monochronic   ☐ Polychronic
- ☑ Individualistic   ☐ Collective
- ☑ Short Term   ☐ Long Term
- ☐ Egalitarian   ☐ Authoritative

Them

Countries
Taiwan

- ☐ Monochronic   ☑ Polychronic
- ☐ Individualistic   ☑ Collective
- ☐ Short Term   ☑ Long Term
- ☐ Egalitarian   ☑ Authoritative

Notes about assessment of culture

Relationship and respect is paramount. Business will not
succeed until relationship built – avoid any loss of face.

4B. CULTURE PLAN

Plan to build rapport
- Formal greetings (greet oldest first)
- Wait until they tell us if we can use their first name
- Give a gift, they may refuse the first offer so re-offer
- Do not open the gift that they give to us

How the meeting must run
- Avoid structure
- Devote time to relationship building
- Do not time bound the meeting
- Listen for the context of what they are saying

What to say
- Use indirect language
- Reinforce respect and thank them

How to act
- Present and accept business cards with both hands

What not to say
- Do not cause them to lose face
- Don't be too direct

Gestures to avoid

Personality and negotiation 06

This chapter explores how individual and team personalities are relevant to negotiation and it provides a framework to understand and define this. It also provides an approach that attempts to understand the personality of the other party. A link between personality and the type of negotiation is established together with a means to adapt personal style where needed and compensate for specific personality traits.

Pathway questions addressed in this chapter

10 How do my individual personality traits (and those of others who will negotiate with me) help or hinder a specific negotiation?

11 What behaviours, style and demeanour will help me succeed at negotiating?

12 How can I know my opponent and how best to interact with each individual in order to put myself in the strongest position possible?

Red Sheet steps covered in this chapter

5A, 5B and 6A

The relevance of personality

Good negotiation is about personality, process and repertoire. As we learnt in Chapter 1 there are many personality traits that can both help and hinder negotiation. Our personalities affect our thoughts and feelings, drive our behaviour and make us unique. Personality is something that arises from deep within us and remains fairly consistent throughout life, though the degree to which our personalities can change is a matter of debate.

The work of Sigmund Freud around 100 years ago suggests personality cannot be modified after childhood (Freud, 1999, originally *c* 1917). He also proposed ways to deal with the things deep within that shape our behaviour, suggesting we can adapt. Neo-Freudians such as Carl Jung, Alfred Adler and Karen Horney accepted many of Freud's ideas but they argued human motivation is more complex and that we have a greater capacity to shape the person we become.

Many psychologists have attempted to classify and measure the different characteristics of personality. Sigmund Freud and Alfred Adler pioneered work in this field early in the last century. Since then many models have emerged. Carl Jung (1921) categorized people into four primary types of psychological function:

- *sensation* and *intuition* – the 'perceiving' functions;
- *thinking* and *feeling* – the 'judging' functions.

This work now forms the basis for the Myers–Briggs Type Indicator (MBTI) tool used across the world. Allport and Odbert (1936) suggested there are traits and rules of personality that can be generalized, defined and universally attributed to large numbers and types of people as well as characteristics that are unique to the individual. They identified three types of personality trait:

- *Cardinal trait.* A single trait that dominates an individual's life, personality and behaviour. Cardinal traits are uncommon as most people's lives are shaped by many traits. But history reveals individuals with cardinal traits so distinguished that their names become synonymous with the qualities of the trait, eg Christ-like, Freudian, Machiavellian, Narcissistic and so on.
- *Central traits.* The general characteristics that form the basic foundations of personality, eg outgoing, conscientious, anxious, agreeable etc.
- *Secondary traits.* Traits that are related to attributes of preferences and typically appear in certain situations or under specific conditions, eg becoming aggressive when under pressure.

More recently Costa and McCrae (1992) identified five dimensions to personality, known as the OCEAN model or 'The Big Five'. They are:

- Openness;
- Conscientiousness;
- Extraversion;
- Agreeableness;
- Neuroticism.

Personality has an influence on negotiation because personality influences how we perceive the world and make decisions, and that drives how we behave. If some or all of personality is inherited and shaped by early environment through education and experience, then this accounts for the fact that we see culture-specific behaviour.

While we may or may not be able to change personality, if this is possible at all in adulthood, then spending many hours on a psychoanalyst's couch as preparation for a negotiation is somewhat impractical. Notwithstanding how fixed or otherwise our personalities are, it is possible to choose an identity and this is how we can gain an advantage in a negotiation. Personality is distinct from identity. Indeed an assumed identity may be heavily influenced by personality, but with skill and practice it can be different. It can, in fact, be whatever you want it to be. The problem, however, is that, in assuming an identity that is very different from your own personality, there is a risk that under pressure, the natural human response is to revert to inherent personality traits. With self-awareness of who we are and an understanding of the personality traits that drive our behaviour it is possible to choose a different behaviour (Dilts and DeLozier, 2000), and thereby adopt a different identity. This is at the heart of effective negotiation. This new identity and adopted negotiation personality style is called our 'negotionality'. Doing this in practice takes three steps: determine who we are, determine who we need to be, and from this identify our adopted negotionality (see Figure 6.1). To support this, further reading around Neuro-Linguistic Programming (NLP) and Cognitive Behavioural Therapy (CBT) may well help.

Figure 6.1 The steps to negotionality

1 Who are we?	**2** Who do we need to be?	**3** Develop 'Negotionality'
Understand individual and team personality traits.	Determine the optimum mix of ideal personality traits and behaviours. This must be negotiation specific considering value and relationship objectives, power held and prevailing culture.	Match behaviour to the negotiation and developed style accordingly. Retain emotional control over individual personality traits.

Understanding our personality

Before we can create our negotionality for a specific negotiation, we first need to understand our natural personality and that of any team members who will be participating.

COW SOAP

While the Costa and McCrae (1992) Big Five personality dimensions model provides a framework to classify personality traits in life generally, within the context of a negotiation it lacks certain dimensions and the emphasis is not entirely relevant. For example, neuroticism in its fullest sense is not hugely relevant to understanding personality in a negotiation context, although negotiators should posses a degree of 'personal calm'. Furthermore, the degree to which an individual is driven and their will to win is highly relevant, though not emphasized within the Big Five model. Yet 'drive' is a personality trait as we cannot go on a course to learn competitiveness, nor is it something we choose to do; we are either driven and want to win or we are not. The same could be said of someone who is 'solution-focused'; we can go on a problem-solving course and learn a process; however, solving problems seems to be a skill some people just naturally possess. This may not be inherited but could be a product of our early experiences. Whether psychologists would accept these as true personality traits is not important. Instead what is important is that we have a model to understand the traits, dynamics and/or behaviours that are relevant for negotiation and that appear to arise from deep within us, and for this we need COW SOAP!

The COW SOAP model comprises the seven aspects of personality relevant to negotiation (Figure 6.2): Conscientious, Outgoing, Will to win, Solution focused, Open-minded, Agreeable and Personal calm. This model forms the basis for assessing personality and then developing negotionality.

Playing the ACE

While COW SOAP helps understand personality – the traits we have little choice over and can, with awareness, only compensate for – there are further aspects of negotionality where we do have a choice and can develop personal effectiveness (Figure 6.3). These are Assertiveness, how we approach Conflict, and Emotional competence, collectively called the ACE model. This sits alongside COW SOAP to form the complete model and is explored over the next three sections.

Figure 6.2 The COW SOAP model

The COW SOAP model of negotiation traits that are an inherent part of personality

C	**Conscientiousness**	Hardworking, organized and self-disciplined with attention to detail. High-scoring individuals are typically very reliable and will persevere to get things right.
O	**Outgoing**	Socially confident and easily met in conversation, comfortable speaking about their ideas and making new social connections quickly.
W	**Will to win**	Competitive and highly ambitious. The need to achieve goals is more important to the individual than personal relationships.
S	**Solution focused**	Can assimilate new information accurately and rapidly and identify effective solutions. Collects and analyses data and makes data-based decisions.
O	**Open-minded**	Ability to work well in the absence of structure. Creative, imaginative and often curious. Is comfortable working in a vague, fluid or rapidly changing environment.
A	**Agreeable**	Good natured and helpful. Places the needs of others in front of one's own needs. Acts selflessly and tries to meets the emotional needs of, and nurture, others.
P	**Personal calm**	Relaxed, at ease and secure. Controls own emotions and individuals scoring high are often patient and even tempered.

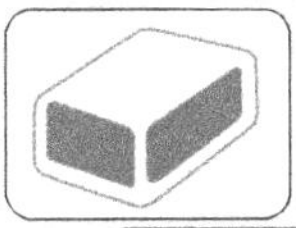

Assertiveness

Assertiveness is how comfortable we are in asserting our own ideas, views or needs with others and the degree to which we remain insistent about these in the face of disagreement, criticism or adversity. The underlying purpose of assertiveness is to satisfy our own concerns, wants or needs. *Dorland's Medical Dictionary* (32nd edition) defines assertiveness as:

A form of behaviour characterized by a confident declaration or affirmation of a statement without need of proof; this affirms the person's rights or point of view without either aggressively threatening the rights of another (assuming a position of dominance) or submissively permitting another to ignore or deny one's rights or point of view.

Are assertive people born assertive? From my early school days I can remember there were always kids in the class who seemed to get what they wanted more than me. Today, when I observe my kids interacting with their friends there are some children who are happy to be subservient to others and some who seem to just assert themselves and what they want to do over the others. It is interesting to note that there is usually a correlation between the assertiveness of the child and at least one parent. Perhaps this is nature, perhaps nurture or both. Nevertheless, assertiveness is a behaviour certain people use with ease.

Figure 6.3   The ACE model

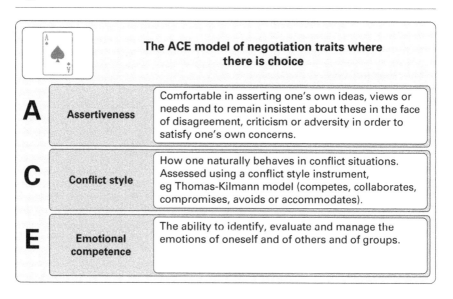

Assertiveness is an important skill for negotiations, especially in individualistic cultures, and lies at the heart of laying out a position, making a request and being able to hold fast when under pressure from the other party. It is a behaviour and skill that makes one individual apparently more important than another without being aggressive. Assertiveness is diluted in collective cultures where such behaviour would be at odds with cultural norms. What a Western society might view as good, healthy assertion could be seen as rude and disrespectful in Eastern society. This is because in collective cultures importance is given by status. People respect this and would never seek to challenge or behave in a way that suggested challenge. Cultural dimensions must therefore be considered alongside personality and creating negotionality. For example, a negotiation with the Japanese may not go too well unless a highly assertive person learns to adapt his style.

Assertiveness manifests itself in a number of ways depending upon the circumstances. In the case of my children and their friends, the assertive ones would perhaps talk more loudly, use directive language and take the lead in deciding what the group would do. One child even knew how to gently grab the arm of another child and turn them face on so they had to listen. In Western societies assertiveness in adults is more sophisticated and is a mix of language, gestures, body language and physical positioning (see Table 6.1). While some people are naturally more assertive than others, a crucial skill is the ability to choose when to be assertive and when to hold back. This comes with emotional competence and reflects a degree of personal development. There are plenty of people who can't help being assertive and others who struggle to put themselves forward, both paying the price that polarization brings. However, it is possible to learn to make a choice and this can then be very powerful. Assertion is not a permanent state; it is a form of acting. Techniques for learning to be more or less assertive exist and there is a vast range of training and literature available so further reading is recommended. However, if developing assertiveness is your aim then here are some suggestions for things you can do to help improve your negotiation capability:

1 **See yourself being assertive.** Several days ahead of the negotiation picture yourself in the negotiation acting with confidence, holding court, making your point known with ease, not being pushed around. Keep repeating this in your mind.

2 **Position yourself** in the prime spot or seat if you can, sit upright, look attentive and make eye contact with the person you are engaging.

3 **Express how you feel** about a situation and be direct in what you say, use 'I', eg 'I don't feel I can accept that' or 'I feel we might be close here but I'm not getting everything I need'. 'I' might need to be tempered in a group negotiation when not in a lead role to 'we'.

4 **Listen carefully** and understand the other's point of view.

5 **Stay honest,** direct and accountable.

6 **Don't confuse assertion with aggressiveness;** stay calm and composed.

Table 6.1　Components of assertiveness (individualistic culture)

Component	Assertive	Passive
Intervention	• will stand up for one's own rights • will make known own desires and feelings; will not be side-tracked by others • will show maturity when others are being offensive, hostile, blaming or attacking • happy to risk being misunderstood • will seek a win/win and recognize the rights of both • will not attack others' self-esteem and responses • will time interventions carefully • seeks respect for own feelings • shows personal accountability and makes others accountable	• avoids expressing feelings, needs and ideas • avoids confronting a situation, hoping it will get resolved on its own • will complain to others rather than the person who needs to hear the complaint • ignores personal rights • allows others to infringe upon them • indirect and inhibited • lets others choose for them • may develop a 'whatever!' attitude
Use of language	• uses 'I' statements to tell others how they feel about a situation • talks factually not emotionally • determined tone of voice, never shouting • will actively listen to understand other's point of view	• finds it difficult to say 'no' • will choose to remain silent if possible • will 'whine' about things and blame or accuse others • uses indirect statements • may be dishonest in what is said • often speaks quietly and without confidence

Table 6.1 *continued*

Component	Assertive	Passive
Body language	• maintains direct eye contact • appears interested and alert • sits or stands erect, perhaps leaning forward slightly • uses relaxed, conversational gestures • inclusive gestures such as 'showing palms'	• avoids eye contact • closed body language • posture often timid, eg might hold head low or avoid standing erect when in a group
Physical positioning	• will place him/herself in the prime spot, at the forefront of the area or centre of the group	• will detach from centre of the group or avoid direct engagement

Ready for a fight? Conflict style

What do you do in a conflict situation? Hide? Run away? Shout back? Try to find some middle ground? It is important to know. Some people will attempt any way possible to avoid conflict, perhaps with a well-developed repertoire of tactics to call upon to defuse situations; or better, will avoid being there in the first place. Others stand up and argue back at just the slightest hint of a disagreement.

Conflict is a natural part of human life and appears in different forms according to culture. Conflict is a disagreement through which parties involved perceive a threat to their needs, interests or concerns. It is important to note that 'perceived threat' lies at the heart of conflict. It is not just having a different point of view; it is also how people feel about the disagreement and the emotional responses it triggers with respect to their needs and interests. Needs are often defined as something obvious and near-term; however, they are in fact more like icebergs. The 'visible', or obvious, need at the surface does not fully reflect the real need below the surface, which is often far more complex, involving relationships and emotional components. Suggest to an employee that he or she should move desks because a colleague is in the office more and therefore should get the window seat and conflict might result. The employee might present many good arguments to indicate this is not a good idea, but it is unlikely the real reason, ie not wanting to lose a good spot, will be one of them. Conflict usually tends to be accompanied by levels of misunderstanding that serve to exaggerate the perceived disagreement, and that is how many wars have started.

Conflict is a necessary part of negotiation but can be avoided by focusing on interests (Fisher and Ury, 2012). Again this is culture-specific but aggression in the face of collaboration or accommodating the other's request too easily will be detrimental to negotiation outcomes. There are many instruments or models that can be used to evaluate personal conflict style. Most of them are based upon the work of Robert Blake and Jane Moulton in the 1960s that considered the degree to which an individual has concern for people vs concern for the task. The Kraybill Conflict Style Inventory built this a step further and identified five styles of response: directing, harmonizing, avoiding, cooperating and compromising.

However, possibly the most widely known model is the Thomas-Kilmann Conflict Mode Instrument or TKI (Thomas and Kilman, 1974 and 2002). This too builds on the work of Blake and Moulton but uses the two dimensions of assertiveness and cooperation and identifies five conflict styles, namely: competing, avoiding, accommodating, collaborating and compromising. If you're serious about negotiation, then understanding your individual conflict style is highly recommended; you can find out more about TKI from the Myers-Briggs website (themyersbriggs.com) and also from the Thomas-Kilmann website (kilmanndiagnostics.com (archived at https://perma.cc/YF5T-74WT)). Each offers options to take the TKI online and obtain your own personal conflict style summary.

Figure 6.4 gives the conflict styles for negotiation based upon the Thomas-Kilmann conflict style model. These are either our natural responses to conflict or, with emotional competence (see below), the responses we can choose for a given situation. Culture must be considered when choosing a conflict style; for example, an individualistic negotiator adopting a competing style in a collective culture will fail. Equally, choosing to be highly accommodating in a straightforward value-claiming negotiation where we hold the power will leave money on the table.

Understanding personal conflict style and ideally the ability to switch styles, is therefore essential. This is not that easy, however, and may, for some, feel like a big mountain to climb. Choices should be made carefully with the negotiation in mind.

Figure 6.4   Conflict styles for negotiation (based on and adapted from the Thomas-Kilmann Conflict Style Instrument)

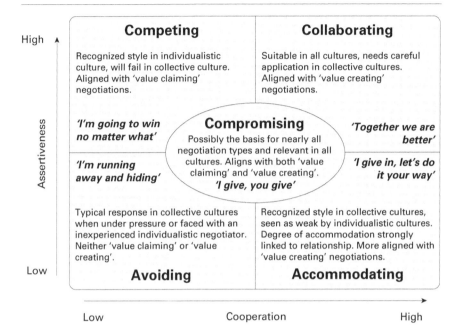

Emotional competence

This section is concerned with the ability to understand and manage our emotions and those of others, and to express emotion. This is arguably one of the most important attributes of a negotiator.

There is much terminology in this space, and, it seems, quite some debate as to how things fit together. 'Emotional Intelligence' (EI or EQ) is an all-encompassing term and means the ability to identify, assess and control our own emotions and those of others. Goleman (1996) identified five domains of EQ:

1 Knowing your own emotions.

2 Managing your own emotions.

3 Motivating yourself.

4 Recognizing and understanding other people's emotions.

5 Managing relationships and managing the emotions of others.

An autistic person might typically be highly intelligent with great capacity for assimilating certain fact-based information, but have low EQ. If you smile at him, he may struggle to naturally recognize the smile as a sign of friendliness or happiness. He might overcome this by learning to recognize the smile and associate it as a sign of friendship. This learning process would be slow and might involve the person carrying around a card of a happy face with a word to say what it means, and in time he would learn to associate the two. While autism is an extreme example of low EQ, EQ is increasingly considered alongside IQ as a measure of personal capability and one many employers now consider when hiring staff. While EQ is primarily concerned with understanding and controlling emotion, Emotional Competence (EC) takes it a step further, measuring how we then express our inner feelings. Both understanding and expression are important in negotiation and so it is emotional competence that forms part of the ACE model.

Saarni (1999) describes eight components of emotional competence:

1 Awareness of one's own emotions.

2 Ability to discern and understand others' emotions.

3 Ability to use the vocabulary of emotion and expression.

4 Capacity for empathic involvement.

5 Ability to differentiate subjective emotional experience from external emotion expression.

6 Adaptive coping with aversive emotions and distressing circumstances.

7 Awareness of emotional communication within relationships.

8 Capacity for emotional self-efficacy.

EC is a core skill of good salespeople; we touched on this in Chapter 2 when we considered how empathy (which is a core component of EC) seems to aid the sales process. We considered how certain salespeople seem to naturally have the right personality traits for selling and, as in the case of empathy, develop this capability through continuous practice and social experience (Mead, 1934). For purchasing professionals, EC is therefore an important measure of how effective we are likely to be at adapting personality. It is different to all the other COW SOAP ACE traits and behaviours because it considers our ability to adapt across all other traits and to make cultural adaptions, thus creating our negotionality.

Assessing COW SOAP ACE traits

A full personality psychometric assessment against the COW SOAP ACE traits will provide an empirical measure. However, a more practical alternative is to simply assess yourself and any other team members. This is not a precise science but a gauge of personality, and one that is usually reasonably accurate; no one knows you better than you, but to be doubly sure, ask those around you to assess you also, ideally including people who know you personally and those you work with. Encourage team members to do the same also. Table 6.2 gives the possible responses for each trait and Figure 6.5 lists the descriptors for COW SOAP to aid the process of self-assessment. Work through each trait in turn considering which words would most describe you or another, and therefore how high or low this trait is.

Table 6.2 Possible responses for COW SOAP ACE personality assessment

COW SOAP	ACE		
All traits	**Assertiveness**	**Conflict Style**	**Emotional Competence**
'H' (High)	**'H'** (High)	**'Cpt'** (Compete),	**'H'** (High)
'M' (Med)	**'L'** (Low)	**'Col'** (Collaborate)	**'M'** (Med)
'L' (Low)	**'Choice'** (able to choose)	**'Cmr'** (Compromise)	**'L'** (Low)
		'Av' (Avoid)	
		'Acc' (Accommodate)	

Developing negotionality

'Negotionality' is the specific identity created for a specific negotiation. It is the mix of personality traits, deliberately emphasized or suppressed together with some deliberate behaviours. This process might also be known as acting!

The idea that we 'act' when negotiating can be a difficult concept to accept. I once met a buyer who was most alarmed at the thought of pretending to be someone other than her true 'self'; in fact, the lady even suggested this was unethical. The reality here is that we have a choice as to how we act and behave in a negotiation and it is important to choose our approach well if we want to succeed and ensure any approach aligns with the type of negotiation we are conducting. For example, in a one-off value-claiming negotiation where there is no prior relationship and the balance of power is in our favour, playing the part of a tough negotiator who shows little mercy might be exactly what is needed. Whereas in a long-term value-creating

Figure 6.5   Descriptors of COW SOAP personality traits

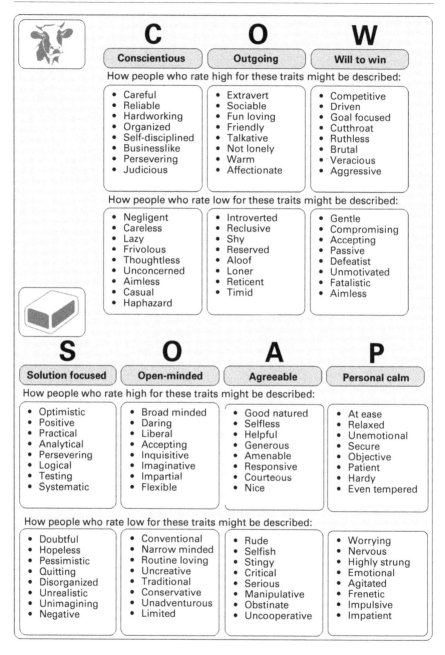

relationship openness, trust and simply being 'who we are' may yield the greatest result. Whatever the scenario, it is important to ensure that the 'negotionality' adopted is a conscious choice based upon the circumstances of the negotiation.

Figure 6.6 Factors that shape negotionality

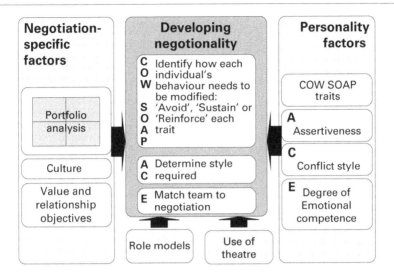

Several factors must be considered when determining negotionality. There are the COW SOAP ACE personality traits for each team member, and then the factors specific to the negotiation, including the type of negotiation using portfolio analysis, culture and the value and relationship objectives (Figure 6.6). With these in mind, making adaptations, modifying behaviours, selecting style and checking that the most appropriate individuals are matched to the negotiation, determine negotionality.

Portfolio analysis

Portfolio analysis is one of the most important tools for purchasing practitioners. In this book I can only provide a high-level summary; however, the tool is explored in much greater depth within *Category Management in Purchasing* published by Kogan Page and so further reading is recommended.

Portfolio analysis is a strategic tool that is applied for specific categories of spend (groups of products or services that an organization purchases where the grouping reflects how marketplaces are organized). It enables us to identify how much leverage might be available to us. Over the years, suppliers have done a good job in retaining the leverage or preventing buyers from obtaining it, and even where the buyers have had the leverage, suppliers have often managed to behave as if it was the other way around.

Within a negotiation we are searching for leverage, and the degree to which we have leverage determines what approach we should use. If we have great leverage over the supplier then a value-claiming approach might be entirely appropriate; however, if things are more balanced or even in the supplier's favour then value creation would be most likely. Of course culture adds a further dimension of complexity here too and then, once we understand the entire nature of the negotiation, we need to consider the most suitable negotionality.

Portfolio analysis (Figure 6.7) is based upon the work of Peter Kraljic (1983) whose original tool was designed to enable buyers to determine the specific approaches required for each area of spend according to the potential profit impact and supply risk or market difficulty. We use this tool in negotiation planning to help classify and determine the nature of the negotiation we are about to conduct.

While we might be planning a negotiation with a supplier, we should not plot the supplier on this matrix but rather the specific category (or categories) we already buy, or are negotiating to buy, from the supplier. If this negotiation is for one category of spend, but yet there are many others the supplier is also responsible for that sit outside the scope of this negotiation, these should be plotted too in order to understand the total leverage position. Therefore, to apply portfolio analysis, use the matrix shown in Figure 6.7 and position each category in one of the four quadrants, avoiding placing anything on the lines. This classification must be made based strictly upon the interpretation of the two axes, degree of market difficulty, and degree of profit impact.

Degree of market difficulty

Called 'supply risk' in Kraljic's original paper, this is concerned with all the factors that might restrict our freedom of choice when sourcing the category. These include:

- inability to switch suppliers easily;
- only one or a small number of suppliers can supply this;
- the category is complex, therefore it is necessary to work closely with suppliers before they are able to supply;
- availability, eg there is limited supply or capacity in the market, or storage and distribution channels introduce risks in supply;
- competitive demand.

Figure 6.7 Portfolio analysis (adapted from Kraljic, 1983)

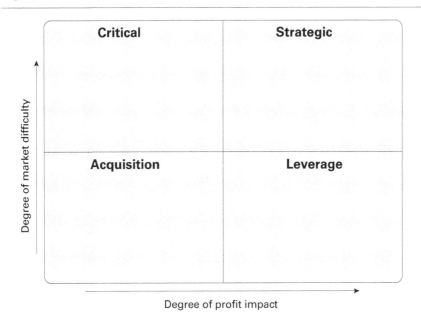

Degree of profit impact

In some versions this axis is changed to 'spend'. However, considering spend alone can introduce some difficulties in using this model, we might spend very little on a category that contains component parts, but the quality of a particular component may be critical to the quality of the final product. Thus, if we encounter any quality problems with the component, this could dramatically impact our overall profit. Using spend alone for the component would be low, but this becomes high when using Kraljic's original 'profit impact' approach.

Degree of profit impact is concerned with the degree to which a small improvement per unit purchased would have a significant and positive impact on the overall profit of our organization. This could be a saving per unit, dramatically multiplied due to high volume or high spend, but could equally be mitigation of risk, improved effectiveness or something that will improve future profit potential. Therefore it is relevant to look beyond simply how much we spend on a category. Factors that heighten the degree of profit impact are:

- spend on this category relative to the overall spend of the organization (not the market or size of individual suppliers);

Figure 6.8   Portfolio analysis – the power balance

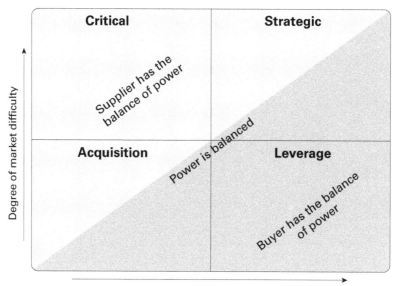

- the percentage that this category represents against total purchase cost of the final goods or service;
- volume purchased;
- impact on final product quality;
- impact on business growth.

The classification of categories within portfolio analysis helps us understand the balance of power between buyer and supplier and thus determines the required negotionality. Figure 6.8 shows how power shifts through the model. If a category is on the right-hand side in either leverage or strategic, the high profit impact means there is much to gain and it is worth putting energy into maximizing the overall position. In leverage this might demand value-claiming approaches in support of securing the best price or terms in the market. In strategic, it could mean value creation and working in a long-term relationship with the supplier to secure optimum value and minimize risk.

If we are on the left-hand side, then things are different. For a category in critical, we are sourcing in a difficult market where this category represents little profit impact. It is therefore likely that the sourcing process and supplier engagement is consuming effort and energy for little return. There is also likely to be risk here. For example, if, in this difficult market, the supplier simply decides not to compromise or use value-claiming approaches on us, we may have limited alternatives. Furthermore, if we are in critical, it is entirely possible (but not a given) that spend is low and we have little leverage in the marketplace. If the category or individual components are essential to the operation, then there is a problem.

We cannot just ignore categories in critical. Instead, we need to understand why we are there, what we can do to change it and adopt value-creation approaches within a negotiation that seek to build a relationship and find reasons to make us more attractive overall to the supplier.

Equally, a category within acquisition warrants little effort and energy, as the potential returns are small. However, here the market is easy, so switching suppliers is easy. There is also scope to simplify the purchasing process, perhaps even automating it entirely, most likely using value-claiming type negotiation. Figure 6.9 provides the implications for negotiation in each quadrant, including potential BATNAs (Best Alternative To a Negotiated Agreement – see Chapter 9).

Portfolio has one final dimension that must be considered in negotiation. The diagonal power balance line shown in Figure 6.8 can shift to the right or left. As shown, this is typical of a large organization with a sizeable spend, sourcing in a global marketplace. However, this line would move right for a small business which has little strength in the marketplace thus diluting

Figure 6.9 Portfolio analysis – implications for negotiation

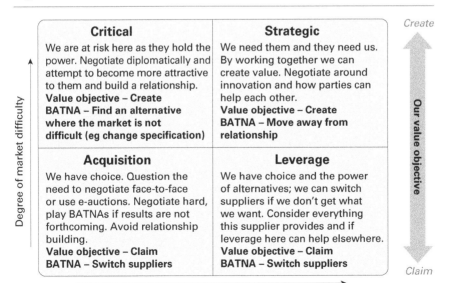

Figure 6.10 Required negotionality vs portfolio analysis and culture

Critical

Personality	Mono	Poly
Conscientious	High	High
Outgoing	High	High
Will to win	Low	Low
Solution focused	High	High
Open minded	High	High
Agreeable	High	High
Personal calm	High	High

Style	Mono	Poly
Assertiveness	Off	Off
Conflict style	Acc	Acc
Emotional competence	Essential	Essential

Strategic

Personality	Mono	Poly
Conscientious	High	High
Outgoing	High	High
Will to win	Med	Low
Solution focused	Med	Low
Open minded	High	High
Agreeable	High	High
Personal calm	High	High

Style	Mono	Poly
Assertiveness	Moderate	Off
Conflict style	Col	Col
Emotional competence	Essential	Essential

Acquisition

Personality	Mono	Poly
Conscientious	Med	Med
Outgoing	Low	Med
Will to win	Med	Low
Solution focused	High	Med
Open minded	Med	Med
Agreeable	Low	Med
Personal calm	Low	Med

Style	Mono	Poly
Assertiveness	On	Off
Conflict style	Cpt	Col
Emotional competence	Desirable	Desirable

Leverage

Personality	Mono	Poly
Conscientious	Med	Med
Outgoing	Med	Med
Will to win	High	Med
Solution focused	Med	Low
Open minded	Low	Med
Agreeable	Low	Med
Personal calm	Low	Med

Style	Mono	Poly
Assertiveness	On	Off
Conflict style	Cpt	Col
Emotional competence	Desirable	Essential

Spend/potential to impact our/the buyers' profit

Market difficulty (buyer) Strength in market (seller)

available leverage. It would move left if we were a multinational giant corporate with huge buying power. Again this shapes the negotionality required for a specific event.

The ideal negotionality using COW SOAP ACE for a specific negotiation is shaped by our position within the portfolio analysis grid, moderated according to culture. For example, if we are negotiating an area of spend that sits in leverage, then assertiveness and a will to win would be helpful, unless of course that negotiation is with a polychronic or collective culture in which case it could fail. Similarly, in critical or strategic then being open-minded, agreeable and solution focused are important to find mutually beneficial outcomes as part of a value-creation approach. Figure 6.10 gives the required negotionality against portfolio analysis quadrants and culture, and this figure forms a vital point of reference in negotiation planning. Note that the axis labels are slightly different and provide for use by both buyer and seller, as per the Red Sheet.

Reinforce, avoid or sustain – adapting style

Equipped with knowledge of 'who we are' we can now plan 'who we will be' for a given negotiation. As I suggested earlier, this is fundamentally about acting, but to do this we need a script to direct us, and this comes from the gap between our personality using the COW SOAP ACE model and the required negotionality for the specific negotiation, derived from Figure 6.10. The difference determines the specific responses needed for each trait and possible responses are given in Table 6.3.

There are many ways to adapt style but fundamentally it is about deliberately assuming a specific identity or chosen character for the negotiation. This needs to be done carefully as over-acting here can be counter-productive. This is where the development of our personal negotiation repertoire begins. If the negotiation calls for high levels of agreeableness and that is not our natural personality, then practise emitting the tangible signs of agreeableness: make small talk, take an interest in them, smile, make eye contact, remember the names of their children, share something personal, be human and so on. The process of adapting style should begin long before the negotiation itself and there are a series of techniques that can help here:

- *Role model.* Identify someone who has the trait or behaviour you are trying to emulate. Think about what they do or did that that made them that way. Replicate this yourself, adding your own personal flavour.

Table 6.3 Possible responses for COW SOAP ACE negotionality development

COW SOAP	ACE		
All traits	**Assertiveness**	**Conflict Style**	**Emotional Competence**
'A' (Avoid) **'S'** (Sustain) **'R'** (Reinforce)	**'On'** (Be more assertive) **'Off'** (Avoid being assertive) **'Mod'** (Moderate: use selectively and moderate the degree of assertiveness)	**'Cpt'** (Compete) **'Col'** (Collaborate) **'Cmr'** (Compromise) **'Av'** (Avoid) **'Acc'** (Accommodate)	**'✓'** (Team member sufficiently emotionally competent for the negotiation) **'✗'** (Team member lacks the required EC for the negotiation)

- *Build your repertoire.* As for all acting, playing a new role is not about changing who you are but being able to change what people see. Much of this is repertoire – the stock of skills, behaviours, things you say, body language, gestures and so on that you draw on as needed to suit the situation. Determine what these things might be for the character you are creating and start building your own repertoire. It helps to keep a note of these somewhere.

- *Get into character.* Practise being the character you need to be. For gestures and body language, sit in front of a mirror or get colleagues to observe you. For everything else our daily lives are full of opportunities. If you need to develop assertiveness then seize the opportunity in the restaurant when the service is poor and see how you get on or get a colleague to practise role-play with you.

- *Mental movie.* In the time leading up to the negotiation, create a full-colour movie in your mind of you in the negotiation doing really well and playing the character you have chosen. Picture yourself full of confidence, in control, handling everything that is thrown at you, but most importantly being the character you need to be. This is a very powerful mental preparation technique that instructs your subconscious as to what you need to do on the day; your brain will do the rest while you sleep.

Adaptation is possible for all of the COW SOAP ACE traits or behaviours except for emotional competence and this is something that an individual either has in good measure or does not. While we can develop emotional competence over time it is not something that can be switched on for a negotiation. An understanding of what is needed for the negotiation and who is available allows us to select or deselect the negotiation team accordingly, avoiding, for example, placing someone who exhibits little emotional competence in charge of a portfolio analysis critical quadrant negotiation in a polychronic culture.

Assigning roles in a negotiation

In a team-based negotiation each team member must understand his or her role during the negotiation. It is also important to agree some ground rules for interaction, specifically:

- who is leading;
- rules for team members to engage, eg no restrictions or leader fields questions and directs them to team members or a mix;
- how to communicate, eg a secret code to signal a problem, prompt action, suggest a time-out or trigger a pre-planned intervention, such as one member starts to play the bad guy.

The roles that are assigned depend upon the objectives for the negotiation, the type of negotiation and how many people are on the team, but possible roles include (not all of these are always needed and often these are combined):

- *Team Leader.* The person responsible for the negotiation and the actions for the team.
- *Listener and summarizer.* This person listens carefully to what is discussed with the aim of picking up on subtleties within what is spoken. This individual is then best placed to provide summaries when called to. It is advisable to agree a code word this individual can use if he or she believes the leader has not picked up on something.
- *Note Taker.* Maintains a vital record of discussions; essential to help play back what was discussed during any time-outs.
- *Mr Data.* The individual equipped with all the supporting facts and data.
- *The Sweeper.* Someone who sits and watches the reactions and body language of the other team. Again a code word can help here if the sweeper is detecting something that might be unnoticed by the leader.
- *Hard-liner.* Person who maintains a hard position throughout.
- *Good Guy.* Deliberately amicable, friendly, empathic and approachable.

- *Bad Guy*. Deliberately adversarial and appearing to be an obstacle to an outcome, possibly even prone to outbursts. (see also the tactic 'good cop/ bad cop' in Chapter 11).

- *The Expert*. Subject matter expert who will know more than the other party and so is not easily challenged, and with a clear brief to devalue their position using his or her expertise.

Roles can change during the negotiation and certain roles may only be needed for specific interventions. For example, good guy/bad guy is a specific tactic that might be played at a certain time. In determining roles for a team, decide who will do what and for what part of the event.

Actually doing it

Red Sheet steps 5A and 5B – Negotionality

Purpose of these steps

Steps 5A and 5B of Red Sheet are about determining the required negotionality for the specific negotiation and about identifying a personal plan to adapt personality and behaviour for the negotiation. This step is in two parts, half sitting within the 'Situation' section of Red Sheet and the other as part of the 'Target' section. Figures 6.11 and 6.12 give a worked example.

Completing this step

Work through steps 5A and 5B as follows:

1 Start by listing all the team members who will be part of the negotiation team. For each list their name and assign their negotiation role. Note Red Sheet assigns each an 'OT' label, eg OTL (Our Team Lead) or OT1 (Our Team Member No 1).

2 Identify the relevant quadrant(s) within portfolio analysis for this negotiation and mark accordingly.

3 Complete your own profile and that of all your team members using COW SOAP ACE then move to part 2 of this section.

4 Determine the negotionality required from the matrix according to culture type and portfolio quadrant. Enter these values into the 'required' column. Note for ACE the same is required for all team members.

Figure 6.11 Red Sheet step 5A – Negotionality (worked example)

5A. NEGOTIONALITY®

Our team

No.	Name	Role in the negotiation
OTL	Mike Mills	Team Leader
OT1	Peter Williams	Technical Expert
OT2	Xi Lu	Mr(s) Data
OT3	Diane Radby	Sweeper
OT4	Sam Coleman	Listener/Summary

Portfolio Analysis

Determine the quadrant for the category being negotiated (mark with a 'X')

	Critical	Strategic
	Acquisition	Leverage

Market difficulty (buyer)
Strength in market (seller)

Spread/Potential to impact our profit
Spread/Potential to impact the buyer's profit

Personality assessment for our team. Insert 'H, M or L' (High, Medium or Low) for all except assertiveness and conflict style where the possible responses are given below in brackets

		OTL	OT1	OT2	OT3	OT4
C CONSCIENTIOUS	Hardworking, organized and self-disciplined with attention to detail. High-scoring individuals are typically very reliable and will persevere to get things right.	M	M	H	M	H
O OUTGOING	Socially confident and easily met in conversation, comfortable speaking about their ideas and making new social connections quickly.	H	L	L	H	M
W WILL TO WIN	Competitive and highly ambitious. The need to achieve goals that are important to the individual is more important than personal relationships to the individuals scoring highly here.	M	L	L	M	M
S SOLUTION FOCUSED	Can assimilate new information accurately and signify and identify effective solutions. Collects and analyses data and makes data-based decisions.	H	H	M	H	M
O OPEN MINDED	Ability to work well in the absence of structure. Creative, imaginative and often curious. Is comfortable working in vague, fluid or rapidly changing environments.	M	H	H	L	M
A AGREEABLE	Good natured and helpful with a strong desire to place the needs of others in front of one's own needs. Acts selflessly, tries to nurture and meet the emotional needs of others.	H	M	M	H	H
P PERSONAL CALM	Relaxed, at ease and secure. Controls own emotions and individuals scoring high are often patient and even tempered.	M	M	M	H	H
A ASSERTIVENESS	Comfortable in asserting one's own ideas, views or needs and to remain insistent about these in the face of disagreement, criticism or adversity, in order to satisfy one's own concerns. (High, Low or Choice)	C	L	L	L	C
C CONFLICT STYLE	The individual's behaviour in conflict situations. Compete (Cpt), Collaborate (Col), Compromise (Cmi), Avoid (Av) or Accommodate (Acc)	Col	Av	Acc	Acc	Col
E EMOTIONAL COMPETENCE	The ability to identify, evaluate and manage the emotions of oneself, others and of groups	H	M	M	H	H

Figure 6.12 Red Sheet step 5B Negotionality (continued) – determining required behaviours

5B. NEGOTIONALITY® PLAN

Negotionality required for this negotiation:

Determine the culture of the other party (section 4A) and the Portfolio Analysis quadrant for this negotiation (section 5A) and tick the relevant box here: then identify the required negotionality from the matrix below. Enter into the 'Required' column on the right of this section and then determine the negotionality behaviour modifiers for each team member.

Critical

		Mono		Poly	
Personality	Conscientious	High		High	
	Outgoing	High		High	
	Will to win	Low		Low	
Drive	Solution focused	High		Med	
	Open minded	High		High	
	Aggressive	High		High	
	Personal calm	High		High	
Style	Assertiveness	Off		Off	
	Conflict style	Acc		Acc	
	Emotional competence	Essential		Essential	

Strategic ✓

		Mono		Poly	
Personality	Conscientious	High		High	
	Outgoing	High		High	
	Will to win	Med		Low	
Drive	Solution focused	Med		Low	
	Open minded	High		High	
	Aggressive	High		High	
	Personal calm	High		High	
Style	Assertiveness	Moderate		Off	
	Conflict style	Col		Col	
	Emotional competence	Essential		Essential	

Acquisition

		Mono		Poly	
Personality	Conscientious	Med		Med	
	Outgoing	Low		Med	
	Will to win	Med		Med	
Drive	Solution focused	High		Med	
	Open minded	Med		Med	
	Aggressive	Low		Med	
	Personal calm	Low		Med	
Style	Assertiveness	On		Off	
	Conflict style	Cpt		Col	
	Emotional competence	Desirable		Desirable	

Leverage

		Mono		Poly	
Personality	Conscientious	Med		Med	
	Outgoing	Low		Med	
	Will to win	High		Med	
Drive	Solution focused	Med		Low	
	Open minded	Low		Med	
	Aggressive	Low		Med	
	Personal calm	Low		Med	
Style	Assertiveness	On		Off	
	Conflict style	Cpt		Col	
	Emotional competence	Desirable		Essential	

Market difficulty (buyer) - Strength in market (seller)

Spread/Potential to impact cur profit
Spread/Potential to impact the buyer's profit

Negotionality Behaviour Modifiers

Enter the required behaviours from the relevant column in the matrix on the left. Then, for each team member, enter the actions to change behaviour and compensate for personality traits:

	Required?	OTL	OT1	OT2	OT3	OT4
C	H	R	R	R	R (reinforce)	S
O	H	S	S	R	R	R
W	L	A	R	A	S	A
S	L	A	A	A	A	A
O	H	R	R	A	R	A
A	H	S	R	S	S	S
P	H	R	R	R	S	S
A	off		(enter 'On', 'Off' or 'Moderate')			
C	Col	Collaborate	(enter 'Cpt', 'Col', 'Cmr', 'Av', or 'Acc')			
E	✓	✓	(enter '✓' or 'x')			

(enter 'A' - avoid, 'S' - sustain, 'R' - reinforce)

5 Determine the negotionality behaviour modifier for you and each team member based upon matching your personality profile with the required negotionality. Then determine the specific response or action you need to take, eg avoid, reinforce or sustain.

Getting to know our opponent

The four personality types

Understanding the personality of the other party is just as important as understanding ourselves. If we can anticipate *who* they are, and what drives and motivates them, then we will be able to tailor our behaviour and approach. This is an essential component in good negotiation but one that frequently is not considered before the event.

In the world of hostage negotiation one of the first activities for a police or security forces negotiator is to find out everything they can about the perpetrators, particularly their personality, history, motivators, track record, mode of operation and so on because this shapes the tactics the police will then use. A religious fundamentalist who believes he or she is acting on behalf of a higher power will exude a determination that transcends appeals to do the right thing. Having his mother call for her son to give himself up through a megaphone is unlikely to work. However, such a tactic might work for a desperate refugee who would not normally commit such a crime. Dilts and DeLozier (2000) suggest that behaviour is a product of who we are – our inner 'purpose' or personality together with beliefs.

So understanding 'who' we are negotiating with is crucial intelligence for any negotiation and this starts by attempting to determine their personality type. The problem, however, is how we gain this understanding. It would be somewhat unexpected for a hostage taker to agree to complete a personality assessment and send it back to the police negotiator. Instead, police work on compiling a personality profile, an activity that starts the moment a security incident occurs and continues through the entire negotiation with every engagement and interaction helping to further build the profile. At the points where contact is made, good police negotiators will sometimes try different lines of engagement to attempt to provoke certain responses as a means of determining the personality type of the perpetrator.

In the world of procurement and supply chain negotiations where we are negotiating with suppliers not terrorists, and megaphones are not necessary,

Table 6.4   The original four humours, temperaments and characteristics

Humour	Fluid	Season	Element	Organ	Personality Characteristics
Sanguine	blood	spring	air	liver	courageous, hopeful, amorous
Choleric	yellow bile	summer	fire	spleen	easily angered, bad-tempered
Melancholic	black bile	autumn	earth	gall bladder	despondent, sleepless, irritable
Phlegmatic	phlegm	winter	water	brain/lungs	rational, calm, unemotional

the same challenges for understanding the personality of the other party exist. However, if behaviour is a product of who we are (Dilts and DeLozier, 2000) then we can both identify personality from behaviour and predict behaviour based upon personality. Here we turn to the Greek physician Hippocrates.

Hippocrates (*c* 400 BC) suggested humans were both soul and body with four 'humours', meaning fluids that had to be in balance in order to be free from illness, with each fluid influencing human moods, emotions and behaviours. The four humours are Sanguine (blood), Choleric (yellow bile), Melancholic (black bile) and Phlegmatic (phlegm or mucus). This theory supported medical practice right up until the 18th century. Galen (*c* AD 200) built upon Hippocrates' work and developed a typology of temperament to explain different behaviours in humans. Table 6.4 summarizes this early work.

These four temperaments remained important in designating personality with correlations to the work of, and further developments by, Alfred Adler, Carl Jung and MBTI, Eric Fromm and Keirsey Bates. The four temperaments model was further developed and updated by Eysenck (1992) who carried out a study into personality differences and concluded that temperament is biologically based. Eysenck suggested personality was a product of neuroticism (tendency to experience negative emotions) and extraversion (tendency to enjoy positive events). Eysenck paired these two dimensions and noted the results of his study were similar to the original four temperaments. The resultant amalgam of his work and the original four temperaments model is one model used widely today. However, Littauer (1992) developed a different take on the four temperaments and her book *Personality Plus* became an international bestseller as it provides a simple means to easily understand personality of others and adopt an approach that will resonate with them. Securing a copy is highly recommended.

To arrive at a single, easy-to-use model that allows us to quickly determine the personalities of those we are negotiating with, the most credible research needs to converge, and here we need a means to reference the four personality dimensions. There are many different variants of this model out there, each with its own colour-based model, with each personality type having its own colour. The association of colours with each personality type creates a simple means of recall. While the original humours and bodily fluids have their own natural colour (black, red, yellow and green), and many representations of this model use these colours, they do however seem at odds with the nature of each personality. Authorities on this subject and companies practising in this field have offered many variants of the four temperaments with a range of colour combinations to suit, each attempting to create a unique model but creating a somewhat confused colour landscape, something to be conscious of if researching this area more deeply. Indeed, earlier editions of this book presented this model using my own four-colour model. However, I have moved away from this as I found the model created confusion where negotiators were already familiar with an alternative four-colour model. I have therefore adopted a four-dimensional personality type model using descriptors for each type. These are *Harmonizing, Fun-loving, Perfectionist* and *Leader*. This approach can therefore be easily referenced against, and aligned to, any of the four-colour models in use out there.

Figure 6.13 provides the four personality types and is adapted from and based upon the work of Littauer, Clark and Eysenck, and the original four temperaments. This model has also been developed to specifically relate to a negotiation context and align with the rest of the Red Sheet methodology. It includes four separate axes and it is this model that we shall use to support negotiation planning and, in particular, a means to conduct a rapid assessment of another party.

Assessing the other party using this model should happen both before and during the negotiation. Familiarization with this model allows us to determine the personality type of others with ease when meeting and interacting with them. To help internalize this, I recommend applying it to people you encounter. Start by classifying family, friends and colleagues; with practice it will become an inherent part of daily interactions and one that gives you the ability to select approaches that net the greatest response from others. Remembering and 'using in our minds' the personality types helps

Figure 6.13 The four personality types

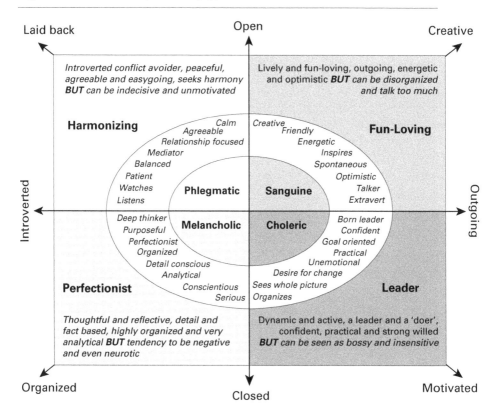

here: the person who always chairs or shapes proceedings in the meeting, and pushes for actions to be delivered is 'Leader'; the lively, bubbly lady who is always chatting at the water cooler and is always the first choice to organize the Christmas party is 'Fun-Loving'; the person who calmly gives lots of great reasons why his actions haven't been completed but somehow is difficult to get angry with is the 'Harmonizer'; and the quiet lady who routinely produces the weekly analysis, distributed without comment but always perfect is the 'Perfectionist'. I would, however, suggest caution in sharing your assessments openly without context; telling your wife she is not, as you previously thought 'Fun-Loving' but more 'Perfectionist' may not come across as the compliment you intended.

In negotiation planning, our aim is to find out what we can about the other party and to determine their personality type(s), ideally before we engage with them so we can tailor our approach accordingly, but in any event this should be an ongoing process. Start by finding out about the names and roles of those on their team. This may already be known. If not,

Figure 6.14   The four personality types explained

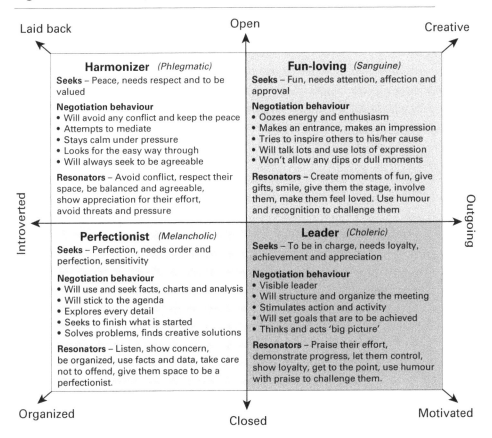

take the time to establish this, which can easily be done under the guise of making arrangements for the meeting, producing agendas or to enable prior security clearance etc. Next, research them and their personality and this is where we use our model of four personality types as defined in Figure 6.13 and also Figure 6.14, which shows how the four types relate to negotiation and typical negotiation behaviours. There are three approaches to do this: research, observation and testing. All should be used as needed in order to be comfortable we fully understand the other party.

Research

Today, like never before, it is possible to research an individual before you engage with them and gain lots of information about them. Just entering someone's name into a search engine often yields a wealth of information, especially if they frequently interact on the web using social media. Avenues of research include:

- **Web search.** See what you can find out about them and their company on the internet.

- **Social media.** See if you can find them using social media. Check LinkedIn, Facebook, Twitter and, if you can, read their posts and profiles. Often this alone is enough to determine their colour.

- **Find out who knows them.** Has anyone from your business or in your network met with them or had experience of them before?

- **Where in the organization do they sit?** Find out whom they report to, often published on company websites.

- **Find out whom they need to please...** to whom are they accountable? Who is their client? Who do they need to look good for? This may not be who you think. An individual I worked with would not agree to any significant business decision until he had discussed the matter with his wife; if she approved, he would approve. If you can work out whom they need to please you can begin to make it personal. This is a very important, yet often missed, subtlety within individual motivation and one reason why negotiating with with a teenager who believes she doesn't need to answer to anybody can be difficult.

Observation

There is no better gauge of personality than to experience it first-hand and your assessment of the other party shouldn't be limited to desk-based research. As you engage with them, simply watch them; observe what they do. Do they take control of the meeting or reside in analysis? Be careful not to make rash judgements based upon one action, as effective people learn to practise attributes seen in all four personality types, but build up a picture over time.

Testing

When the police are negotiating the release of a hostage they often don't have the benefit of social media profiles or first-hand interaction and so have to establish personality from a voice on the phone. Here, as I mentioned previously, tactics aimed to provoke certain responses can help. For example, a negotiator might briefly try to 'wind up' the perpetrators and attack them for, say, not having thought things through, to see what reaction they get; do they rise to the bait or run away? Testing personality can reveal much and Table 6.5 provides some suggested tests together with likely responses for each personality type.

Table 6.5 Negotiation personality type tests

Test	Leader	Fun-Loving	Harmonizer	Perfectionist
Try to take the lead on something	attempts to prevent you or take the lead over you	excited by your leading	appears to allow you to lead but often with quiet dissent	lets you lead
Make a highly ambitious, off-the-wall suggestion	seeks to bring you back to practical realities	likely to support your idea	draws your attention to all the hard work involved without disagreeing	will look for facts to support your proposal
Suggest a decision is required for something trivial	decisive with sound basis	spontaneously decisive	prefers you to make the decision	will seek to analyse and make fact-based decision
Inject moments of fun and humour	polite humouring only; anything more might be yielding to a leadership challenge	joins in	positively agreeable	little response
Smile at them	superficial smile; mirroring on own terms	enthusiastic smile	self-conscious smile	looks away, perhaps brief self-conscious smile
Outline something using facts and lots of detail	frustrated tolerance initially but will then demand the 'bottom line'	will be enthusiastic, helping to embellish dull moments	patient listening	purposeful listening; will seek to demonstrate real-time assimilation

Once again a health warning is appropriate here. The responses I've provided are representative and typical of personalities who perfectly mirror the classification; such things can never be fully predicted. Also, those who are emotionally competent will play different roles with ease to suit the situation. Furthermore, any testing of personality needs to be done carefully and subtly so it goes unnoticed. Attempting to be deliberately confrontational could be very detrimental to a critical negotiation.

Pressing their buttons

Most of the personality models that use the original four temperaments in some way are based on the ability to understand self and others and learn how to adapt personal behaviours to be more effective. Jerry Clark (2006b) uses his four-colour model to describe a series of influencing approaches tailored for each personality type. He cites examples of great sales success stories by individuals that do this. So for negotiation planning, the four personality types can help us to select and plan our style, demeanour and method of engagement in order to maximize potential outcomes. This might include what we do to put them at ease, help them to like us, get them to trust us, secure their interest and win them over. It is, in essence, about designing our approach to resonate with them and build rapport. Resonance is the key here as certain things we can choose to do when we are interacting can stimulate the greatest response from the other party. Table 6.6 gives a detailed list of resonators together with actions to control negative traits and things to avoid for each negotiation personality type.

Table 6.6   Resonators, controllers and things to avoid for each negotiation personality type

Personality type	Resonators	Controllers	Avoid
Leader	• show them respect, let them control, show loyalty • give them some authority • praise what they do to the rest of the group • make a point of being impressed by what they achieve and how they keep things going • let them open the meeting	• when they intimidate, shout or threaten: show them ways through, stay calm, don't confront • too controlling: gently remind them of the limits of their authority • impatience, impetuosity, inflexibility: don't challenge but ask them to consider the merits of an alternative approach	• rebelling against them • confrontation, let them feel in control • trivia and detail

Table 6.6 *continued*

Personality type	Resonators	Controllers	Avoid
Fun-loving	• they enjoy spending – give them the opportunity! • smiling, charm, humour • ask what they think and thank them for their input • mirror their excitement and enthusiasm • praise them • be supportive to them if they appear to be struggling • if appropriate, use gentle touch to help them stop talking • make it fun	• talking too much: interrupt them by thanking them, or use humour • too much socializing: bring them back to the task in hand	• cutting them off, let them speak but if you do need to interrupt, thank them or use humour • overwhelming them • putting them down • too much detail • being dull
Harmonizer	• give them an easy way through • appreciate them • make a point of reflecting on the intangibles they bring • ask them to mediate • invite them to share their observations • build a relationship with them	• procrastination: be firm, don't let them do it • indecisive: create limits or deadlines to elicit a decision • stubbornness: determine and help solve with them the underlying issue • detached: get them involved • sarcasm: recognize this is a sign they feel out of control	• putting them under pressure or threatening them • using conflict with them
Perfectionist	• demonstrate high standards and perfection • show great sensitivity • show them you understand them • play to their need to analyse; use charts and spreadsheets with them • encourage them to think outside the box • sincere praise for their extra efforts	• moody: affirm their mood; don't try to change it – ask them how to solve the problem • reluctance to spend: create a need to act based on facts and data • lost in detail: interrupt them and thank them	• joking around or being insensitive to them • trying to lighten them up; appreciate their depth • any signs you don't fully appreciate their analytical output

Assessing our opponent

It is at this point where we can bring together our research and assessment of those we will be negotiating with. Step 6A of the Red Sheet helps us structure our thinking here (Figure 6.15 gives a worked example). Once we have determined the individuals we will be negotiating with we can decide what their personality types are. At this point in our planning, it is a good time to consider and note anything else we know about them, perhaps pooling knowledge from our side, to give us as complete a view as we can of our opponent. With this assessment complete (Red Sheet step 6A) we can begin to determine the specific actions and approaches we will take in terms of our style and demeanour that will enable us to have good power in the negotiation as well as to build trust and rapport. We will find out more about how we can do this, and how we complete Red Sheet step 6B, in the next chapter.

Actually doing it

Red Sheet step 6A – Opponent

Purpose of this step

Step 6A is concerned with assessing, as best as we can, the other party's team and identifying what we know about them. Figure 6.15 gives a worked example and the template can be found in the Appendix.

Completing this step

1 List the individual(s) you will be negotiating with and their position.

2 If you can, classify the personality type of their team by inserting their team identifiers (eg TTL, TT1 etc) into the relevant negotiation personality type quadrant.

3 List anything else you know about them, eg who they report to, who they need to please, what motivates them etc.

Figure 6.15 Red Sheet steps 6A and 6B Opponent and Intangible Power Plan

6A. OPPONENT

Our team No.	Name	Role in the negotiation
(TL)	Lin Chong	Sales Director
(TT1)	Zhang Wei	Operations Manager
(TT2)	Chen Jimmy	Account Executive
(TT3)	Hung Lo Wan	Engineer
(TT4)		

Their negotiation personality (our best assessment)

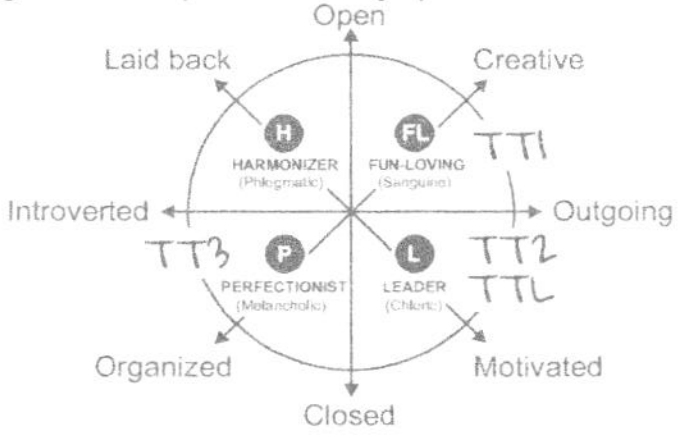

Open / Creative / Outgoing
Laid back
FUN LOVING (FL) (Sanguine) — TT1
LEADER (L) (Choleric) — TT2, TTL
HARMONIZER (H) (Phlegmatic) — TT3
PERFECTIONIST (P) (Melancholic)
Introverted
Organized / Closed / Motivated

What else do we know about them?

1. We think their new Taiwanese factory is only operating at 50% capacity - they need more work to get ROI

2. Business owner known for integrity in business

3. Sales director is an ex-PMC Ltd employee

6B. INTANGIBLE POWER PLAN

Plan for 'our style' and demeanour to project power and how we will build trust and rapport.

1. Use indirect language and reinforce/embellish with positive components.

2. Avoid any suggestions that 'time is short', instead talk about 'talking as long as necessary to get this right'.

Power

07

This chapter explores power in negotiation. It defines the prime factors that can enable power in a negotiation, the importance of knowledge in terms of understanding what power you or the other party actually has and it provides practical approaches to projecting your power and diluting that of the other party.

Pathway questions addressed in this chapter

13 What power do I hold relative to my opponent?

14 How do I increase my negotiation power position and/or undermine that of my opponent?

Red Sheet steps covered in this chapter

6B, 7A, 7B and 7C

It's all about power

Types of power

If you have the power in a negotiation then surely you will get what you want? It sounds plausible but the reality is often very different and ignorance of the actual power available and more importantly what to do with it is commonplace, as is failure to properly prepare and research a position.

Power is one party having, assuming or being acknowledged as having a stronger position over the other. Power can be both something that can be tested or measured but is also perception, based upon the ability of one party to appear more powerful than they are and the susceptibility of the other party. Power can also come from the use of clever tactics that outwit the other party. For example, physical strength is a primary source of power for wrestlers and this power can readily be put to the test; it is also linked to the size of the wrestler, hence why wrestlers are equally matched in the ring. But this is not the only source of a wrestler's power. Any wrestling match will be preceded by an elaborate show of bravado from the competitors, each attempting to 'psych out' or intimidate and place doubt in the minds of their opponent. Wrestlers will also use the power of clever tactics and sometimes it is not strength that wins but tactics alone that will bring a Goliath down.

We can see different forms of power at work around us in everyday life. Army recruits would not dare to question the sergeant major who bellows them into submission; a patient heeds every piece of advice and instruction her doctor gives her; and a child tries hard to win the approval of a parent. While the sergeant major, doctor and parent all have power, each is different – power based upon fear of consequences, respect for expertise and the reassurance love and favour brings, respectively. Similarly, in a negotiation there are different factors that can create a position of power, either real or apparent, and these are unique to each negotiation. French and Raven (1959) describe five separate and distinct types of power: these are coercive, reward, legitimate, referent and expert, and Table 7.1 provides an explanation, together with how these might apply to a negotiation.

The 5×5 power sources

The French and Raven work considers power in a general and organizational context. In the context of a negotiation, while they begin to help us understand the types of power that might be at play, they do not, on their own, provide a means to practically shape and control power in a negotiation. For example, a negotiator may be able to successfully apply legitimate power by making the other party feel they have some sort of obligation, but the negotiator must use a series of carefully applied tactics and techniques in order to achieve this. Coercive power is only possible, say, in a value-claiming negotiation, if the other party doesn't have the option of simply walking away. Practical application of power, and deflection of the other's power, requires us to consider both the type of power as well as the potential sources of power and what creates these in the first place. Therefore we must consider power sources, of which there are two types: tangible and intangible.

Table 7.1 Types of power (from French and Raven, 1959)

Component	Definition	This Power in a Negotiation Context
Coercive power	Forcing someone to do something that he/she has no desire to do with a goal of compliance otherwise punitive action could follow. Threats lie at the heart of coercive power and so this type of power is often associated with bullying or abusive behaviour in extreme circumstances.	• coercive behaviour would typically underpin hard value-claiming negotiations – 'agree to this or I walk away' • not compatible with relationship development • only possible where the other party believes you are in a more powerful position then they are
Reward power	Power from the ability to reward someone for the things they do. This power is based upon the premise that human nature is such that we are more likely to do something if we are likely to get something back for doing it. Power is only strong so long as you continue to have something the other party values to give back; the more you reward someone the more you normalize this and their expectations increase.	• used in a negotiation to offer returns beyond the negotiation (whether actual or promised by trust) eg 'agree to the deal as presented and next time I will ensure we look after you' • personal reward for doing a particular deal is the basis of corruption
Legitimate power	Power from the ability to engender feelings of obligation or the notion of responsibility in another. Legitimate power often comes with title, ie you obey the boss because they are your boss. Legitimate power is particularly prominent in authoritative, collective and polychronic cultures.	• power based upon obligation to an individual or what they stand for eg insurance salesperson – 'you owe it to your family to buy life insurance in case something happens to you' • requires legitimacy to be established first place • legitimacy in negotiation is only partly established by title but also by the actions of the individual to establish a position of supremacy eg personal style, actions, what is said or social comparison

Table 7.1 *continued*

Component	Definition	This Power in a Negotiation Context
Referent power	This type of power is associated with role models or individuals others might look up to and is concerned with the ability to create a sense of approval or acceptance for another's actions.	• inexperienced negotiators can yield to referent power if they believe the other party is a much better negotiator and will, often without realizing it, seek approval from the other for their negotiating ability. An experienced negotiator will spot this and seize the opportunity to reinforce power with some well-chosen interventions eg 'you're not making this easy for me' or 'you're clearly highly experienced at this', all designed to suggest approval
Expert power	Power based upon being the source of information, knowledge and expertise and so compelling others to trust them. This form of power is associated with professional roles such as doctors and lawyers where people trust their judgements and will take their advice.	• relevant where a party is the expert, eg attempting to negotiate with a supplier who is a specialist in their field who you want to provide an innovative solution • those providing a truly unique solution hold great power here, eg hiring a named designer

Tangible power sources can be researched, measured, established, observed and defined and where specific interventions can change the power available. For example, switching from buying a branded product to a generic alternative opens up the market, increases market power and reduces the power of dependency the branded supplier would otherwise hold. Effective use of tangible power sources requires knowledge to understand the actual power held by both parties. Tangible power is countered by finding alternatives.

Intangible sources of power are less observable but more felt, create perceptions and shape and guide the actions of others, often without realizing it. The ability to use intangible power in a negotiation comes with the emotional competence of the negotiator. It is countered through awareness of, and not being led by, the tactics a negotiator might use.

Figure 7.1　The 5×5 negotiation power sources model

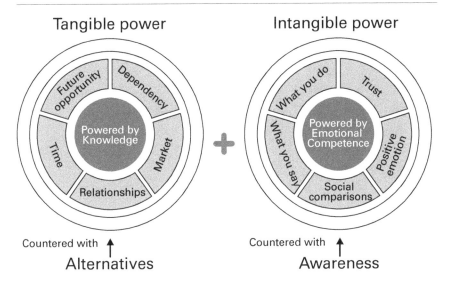

Of all the potential tangible and intangible sources of power in a negotiation, most fall into five headings, giving way to the 5×5 negotiation power sources model shown in Figure 7.1 (expanded in the following sections). The 5×5 model begins to bring together much of that already explored in previous chapters as well as those to come, and provides a powerful and practical tool for negotiation planning. Each power source relies upon one or more of the French and Raven (1959) power types. By considering the power sources and the type of power each utilizes, it helps define the context for how we will actually use our power in a negotiation and this is given in Table 7.2. For example, if we know the other party is dependent upon us, and they have no time to find any alternatives, we might consider using coercive power and a value-claiming negotiation approach, unless of course there was a longer-term relationship at stake.

Tangible power

There are five key tangible sources of power in a negotiation situation that we need to understand and ideally control: dependency, market, relationships, time and future opportunity. In each case, power requires knowledge, gained through thorough research and analysis, and can only really be diluted by finding alternatives, as this section will explain. Steps 7A, 7B and

Table 7.2   Power sources mapped to French and Raven (1959) power types

Power Source	Coercive	Reward	Legitimate	Referent	Expert
Tangible power sources					
Dependency	✓		✓		✓
Market	✓				✓
Relationship	✓	✓	✓	✓	✓
Time	✓				
Future opportunity		✓	✓		✓
Intangible power sources					
Trust		✓	✓	✓	✓
Positive emotion			✓	✓	
Social comparison		✓	✓	✓	✓
What you say	✓		✓	✓	✓
What you do	✓		✓	✓	✓

7C of the Red Sheet provide the process for assessing tangible power and determining our overall plan as well as any further information actions needed to expand our knowledge (to improve our power position).

Knowledge is power

Knowledge is power! So Francis Bacon once said, and when it comes to negotiation he was right. Having the knowledge of the power we actually hold, and that of the other party, is essential. Without it the only option is to bluff.

Tangible power is a product of that which is real and definable and, by its very nature, only exists if there is a differential between parties. If both sides hold equal power, and know it, there is in effect no power and no leverage. Tangible power is therefore relative to our position against that of the other party. Determining the tangible power requires us to consider what power is real and what is 'projected power'. For example, a good negotiator with little power may be able to give the impression that he or she has power.

If the other side is uninformed or inexperienced this may well work too. Projecting power is therefore a key negotiation tactic that we can use to our advantage but it can also be used against us if we do not understand our true power position and that is why knowledge is so essential.

Knowledge is a product of research and information gathering. Knowledge gathering is often neglected yet it can make a dramatic difference to negotiation outcomes. As with most research-based activities it is easy to assume that we already know enough. In a negotiation context bias in self-belief can also fool us into thinking we can bluff our way through without the need for good sound data. This is a dangerous mindset that can doom negotiation to fail.

In 2002 Donald Rumsfeld, the then Secretary of Defense for the United States, stood up at a press briefing addressing the absence of evidence linking Iraq with the supply of weapons of mass destruction and said:

> There are known knowns; there are things we know that we know. There are known unknowns; that is to say there are things that we now know we don't know. But there are also unknown unknowns – there are things we do not know we don't know. And if one looks throughout the history of our country and other free countries, it is the latter category that tend to be the difficult ones.

While Mr Rumsfeld's quote appears to have gone down in history with both praise and scorn, his words could have been written around research for a negotiation as they profoundly summarize the challenge, in particular the need to look beyond what we see before us so we might find alternatives and opportunities. We might know the supplier and their capabilities, we might be aware we don't know what is happening in the market, but we could find out. However, have we stopped to think about the supplier's financial position? Are they doing well or struggling? Because the chances are they are not going to reveal this to us, and published information will have a time lag so will not help us. The point here is that in negotiation preparation it is the 'unknown unknowns' that are most important and these could either catch us out or provide a great, but yet unrealized, opportunity.

Knowledge gathering in negotiation planning is about converting 'unknown unknowns' into 'known knowns' through research. There is no magic research plan that can help here. Instead we need to research as much as we can, in as many areas as possible, and slowly valuable knowledge will begin to materialize; as each research door is opened, new doors that hadn't previously been thought of appear, and so on. This is the power and beauty of good research and something that anyone who has completed a dissertation or thesis may well relate to.

Research and knowledge gathering therefore serves several purposes:

1 It establishes what tangible power we hold.
2 It establishes the tangible power the other party holds.
3 It helps us identify the actual differential between them and us.
4 It helps us determine if the other side fully understands their position.
5 It helps identify alternatives and opportunities.

Table 7.3 provides a list of research areas and potential sources for negotiation knowledge gathering. The list is neither exhaustive nor prescriptive and what and how much information is gathered depends upon the negotiation. However, it is possible that much of what is needed may already exist within the organization both within and outside the procurement or supply chain function. For example, if the organization has adopted Category Management or Supplier Relationship Management then both these initiatives demand comprehensive research into the supplier, market, internal aspects and the category being sourced and this can be found within category or relationship strategies.

Table 7.3 Areas for research in negotiation planning

Research Areas	Information to Collect	Possible Sources
Their team	• who are their negotiation team? • what is their role? • what do we know about them? • what is their negotiation personality type? • what personally motivates each individual?	• ask them • internet search • social media • ask others who know them • check their organizational structure
The supplier	• scope of business • turnover and percentage we represent • financial position • other clients or projects they are working on	• check their website • annual reports • financial check eg using companies such as Dun & Bradstreet • ask them

Table 7.3 *continued*

Research Areas	Information to Collect	Possible Sources
The product or service (business requirements)	• scope • legal requirements • assurance of supply requirements • quality, technical and specification requirements • service standards needed • commercial requirements • future aspirations around innovation	• ask stakeholders • specifications • past history • talk to marketing about what customers want in the future
How we use/ will use it	• who buys this? • how do we use this? • volumes, now and future • current performance or satisfaction	• ask stakeholders • spend data/purchase order history • see for yourself (eg visit the factory, see how it is used) • talk to marketing about what customers want
Other suppliers	• what other suppliers are there in this market? • what are the other suppliers doing?	• internet search • trade bodies
The market	• what determines market boundaries? • what other or related markets exist? • what is happening in the market and why? • how competitive is the market (use Porter's Five Forces analysis)?	• industry publications • internet search • ask experts • ask suppliers • research raw material or commodity prices using published indices • trade shows • newspaper and trade press articles • financial reports

Figure 7.2   The visual power gauge concept

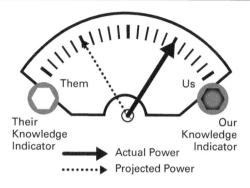

When the 'unknown unknowns' have been banished, the relative power position we find ourselves in needs to be easily understood so we can convert it into practical action during the negotiation. To this end, the Red Sheet methodology provides a visual indicator system, based upon an instrumentation gauge (Figure 7.2). The concept is simple: just like the needle on a gas gauge in a car shows the current fuel reserves, somewhere between empty and full, our power gauge shows the balance of power somewhere between 'them' and 'us'. Red Sheet provides five gauges for each tangible power source, used by drawing a pointer or arrow to show the actual power position and a second pointer to indicate their projected power (how the supplier is attempting to make us feel). This powerful visual summary of actual and projected power side by side lays the groundwork for the tactics we might subsequently choose to use in the negotiation.

The visual power gauge also features a knowledge indicator for both parties, each like an instrument panel lamp, which is simply coloured in when using the Red Sheet to indicate if, within our assessment, we feel we have adequate knowledge of our position and whether or not we believe the other party has good knowledge of their position. If, for example, we determine our power position to be high but have not engaged in much research and so don't really have the knowledge then we are just guessing and guesses become bluffs and so we are likely to fail. Similarly, if our research suggests they are in a strong position but we don't think they know it, then we can use this to our advantage. Checking knowledge is an important adjunct to our assessment as it serves to confirm our position and highlight opportunities.

Knowing what the 'final price' should be

'How can I know what I should pay for this?' is a fair question when planning a negotiation and one I frequently hear asked, especially by those starting out. It is a common misconception that somewhere out there lies a magic tool or approach used by the professionals to gain this insight. Negotiation would be easy if we could arm ourselves with quality information about where the end point lies. In practice, however, this is not so easy.

There are some negotiations where, with effort, research and planning, it is possible establish with some or even a good degree of accuracy what we should expect to pay, yet for others – and possibly in the majority of cases – we are blind, or at least semi-blind. There are many reasons for this. Complexities, history, market dynamics, market difficulty all cloud our insight, but fundamentally it is not in the supplier's interest for us to know the end point, as clearly this would limit their power and possibilities, so suppliers will seek to keep as much as they can hidden from us in order to protect their margin.

Establishing what we should be paying with any degree of accuracy depends on what we are buying. If we are a retailer sourcing bread then it is relatively straightforward to determine what bread should cost by considering the ingredients and volumes used, most of which are commodities where price information is readily available, together with an assessment of labour, manufacturing, transportation and other costs. With effort it is possible to develop a dynamic cost model that tracks commodity price changes and calculates what we should be paying for bread at that point in time. This can be vital intelligence for a negotiation that limits the supplier's options assuming the analysis is accurate. However, if we are buying branded bread which the end customer expects to see on our shelves, then the cost breakdown becomes less potent; the discussion shifts more to how we can secure the most value back for a price point higher than what the breakdown suggests. We are in effect buying the additional value of the brand and this may not be quite so negotiable.

Using a cost breakdown in a negotiation can be a powerful weapon providing we are confident in our analysis. If our facts and data are underpinning our position of wanting a price reduction then if the supplier engages in the debate there are only two responses he can give:

- To yield to the argument and concede on price, perhaps shifting discussions to what a fair amount of profit might be, or what value-adds could be provided.

- To reject the argument, perhaps on the basis that the analysis is disputed, in which case the next question becomes 'Please can your provide the correct figure?'

Using a cost breakdown in a negotiation to any effect requires the supplier to engage with the discussion and once engaged it becomes difficult for them to back out (for the reason above). In a recent discussion with a builder who I had engaged to provide a quote for some work, I asked if he could give me a breakdown of his price and show me the labour and key materials components. Clearly this was a question he was used to batting back as his response was: 'I don't give breakdowns of price. I can list all the activities and materials within the job, but my price is my price and I believe it is fair for what we do.' A smart response and one that disarmed any possibility of negotiation around individual elements, but rather shifted discussions to a simple decision as to whether my need and prior homework regarding what I should expect to pay versus his availability and reputation meant the price was right. It was, and the deal was done without any further attempts on my part to secure a bit more so as to incentivize him to do a good job for me. After all, my power was limited to how much we wanted or needed that work at that particular time vs his reputation.

Suppliers therefore typically seek to avoid ending up in such discussions unless they are confident their position stands up to transparent scrutiny or they know they can hide profit, say within the way overheads are dealt with or via hidden kickbacks from their suppliers. The notion of 'open book' costing, where suppliers volunteer the breakdown, is therefore one to be cautious of unless there is confidence in the validity of any figures a supplier might present. Furthermore, if the first time such figures are presented is during a negotiation then it is important to buy time to properly review and analyse what is being presented.

There are therefore a number of factors that create negotiation blindness around price points. These are:

Factors from our side that create negotiation blindness

- lack of research or understanding on our part;
- buying branded, unique or high-value add goods and services.

Factors that suppliers use to create blindness (or projected power)

- maintaining secrecy around commercial information and anything that would allow a cost breakdown to be established;
- added-value bundles (see Day One analysis);

- making out they have a stronger position and we need them even if we don't (projected power).

The Purchasing Price Cost Analysis tool

We can, for some negotiations, overcome this negotiation blindness to a degree using the 'Purchase Price Cost Analysis' (PPCA) tool – sometimes called a *should cost* or *cost breakdown* analysis tool – where we take the product or services we are seeking to negotiate over and develop a cost breakdown. With a good breakdown, and knowledge of what something should cost, we can be armed with excellent intelligence to inform our negotiation and provide supporting facts and data.

PPCA is not suitable for every negotiation. If we hold little power over the supplier, for example because we are sourcing something unique, branded, perhaps in low volumes, then PPCA will do little more than provide the supplier with some amusement, followed by a polite rejection of our demand for a reduced price. It is therefore essential to decide if PPCA is an appropriate tool to support our negotiation. To do this, we use Day One analysis which we explored in Chapter 4. Figure 7.3 shows the applicability of a PPCA against each quadrant for a negotiation.

Figure 7.3   Using Day One analysis to determine if a cost breakdown is feasible (PPCA)

	Tailored ✓ ✓ ✓	**Generic** ✓
More than one	PPCA can really help negotiations in this quadrant. We have the power of alternatives, but switching suppliers may have implications. PPCA can help inform our negotiation position in terms of the right price point to aim for in the negotiation. Using the PPCA in the negotiation can also be a powerful tactic to work towards the right outcome.	We have the choice and the power of alternatives, so we can switch suppliers to get what we want. Market should determine price points so using PPCA to support negotiations for this quadrant serves little purpose. However, maybe worthwhile if simple or to help understand the lowest market price.
	Custom ✓ ✓	**Proprietary** ✗
One	PPCA can help here. Whilst we are committed to this relationship and lack the power of alternatives, the supplier also needs us. PPCA helps inform a transparent approach to pricing so we can be clear about what additional value we might want within the relationship.	PPCA serves little purpose in the proprietary quadrant. The supplier holds the power and if we cannot switch then we lack alternatives. Using PPCA here is unlikely to secure an outcome as pricing will be based on value or brand. Instead focus on negotiation around added value elements.
	One	More than one

Number of suppliers (vertical axis)

Number of buyers (horizontal axis)

PPCA can work well to support negotiations for products or services in the *tailored* and *custom* Day One analysis quadrants. Some *generic* items can benefit from PPCA but only if they are non-complex and can be done as a 'quick test'. For example, if we were buying buildings maintenance, to understand the cost we might calculate what the service should cost based upon the hours worked at known market rates, together with any materials used. There is, however, little point spending much significant time on items in this quadrant, because if we understand the market and the price points of competitors, then we should already know what the market price should be. Nor is there any point using PPCA if we are in *proprietary*. Here we are paying for something unique that only this supplier can provide, here we are mostly likely to be blind to actual cost, and in any case the supplier is unlikely to be interested in such discussions, but rather our negotiation is around the best we can achieve and perhaps how much added value we might be able to secure.

Developing a PPCA is straightforward, but it is one of those activities that buyers seem to shy away from when planning a negotiation. The process for doing this is given in full in my book *Category Management in Purchasing* but in essence comprises three steps:

1 Sketch out all the direct cost components that sit behind a product or service. If it's a product, take it apart if possible and look at all the bits that make it up. For a service, list all the different activities that happen, any materials used and any expenses incurred. Include materials as well as direct overheads such as labour, process and distribution costs and identify or estimate what each component should cost.

2 Next make a list of the indirect cost components. These are all the costs that support the overall running of the business including overheads. These are harder to estimate but check annual reports or visit the supplier to see their operation. As a general rule of thumb indirect overheads often represent 50 per cent of the combined direct materials/costs and direct overheads.

3 Finally, for the areas that could not be completed, agree actions to do the further work and research and complete the analysis. Refine the analysis with further data gathering as needed to improve the robustness of the PPCA.

The use of a PPCA in a negotiation should be planned carefully. Believing that the PPCA is 100 per cent correct and presenting the analysis as a non-negotiable argument can be counterproductive, and even drive the supplier to play their BATNA. Instead, exploring the basis for the supplier's required price position with them using PPCA data can stimulate the right discussion and demonstrates to the supplier how serious we are. It is important to remember that our PPCA will almost certainly have a margin of error, yet with discussion we may be able to get closer to the true position and this will help us determine where the end point for our negotiation might lie.

The power of alternatives with a good BATNA

Having an alternative is the single most effective way to dilute or remove the other party's power in a negotiation and this is where we introduce the 'BATNA' or Best Alternative To a Negotiated Agreement. The concept of the BATNA was developed by Fisher and Ury (1991) and is concerned with identifying in advance alternative courses of action we will take if we do not get what we want from the negotiation.

BATNAs operate at different levels, having an alternative to the entire deal or individual alternatives for components of what is being negotiated. For example, imagine a friend is trying to buy a car and she has set a price she will not go beyond. She has also decided that if the salesperson refuses to meet her price then she will go and buy another car from another seller; this is a deal BATNA. However, within the negotiations she may also have decided to try and get a good trade in for her old car with the alternative that if she doesn't get the right offer she will remove it from the deal and sell it separately.

BATNAs should therefore be developed for as many individual components of a negotiation as possible, including the entire deal itself. BATNAs need to be worked up in advance and this is where our knowledge gathering can help; however, developing BATNAs is not just about going through the motions but the alternatives must be real and we must be fully prepared to follow them or they will lack potency. Knowing for certain we have an alternative builds confidence, self-esteem and courage to push harder during a negotiation. For example, if someone who needs a job gets offered a job they are likely to feel relief and gratitude. These emotions would weaken the individual's nerve around asking for more money before agreeing to accept the role. The job would, most likely, be accepted as presented. However, things change if there are two separate, equally attractive offers of a job at the same time. The power of having an alternative can provide the courage to try asking for a higher salary from one or even both prospective employers.

I frequently hear 'but there is no BATNA for this situation'. This mindset is performance limiting. There is always a BATNA: it just might need some brain power to work out what it could be. But, crucially, finding it might require removal of any emotional attachment to a particular outcome. Remember the friend I described earlier, the car salesman? He described watching for visible signs that someone was ready to buy a particular car. Cleverly he would reinforce this by helping them see themselves owning and enjoying the car. This is a salesperson's dream, as once someone has formed an emotional attachment to acquiring something then they have ruled out in their minds any alternatives. That gives the salesperson the power and all that is required is to make the customer feel they are getting a great deal and the emotional attachment will do the rest. Finding a BATNA is not necessarily easy and might require alternative scenarios you would prefer not to go with to be contemplated, but this is where negotiators must choose between securing a great negotiation outcome or agreeing to terms as presented in order to get the precise thing you have set your heart on. There is a place for both approaches and so using the power of alternatives is a choice we have depending upon what we want.

Many potential BATNAs are often possible, it just requires a bit of creative thinking to find them and brainstorming with others can help. Potentially these could include:

- walk away;
- go to another supplier;
- buy an alternative product/service;
- delay;
- change specification;
- remove a component from the deal;
- change who we are negotiating with;
- maintain the status quo – keep current arrangements;
- go negotiate with another part of their organization/go above them;
- any alternatives found within category strategies (if the organization has adopted Category Management).

All experienced negotiators will develop BATNAs. That means that the other party will be doing this too, so good planning means attempting to anticipate the other party's potential BATNAs in advance and identify how we might respond. Wolfe and McGinn (2005) suggest that the ultimate power in a negotiation is the difference in the alternatives. For example, if their alternative is to lower the price and settle for less but we are prepared to walk away, then we have greater power.

Developing BATNAs is therefore an essential part of negotiation planning and one that requires avoiding emotional attachment. Being creative to develop alternatives can be enormously powerful. Never leave home without a BATNA!

Degree of dependency

This is the degree to which one party is dependent upon the other and the overall imperative for one or the other party to realize a given outcome or maintain the broader relationship. Dependency can take many forms and is primarily about the absence of easy alternatives and can create a scenario where the dependent party becomes subservient to the other party.

During the 1990s the concept of outsourcing rose to popularity as organizations sought benefits by removing entire parts of their organizations in favour of using an outsourced provider who promised economies of scale and expertise. While there are many examples of successful outsourcing, there are also tales of wholesale failure where costs increased, quality decreased and companies found themselves 'locked in' because the supplier had accumulated vital know-how about how the service was provided, thus preventing them from switching suppliers. Here, the supplier had in effect created a dependency that could not easily be removed.

Assessing the power balance in terms of dependency is about considering all the factors that create dependency. Factors that create dependency on both sides are given in Table 7.4. Reducing dependency is about considering what alternatives exist or what would need to happen to create alternatives.

Market

Market power is distinct from any power derived from market difficulty due to complexity or factors that limit choice; that is part of dependency power described above. Market power is the degree to which prevailing or predicted market conditions are favourable or unfavourable depending upon which side we're on.

Marketplaces are systems, structures, relationships or institutions where there is some exchange of goods, services or information for money or something of value. They can be simple or complex and exist in many forms: a physical space; a non-physical or online market; labour; commodity; currency or stock market; an artificial market (ie one that is constrained by government regulation) or even an illegal market such as the trading of drugs or arms.

At the heart of market power is a good understanding of the market itself so good knowledge gathering is essential. Without it we're negotiating blind. To determine market power we need to answer three questions:

Table 7.4   The power of dependency

	Dependency on them	Dependency on us
Framing question	How important is this supplier to us and why?	How important is this spend to the supplier and why?
Factors that determine dependency power	• the supplier is important in terms of our future business direction, eg they have innovation or key personnel we need or because of current collaborative projects • switching suppliers is not easy • product or service is highly complex • relationship with this supplier is important beyond this negotiation • supplier holds important knowledge or know-how about the area of supply that we lack and cannot easily amass (eg outsourced provider with critical process knowledge) • we have no choice but to buy a specific named, branded or patented product/service (eg client specified, regulatory approved etc)	• supplier is dependent on us for the future success of their business (eg because of collaborative projects or investments in capacity) • we represent a significant percentage of supplier's sales or turnover • our brand, or being seen as a supplier to us, is important to them • our business with the supplier enables another area of revenue generation, eg by-product from manufacturing for us is used elsewhere • supplier's financial position is weak and they need this business
Tests for alternatives (BATNAs)	• if we don't secure the outcome we want, how easy or quickly can we find an alternative? • what alternative suppliers are there? • what alternative or substitute products/services are there?	• if the supplier lost this business, how quickly could they offset the loss?

1 What exactly is the marketplace?

2 What is happening in the market?

3 What alternatives are there?

Determining the marketplace

The first question might seem easy, but in reality negotiators often fail to understand the exact market they are in. The key here is to understand the boundaries of the marketplace and then it is possible to determine what would need to happen to push beyond these. Markets can have natural and artificial boundaries. For example, taxi firms exist the world over, but don't constitute a global market. It is a collection of small markets, each bound by practicality, licences to operate, and ultimately the limited demand for long-haul taxi services. Factors that determine markets are:

- form – the type and nature of the market, eg a physical space, online etc;
- size – how big the market is, usually measured in total volumes sold, people employed or how much is spent in the market, eg the size of the US fast food market is estimated at $120bn per annum;
- scale – the geographical reach of the market;
- location – where the market is based and what its boundaries are;
- types of participants – eg whether they are individuals or companies;
- types of goods or services – what they are, the function they perform or the need they fulfil;
- generic choice – the generic or proprietary nature of what is being sourced;
- restrictions – any factors that limit a market or the freedom of trade such as government sanctions or regulation reducing the quality or quantity available.

In each case these factors introduce boundaries. A physical space is limited by the space available and where it is; geographical reach depends upon economic practicalities and if you set out to buy 'an Apple iPad' rather than 'a tablet computer' then you have limited your potential marketplace by selecting a proprietary product. Typically, the closer the boundaries are, the less choice we have, and the more our potential power in the market is diluted. Consequently suppliers will seek to reduce our options so that we have, or are made to believe we have, little choice, thus increasing their power by reducing the apparent size of the market they occupy.

Market power is therefore related to the boundaries of the market but it is also determined by what is happening in the market.

Understanding what is happening in the market

This is ultimately determined by supply and demand at any given moment and how it is changing or predicted to change over time. The economics behind this is an entire subject all of its own, but in simplistic terms: where there is no artificial intervention, markets will grow or contract but will always naturally gravitate to a state of equilibrium where supply matches demand. An imbalance with high demand and limited supply will attract higher price points and new entrants, while low demand and over-supply will tend to cause price to fall and drive suppliers out of business or force them to diversify. However, markets can be slow to respond, creating moments of imbalance. An over-supply means buyers have the advantage; where there is high demand and limited supply the supplier has the upper hand. With careful monitoring, good timing and the ability to act it is possible to seize advantage from changes in the marketplace. This can be seen at work in trading rooms around the world where stocks or commodities are bought or sold on a daily basis; money can be made by informed speculation and knowing when to buy or sell.

Understanding what is happening in a commodity market is relatively straightforward. Commodity prices vary according to market conditions and familiarization with published commentaries, indices and trading results will soon provide good insight. It is also possible to understand trends and what might cause them; for example, a bad summer with extremes of weather might cause crop failures, reducing supply capacity and pushing prices up. If that wasn't enough then there are plenty of experts out there ready to share their knowledge.

For goods or services that are more than a commodity, understanding what is happening in the market begins to get a little more complex. Where products are simple and generic, the market can sometimes be understood by considering the raw materials and what is happening in respective markets for each. For example: to understand what is happening in the market for chlorine we need to understand the key components that influence chlorine price:

- current cost of raw materials – salt and energy;
- current cost of haulage – oil prices;
- demand for caustic soda (a by-product of chlorine manufacture, produced in equal proportions);

- current manufacturing capacity – chlorine production requires large-scale manufacturing so capacity can only be added or removed in large blocks. A closing factory will impact price.

For goods or services that are more complex or proprietary in some way the link to individual cost drivers becomes less distinct or even disconnected. For example, there is a market for perfume but the selling price is not typically sensitive to fluctuations in raw materials. Monitoring glass prices or the availability of rose petals will not help us understand what is happening in this market. Instead raw material fluctuations are absorbed by huge margins. The selling price is set by the supplier, based upon what those in the market are prepared to pay for the perceived value a specific brand or fragrance will bring. Yet this is still a market and demand still fluctuates; the difference is when demand falls the perfume houses don't tend to respond by cutting prices, but rather by attempting to reinvigorate demand using aggressive marketing campaigns.

Understanding what is happening in a market is therefore a science all of its own and depends upon what we are buying. Where there are direct correlations to commodity or raw material prices then researching these is essential to understanding market power. Beyond this researching the market requires some detective work, as any supplier is unlikely to tell us unless a market is moving in his favour. The good news is that in any given market there are plenty of experts and good sources of information that can provide vital intelligence and these are included back in Table 7.3.

Determining alternative markets

It may be possible to increase our market power and dilute that of the other party by finding alternatives and opportunities. This means seeking to push beyond the current market boundaries and find opportunities in the way the market is moving. Once again it is good research that can help here to provide the knowledge of what is possible.

By understanding boundaries we can explore what is constraining us from increasing our power in a marketplace. Pushing beyond the boundaries can bring leverage. For example, looking beyond traditional markets to low-cost country sources might expand the potential market providing there is capacity with hungry suppliers. Looking at the function of what is being sourced rather than the types of goods or services changes the mindset and can push the boundaries by opening up whole new marketplaces. For example, there is a defined marketplace for air travel; however, if the function is business meetings with global counterparts then there is a much bigger marketplace for getting people from A to B and a completely different set of marketplaces for connecting people remotely using technology.

Arming ourselves with knowledge of what is happening in a marketplace enables us to place our negotiation within this context; to consider the timing of our negotiation, alternative or broader markets available to us to shape what goals we pursue and the tactics we adopt. For example, in 2012 as food producers in the United Kingdom saw the cost of raw materials increase sharply following a series of poor crop yields and rising energy costs, negotiations with retailers were focused on suppliers attempting to secure price increases. The global downturn was not over and was still very much restricting consumer spend, so the supermarkets were desperate to maintain their competitive position. But despite their power it was clear that at some point price rises would need to be accommodated and passed on to the consumer.

One supermarket chain recognized market power was against them and adopted two negotiation tactics: first, they delayed having the negotiation with the supplier as long as they could; second, when they did negotiate, they pushed for their suppliers to hold current pricing as long as possible – with the promise of an uplift in price at a point in the future, thus forcing the supplier to absorb the impact in the short term. In contrast during the 2020 pandemic lack of supply disrupted and permanently redefined many supply chains and in some cases switched the balance of power, making retailers desperate to keep certain supplies flowing. Retailers were forced to adapt their response away from hard leverage to trading goodwill with an eye to the future. By understanding what is happening in the market and the external environment it is possible to design a negotiation approach that seeks to seize opportunities or deflect threats depending upon whether the market is for or against us and time our interventions accordingly. Table 7.5 defines the factors that drive market power together with test questions for alternatives.

Relationship

Don't underestimate the power of relationships! Relationship power is often hidden but can present a formidable force in a negotiation that can help or hinder. Relationship power is the degree to which one party has established a history that gives them an advantage or holds influential relationships with key people in our organization.

Table 7.5 Market power

	Market in their favour	**Market in our favour**
Framing question	What is happening in the market? Which way is it moving?	
Factors that determine market power	• sole supplier or market is concentrated with a few dominant players • they are a significant supplier in this market • supplier operates in multiple marketplaces and is not reliant upon just this market for revenues • we are buying a unique, differentiated, branded or patented product or service • demand is high and exceeds supply, little or no spare capacity in the market • distribution channels are controlled • difficult for new companies to enter the market (eg due to regulation, investment required etc)	• market competitiveness is high (suppliers fight to secure and retain small margins) • we are a significant player in the market (eg buying in high volumes, high spend) • we can switch suppliers easily (eg we are buying a generic product and alternatives exist) • there are few buyers • supply exceeds demand – eg over-capacity in the market, low demand • new entrants possible and likely • there are high exit barriers
Tests for alternatives (BATNAs)	• are there substitute products or services (things that fulfil the need in a different way) that open up new markets? • can we make the product/ service more generic and switch suppliers? • can we expand the potential market boundaries, eg low-cost country sourcing? • can we remove the need?	• could the supplier forward-integrate (start doing what we do)? • can the supplier afford not to compete in this market (eg has significant interests in other markets)? • could the supplier collaborate with another supplier and dilute our power?

History

If a supplier has supplied us prior to a negotiation then they have history. Depending upon what they supplied this may give them an advantage over competitors and it may even make them more attractive to us as they know our business. However, if as part of this history the supplier has accumulated know-how about how to provide the goods or service in question, and we don't readily have access to this, then in this situation the supplier has power. Examples of the power of history exist in service provision and outsourcing where a supplier becomes familiar with the nuances of a customer's business. Often such knowledge cannot fully be defined, as it exists within the learnt experience of the supplier's staff. Diluting power here and finding an alternative requires considering what must happen to switch suppliers and re-learn any vital know-how. History can work in our favour too if we have shown support to a specific supplier to grow their business. If we were the client that gave a small supplier their first big break this, in itself, creates a sense of obligation.

Influential relationships between individuals

As we saw earlier, suppliers work to develop relationships and build trust. However, this is not something that is confined to the procurement or supply chain team. If allowed to, suppliers will seek to establish individual relationships with as many key people in our business as possible. Depending upon what the organization permits, and sometimes despite this, relationships are cultivated by friendly exchanges, offering support, meetings over lunch or even tickets to sporting events. Across all the organizations I've worked with around the world, only a handful ever seem to successfully manage, or have an agreed protocol, for how those in the wider business should engage with suppliers. Functions other than procurement typically see it as part of their role to have a free and unhindered relationship with suppliers and might view any interference as standing in their way. R&D teams meet with suppliers to discuss how they can support new developments, marketing want to discuss future possibilities, operations discuss the day-to-day happenings.

While it might seem somewhat constricting if a procurement function controlled every supplier engagement, the issue here is one of alignment or rather the lack of it. Suppliers are often free to seek and win allies across a business, 'dividing and conquering' to establish powerful relationships that can work against procurement interventions and even unhinge negotiations. Conditioning a supplier prior to a negotiation serves little purpose if the supplier then triangulates what they hear from someone else in our organization and hears a different story. This might all sound as though I'm suggesting those outside of a procurement function to be subversive, disloyal and ready to jeopardize outcomes. This is not so, but the reality is that few businesses take the time to educate those outside of procurement about how to engage with suppliers, what to do and more importantly what not to do, and this is a weakness suppliers will exploit. An apparent friendly exchange with a supplier can actually be an intelligence-gathering exercise.

Relationships are not confined to those built by the efforts of the supplier, but may also be a product of historical circumstances. If a key individual within a supplier has a relationship with one of our senior executives, say from working together previously, then there may already be a natural friendship and degree of trust and appreciation between these two. Such a relationship can, in fact, be very powerful and actually help outcomes by doing business with a supplier who doesn't want to let us down. However, these relationships can also act as an impediment to negotiation outcomes if the senior individual is not aligned with our cause. The point here is it is important to understand the relationships that exist and if they provide a source of power in a negotiation for one or the other party.

Relationships aren't always in the supplier's favour. If, for example, we had previously given a small company a big break that helped them grow and develop, then it is possible the supplier will not forget this, thus creating a degree of obligation from the supplier and power in our favour.

Relationship power changes with culture. In monochronic and individualistic cultures relationships tend to be more functional and the need for transparency in business dealings is often a prerequisite. However, in polychronic and collective cultures relationships between individuals and history count for everything and deals will stand or fall on this basis. This makes transparency more difficult as loyalties to individuals transcend loyalties to the company.

Knowledge of relationships is essential for negotiation planning and to understand this we return to the stakeholder map developed within step 3 of Red Sheet and from here determine what relationships exist and the degree and nature of them. It is not out of place to ask a supplier to help us understand the different points of contact they have. Once all the points of interface and who has relationships with whom are understood, the power these hold can be considered. Relationship power can be countered by seeking alignment, which in practice means working closely with stakeholders so they support the negotiation approach and present a unified message to those suppliers with whom they have a relationship. Table 7.6 summarizes the factors that determine relationship strength and the tests that can be applied to find alternatives.

Table 7.6   The power of relationships

	They hold strong relationships	Relationship in our favour
Framing question	What is the nature of relationships between parties, with whom and how strong?	
Factors that determine relationship strength	• strong relationships with stakeholders across our business, perhaps even not fully understood • many other parts of the business can, and do, choose to place business with this supplier • support for this supplier within our business, perhaps even stronger than support for procurement • supplier provides apparent free support to operations, technical or R&D functions • longstanding history of supply • they have significant knowledge of our business, which gives them an advantage over competitors • supplier holds personal relationships at a senior level with our business • procurement not aware or involved in many engagements with this supplier • relationships and interactions with suppliers are decentralized and cross-functional	• stakeholders support procurement • all our stakeholders are aligned and present a united, pre-agreed position to the supplier • procurement are aware of and involved in all key supplier engagements • no or little history to lock us in (eg due to supplier knowledge of our business) • we have a history of supporting this supplier (eg we have helped them grow) and they view us favourably because of this • relationships with suppliers are managed centrally by procurement • senior or executive individuals reinforce the agreed position with suppliers • suppliers don't have the freedom to engage with individuals across the business, eg there are rules for how suppliers must engage

Table 7.6 *continued*

	They hold strong relationships	Relationship in our favour
Tests for alternatives (BATNAs)	• can we secure internal alignment? • can we use our senior team to reinforce our position? • can we identify the know-how that is giving this supplier an advantage and provide for this with a new supplier? • can we stop the supplier engaging elsewhere? • can we use facts and data to convince those in our organization of the need to change? • can we develop more influential relationships above the sales personnel?	• can the supplier complain to senior individuals in our organization? • is anyone in our organization obliged to the supplier in some way?

Time

Time is money! Time is of the essence! Time is against us! All cries that might be heard within business dealings to compel the other party into action. Time can prove to be a potent source of negotiation power for either party. If there is limited time to close a deal, say because a contract expires or an unmovable event is imminent, then unless there are alternatives, power is in the supplier's favour. If they know it then they can even hold us to ransom too.

Preventing the other party from holding the power of time constraint over us requires good planning to ensure we don't get backed into a corner. The 2012 London Olympics provided an immovable deadline for its suppliers, but good planning by the procurement team ensured that this didn't become a source of power for suppliers. Instead negotiation and contract placement activities were planned well in advance, but crucially a key criterion with the procurement framework used by the Olympic Delivery Authority that was used to qualify and select suppliers was ability to deliver on time. Here 'time' became part of the basic assessment of fitness for purpose early on and a basis to select suppliers who could commit to meeting timescales.

Time power can also come from procrastination and delay and this can be equally hard to counter. In the legal profession finding ways to delay reaching an agreement by asking for a series of small points of detail to be resolved or additional information to be provided is a common tactic, especially if the other has limited funds to keep fighting an expensive legal battle. Hostage negotiators use the same tactic. While it might seem like the bad guys with the guns and the hostage have all the power, what they lack is time. A good hostage negotiator will know this. Sooner or later the kidnappers will need food, water and sleep and will begin to become mentally fatigued and these factors present opportunity for bargaining. If the hostage negotiator believes the situation is contained, taking time is often the best tactic.

Time is only a source of power if there is knowledge of the position of the other party. For example, if a supplier has cash flow challenges and needs to cut a deal quickly then this only works in our favour if we know their position, and they will most likely avoid being upfront about this. Table 7.7 summarizes time power and the tests that can be applied to find alternatives.

Future opportunity

The power of future opportunity is about the current potential one party represents or offers to the other and the benefits that might be realized beyond the immediate deal. Future opportunity has the power to turn a poor deal into an attractive proposition. There are four types of opportunity power:

- **Jam tomorrow.** The promise or suggestion of some additional or future benefit; for example, suggesting to a supplier that there could be much more future business beyond the work being discussed now if they perform well, and just improving their price might be all that is needed to tip the balance and secure the deal needed. Even without guarantees, the suggestion itself creates a degree of obligation or at least the sanction for follow-up. Obligation power can therefore be a benefit that is certain or speculative.

- **Prestige.** The intangible value of doing business with the other party. For example, if we represent a prestigious household brand, suppliers will

Table 7.7 Time power

	Time is on their side	Time is on our side
Framing question	Is time of the essence?	
Factors that determine time power	• is there limited time before a deal must be negotiated? • current arrangements cannot run on past an upcoming end date such as a contract expiry • the goods or services are needed quickly, perhaps even faster than others in the marketplace could respond • we need to spend money before a specific date (eg due to budget or financial rules)	• we are not in a hurry and can take as long as we need to get the right deal agreed • the supplier needs to close the deal urgently • the salesperson wants the sale to count in a current bonus period • the supplier has financial or cash flow difficulties
Tests for alternatives (BATNAs)	• can we extend contracts or deadlines to make more time to look at other alternatives? • can we implement a short-term contract? • can we plan better? • can we switch suppliers and make the 'ability to meet timescale' a key selection criterion? • can we delay?	• can the supplier compel us to make a deal in some way? • could the supplier suggest or create future scarcity? • could the supplier use delaying tactics?

place great value in being able to claim us as their client, especially if they can reference this elsewhere.

• **Specialism.** One party has a unique or specialist capability, product or service that could be highly valuable to the other. Specialisms present most future opportunity power where there is alignment with wider aims and objectives of the other party or potential to prevent competitors from gaining advantage. For example, a small company specializing in developing new flavours might represent a source of great innovation to a multinational food producer and add value to the brand. Despite the flavour house being a small concern they present great opportunity and if the multinational made some exclusive agreement it would prevent competitors having access to the same innovation.

- **Personal satisfaction.** The final component of future opportunity power is any personal satisfaction or benefit that individuals get from a negotiation outcome. An extreme example of this would be bribery and corruption; however, opportunity power also exists where it would be beneficial or desirable for an individual to make a particular agreement, perhaps to help self-development or career progression.

The power of future opportunity is often underestimated and it is easy to sell ourselves short. If a supplier wants the kudos associated with being a supplier to our brand, they are unlikely to tell us; instead this objective will remain hidden. Understanding future opportunity power is therefore about considering carefully what potential we and the other party offer. Table 7.8 summarizes the factors that drive the power of future opportunity and some tests for alternatives.

Creating a tangible power plan

Equipped with an assessment of the power we and the other party hold for each of the five tangible powers, and whether parties know their or the other's power position, we must decide how we will use this insight to shift the power balance in our favour. We do this in two ways:

- use alternatives and BATNAs to increase our power and/or dilute theirs;
- use knowledge (or any lack of it on their part) to project more power or dispel power they are projecting.

We use our power assessment from step 7A to determine the specific things we will do in our negotiation and create a tangible power plan (step 7B of the Red Sheet). There are two dimensions to this:

- Strengths – Consider where our actual or projected power lies, or where the knowledge of power positions is in our favour, and determine specific actions, topics of discussion, BATNAs we will play or lines of enquiry to seize advantage here.

Table 7.8 The power of future opportunity

	They represent opportunity to us	We represent opportunity to them
Framing question	Is there a significant future opportunity?	
Factors that determine opportunity power	• they can help us realize our goals and increase our brand value • they have a unique product or service • they have a specialist capability that we need • they are innovators in an area of great interest to us • if we do this deal, it is possible, likely or even guaranteed we will benefit in the future • there is good alignment between them and us (eg operating location, infrastructure, ways of working)	• we can help them realize their goals and grow their business • brand value – the supplier will gain prestige from being a supplier to us • growth in volumes/ extent of service likely • our business is expanding • growing interest in our innovations • alignment of geographical operating bases • we are good to do business with (style, culture, payment terms, people, ways of working etc)
Tests for alternatives (BATNAs)	• can we backward-integrate and do what the supplier is doing? • are there others who could provide a similar opportunity?	• can the supplier forward-integrate and do it themselves? • could they partner with one of our competitors?

- Weaknesses – For the areas where we are weak determine any actions that might increase our projected power, eg with a cleverly staged bluff, use of facts and data or to anticipate the tactics and approach our opponent might try here and consider ways we might be able to parry their attacks.

For any areas where we don't adequately understand our power position and that of our opponent, we must to do more homework and not leave

anything to chance if we are to secure a good outcome. Gaps in our knowledge can be our downfall but equally they might represent opportunities to
find something that changes the game in our favour. Negotiators typically
fail to identify or act upon such areas, defaulting to less than adequate
research and preparation or leaving it until the event to 'see how it goes.'
This is poor practice and instead areas where we lack knowledge should be
a concern to any negotiator and trigger further thorough research. This
takes time, effort and commitment yet it is by securing good facts and data
that we might find ways to increase our power or better deflect theirs. We
won't always find the intelligence we need, but if we have endeavoured at
length to bridge our knowledge gaps we will be as prepared and equipped
as we can be. Therefore, the final step in developing a tangible power plan
is to identify and act upon any knowledge-gathering actions (and here we
use step 7C of the Red Sheet). Figure 7.5 gives a worked example of both the
tangible power plan and the knowledge actions.

Intangible power

Power in any negotiation is multi-faceted and any negotiation must consider
all the sources of both tangible and intangible power. Intangible power is
less specific but rather power that emerges through the different ways a
negotiation is conducted, runs through all stages and underpins the entire
Red Sheet methodology. Intangible power is projected and countered though
emotional competence. With self- and social awareness, and the ability to
manage ourselves and our relationships, it is possible to project power and
not be influenced by how others project their power. A schoolteacher entering a new class for the first time might enter the classroom walking tall and
immediately attempt to display assertive behaviour over the group. She is in
fact projecting power in a series of ways in an attempt to establish who is in
charge early.

The sources of intangible power in negotiation are given in Figure 7.1
above but include positive emotion, trust and social comparisons (expanded
below) as well as what you say and how you act in a negotiation (the latter
two are negotiation topics all of their own and so are covered in later chapters).

Displaying positive emotion

Displaying positive emotion is about a negotiator appearing enthusiastic,
excited with us and happy towards us as we engage them. This lies at the
heart of interpersonal selling: 'the salesman with the nice smile' and so on.

When negotiators display positive affect, they signal that they are trust-worthy and also that they are ready to cooperate. Displays of positive emotion by one negotiator induce an actual positive emotion response in the other party, putting them at ease, increasing communication (Carnevale and Isen, 1986) and opening up the possibility to discuss interests and priorities – an opportunity a good negotiator and salesperson will seize.

Positive emotion also engenders trust. Research suggests that when some-one displays positive emotion towards us we tend to naturally trust them more (Frank, 1988; Fridlund, 1994; Knutson, 1996) and trust is a key source of negotiation power. Anderson and Thompson (2004) cite excitement, enthusiasm and happiness as the components necessary to induce positive effects on others in a negotiation.

Trust is power

As we have seen, our need to trust is an important and often underestimated component of human interaction; it is also a potent source of intangible power.

Winning the trust of the other party can convert a value-claiming negotiation into a value-creating negotiation inviting discussion and collaboration between parties about possibilities and so creating new value rather than fighting over the distribution of a fixed amount of resources (Bazerman and Neale, 1992; Fisher and Ury, 1991; Thompson, 1990). An example is 'up-selling' and forms part of sales training the world over. Some people are more susceptible, or less experienced, than others at spotting what is happening. I myself can report going into a store with a clear idea about the 'mid-range' TV I was going to buy and emerging several demos later with the biggest ultra-high definition panel in the shop, and feeling good about having been talked up by the salesperson too.

In a negotiation or relationship where there is a power imbalance, the party with less power occupies a vulnerable position, one where they are susceptible to being exploited by others (Chen, Brockner and Greenberg, 2003; Kramer and Tyler, 1996). It follows that those in the lesser position tend to be more anxious and concerned about issues of trust and so will seek reasons to trust the other and to know they won't be exploited (Mannix, 1993; Tyler and Degoey, 1996; Van den Bos *et al*, 1998). As we saw in the previous section, positive emotion helps create trust. A nice smile by the used car salesman to the little old lady who likes the car but 'really ought to call her son before agreeing to anything' can work wonders, sending a powerful 'you can trust me' signal.

However, trust can also be real and genuine and provide a basis to select one supplier over another. For example, in a long-term relationship where we know the supplier, they have never let us down and our engagements seek to create value, the trust that we hold for that supplier is a compelling reason to use them. If a senior executive needs a delicate piece of work done they are most likely to bring in someone they know and can trust. Entrepreneurs of small businesses will often employ and surround themselves with friends and family for the same reason. Trust is therefore not something that must always be resisted, but in a negotiation it is necessary to be vigilant for false trust-building tactics, say from displays of positive emotion and especially when in the position of least power, and differentiate between these and genuine, positive trust built up as part of a relationship.

Social comparisons

If we view the other party as superior in some way then we are more likely to give them the upper hand in a negotiation. This will not be a conscious thing but rather our own self-confidence and self-belief will be compromised because something inside makes us feel this way. Think about people you have met where you felt intimidated or something they did made you feel afraid to confront them. If this happens when you are negotiating, chances are your performance will be compromised.

When we meet or engage with someone or a group or people, we will, without realizing it, seek to compare ourselves to them and determine our position relative to theirs. Where we feel our position lies will then determine how we behave and act. There are many triggers for social comparisons. In collective cultures this is almost entirely driven by status, but in individualistic cultures the cues are subtler. Tone of voice, posture, the way they enter the room, what they say and the language they use are all cues we pick up on. We also make comparisons based upon how they look, how they dress, the car they drive, the watch they wear and so on.

The saying 'dress to impress' is particularly relevant in negotiation. In Italy, for example, how you dress for a negotiation is vitally important if you want to be seen as powerful. A good negotiator should consider everything about his or her demeanour and do as much as possible to maximize the impact of look and conduct. Dress is culture-dependent but prior research will reveal how business is done and what will impress. In France a professional understated but stylish outfit would be typical but the quality of the accessories sends a powerful message. In Japan a smart suit and tie for a man or conservative dress for a woman project the right image (www.kwintessential.co.uk (archived at https://perma.cc/SHQ8-PTY6), 2012). Negotiations also present the opportunity for us to act differently. With practice a negotiator can project power just by walking taller, sitting more upright, being more attentive, considering what is said carefully and adopting a deliberately professional outward appearance. Style and demeanour counts for much and should be considered and planned for in advance. We will return to the subject of body language.

Creating an intangible power plan

In addition to our tangible power plan, we also need an intangible power plan. This is where we determine what our style and demeanour needs to be in order to project power where needed. It is also about how we plan to build trust and rapport. Here we are attempting to do two things:

- use emotional competence together with personal repertoire to perfect our negotiation approach for any given scenario;
- with awareness and experience understand our opponent and adapt our approach to have the optimum impact.

Unlike tangible power, we do not start with an assessment of our intangible power, but rather we determine this, and actions to project power across some or all of the 5 intangible powers according to the planning work using Red Sheet thus far. Specifically:

1 How we will negotiate

2 Whether we are value claiming or creating, for example building trust is more crucial for value claiming

3 Our relationship objective

4 Cultural norms and expectations

5 Tangible power assessment and where we need to project more power

6 The personality type(s) of our opponent(s)

It is perhaps this last one that is most relevant because we will be most effective if we can plan our approach and shape how we will project power based upon the personality type(s) of our opponent. For this reason, the intangible power plan is part of Step 6 (6B of the Red Sheet). A worked example was given back in Figure 6.15 in Chapter 6.

Anticipating their BATNAs

In a value-claiming negotiation where we hold the power and the other party has no or few alternatives we may well get what we want no matter what. Otherwise if the other side doesn't get what they want then they may revert to their BATNAs and potentially walk away yielding a lose/lose outcome. While it is important to consider our BATNAs, it is also essential to attempt to pre-empt theirs and assess how real and likely they are. We may have the best negotiation plan ever devised but if the other side walks away it is worthless.

Walking away is just one response from the other party that can work against us. If someone isn't getting what he or she wants, an alternative response can often be to become more aggressive. This is called the frustrative–aggression principle (Berkowitz, 1969). In recent years there has been a steady increase in piracy in the international waters off the coast of Somalia. At first, the lack of jurisdiction of these waters afforded the pirates the opportunity to 'catch' and board a vessel. Initially no one got hurt, but when the criminals failed to get what they wanted they started to get more aggressive and started killing people. In a negotiation this aggressive type of response can be equally difficult to handle, as it tends to close down dialogue and reduce the opportunity for value creation. When faced with this situation, a negotiator should remain calm, avoid being bullied into submission, avoid mirroring the aggression and gently reiterate his or her position using indirect language such as 'I feel that…' or 'I hope we can…' etc.

Actually doing it

Red Sheet steps 6B, 7A, 7B & 7C – Power

Purpose of this step

Steps 6B, 7A, 7B and 7C of Red Sheet collectively are about determining the power balance between you and the other party for the specific negotiation, and planning interventions – actions you can take to shift the power balance more in your favour. It is also about identifying personal actions to appear more powerful during the event. This step is in two parts; one is within the 'Situation' section of Red Sheet and the other as part of the 'Target' section. Figures 6.15 (last chapter), 7.4 and 7.5 give worked examples and templates can be found in the Appendix.

Completing this step

Work through 7A, 7B, 7C and 6B as follows:

1   Determine the power balance for each of the five tangible powers based upon facts and draw a pointer on each dial in 7A accordingly.

2   Draw a second 'dotted' pointer on each dial to indicate if the 'projected power' balance is different to the actual power.

3   Determine the knowledge you hold and what you believe the other party to hold. If you hold sufficient knowledge, colour in your knowledge indicator; if you believe the other party has good knowledge of their power position, colour in their indicator.

4   Note the rationale for each determination of power.

5   Review all five power balances and determine the specific actions that could shift the power balance more in our favour by taking advantage of strengths and considering how to handle weaknesses. Define the plan in 7B.

6   Determine knowledge actions required to address any gaps in our knowledge. For each identify the source, assign an owner and 'by when' date in 7C. Manage to ensure actions are delivered.

7   Determine the intangible power plan – our planned style and demeanour to project power and how we will build trust and rapport. Develop this in response to the sections of Red Sheet already completed and enter in section 6B.

Figure 7.4 Red Sheet step 7A – Power (worked example)

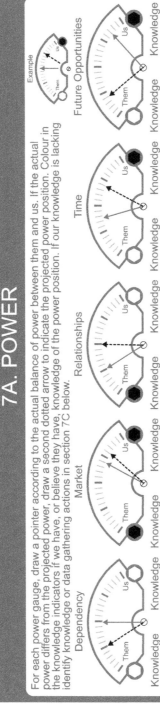

7A. POWER

For each power gauge, draw a pointer according to the actual balance of power between them and us. If the actual power differs from the projected power, draw a second dotted arrow to indicate the projected power position. Colour in the knowledge indicators if we have, or believe they have, knowledge of the power position. If our knowledge is lacking identify knowledge or data gathering actions in section 7C below.

Dependency

Knowledge — Knowledge

Degree of importance. Reliance upon you or the other party and the impact of failing to reach a favourable outcome. Speed and ease with which an alternative could be secured. Rationale:

Alternatives exist but we would prefer not to be focused into looking at these, as it will delay the project. They are projecting power here.

Market

Knowledge — Knowledge

Strength of position in the market place. Changes in market dynamics and availability of alternatives. Rationale:

They need this to work, we think they need to fill capacity. However, they are behaving as if we need them more.

Relationships

Knowledge — Knowledge

Longevity of relationship, extent and influence of relationships and business arrangements between the two parties, degree of stakeholder support across the wider business. Rationale:

They have a long-standing relationship with our CEO. Their sales team have established relationships with our technical team.

Time

Knowledge — Knowledge

Time available before a deal needs to be concluded. Rationale:

We have limited time as we need to reduce current operating costs, they are not aware of this.

Future Opportunities

Example

Knowledge — Knowledge

Potential for one party to benefit and support the other's future plans. Rationale:

Potential for this supplier to take on all future production.

Figure 7.5 Red Sheet steps 7B and 7C – Tangible power plan and knowledge actions (worked examples)

7B. TANGIBLE POWER PLAN

What we will do to utilize or improve our power position

1. Reinforce our CEO's position as fully supportive

2. Sell hard the future vision and potential

3. Avoid any suggestion that we might have time pressures - maintain the illusion that time is no constraint

4. Use latest facts and data re how the market is changing in our favour

5. Create a new project to explore a substitute solution here - ensure our opponent gets to hear about it

7C. KNOWLEDGE ACTIONS

Actions to improve or prove knowledge

Knowledge or data required	Source	Who	By when
Find out how much they need this business in order to fill their factory capacity.	Factory tour	Neg. Team	May 1st
Confirm alternative solutions, should this not be successful.	RFP + Market Analysis	M.M.	April 24th

Game theory in negotiation 08

This chapter explores the games played in negotiations using game theory as a reference point. It defines the main four games that are played and provides practical guidance for identifying these, determining the desired game and switching the game.

Pathway questions addressed in this chapter

15 What is the underlying 'game' my opponent is playing and how do I change the game to my advantage?

Red Sheet steps covered in this chapter

8A and 8B

Using game theory to maximize outcomes

Origins of game theory

Game theory is the study of the choice of strategies between intelligent rational decision makers. Game theory uses mathematical models to explain how individuals choose between conflict and cooperation. The models each help predict outcomes in specific scenarios by modelling an individual's best response to the strategies chosen by others. McCain (2004) states that game theory 'is based upon a scientific metaphor, the idea that many interactions we do not usually think of as games, such as economic competition, war and elections can be treated and analysed as we would analyse games'. The concept first emerged in a book by John von Neumann and Oskar Morgenstern in 1944 following a paper von Neumann published 16 years earlier.

Game theory was introduced as a tool for negotiators within the Red Sheet methodology and provides a powerful approach to help negotiators understand the way a specific negotiation is unfolding and the opportunity to change the approach in order to achieve a more favourable outcome.

At the heart of game theory are, as the name might suggest, a series of games, each described by a mathematical model. There are around 30 games in total that model all sorts of life's scenarios, but of these four are particularly relevant to negotiation. These are Chicken, Trust, Prisoner's Dilemma and Stag Hunt.

There is no right or wrong game and the most appropriate game depends upon the circumstances and may even need to change throughout the negotiation to achieve the best outcome. The key point is that, as negotiators, we have a choice as to what game we can play. While we may not be able to influence the games the other party chooses, with understanding of game theory we can identify their strategy and work to change the game in our favour. I will explore each game in turn.

Why use game theory?

Game theory provides a number of critical features that can add significantly to our negotiation preparation in three ways:

- *Common language.* The language that describes how a negotiation should 'play out' is often not available to us. Game theory helps by providing a common language within a negotiation team to communicate our intent; referencing a whole approach to a negotiation through a single name enables others on our team to immediately understand the required style, what to be cautious of and the desired outcomes.

- *Verification of approach.* The concept of playing a game helps test if our negotiation preparation makes sense and if we are planning to use tactics and techniques that will resonate with our chosen game.

- *Helps switch the game.* If the team members share the common language of each game, then switching game so the entire team switch their approach and mindset in unison becomes simple.

The four negotiation games

Chicken

The game of Chicken is the most common game played in negotiation and the one that inexperienced negotiators play. It is a game where two players engage in an activity that will result in serious harm unless one of them backs down. The most common depiction of this game is when two vehicles are driven towards each other and the first to swerve loses and is humiliated as the 'chicken'. Thankfully, when it comes to driving, the game of Chicken is something found more in Hollywood films than everyday life, but nevertheless this is a real game and one typical of many negotiations.

Figure 8.1   Chicken – choices of each party and outcomes

Chicken		Driver 1	
		Swerve	**Drive straight**
Driver 2	**Swerve**	**Neutral** *Both drivers swerve, there is no champion.* **In a negotiation** – Parties refuse to engage or walk away with no loss but no gain.	**WIN/Win or Win/Lose** *One driver loses face while the other is the champion.* **In a negotiation** – one party is forced to concede.
	Drive straight	**WIN/Win or Lose/Win** *One driver loses face while the other is the champion.* **In a negotiation** – One party is forced to concede.	**Lose/Lose** *Both cars collide head on.* **In a negotiation** – neither party will concede and no agreement is reached presenting both with a problem.

Chicken would be found in value-claiming negotiations where one party uses the strength of their position to attempt to leverage the other and force them to concede. Chicken is not collaborative but is about one party winning over the other. Therefore the only possible outcomes are either WIN/win (or win/lose) or, if the disadvantaged party chooses to walk away, lose/lose (Figure 8.1).

Chicken is the classic hard leverage negotiation approach countered by good BATNAs. In choosing to play Chicken we must anticipate the other's BATNAs to determine how far we can push things. When the other party plays Chicken against us, we might need a good BATNA. Alternatively it may be possible to change the game by proposing a different approach. Table 8.1 gives the characteristics of Chicken.

Table 8.1   Characteristics of Chicken

In a sentence...	'I'll get what I want and not give them anything.'
Direction	Can be applied in either direction. Typical buyer-side Chicken: 'Reduce your price or I'll go elsewhere.' Typical supplier-side Chicken: 'I know you have no alternatives so here's a price increase.'
Value objective	Value-claiming only
Cultural implications	***Monochronic cultures*** – often the way business is done, albeit not effectively in some cases. ***Polychronic cultures*** – within a strong relationship, playing Chicken can cause loss of face in the other party if it is played hard so a more gentle approach might be more appropriate. With no relationship in place Chicken could be played hard. Choosing to play this game in these cultures requires careful thought outside of a relationship as you could end up playing Prisoner's Dilemma without realizing it and being duped.
Countering Chicken	Chicken is countered by alternatives and ultimately the ability to walk away. The fewer alternatives available to the other, the harder Chicken can be played. Having good BATNAs gives you a way out if the other side plays Chicken with you, and if you choose to play Chicken, anticipate their BATNAs and their ability to walk away.

The Cuban missile crisis – the ultimate game of Chicken

The Cuban missile crisis in October 1962 is the closest the world has ever come to nuclear war. In the words of Anatoly Gribkov, the then Soviet General and Army Chief of Operations: 'Nuclear catastrophe was hanging by a thread.' The crisis was a 13-day stand-off between the United States and the Soviet Union together with Cuba. Following a series of political moves by the United States aimed at overthrowing the Cuban regime, the Russian premier Nikita Khrushchev made a proposal to Cuba to place Soviet nuclear missiles on Cuba as a means to deter future invasion but also to improve the Soviet Union's strike capability. Five months later US aerial photography revealed the construction of several missile sites for medium- and intermediate-range ballistic nuclear missiles. A military blockade was put in place by the United States who announced that it would not permit offensive weapons to be delivered to Cuba. An ultimatum was issued to the Soviet Union demanding they dismantle the missile bases already under construction or completed and return all offensive weapons to the USSR. Khrushchev wrote to President John F Kennedy stating that his blockade in international waters constituted an act of aggression propelling human kind into the abyss of a world nuclear-missile war. Soviet ships attempted to run the blockade and US Navy ships were instructed to fire warning shots and then open fire. The crisis reached a peak when a Soviet missile crew shot down a US U-2 aircraft. Despite this escalation, negotiations between Kennedy and Khrushchev continued and a resolution was agreed, ending the confrontation on 28th October 1962. Soviet Union missiles would be removed if the United States agreed not to invade Cuba and to dismantle their missiles in Turkey and Italy.

The Cuban missile crisis was the ultimate game of Chicken with world nuclear war representing the inevitable outcome if parties had continued trying to use power and force over each other to try and secure their individual goals. But nuclear war didn't happen in 1962 because Khrushchev and Kennedy stopped playing Chicken, and instead reached a negotiated agreement. In effect the game changed from Chicken to another game: Trust.

Trust

In the game of Trust one party (the proposer) holds a position of power over the other (the responder) and is therefore able to determine the allocation or distribution of benefit between the parties. The responder is completely passive and has no real power here, and therefore chooses to make a gift to the proposer in advance in the hope that it will influence the split in their favour and that the size of the gift will also influence the size of the split the responder receives. Key to understanding Trust is the fact that the party with least power transfers some value to the other before any deal is concluded and there is no obligation to respond favourably. The giving of a gift is therefore a judgement made by the less powerful party with the hope that it will enable a better end-position and there will be reciprocation (see Figure 8.2).

Trust can work in either direction when one party is dominant over the other; however, the choice to play this game lies with the lesser party who

Figure 8.2   Trust – choices of each party and outcomes

	Person 1	
Trust	**Give gift**	**Give nothing**
Return favour (Person 2)	**Win/Win** *The gift is given and the other party returns the favour* **In a negotiation** – A benefit is given, hoping the other side will return the favour which they do.	**WIN/win or Win/Lose** *No gift is given but yet the other party still gives something back* **In a negotiation** – No benefit is provided but yet the other side still provides something back.
Provide nothing (Person 2)	**win/WIN or Lose/Win** *The gift is given but the favour is not returned* **In a negotiation** – A benefit is given, hoping the other side will return the favour but they do not.	**Lose/Lose** *No gift is given by either party* **In a negotiation** – no benefit is given by either side.

decides to make some sort of gift to influence the outcome. Without any gift the game is simply that of a dictator who holds all the power and can decide whether to concede or not, with the lesser party holding no power or influence at all. However, the gift introduces some power to the lesser party through obligation.

In practice this gift can take many forms. A supplier can offer some sort of loyalty bonus, free time, or agree to accept unfavourable terms to a powerful buyer in the hope that they will win or retain key business. A buyer can offer flexibility on timing, to promote the supplier to their customers or suggest the supplier can use them as a reference site. In the 1960s when Cubby Broccoli approached Aston Martin to ask them to supply cars for the next James Bond film the meeting was conducted over a nice lunch. Broccoli knew that the Aston Martin management were reluctant to engage as, at that time, Bond was not the success it is today and the value of product placement was not something firms considered then. Here, lunch was the initial gift and one that provided the opportunity for Broccoli to make the proposition attractive. Gifts therefore may not be a specific thing but rather an action to make the lesser party a more attractive proposition to the other. Table 8.2 gives the characteristics of Trust.

Trust is often the game played when friends negotiate and they don't want to offend the other. Not wanting to offend someone has the same effect as putting them in the position of power and letting them decide the proportion of the split available, the initial gift being friendship. In

Table 8.2   Characteristics of Trust

In a sentence...	'I'll give you a gift and hope that you will return the favour and cut me a good deal.'
Direction	Can be either direction.
	Typical buyer-side Trust: 'I'm happy to be very flexible on timing to fit with your programme. If you say prices need to rise then so be it but by how much?'
	Typical supplier-side Trust: 'Now I'll just get the bill for our lunch… let's talk about the deal.'
Value objective	Value-claiming on the part of the party with the power if they choose not to return the favour. Value-creating if the favour is returned.
Cultural implications	Multi-cultural
	Monochronic cultures – success depends upon the individual.
	Polychronic cultures – highly effective only where a relationship exists.
Countering Trust	Trust is countered by identifying when negotiations are placing an implied obligation in return for something and deciding whether to reject this, accept it 'on trust' or formalize it within the negotiations.

negotiation, Trust is the only game possible when we lack power. The challenge is to consider an appropriate gift that is possible, acceptable and attractive. Trust can be countered by not accepting the gift, quantifying it and incorporating it into the deal or simply not returning the favour.

Trusting for sweets

Hugh is sent to the shops by his mum to get some groceries; he is told that he can buy some sweets with the change. This he does and when he returns home his big sister Emily spies the sweets and decides she would like some, but also knows that they are Hugh's in return for running the errand and he has no obligation to share. Hugh knows he ought to share his sweets and that doing so without being told to will be viewed favourably by his Mum. However, Hugh is trying to decide if he should split them 50:50 or

▶

just give his sister a few sweets; after all they are his in return for running the errand. Without mentioning the sweets, Emily puts on her best friendly sister routine and invites Hugh into her bedroom where she announces that Hugh can, if he wants, have her old iPod that she no longer needs as she has a new one. Hugh is overjoyed by the gift and then offers his sister half of the sweets he has bought.

Prisoner's Dilemma

This is perhaps the most famous and most studied but yet the most difficult game to understand. In the game of Prisoner's Dilemma two parties meet and agree a deal or a course of action, and then part company to go and effect the deal, each deciding if they will honour the deal or defect. The name of the game comes from a story used by Albert Tucker at Stanford University to bring the game to life and later reported in the *Philadelphia Inquirer* (Hagenmayer, 1995). Tucker told a story of two burglars that the police capture and arrest near the scene of a burglary. The two are taken away separately and placed in separate interview rooms. Police interrogate each suspect intensely in an attempt to get a confession. Each is told separately that they must choose carefully whether to confess and implicate the other. If neither confesses then the police will be unable to get a prosecution and so will only be able to charge both suspects on minor firearms charges and so each will serve one year in prison. If both burglars confess and implicate the other, both will serve a 10-year sentence. However, if one burglar confesses and implicates the other, but the other burglar does not confess, then the burglar who collaborated with the police will go free while his accomplice will serve 20 years in prison.

The outcomes (benefits or penalties) of Prisoner's Dilemma depend upon the choices each makes, but crucially there is greater benefit available to one by duping the other, providing the other party doesn't try the same thing. At the heart of Prisoner's Dilemma is self-interest driving actions that appear rational to the individual in the situation. However, when both parties place self-interest first they end up both being worse off (see Figure 8.3).

Prisoner's Dilemma in negotiation is a game to be watched out for and to ensure not to get duped by it. It is usually circumstance that creates a Prisoner's Dilemma scenario where there is the opportunity for parties to decide whether or not to honour a deal made after an initial meeting or negotiation. A supplier retracting their offer after a deal was agreed is not

Figure 8.3 Prisoner's Dilemma – choices of each party and outcomes

Prisoner 1

Prisoners	Don't confess	Confess
Don't confess (Prisoner 2)	**Win/Win** *Prisoners stick with their agreed story; each gets one year in jail* **In a negotiation** – Both parties make a commitment and honour what was agreed.	**Lose much/Win much** *One prisoner confesses; he goes free, the other gets 20 years* **In a negotiation** – Both parties make a commitment but one defaults, cheating the other.
Confess (Prisoner 2)	**Win much/Lose much** *One prisoner confesses; he goes free, the other gets 20 years* **In a negotiation** – Both parties make a commitment but one defaults, cheating the other.	**Lose/Lose** *Both confess and get 10 years in jail each* **In a negotiation** – Both parties make a commitment and both default costing each other much.

Prisoner's Dilemma but rather a change of heart as the supplier's position remains neutral. They will not benefit from this choice: they have simply chosen not to do the deal.

Instead consider this example. A company negotiates a preferred arrangement for legal service with a law firm. The agreement is made on the basis that: 1) the law firm has only top-quality lawyers carrying out the work, not paralegals billing at lawyer rates; and 2) the buyer will ensure that this law firm is used exclusively for all legal services. Once the deal is done each party must then decide if they will honour the deal. The law firm knows that they can get away with paralegals doing most of the work unless something goes wrong. The buyer knows that there are some other firms they would still like to use and this can be done discreetly in order to keep the exclusive partner rates of the preferred firm because, after all, they don't know what the total spend is.

A second key characteristic of Prisoner's Dilemma is that it involves both parties having a choice as to whether to honour the deal or default. If only one has this opportunity then this is not Prisoner's Dilemma but rather Chicken played to a win/lose conclusion. For example, if you buy an apparently 'genuine Rolex' from a man selling watches out of a suitcase on a street corner, but when you get it home the back falls off to reveal a cheap quartz electronic movement, then you have been duped. It is unlikely the same seller will be in the same place the next day to receive your complaint. This is not Prisoner's Dilemma. However, if you had a choice too, say to decide whether or not to pay with counterfeit money which the seller discovers

Table 8.3   Characteristics of Prisoner's Dilemma

In a sentence...	'We'll both agree to a course of action but we both know our own self-interest might lead us to default.'
Direction	Can be attempted by either party but the conditions for default on both sides must exist.
Value objective	Value-claiming if you default, value-creating if both parties choose to honour the deal.
Cultural implications	*Monochronic cultures* – will be found in some scenarios.
	Polychronic cultures – Prisoner's Dilemma may not be played if there is a relationship, as any risk of default would damage the relationship. Here trust and honour are crucial to any deal and so default of any kind would be deeply offensive and cause loss of face and irreparable damage to the relationship. However, if there is no relationship Prisoner's may be the game of choice.
Countering Prisoner's Dilemma	Prisoner's Dilemma is countered by removing the opportunity for default.

later, then the scenario becomes Prisoner's Dilemma and both parties walk away from the deal and only discover afterwards whether or not the other has honoured their stated commitment, eg real Rolex or real money. Table 8.3 sets out the full characteristics of Prisoner's Dilemma.

Prisoner's Dilemma and the catch of the day

In the 1970s, as the world's fish stocks dwindled and certain species become threatened due to demand and over-fishing, some countries introduced a system of fish quotas in the waters around them, collaborating and making agreements with neighbouring countries where possible so there is a total allowable catch (TAC) for each species in a given fishing ground. Since its introduction, the enforcement of the quota system has not been easy. Different approaches have been tried, most with limited success in the early days because individual fishermen had no long-term stake in a fishery but rather were focused on maximizing their immediate harvest and so would find ways around the restriction. This also happened at a country level where different choices regarding compliance were made.

Within fishing grounds located between two countries with a shared quota, if both countries ensured their fishermen honoured the quotas, the catch each day would be mediocre yet stocks would be sustainable. However, if one country decided to turn a blind eye to its fishermen taking more than agreed, then the catch would be plentiful and this would boost the economy, but the resultant over-fishing would lead to fewer fish next year. If both countries did this then both would gain in the short term but when the fish ran out both would need to find other fishing grounds.

Today there are some 250 fishing quota arrangements in place around the world and technology is used to enforce them.

Stag Hunt

The game of Stag Hunt describes a conflict between taking the safe option and social cooperation and is explained as follows. Two individuals go out on a hunt. Each can choose whether to hunt for stag or hare. Each hunter must choose what to hunt without knowing the choice of the other. An individual can hunt hare by himself but a hare is worth less than a stag; but if he hunts hare then he knows he will eat. A stag is difficult to catch so if an individual hunts stag then he must have the cooperation of his partner in order to succeed. If there are more than two hunters then the chances of a successful Stag Hunt increase sharply.

Stag Hunt is a game of cooperation and the key to understanding the game is the additional benefit that both parties receive if they work together. The way the game is described might sound similar to Prisoner's Dilemma in the sense that each party chooses their course of action without the other knowing and if parties choose differing actions there is a winner and loser. However, the key difference is there are two different states of joint benefit: if both parties defect and hunt hare, neither are disadvantaged as both can eat; if both hunt stag then both benefit much more. In the game of Stag Hunt parties make individual choices based upon what is rational for them and how they anticipate what is rational for the other party. In Prisoner's Dilemma there is a conflict between individual rationality and mutual benefit and so there is no way to anticipate what is rational for the other party.

Skyrms (2004) suggests rational choice is also a key component in Stag Hunt. If two women row a boat then the outcome is the best for both as

Figure 8.4   Stag Hunt – choices of each party and outcomes

		Hunter 1	
Stag hunt		**Hunt stag**	**Hunt hare**
Hunter 2	**Hunt stag**	**Win much/Win much** *Both choose to hunt stag and both make more money by doing so* **In a negotiation** – Both parties collaborate and work together to grow and share the benefits.	**Lose/Win some** *One chooses to hunt stag and fails while the other gets some hare* **In a negotiation** – One party tries to collaborate but loses out as the other does not.
	Hunt hare	**Win some/Lose** *One chooses to hunt stag and fails while the other gets some hare* **In a negotiation** – One party tries to collaborate but loses out as the other does not.	**Win some/Win some** *Each hunts hare and makes only what their catch fetches* **In a negotiation** – Neither party will collaborate so benefits are constrained to the deal in hand.

they make headway. If both choose not to row neither have lost anything as both stay in the same place; however, if the one in front rows and the one at the back does not, it is the worst outcome for the one rowing as she expends all her energy but the boat makes little headway. In this case it is rational to assume that both would row as they do it by agreement or convention. So in playing Stag Hunt it is important to consider if the other side would see cooperation as the rational way forward. Figure 8.4 gives the responses.

In a negotiation this game presents an opportunity for significant value creation between parties but only if both parties can find a way to access it and often the route to that value is not clear or parties might find it difficult to trust the other. Stag Hunt is therefore the game that supports value-creating negotiations. In practice it requires parties to look beyond the immediate deal and make compromises and commitments to each other so that both parties improve their position. This might mean pooling resources, agreeing a long-term programme, extending the scope of the deal so both parties can share the payoff and so on. It might also mean both parties making different gestures that help the other party but resulting in a net benefit to both. For example, a buyer might agree to promote a supplier to their customers to increase volumes while the supplier attempts to reduce costs using the resultant economies of scale.

Stag Hunt should be the typical game played for buyer/seller relationships that surround a major contract such as an outsourced arrangement, but when outsourcing fails it is often because one party is trying to play Chicken. Table 8.4 gives the characteristics of Stag Hunt.

Table 8.4   Characteristics of Stag Hunt

In a sentence...	'If we work together we will both do better.'
Direction	Non-directional. Requires both parties to decide to collaborate towards a mutually beneficial outcome. Could involve more than two parties.
Value objective	Value creation.
Cultural implications	Universal.
	Monochronic cultures – often trepidation that such an approach is genuine or could work or belief that the game is actually Prisoner's Dilemma.
	Polychronic cultures – it is the way business is typically done but only within a strong relationship.
Countering Stag Hunt	Why would you, unless your value objective is to claim benefit no matter what and you specifically don't want to work together?

Neighbours playing Stag Hunt

A large hedge forms the boundary between two neighbouring properties. The hedge is shared so both parties are responsible for maintaining it. If both choose to leave the hedge it will grow tall and bushy but neither party will be wasting money on the services of a gardener. If both parties decide to cut the hedge regularly it will look neat and tidy for both. However, if only one party decides to cut the hedge on his side and the other decides to save his money, then only one side of the hedge will look neat, but the hedge will remain tall and overgrown on the neighbour's side and this is visible to both neighbours, thus wasting the efforts and money of the neighbour who cut his side.

The right game

Choosing which game to play

Our choice as to which game to play depends upon many factors. The game *they* are playing, or are anticipated to play, is a factor but not necessarily the

Figure 8.5   Portfolio analysis and game theory

Critical	Strategic
First choice of games: **You:** Trust **Them:** Chicken or Prisoner's Dilemma The supplier holds the power here. All we can do is make ourselves attractive and influence deals as best as we can	**First choice of games:** **You:** Stag Hunt **Them:** Stag Hunt Changes if you are unattractive to them (exploit or nuisance in supplier preferencing) or they only have a value claiming objective
Acquisition	**Leverage**
First choice of games: **You:** Chicken **Them:** Any Here you have alternatives, however, and here are categories of spend that don't warrant much time spent on them. Use BATNAs as needed	**First choice of games:** **You:** Chicken **Them:** Any Play less assertively in polychronic cultures. Use BATNAs if they don't respond. Check your relationship objectives before collaborating

Degree of market difficulty (vertical axis)

Degree of profit impact (horizontal axis)

basis on which to choose our game. Parties often choose to play Chicken because they know no other way, and responding with Chicken just because they are playing it can be counterproductive. Similarly the other party might really want to work collaboratively and grow the relationship with us but if we have plenty of alternatives there may simply be no need to do this. Therefore, it is important to determine which game would potentially yield the best outcome (and this might be more than one game played at different points in time) and work out what to do in order to play our game(s).

By the time we get to this step within our Red Sheet planning we have already gained a series of insights and it is by considering all these together that we can determine the best game to start with. For example, if we are value claiming, for a leverage category where we hold the power, which is core business to the supplier in a monochronic culture, we should play Chicken. A critical category, from a supplier not too interested in us, would suggest a Trust game is more appropriate.

Portfolio analysis provides the most direction here and so this should be the first thing to review (Figure 8.5). Consider the quadrant the category of spend being sourced lies within. For each quadrant there is a natural game that, in the absence of any other factors, would be the first choice (Figure 8.6). Then consider the other factors and if any of these change the

Figure 8.6 Choosing the game

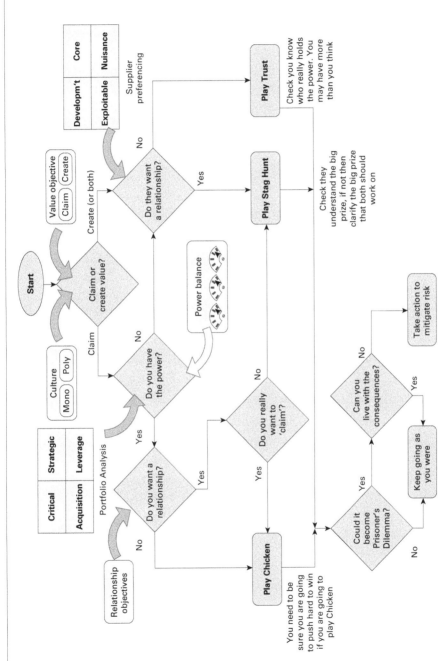

game. Game choice is a judgement and there is no precise science in how to choose, but here good old human brain power is required in order to assimilate all the information and insights available and determine the most appropriate game. Figure 8.6 summarizes this process and shows the various factors to consider.

It is entirely possible that this analysis could completely change the negotiation strategy or force us to question why we are negotiating at all. For example, if the initial analysis suggested we should play Stag Hunt because portfolio analysis placed the category as 'strategic' and we need to create value and build a relationship, but our review suggests the supplier is uninterested and even sees the account as exploitable, then trying to play Stag Hunt might fail. Worse, we could end up negotiating with a defaulting party playing Prisoner's Dilemma. Consequently playing Trust and increasing our attractiveness might be more appropriate or deciding simply to play Chicken but being prepared to lose and walk way.

Once a game is determined it is worth checking that we are ready to play our game and that by playing it we will not fail, jeopardize outcomes, or damage a relationship. Table 8.5 provides a list of check questions to validate game selection and any resultant gaps identified should be acted upon.

Spotting the game

With practice, it is possible to determine the game other people are playing and this knowledge helps open up all sorts of choices and possibilities. Games are being played all around us, but people are not typically aware of a game they might be playing. Game theory is a way of explaining different aspects of human nature and behaviour. Yet game theory is not something that is part of mainstream business development programmes. Sales teams don't typically decide they are going to play Chicken or Prisoner's Dilemma: these games just happen to be what they end up doing, perhaps without being aware. Parties within a strategic relationship may not be aware they are playing Stag Hunt.

In planning a negotiation it is helpful to be able to spot the game in play, but this could change throughout a negotiation and during a relationship and we need to detect this too. For example, a first engagement with a supplier might be pure Chicken, but in time as both parties get to know one another and see benefit in working together the game might switch to Stag Hunt. Assessing the game should therefore consider:

- the game they played last time (assuming we have engaged with them before) and the game we played with them then;

Table 8.5 Check questions for validating game selection

Game	Check questions – Implications and considerations
Chicken	• What must we do to make them swerve?
	• Are we confident in our position?
	• Are our arguments robust?
	• Are we prepared to hold course (otherwise consider another game)?
	• Can we live with the consequences of forcing them to swerve, eg implications for relationship?
Trust	• Who really has the power; do we know for certain?
	• What sort of gift will truly be valued? What would they really want? have we been creative enough in our thinking?
	• Are there any factors that would prevent them accepting the gift?
	• What is easy to give but would make a big impact?
Prisoner's Dilemma	• How will we know if we are playing Prisoner's Dilemma?
	• Are we likely to need to let the other party down on the deal?
	• Can we live with the consequences if we do let them down?
	• Can we open lines of communication to avoid Prisoner's Dilemma?
	• What are they expecting us to do?
	• What are we expecting them to do?
	• What else could we do to build a successful conclusion to this game?
Stag Hunt	• Do we know the prize we want to aim for?
	• Does the other party agree?
	• Could the other party be chasing something else?
	• What is the consequence of chasing the wrong thing and can we live with it?
	• Do we really want this prize?
	• What resources do we need to catch the bigger prize?
	• How do we review progress along the way?

• the game we anticipate they will play ahead of an event;

• the actual game we observe them to be playing during the event, and if they switch games.

Game spotting is a skill and the explanations in this book provide the first spark to learn this. Getting good takes practice and the best approach here is to use everyday situations to practise spotting which games people play: buying something in a shop; negotiating for a new car; getting the kids to do their homework; or discussing with a partner where to go on vacation. With practice, the power of game theory will open up. To help get started here are 10 examples of games: try to determine which is being played. The answers are given at the end of the chapter.

What game is being played?

1 A small software company tells you: 'Look, there's no point us trying to negotiate because I want this contract so I'll do the work for the price you want, but it would really help if you could recommend us to your customers'.

2 A man tries to buy a TV in a store. The price is £500, but he says he can only go to £400. When the manager shows him a smaller TV the man insists he wants the first one. In the end the manager offers him a discount of 10 per cent.

3 An employee asks for a raise. The manager says it's not possible now but says when the annual review comes around she will 'look after him'.

4 A supplier of gardening services agreed to attend each site weekly and is billing you for this. You have agreed to pay them weekly in advance and this you are doing, but it seems in practice they are not attending so frequently.

5 A buyer runs an e-auction for the supply of paper beverage cups. Six suppliers participate and the auction is set up so there may be a post-auction negotiation with the two bidders who win the auction.

6 A college project requires four students to complete a piece of work, each has to carry out a separate piece of research that when combined will be submitted for assessment. Each of the students will only pass the module if the entire work is complete.

7 You buy something from eBay, the seller e-mails you after the auction and suggests the usual payment methods are not suitable and instead he will mail you the item if you agree to put the cash in an envelope and mail it to him.

8 A valued supplier of a highly critical complex component is having quality problems. Demand for such components is falling and the supplier's cost of failures has increased. The buyer is worried the supplier might want to pull out so offers to supply a process expert for free to work with them and help improve the situation.

9 A teenager asks to say out late. Her parents say no because she hasn't done her schoolwork. She stays out late anyway despite the consequences.

10 The same teenager shows her parents her completed homework and talks about how her grades are improving and then asks if she can stay out late. The parents agree.

Switching the game

If they switch game it is a sign that something has changed, perhaps in our favour or otherwise, and spotting this is important if we are to remain in control. We too can switch games and doing so might help us take a more productive tack towards achieving our objectives. The games we play should be determined in advance as part of negotiation planning; however, it is sometimes appropriate to consider playing a series of games depending upon how the negotiation proceeds. In this case it is necessary to consider what the triggers are for switching and, if we are part of a team preparing for the negotiation, that everyone understands them.

For example, imagine a negotiation scenario where the supplier played Chicken last time and this is what we anticipate them playing at this event. We decide that we should play Chicken and see if we can get what we want. If it looks like the other party is not going to concede to the level we require then we will switch to Stag Hunt, the trigger being a refusal from the other party to meet a specific price point. We will suggest we hold off our discussions and consider a new collaborative approach that could benefit both.

Planning how we might switch games is ideal, but there are circumstances where the unexpected happens or the other side does something we hadn't anticipated. Here it may be possible to switch 'on the fly'; however, this is not generally recommended as the unexpected turn of events has left us unprepared. If possible buy some time to rethink by asking for a time-out or saying you will need to come back again after you have talked to your people.

Games can be switched in different ways and Table 8.6 provides a list of how to switch once you have reached your trigger.

Table 8.6 Switching games

Game they are playing	How to switch
Chicken	**To Stag Hunt** – stop proceedings, suggest there might be a different way to look at things, outline the bigger potential benefits if both parties collaborated, 'sell' the idea hard. Only commit to a new course of action if you are certain they are on board also, otherwise you might have ended up in Prisoner's Dilemma.
	To Trust – give a gift or benefit of some sort unconditionally.
	To Prisoner's Dilemma – create the conditions that would allow you to play this game, ie the opportunity for you to default on something.
Trust	**To Chicken** – reject the gift or value it and incorporate it into the deal. Reiterate your position and your demands.
	To Prisoner's Dilemma – create the conditions that would allow you to play this game, ie the opportunity for you to default on something.
	To Stag Hunt – accept the gift or recognize it as a step towards collaboration, perhaps with reciprocation. Move discussions towards considering a more collaborative approach that better benefits both sides.
Prisoner's Dilemma	**To Chicken** – remove the opportunity for default by changing the way the deal is being done or secure commitment (eg within a contract or payment terms once you have verified things have been delivered to your satisfaction). Once the appropriate protection mechanism is in place play Chicken.
	To Stag Hunt – stop proceedings, suggest there might be a different way to look at things, outline the bigger potential benefits if both parties collaborated, 'sell' the idea hard. Only commit to a new course of action if you are certain they are on board and/or you have removed the opportunity for them to default.
	To Trust – give a gift or benefit of some sort unconditionally and hope for the best.
Stag Hunt	**To Chicken** – reject calls for collaboration. Reiterate your position and demands.
	To Trust – give a gift and see what they do (expect collaboration).
	To Prisoner's Dilemma – agree to collaboration and working together but secretly reserve the right to change your mind and default.

The answers

The answers to the test earlier in this chapter are:

1 Trust – the software company has no power and so gives the gift of the price point the buyer wants in the hope it will get future business.

2 Chicken.

3 Trust – the employee is giving the gift of continuing to work on his current salary and the manager will later determine the allocation of any raise.

4 Prisoner's Dilemma – the gardening services company is choosing to default on their agreement but you have not.

5 Chicken.

6 Stag Hunt – if all cooperate, all pass; however, if one doesn't cooperate then no one will pass and the others will have wasted their effort. If all decide not to do the work then all are no better or no worse off; they won't pass but won't have had to do any work either.

7 Prisoner's Dilemma – should parties agree to this arrangement outside the protection eBay affords, then each is able to decide to honour the commitment or to defect.

8 Trust – the supplier has the power as there is a risk they want to pull out, so the buyer makes a gift of free process support to help influence the supplier's actions.

9 Chicken – the teenager uses her power of independence.

10 Trust – the teenager gives her parents a gift to influence the subsequent negotiation.

Actually doing it

Red Sheet Steps 8A and 8B – Game

Purpose of this step

Steps 8A and 8B of Red Sheet are about determining the game you plan to play in a negotiation and how you might switch games. These steps are in two parts, half sitting within the 'Situation' section of Red Sheet and the other as part of the 'Target' section. Figure 8.7 gives a worked example and a template can be found in the Appendix.

Completing this step

Work through steps 8A and 8B as follows:

1 If there has been a previous engagement, or the game is already 'in play' with the supplier then determine the current game both you and they are playing and tick the appropriate boxes in 8A.

2 Based upon what you know about them decide what game you anticipate they will play at the event. Tick the relevant box and note your rationale in 8A.

3 Based upon your review of the various factors that determine the best game to play, determine what game you should open with and tick the relevant box in the 'Games we will play...' section in 8B and record how you plan to do this.

4 If you anticipate the need to switch game then identify the trigger to switch (ensuring any team members understand this) and note the next game you will play (also in this section 8B) as needed.

Figure 8.7 Red Sheet steps 8A and 8B – Game (worked example)

8A. GAME

Determine the game that has been or is currently being played and which game we anticipate they will play at the event.

Chicken | Trust | Prisoner's Dilemma | Stag Hunt

Chicken
A game in which two players engage that will result in significant loss to both sides unless one of them backs down. It is commonly applied to a game where two motor vehicles are driven towards each other at speed, the first to swerve loses and is humiliated as the 'chicken'.

Stag Hunt
Two individuals go on a hunt. Each of them can choose to hunt a stag or hunt a hare. Each must choose an action without knowing the choice of the other. If either individual hunts stag, they must have the co-operation of the other in order to succeed. Either party can hunt for hare alone, but a hare is worth less than a stag.

Trust
One party offers a gift, benefit or concession to the other on the basis that the other party will give back something in return, however the allocation or size of benefit given back in return is determined by the other party. The initial party trusts the other party to make an appropriately sized return gesture.

Prisoner's Dilemma
Two parties make a trade off, the outcome of which is unknown to both parties until the trade off is complete. Parties might have an understanding of what will be traded, however each can chose to honour this or defect. If both co-operate and honour what was agreed both win, however if one defects he wins much whilst the other loses much. If both defect, both lose.

Current game
The game that has been played previously or the current game being played

	Chicken	Trust	Prisoner's Dilemma	Stag Hunt
Us		Us ☑	Us	
Them		Them ☑	Them	

The game they will play
The game we anticipate them playing at the event

	Us	Us
Them ☑	Them	Them

Rationale for our assumptions:
They are currently giving various incentives that are unnecessary as part of the relationship development.

8B. GAME PLAN

Chicken | Trust ☑ | Prisoner's Dilemma | Stag Hunt

Game 1
How we will play: *We will open with a gift*

Trigger to switch game: *when they ask for the first concession* ☑

Game 2
How we will play: *Sell the future potential and seek collaboration*

Trigger to switch game:

Game 3
How we will play:

Trigger to switch game:

Building the concession strategy

This chapter defines how requirements for a negotiation are developed and how these then determine both the most and least desirable outcomes. Concession strategy is explored and the chapter provides a range of tactics and techniques to help improve this strategy. Finally the chapter outlines the role and application of BATNAs in a negotiation.

Pathway questions addressed in this chapter

16 How do I determine the specific points or requirements to negotiate?

17 How can I manage and stay in control of trades and concessions?

19 What tactics and techniques will help me be successful?

Red Sheet steps covered in this chapter

9 and 10.

Creating and deploying a winning concession strategy

The concession strategy lies at the heart of a negotiation and it is the thing that determines how we should manage the way the negotiation plays out. Yet the concept of a concession strategy and actually using it to drive how we negotiate seems to be something that is difficult to grasp. Few texts and training providers in this area get to the heart of this concept – how one can actually develop and deploy a winning strategy – electing instead to provide the theory and leave the individual to figure out how to bring it to life. This possibly accounts for why, based upon my experience, the concession strategy is the least planned-for and most avoided component of negotiation preparation.

The concession strategy is a difficult concept because it is not one single thing. It is not a process, not a tactic nor a set of rules we can apply. It is an amorphous melange of how we define everything we need and want from a negotiation, what we can and cannot accept, how we manage all the different things we need to negotiate and a planned means to move towards a goal in a way that maximizes our success. An effective concession strategy is one that equips us to visualize all the moving parts of a negotiation in our mind and then enables us to manage our actions and interventions in a planned and considered way to achieve our goal. This chapter will attempt to provide an approach to help do this, and so we will explore the six components that collectively make up a good concession strategy. These are:

1 Defining our requirements

2 Determining our MDO, LDO, BATNA and ensuring the ZoMA

3 The four phases of negotiation and how we will navigate through them

4 The process of trading concessions

5 Winning techniques for concession trading

6 Attempting to guess what they want and what their BATNAs might be

I will explore each in turn.

1 Defining our requirements

Negotiation is about reaching agreement between parties by conferring. If you go out to buy a new TV and you know precisely the make and model you want because you've seen it at a friend's house, then it is likely there is just one point that needs to be agreed and that is the price. If you don't get what you want you can go somewhere else. However, in business negotiations there might be a series of separate agreements that, when combined, represent the overall negotiated agreement.

To plan a negotiation, all of the individual points where we want to reach some sort of agreement need to be identified and planned. These are our 'negotiation requirements' or 'negotiables' and form our shopping list of the essential and desirable outcomes we need and want respectively and therefore the individual topics for discussion. Negotiations with suppliers might cover a range of different topics and could include:

- price;
- payment terms;
- agreed volumes/size or duration of contract;
- specification, features, benefits, levels of quality, service levels;
- timing;
- how the relationship will work.

Start with the business requirements

Our starting point for defining our negotiation requirements is therefore 'if we can have everything we want from this negotiation, what would we ask for?' To answer this question we need to first understand all the many and different requirements that define and shape what we are buying and might already have been used to communicate our need to the supplier or supply base as part of effective tendering, supplier selection, contracting and performance measurement. The problem, however, is that these are usually way too extensive to be useful but they do provide a good starting point. Typically these wider requirements might include:

- the requirements for the goods or service we are buying (specification, quality required, service levels that must be achieved, timing etc);
- any requirements the supplier must meet (accreditations, compliance with legislation, proven track record etc);
- the requirements for how the business might want to implement any long-term sourcing arrangement for the area of spend (sufficient supplier capacity, support for implementation etc);
- any requirements pertaining to the relationship we want with the supplier (alignment of future plans, willingness to collaborate etc).

We need a consolidated definition of all of these and here we turn to one of the most important tools used in strategic sourcing: the RAQSCI (Regulatory, Assurance of supply, Quality, Service, Cost/Commercial and Innovation) business requirements model. In its simplest form business requirements is about having a predetermined definition of what we are trying to buy as

Figure 9.1   Business requirements: the RAQSCI model

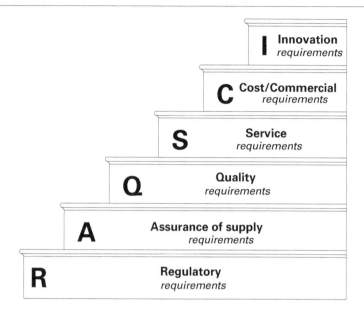

opposed to simply letting the supplier propose what they can sell, and being clear how the arrangement must work. Business requirements are not something that can be developed by a procurement or supply chain function alone; instead they must be a consolidated and aligned definition of what the entire business needs and wants and should be developed following business-wide consultation. If the business has adopted a strategic sourcing approach such as category management then it is most likely such requirements might have already been developed at a category of spend level. The RAQSCI model is illustrated in Figure 9.1, with each element representing the individual themes or headings under which all the requirements are developed.

There is a sequence or hierarchy to these business requirements, and for this reason the model is shown as a staircase. With a staircase, you have to step on the first step, then the second and the third before you can get to the fourth. In the same way with business requirements; it is pointless considering commercial requirements such as payment terms or having designated points of contact if assurance of supply cannot be met and the goods may not turn up. This hierarchy is crucial as it refocuses attention in a prioritized order on what is important. In practice a full list of business requirements might look something like that in Figure 9.2.

Figure 9.2 Example set of business requirements

Business Requirements – Electronic PCB Assembly				
Regulatory requirements	Need?	Want?	Now?	Future?
Full demonstrable compliance with all relevant in-country legislation	✓		✓	
Assurance of supply	Need?	Want?	Now?	Future?
Satisfy our internal audit requirements for quality, environmental and safety	✓		✓	
Must satisfy financial checks with ESGROW provision	✓		✓	
Compliance with our Corporate Social Responsibility policy	✓		✓	
Sufficient capacity for 100,000 assemblies per annum	✓		✓	
Minimum two facilities equipped to manufacture all assemblies	✓		✓	
Quality	Need?	Want?	Now?	Future?
ISO9001 accreditation	✓		✓	
Compliance with full specification for each assembly	✓		✓	
Full demonstrable static handling through all stages of production	✓		✓	
Batch rejection rate less than 1%	✓		✓	
All assemblers must be trained to our specification TWC343 version 2		✓	✓	
Service	Need?	Want?	Now?	Future?
Agreed day-to-day points of contact for account, operational matters and finance	✓		✓	
Online access to production schedules		✓	✓	
Ability to track status of each batch in production		✓	✓	
Maximum lead time of 30 days		✓	✓	
Weekly reporting of production and quality results as per TWC199		✓	✓	
Cost	Need?	Want?	Now?	Future?
Total cost of ownership per assembly must be less than current cost (excluding transition cost)		✓	✓	
Payment terms ideally 60 days but no less than 14 days		✓	✓	
Agreement to our terms and conditions	✓		✓	
Innovation	Need?	Want?	Now?	Future?
Improved production techniques to reach zero defects		✓		✓
Regular collaboration forums and mechanism to take ideas forward		✓		✓

Defining the negotiables

Once the full business requirements are understood we can begin to extract the specific requirements for the negotiation or 'our negotiables' (Figure 9.3). Starting with our full business requirements we begin by discounting any non-negotiable elements. These are the things that must be satisfied in any case and so don't need to form part of the negotiation. For example, a food producer might have a clear set of business requirements supporting the sourcing of a particular food ingredient. These might require any supplier

Figure 9.3   Defining the negotiables

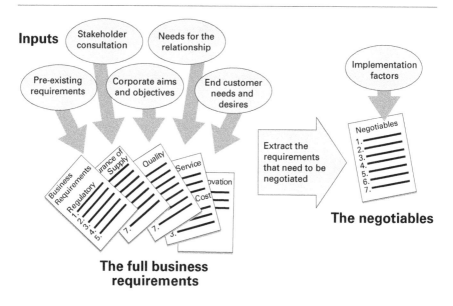

to comply with relevant food safety and hygiene regulations and demon-strate suitable accreditations. This is a prerequisite need and there is no point engaging with any supplier unless we are certain they can meet this basic requirement. These non-negotiable elements are typically the basic needs and in our business requirements hierarchy would be those on the first few stairs (Figure 9.4). They should be satisfied as part of a pre-qualification activity, perhaps through a tendering process, so we are only negotiating with those who can meet our needs. In our TV example above, there would be little point in walking into a bakery and asking what deal they could do on a new TV.

Figure 9.4   Extracting the negotiables from our business requirements

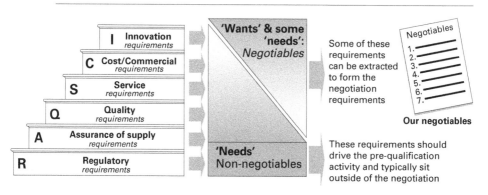

The aim in developing the negotiables is to identify only the points that need agreement and can realistically be addressed during a negotiation; ideally there would be around five or seven of these. Generally the more negotiables or requirements we have, the more complex the negotiation becomes unless we are sufficiently confident to use this complexity to our advantage. In extracting the negotiables from the full business requirements, once the non-negotiables have been discounted there are typically many others that do not need to be discussed. Examples of these would be where we don't anticipate any disagreement or we have already established the supplier's capability or things outside this immediate relationship such as future aspirations. So the ultimate end-point is a simple list of the negotiables or the specific points we intend to negotiate on. Getting these right typically requires discussion, debate and several iterations however, but they represent the main foundations for how the negotiation will happen. For multi-party negotiations separate lists of negotiables are needed for each party as what we want or need could differ between parties.

Our negotiables frame the scope of our negotiation and within this there is the assumption that we have a degree of control and can predict what is and is not in scope. In a negotiation where we have pre-qualified a supplier as part of a tender process we are on pretty safe ground; however, there are scenarios where we could end by suddenly finding that the other party had different ideas or challenges our non-negotiables. For example, consider a critical category of spend, where the supplier holds all the power and we have few or no alternatives. It might be reasonable to assume the terms and conditions agreed within a current contract with the supplier are non-negotiable but if the supplier has other plans they may well be prepared to suggest that 'things have moved on' and they 'need to revisit the contract'. While we might have legal protection and remedies open to us, in practice legal action would be costly and difficult, and perhaps the supplier is even counting on this. We therefore need to be confident that our negotiables include all the areas that the negotiation will need to address, and a check back of the power balance can help here. We also need to anticipate as best we can their negotiables and I'll cover this later.

No pain, no gain

Negotiations ebb and flow as they play out. Sometimes it is possible to take discussions in a particular direction and sometimes we can only get swept along. The skill in negotiating comes from being in control of how we sail through the difficult waters. Our negotiation plan helps to give us this control as it provides the map to ensure we are navigating to and from all the right places.

However, unlike following a map there is not necessarily a sequence to how we work through all of our negotiation requirements. In fact it might even be detrimental to our outcomes if we tried to do this or allowed the other side to do this to us. Good negotiators will work on all requirements simultaneously, making trades of one against another but always keeping the overall 'big picture' agreement in mind.

The problem here is that it is difficult to keep multiple threads of discussion in our mind in the heat of a negotiation and remain in control. This of course gets even more difficult when we have a long list of negotiation requirements. Also, some of our requirements might be much more important than others so we need to ensure we don't over-compromise in the wrong places. To address this we can assign a 'pain factor' to each of our requirements. In other words, how much pain it will cause us to not reach the agreement we want. Thinking of our outcomes (or not reaching them) in terms of pain rather than importance changes our perspective slightly. This can shift our focus towards consequences and away from just winning which tends to drive a slightly different approach to decision making. Figure 9.11 shows an example of negotiation requirements with the pain factor assigned for each using a simple high/medium/low system.

2 Determining the MDO, LDO, BATNA and ensuring the ZoMA

The MDO and the LDO

Any good negotiation textbook will reference the MDO and LDO or similar acronym meaning the same things. Here we are talking about our Most Desirable Outcome (MDO) and our Least Desirable Outcome (LDO). LDO is sometimes called LAA (Least Acceptable Agreement). Together these define what we would like to achieve but also provide for the minimum we will accept without sacrificing our imperative interests (Figure 9.5).

The purpose of the MDO and LDO is to establish clear aims for a negotiation while remaining in control so we don't overly compromise our position. They are an essential part of negotiation planning and enable a negotiator to enter a negotiation with all the relevant facts and data rolled up into two simple indicators.

Figure 9.5   The MDO and LDO

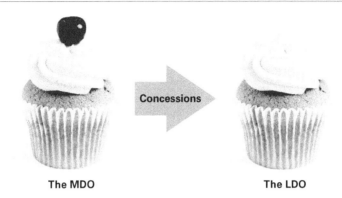

The MDO   **The LDO**

MDOs and LDOs are needed for each of the individual points of agreement within the negotiation defined in our negotiation requirements. There is also an overall MDO and LDO which might represent the sum of the individual MDOs and LDOs.

In Chapter 1 we explored the Zone of Mutual Agreement (ZoMA) and this represents the overlap between our LDO and their LDO (see Figure 9.6). If there is no overlap then agreement is not possible unless one or the other side is prepared to go beyond their LDO.

Figure 9.6   MDOs, LDOs and ZoMA

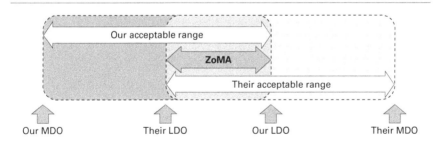

Determining the MDO

In the words of US motivational speaker Les Brown: 'Shoot for the moon. Even if you miss, you'll land among the stars.' That's a great philosophy for negotiation. If we aim high there is a good chance we might end up high, or at least medium, or at least if we end up low then the other party will have had to work to get us there and we will know we got the best outcome possible. The problem, however, is that many negotiators don't aim high enough or are too quick to concede. In the United Kingdom our culture is often too polite to encourage people to negotiate, but for the plucky few who will try this in shops or when engaging a contractor a discount of 10 per cent would be considered a good result and 20 per cent would be amazing. However, in Russia a negotiator would start at 20 per cent of the asking price and go from there, taking no prisoners along the way. There are distinct cultural differences in aspirations in negotiation and it is important to understand these or we could fail. I should point out that these differences also apply to the way sellers set their pricing too, building in different levels of 'margin' according to what they expect to be negotiated out.

Developing an MDO is not just about determining a good starting point but an aspirational MDO can help us maintain our position in a negotiation. As we reveal our MDO to the other party during the negotiation, the other side then has to move us much further to bring us into the ZoMA and this increases the likelihood of the deal being closer to their LDO than MDO. In other words, they have to work hard just to get us to a point where agreement is possible. Therefore, when determining MDOs, we should aim high where possible, assume we won't get everything we want, and remember that compromise is inevitable so the more headroom we can give ourselves the better.

The process of defining the MDO might appear straightforward, as it is easy to decide what we would ideally like to achieve. Here our negotiation requirements form the starting point as they lay out what must be achieved. However, some aspirational enhancement might be needed to shift these into a series of good MDOs. The questions that need to be answered for each requirement are:

1 What is the requirement that needs to be satisfied?

2 If we could do anything here what would we do?

3 Given our position, power, market conditions and other influencing factors what would be a realistic stretch here without jeopardizing the negotiation?

4 Do we believe the other party will have knowledge of what a realistic position might be, eg through facts and data?

The last two questions present the most challenge because a degree of judgement is required. If we are playing trust because we have no power, revealing a preposterous MDO position within our negotiation could just make the other side laugh enough to walk away. However, if we have the power and we are playing Chicken with plenty of alternatives, then why not? So aspirational enhancement of our negotiation requirements to create a good MDO requires careful thought based upon the alternatives (BATNAs) available. MDOs should therefore be determined from the negotiation requirements by reviewing all the insights developed within our Red Sheet planning so far; particularly the game we will play (step 7), balance of power (step 6), portfolio analysis (step 4) and culture (step 3). If the negotiation is team-based then MDOs (and LDOs also) should be worked up by the team.

Determining the LDO

Whereas finding good MDOs is a bit of informed guesswork, the LDO requires more certainty. Having a clear and accurate set of LDOs for all the negotiation requirements is critically important. Get this wrong and the consequences could be catastrophic.

If we negotiate without an LDO we have no reference point to know what a good or bad outcome might look like. A friend talked of how, following sober reflection, he felt he'd been cheated after trading in his car for a new one. My friend shared that he felt as if 'he had had his pants taken down'. Meaning he felt he had ended up doing a deal well away from that which he had anticipated. When I asked him what he had anticipated and what his 'walk away' position was, he admitted he hadn't thought of one but he just knew afterwards he'd been swept along by the salesman's patter. Similarly for an eBay purchase or a purchase made in some other auction it is easy, for the thrill of winning and in the euphoria of the moment, to enter 'just one more bid'. Setting a limit not to go above is the LDO in this scenario. However, here it is also important to manage to stick to it or, as in my case, you will end up with a garage full of stuff you paid too much for. So without an LDO and the conviction to stick to it, it is easy to get swept along or lose perspective and it is the seller's aim to push us as far as he can.

Similarly, negotiating with the wrong LDO can be equally catastrophic. It would usually be folly to do a deal that would harm our business, say because a deal is unsustainable or unprofitable. However, there are circumstances where it is appropriate to either set an unsustainable LDO or go below an LDO. An example might include retailers demanding promotional campaigns such as 'buy one, get one free' from suppliers, which are often loss making, but they are for a limited duration, the supplier will be promised future volumes or preferential in-store positioning and will be featured in the store's promotional marketing. The point here is it is important to be in a position to make a conscious and informed decision to do this quantifying and justifying the action against other benefits, in consultation with the wider business as needed.

LDOs must also be accurate and based upon facts and data where needed. A buyer with a negotiation requirement for volumes with an LDO based in US fluid ounces might be pleased with a negotiation outcome until later, once contracts have been signed, it emerges the supplier was using imperial fluid ounces. Here the difference of 4 per cent in the supplier's favour, in a high-volume, low, margin deal, could make the difference between profit and loss.

Determining LDOs requires research both internally and externally. If a team is involved in the negotiation planning LDOs should be developed collaboratively. Once again we are starting with our negotiation requirements and determining LDOs for each by attempting to answer the following questions:

1 What is the minimum we could possibly live with here if we absolutely had to?
2 Given all the other requirements, if we ended up at our LDO for each would our overall position be just acceptable?
3 Given this, what is a comfortable and sustainable LDO for each requirement?

Figure 9.11 shows the example negotiation requirements with MDOs and LDOs determined. Where we make an agreement between these points is down to how effectively we negotiate.

Determining our BATNAs

The concept of the BATNA (Best Alternative To a Negotiated Agreement) was explored in Chapter 7 and is concerned with using the power of alternatives by creating choice as to whether or not we need to make a particular agreement or could do something different. BATNAs exist both at the level of the entire deal and some of the individual negotiation requirements. BATNAs are an essential negotiation weapon, but to be useful, a negotiator needs as many as possible, working at all levels of the negotiation. Generating BATNAs, however, does not come easy for the inexperienced negotiator. This is because they require creative thinking 'outside the box'. Fisher and Ury (2012) suggest there are four reasons why negotiators fail to develop enough BATNAs:

- **Premature judgement.** It is easy to stick with the thing we know as inventing BATNAs involves thinking up a scenario that doesn't currently exist.

- **Searching for the single answer.** If we are not open to the unconventional we will miss potential game-changing possibilities and stick only one answer in mind.

- **The assumption of a fixed pie.** Value-claiming negotiations limit possibilities. What would happen if we tried to create value?

- **Thinking that 'solving their problem' is their problem.** If we can sort out the other side's concern with its own immediate interests it might open up more possibilities.

With these constraints in mind BATNAs need to be developed and where a team is involved BATNAs should be brainstormed with the group, ideally supported with some good facilitation. Questions that help with BATNA development are:

1 What is the basic need we are trying to satisfy here?

2 How else could we satisfy the basic need?

3 Can the need be fulfilled in other ways such as by using a substitute product or service, or a generic alternative?

4 Can we eliminate or delay the need?

5 Can we fulfil the need ourselves?

6 Can we change our overall direction and do something different?

7 Is there something that would help them and make them more open to making an agreement?

8 Is there a way to create rather than claim value?

9 What happens if we just walk away and do nothing?

10 If we could do anything what would we do?

BATNAs may have a natural prioritization or sequence. For example, if we can't reach agreement on one outcome can we reach agreement on another lesser outcome with the supplier; failing this, can we walk away?

Effective use of BATNAs is simply a case of being prepared for real to do something different. In some cases, at a deal level, this might mean taking the entire business in a completely different direction and so such a BATNA would need to be fully agreed in advance by the relevant stakeholders and decision makers. For example, a major TV content streaming company might enter negotiations with an established satellite/cable TV company who also creates exclusive content. The streaming company would seek to strike a deal so they too can offer is new content, recognizing consumers expect to see these in any package. However, in the negotiation the satellite/cable TV company might recognize the competitive advantage retaining exclusive rights to these channels brings and so hold fast to a very high MDO. Here the streaming company is faced with either doing a bad deal or using a BATNA. They could go and complain to the regulator, which could eventually leverage a ruling, or they could decide to go and create their own alternative programming designed to compete directly with what the satellite/cable TV company offers. This might mean a new business venture or a departure from the traditional core business of the company, and so here the BATNA is not simply an alternative deal but rather a whole new strategic direction for a company. Corporate strategy is therefore often determined or shaped by the outcomes of specific negotiations.

3 The four phases of negotiation

A negotiation event has four distinct phases (Figure 9.7): open, explore, bargain and deal. I will cover the *open* phase in the next chapter when we consider event planning. Once the negotiation is under way parties will start by attempting to understand and *explore* their respective positions. Using questions, proposals and conditioning this phase involves parties attempting to smoke out each other's LDOs while selectively revealing some or all of their MDOs. As parties form a view of each other's position the negotiation enters the *bargain* stage. Here trades begin and concessions are made and parties continue to test what is needed to conclude the *deal*, which is the final phase where parties crystallize their agreement.

Often these blur together and the subtle differences may even go unnoticed; as discussions progress the negotiation will slowly advance through the phases of this unspoken process to reach a conclusion. Understanding these phases enables us to apply greater control to the way a negotiation plays out. Reading when the other party is attempting to shift from one phase to the next gives us vital insight into their comfort with what is on the table and their readiness to make a deal. Also, making deliberate interventions to move the negotiation to a new phase can drive closure on our terms. There are many tactics and techniques that can help through each of these stages and I'll outline these later in this and in future chapters.

Figure 9.7 The four phases of a negotiation event

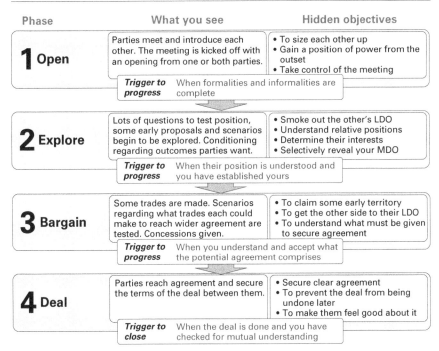

Phase	What you see	Hidden objectives
1 Open	Parties meet and introduce each other. The meeting is kicked off with an opening from one or both parties.	• To size each other up • Gain a position of power from the outset • Take control of the meeting
	Trigger to progress When formalities and informalities are complete	
2 Explore	Lots of questions to test position, some early proposals and scenarios begin to be explored. Conditioning regarding outcomes parties want.	• Smoke out the other's LDO • Understand relative positions • Determine their interests • Selectively reveal your MDO
	Trigger to progress When their position is understood and you have established yours	
3 Bargain	Some trades are made. Scenarios regarding what trades each could make to reach wider agreement are tested. Concessions given.	• To claim some early territory • To get the other side to their LDO • To understand what must be given to secure agreement
	Trigger to progress When you understand and accept what the potential agreement comprises	
4 Deal	Parties reach agreement and secure the terms of the deal between them.	• Secure clear agreement • To prevent the deal from being undone later • To make them feel good about it
	Trigger to close When the deal is done and you have checked for mutual understanding	

4 The process of trading concessions

Securing an outcome as close to our MDO as possible is always the reason why we are negotiating in the first place. The challenge is that the other party will almost certainly be seeking the same thing. There are circumstances where a negotiation might result in one party agreeing to everything the other wants without question; however, these tend to be limited to job offers for junior people, consumer purchases, where one party fails to realize the discussion they have ended up in is actually a negotiation, or where there is simply no acceptable alternative. Whilst there may be some scenarios where we can get what we want by stating our demands and refusing to budge, often such an approach can fail, driving the other party to play their BATNA, perhaps walk away and the negotiation to end without agreement.

Core to most negotiations, there are concessions where parties move from their respective starting positions, typically some distance apart, towards a point where parties can make an agreement. A concession is, according to my dictionary, 'something that is granted, especially in response to demands'. Negotiating to reach an agreement involves making 'concessions', but as negotiators we have a choice as to whether to grant a concession. While the other party cannot make us concede, failing to grant concessions might jeopardize reaching an agreement. Equally, conceding too much will damage our position. Effective negotiation requires an approach to manage how we make concessions. It is worth nothing, however, that whenever a party agrees to 'come to the negotiation table' they are effectively signalling they are ready to give a concession. This alone can often be a vital sign that we can secure a better negotiated agreement.

Step by step

The concept of concessions can be visualized as two individuals standing apart from each other with many metres between them. Agreement is when they meet and shake hands, but to get there each has to take a series of steps. Neither is prepared to walk all the way to the other, but each is ready to make some steps with the expectation that the other will do the same. Neither wants to move too far from their current position yet they will have to if they want to reach the other. Somewhere between them is a point where they can shake hands and make an agreement (the ZoMA) and the territory between individuals and the point of agreement represents the gap between their MDOs and LDOs. This territory might expand or change if the other side has negotiables that introduce new dimensions not anticipated by the other.

When we negotiate our concession strategy is how we plan the way we will make steps towards the other party and encourage them to come towards us. A concession strategy is therefore the planned approach for the series of interactions and exchanges during the negotiation event that seek to secure concessions from the other side and enable us to give considered concessions, with the sole aim to achieve our overall objectives for the negotiation and achieve an outcome as close to our MDO as possible.

Concession strategies work in concert with our repertoire of tactics and techniques that help us execute our strategy. Concession strategies vary from negotiation to negotiation. If we are seeking a WIN/win outcome to our negotiation then we need a concession strategy that applies negotiation tactics designed to make them come further to us than we go to them – remember in such negotiations you don't get points for being fair, it is all about value claiming the bigger 'WIN'. If we are seeking a win/win then we are very happy to meet in the middle because there is a bigger, and perhaps more long-term, prize available to us.

Many negotiators fail to develop or consider concession strategies ahead of the event and so end up taking steps they are not fully in control of. It is easy to assume that the steps we take are of little consequence so long as we reach an agreement both parties are happy with. However, this could not be more wrong as, in fact, the steps we take and the way we make them towards reaching agreement often determine where the final point of agreement lies.

Our concession steps are not only a means to move towards an agreement, but each one tells a story and sends a signal to the other party that they will use to try and determine where our LDO might be. The size of the steps we take, the speed of our steps, the way we take steps represent the focal point where all of our insights, intelligence and negotiation preparation should come together. It is crucial that these steps, or concessions, are not simply left to chance or we will hand power to our opponent.

Negotiators will usually fix their endpoint in their mind and then negotiate to it. This means that in our minds we have already given ourselves permission to go to a certain point and perhaps even, and without conscious thought, divided up the territory between the first stated position and the end point. If we have done this using our LDO then in our mind we have already prepared ourselves to give concessions to end up there, and this 'mental permission' has already set us up to accept the least best outcome. We are, in effect, setting ourselves up to fail before we have entered the room. The psychology here is important and is the same that sports men and women face when competing. If a sports person competes thinking they won't win, they surely will not. But with positive mental attitude, supported by coaching using NLP techniques, and the belief they will win, prepared for with position performance and outcome visualization ahead of the event, then the changes of success are much greater. Go into a negotiation believing in the MDO and we will negotiate better, and so this is not something we should leave to chance. With experience we can learn to fix points at or closer to our MDO in our mind and that can make us stronger in the negotiation itself.

The concession strategy we develop is therefore not just about managing trades, but it is about managing signals to the other party that help our position. Good concession strategies are the ones that consider the psychology behind each step. Some dynamics here include:

- **Step size** – The size of our concession steps, especially our first step, tells a story. A big first step, perhaps because the other party has managed to condition us to believe our position is absurd, can signal that there is much more to be had, ie if they have taken a big step, we can probably get them to take one or two more lesser steps. Equally, small steps from the outset can signal there is little more to be had.

- **Step speed** – Giving concessions too quickly can suggest the party needs to make a deal and may even suggest they are desperate. Similarly, not budging or being slow to trade can signal there is none or very little to be had. This also serves to prolong the negotiation, perhaps even wearing down the opponent but not without the risk of pushing them to walk away.

- **Number of steps** – For most large or complex negotiations we expect there to be a number of steps. If we approach such a negotiation with the belief that there will be just one step, and give our final position, then we can risk the other side keeping going and perhaps even pushing us below our LDO. That said, making a single step can also be a powerful tactic (called *full reveal* – covered later). Unless we manage expectations to the contrary, parties will often expect there to be two, three or more steps and will plan accordingly.

None of these is a reliable gauge of what is actually happening in the negotiation, nor are any definitive rules to guide us as skilled negotiators will play concession steps like a skilled poker player plays a hand, sometimes bluffing, sometimes not, all so the opponent cannot gain any insight, advantage or spot an emerging pattern regarding the other's position. We must do the same. The game with concessions, as in poker, is to keep the other side guessing. The dynamics here, and the way the psychology behind concession steps works, changes with the negotiation scenario, with culture, with experience and with the individual. A negotiation to secure a bit of discount in shop will usually only have one small step; a negotiation with a Russian businessman is likely to involve many large steps.

The negotiation checkerboard

So far I have described the process of trading concessions and the concept of managing steps where we are negotiating one single variable. In practice, as we have seen, most negotiations have a series of negotiables addressing our different requirements and desired outcomes. It helps to visualize this as a checkerboard and Figure 9.8 shows this. We are on one side with our counters at their starting position and they are at the other end with their counters at their starting position. Running the length of our side of the checkerboard are our different negotiation requirements. Each strip between

Figure 9.8 The negotiation checkerboard

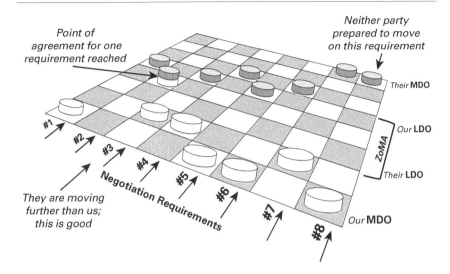

them and us represents one negotiable. We begin with our counters for each negotiable at their starting squares which represents our respective MDOs for each negotiable or requirement. In the middle somewhere are our LDOs for each requirement and we know where these are. However, their LDOs are also there somewhere but they are not visible to us; hopefully there is a ZoMA for each negotiable requirement.

Our aim is to get the other party to advance as many of their counters towards us as possible while avoiding advancing ours as much as possible. The game is played by making a series of advancements, and possibly even retractions, trading one more for another, all the while keeping an eye on the entire board and trying to judge where points of agreement lie and where their LDOs are. If there are too many of our counters heading for the centre while all their pieces are still at the other end we are conceding too much or we don't have the power we need and might want to think about playing an alternative game (BATNAs). Similarly if there is little movement then we may not be conceding enough or negotiating poorly.

Negotiators can easily get lost in a negotiation that has many negotiables, and if this happens the other party can gain power over us by securing a series of seemingly acceptable concessions at an individual level, but when the big picture is considered it becomes apparent too much was given away. This is a tactic that skilled negotiators will use. Visualizing the checkerboard can help to make sense of a negotiation and help maintain perspective so we not only remain in control of the big picture and the balance of concession trades, but also so we can use this to our advantage over our opponent.

Building a winning concession strategy

We develop our concession strategy by planning the way we will move away from our MDO – towards, but ideally not reaching, our LDO. This should not be left to chance nor should the level of individual concessions be left to be determined during the negotiation event (although sometimes this is unavoidable). Where possible, a series of discrete steps between the MDO and LDO for each requirement should be planned in advance (Figure 9.9). The size of each step is predetermined so that when we need to give a concession we have already planned how big or small that concession will be so as to consider the signals we want, or are prepared for, the other party to receive by our actions. Together, all our pre-planned concession steps comprise our overall concession strategy for all negotiables. Referring back to the checkerboard concept, this means determining our position for every square on the checkerboard this side of our LDOs.

Specifying the individual steps is not simply a case of dividing up the gap between the MDO and the LDO as this would establish a recognizable pattern and would have little impact. Instead the nature of the concession steps should be based upon our negotiation planning and insights thus far, determining the increments or decrements according to our position and how we want to play out a particular game and chosen approach.

For example, in a monochronic Chicken negotiation where we hold the power, an appropriate concession strategy could be to try to maintain a position close to our MDO and to hold fast to this until the very end in an attempt to get them to lose their nerve or wear them down. We could choose to use a series of small and diminishing steps to give the impression they are moving us close to our final position (as in Figure 9.9). However, in a Stag Hunt negotiation, perhaps with a polychronic opponent the steps might be chosen to be deliberately generous and show signs of wanting to collaborate. There is no single definitive way to plan concession steps; however, the crucial point here is that as negotiators we can choose how we give concessions and what signals we want each to send, and we can plan our steps to help us achieve a particular outcome according to our overall position. Therefore careful thought should be given to planning this in advance.

The concession strategy should be regarded as the roadmap for bargaining in a negotiation. However, it is entirely possible that, despite great planning, when the actual negotiation begins, the roadmap suddenly appears worthless, perhaps because we have misjudged something or there are factors we have not understood. Notwithstanding the fact that the other party will seek to make us lose our nerve, there are genuine situations where we

Figure 9.9　The pre-planned steps between MDO and LDO

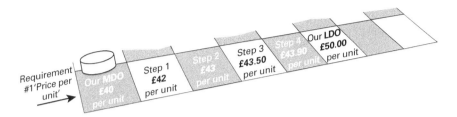

need to abandon our concession strategy. If possible, this should not be done on the fly; instead a time-out should be called to attempt to redefine a new strategy and set new steps.

5 10 winning techniques for concession trading

The tactics and techniques we use in a negotiation are the means by which we move proceedings from one place to another. Good negotiation requires a good repertoire of tactics and techniques together with the experience to know when and how to deploy them. Within this book I have included 100 of the most effective winning tactics and techniques which I will cover throughout the remaining chapters, starting with a series of winning techniques that can help plan concession trading before the event and can help manage concession trading during the event. These are given in Figure 9.10.

Technique 1 is 'something for something' and it is worth spending a bit of time on this as this principle lies at the heart of giving concessions. Remember we have a choice as to whether to give a concession so when faced with a demand to give something, we have four choices. We can:

- not concede;
- give what they ask for;
- give but give less;
- give on the basis that they will give something in return.

There is a place for all four responses, chosen carefully according to what is possible and appropriate. Within any concession is an opportunity to leverage a benefit in return and so concessions represent a source of power.

Figure 9.10   Winning techniques – Concessions

Winning Techniques - Concessions 1

1 Something for something

If you give something, do it on the basis that you will get something back in return and perhaps even make your trade conditional on getting something back. This increases the value of concessions and improves your position.

2 Rule of halves

When giving concessions people often 'halve' the gap between the first stated position and their LDO, and will halve again and again towards, but avoiding reaching, their LDO – their offer can help pinpoint where their LDO lies. Test it and if correct negotiate to your advantage.

3 Meet them

Find a concession where you can 'meet them' easily and agree to something they are asking. This seeks to demonstrate that you are willing to negotiate and want to trade concessions to make a deal.

4 Keep asking until they say no

Keep asking for additional easy concessions until they say 'No'. It is easy to feel we might cause offence and resist asking, but often we have nothing to lose and may well get more than we anticipated.

BY HOW MUCH ?

5 Quantify their demands

When they make a demand get them to quantify it. For example if they say 'your price is too high' then respond by saying 'how high?' The likelihood is they will initially resist quantifying, but keep stating their demand. Stick to your request until they respond and negotiate from there.

Wherever possible this power should be realized by attempting to negotiate 'something for something', a technique that children learn early on:

> Mother: 'Madison, I want you to go and tidy your room this morning.'
>
> Daughter: 'Arrgh! Mum! OK, if I tidy my room can I go to the park with Austin this afternoon?'

Figure 9.10 *continued*

Winning Techniques - Concessions 2

When giving a concession, quantify and emphasize its value – let them feel they are receiving something significant whilst keeping score of all concessions. Use this to summarize how much has been given at key points in the negotiation as a means to resist further concessions.

6 Put a value to every concession

Whenever a concession, gift, trade or offer is made by the other party, take it, thank them and 'bank it' ie proceed from that point as if that concession has been made/taken and revise your figures accordingly. Avoid ignoring a gift or leaving it for later unless there is an ethical reason for doing so.

7 Thank and bank

Be careful not to give concessions too fast or too early or you will be too eager and raise the other's expectations unnecessarily. Speed is one of the most powerful signals to the other party of how much you might need to cut a deal. Don't let the excitement get the better of you.

8 Watch your speed

Where possible, avoid making a firm agreement when trading concessions but rather try to hold doors open. It is harder to undo points of agreement, but instead signal agreement in principle as if you are waiting to get everything on the table before finalizing your commitment.

9 Hold doors open

Building on 9, bring back into contention previously settled issues or agreed concessions if you need negotiation room. Do this by finding a reason to bring it back – perhaps as a result of their new position or because 'something has changed' etc.

10 Bring it back

Applying the 'something for something' principle helps strengthen and maintain our overall negotiation position. But it may not always work. For example, Mum could simply have said No or could have part-conceded, saying, 'You can't go to the park today but perhaps we will all go tomorrow.'

There are also scenarios where something for something is inappropriate or will not work. These include:

- value-creation negotiations where the objective shifts to finding ways for both sides to win something rather than give something;
- hard value-claiming negotiations where we have no power; use BATNAs instead;
- where we want to give a gift, perhaps when playing Trust;
- where the approach starts to have a detrimental effect such as where repeated use might damage a relationship and give the wrong impression.

Use hypothetical questioning to secure *something for something*, eg 'It is possible that I could give X but if I did would you provide Y and also Z?'

6 Guessing what they want and their BATNAs

If we can know what the other side wants to get out of the negotiation then we can tailor our concession strategy and entire negotiation planning accordingly. Unless we have a crystal ball or a snitch on the inside we can only anticipate this as best as we can, making use of any intelligence we might have available to us. In the case of a pre-existing supplier, stakeholder engagement can often yield great insight and the rest is about taking time to put ourselves in their shoes and attempting to best guess what they might want and what their BATNAs look like.

What do they want?

How can we know what they want? Most likely their list of negotiables will be very similar to ours, just with different desired outcomes. Both parties might have a requirement to agree a price point or volumes or contract terms; it is just that each might want different things here. So our starting point for anticipating their requirements is to review our requirements and determine what we think their MDO and LDO might be. Here we need to make our best guess, using any intelligence we might have to help, and checking that we think there is a ZoMA. If it looks likely that a ZoMA is not present then check assumptions, consider revising the MDO and LDO or ultimately rethink the negotiation strategy or even why the negotiation is taking place in the first place.

The supplier may have some other negotiables that we don't have on our list and here we should attempt to anticipate these and develop a view of what our MDO and LDO is as well as best guessing theirs.

Guessing their BATNAs

If we think we have great BATNAs to go into a negotiation with, they may well have the same. The question is: what are they? Failing to understand what alternatives they could have or create means we could misjudge our power position. If it is a delicate negotiation and we hold little power then the supplier could walk away.

The process for guessing their BATNAs is the same as that for ours except here we are attempting to put ourselves in their position: brainstorming in a team using the questions 'What alternatives could the supplier use?' and 'If the supplier could do anything what would they do?'

Actually doing it

Red Sheet Steps 9 and 10 – Our negotiables, concession strategy and their negotiables

Purpose of these steps

Steps 9 and 10 of Red Sheet are about the negotiables both sides have, our MDOs and LDOs and what we think the other party's might be also. Step 9 is concerned with determining in advance our concessions strategy. Figure 9.11 gives a worked example and a template can be found in the Appendix.

Completing this step

Work through steps 9 and 10 as follows:

1 Determine your negotiables and list these in step 9. If you intend to negotiate on a 'big picture' basis, ie a global agreement that encapsulates all individual requirements, then consider using the bottom line for this.

2 For each, determine the pain factor according to how important each requirement is and enter high, medium or low as appropriate.

3 Enter your MDO for each line or negotiable in step 9.

4 Determine what you think their negotiables against you will be and enter these in step 9. If you think they have any additional negotiables then list these too and circle back to complete steps 1 through 3 on your side against these.

5 Determine your LDO for each requirement and enter in step 8.

6 Determine what you think their MDO and LDO might be (make your best informed guess) and enter in step 9.

7 Check there is a ZoMA for each; if so tick the boxes between steps 9 and 10. If there is no ZoMA check your assumptions, consider revising your LDO or question if the negotiation should proceed.

8 Determine your individual concession steps according to your overall strategy and enter these into step 9 against each requirement.

9 Define your strategy and anything of note at the bottom of step 9.

10 Determine your BATNAs and list in step 9.

11 Attempt to anticipate their BATNAs and list in step 10.

Figure 9.11   Red Sheet steps 9 and 10 – Our negotiables, concession strategy and their negotiables

9. Our Negotiables® and Concession Strategy | 10. Their Negotiables®

Our Negotiables® (our requirements)	Pain Factor (High, Medium or Low)	Our M.D.O. (1st position)	2nd Step	3rd Step	4th Step	Our L.D.O. (final position)	ZoMA?	Their L.D.O (our best guess)	Their M.D.O (our best guess)	Their Negotiables® or outcomes (our best guess)
ATL393 Main Assembly Price	H	18% reduction	17%	14%	10%	5%	☑	10%	RFP price	
ATL393 PSU Assembly	M	20% reduction	17%	10%	5%	RFP price	☑	15%	RFP price	
ATL393 Motherboard	M	16% reduction	15%	12%	8%	RFP price	☑	15%	RFP price	
Min production runs	L	500 units	1,000	2,500	5,000	10,000	☑	2,500	10,000	As ours
Payment terms	H	60 days	30 days			14 days	☑	30 days	Immediate	
Full prod output by 1st September	H	1st September	1st October	1st November	1st December	31st December	☑	1st November	31st December	
Lead time	M	14 days	30 days			30 days	☑	30 days	30 days	
Min volume commitment	H	No commit	1,000 per yr	2,000 per yr		10,000 per yr	☑	10k per yr	20k per yr	Min volume commitment
							☐			
Big picture - all requirements combined in one							☐			

Our BATNAs:
- Deal BATNA – Fall back to one of the alternative suppliers in the RFP.
- Transition time – Delay closing current facility
- Main Assembly Price Reduction
- Remove from deal and source separately

Our strategy for concessions and trading:
- Small initial concessions in all areas. Hold firm to our position
- Lead on production runs as a 'decoy'

Their BATNA (our best guess)
- Deal BATNA – They may just sit tight or walk away
- Transition time – They may commit to a tight transfer deadline but introduce delays later
- Price BATNA – They might leverage their relationship with our CEO if they don't get what they want.

The negotiation 10
event

This chapter explores planning the negotiation event and considers the essential pre-planning activities such as communication, logistics and room layout as well as approaches to planning, as far as possible, the actual negotiation discussions.

Pathway questions addressed in this chapter

18 What is the best way to manage the meeting or negotiation event?

19 What tactics and techniques will help me be successful?

Red Sheet steps covered in this chapter

11 and 12

Event preparation

Irrespective of whether we are hosting the negotiation or not, there will be a series of arrangements or things that need to be put in place. Action planning is essential, perhaps using a 'what, who, by when' format with individual actions assigned to members of the negotiation team. Table 10.1 gives a suggested checklist for event planning and Figure 10.1 gives an example from Red Sheet step 11.

Figure 10.1 Red Sheet step 11 – Preparation (worked example)

11. PREPARATION

Event Planning Actions

What	Who	When
- Book meeting room & lunch	M.M.	Mar. 30th
- Book a limo to collect them from the hotel	O.R.	May 1st
- Book a table at restaurant for the evening of May 7th	M.M.	Apr. 15th
- Business cards available	All	May 8th
- Negotiation rehearsal	All	May 1st

Communications Plan

Message	To	Media/Means
- Awareness message using elevator speech	All	Email plus face-to-face
- Requirements of proposal concession strategy	H.K. & P.W. S.M. & N.N.	Face-to-face meeting
- Supplier invites (with conditioning message embedded)	TMC	Email plus phone conversation

Pre-conditioning message for the other party

- We are seeking further enhanced proposals that are an improvement on the RFP.
- We have a shortlist of potential suppliers.
- We can take our time to get this right.

Internal elevator speech

May 8th major negotiation with TMC who have the potential to win a new contract for electrical assembly manufacture if they can improve their current offer and satisfy our needs.

Table 10.1 Event-planning checklist

Planning activity	Complete?
Negotiation format determined – formal, relaxed or other?	
Any pre-engagement to develop relationship organized (eg dinner or social meeting)?	
Location determined and booked?	
Room layout and seating plan determined?	
Agenda or details of topics to discuss in advance (if appropriate) sent?	
Arrangements to meet and greet in place?	
Business cards available?	
Refreshments organized?	
Travel arrangements planned?	

Communications planning

Communications planning to support a negotiation is about adopting a structured approach around what gets communicated internally and especially externally. It ensures key stakeholders are fully informed about, and involved in, the process of negotiation planning. It also supports the process of creating alignment within an organization so the supplier receives a single, unified message. Remember that suppliers will attempt to cultivate strong relationships with individuals across any business. In practice, if communication between these multiple interfaces is uncoordinated, it will be possible for the supplier to gain vital intelligence about our actual position and this could be damaging to our negotiation.

Both internal and external communications are needed to support negotiation planning. Internal communication starts with the stakeholder map we developed earlier. This should list all those individuals or groups of individuals whom we need to engage with in some way or who need to be informed. This list forms the basis for the group to which we are planning to communicate. From here we need to consider the messages we need to communicate and how we will do this, ie the media we will use.

Internal communication messages

Typically these cover details of the negotiation, why and when it is taking place and desired outcomes. They should also define what is required of those in the business to help support the negotiation. There may be some specific involvement or support needed but crucially ensuring stakeholders are informed of what should, and should not, be communicated to the supplier is vitally important. Messages may well vary from stakeholder to stakeholder, some may only need to be kept informed of progress, and others might need much more involvement. Through good, well-managed internal communications it is possible to secure alignment, reduce resistance and galvanize support from within the stakeholder community.

Communication media

Determine media and the form of communication according to what will be most effective in getting the individual messages across. Creativity is needed if the message is to cut through all the competing demands for people's time and attention. Communication falls into two categories:

- **narrowcast** – specific one-to-one communications perhaps through face-to-face engagement or by phone, e-mail or informal networking; and

- **broadcast** – general communications to a broad group or even the entire business can help to keep all informed and this is particularly important where outcomes could impact many people. Examples of broadcast communications include: text messages, messaging apps (eg WhatsApp), closed social media groups, e-mail, internal web pages, newsletters, in-house road shows, notice boards, conferences, group e-mails, video, audio and team meetings.

Communications are managed using a communications plan (see Figure 10.1). Give thought to any cultural differences, especially if the stakeholders sit across geographical boundaries, as the approaches may need to be adapted for each geography. Polychronic stakeholders will need more personal engagement whereas an e-mail might suffice in a monochronic culture.

Getting everyone 'on message'

Getting everyone in a team across an organization 'on message' is always a challenge but one technique that can help here is the 'elevator speech'. Imagine you have just stepped into the elevator and the CEO steps in just as the doors are closing, says good morning and then asks you about what you are working on. You have just one minute before the elevator arrives at the ninth floor to say something meaningful. This sort of encounter takes most by surprise unless they have planned for such a happening and so it is easy to end up responding with meaningless prattle.

Elevator speeches aren't confined to elevators but it is a concept that equips people with a simple and easy-to-remember spiel that can be imparted when the opportunity presents itself. An elevator speech is formed by the creation of a simple central message that succinctly summarizes the message to be communicated. This is then published to all those who might need to give this message who must be encouraged to learn it so if they end up in a dialogue with the supplier they know what to say. To be effective an elevator speech must be short and simple. For example:

Internal briefing – forthcoming negotiation with 'The Goof & Bungle Maintenance Company'

On 22nd December a cross-functional team led by Procurement will enter into negotiations with our outsourced provider of building maintenance across all our sites:

- Currently costs are out of line with the market.
- Recently service has declined and we have found many examples of over-billing.
- The aim of this negotiation is to either agree a way forward that brings the contract back in line or determines if we find an alternative provider.
- If this provider is to retain the contract we need a significant fee reduction and they must implement measures to improve service.
- We are also seeking a rebate for over-billing.

Supplier conditioning

Conditioning is about convincing the suppliers you mean business! It is the process of setting boundaries and limiting expectations in the mind of another party so that they respond in a particular way, and signalling that a particular outcome is expected. It could be called a mild form of manipulation; indeed, some of the approaches used are often the same. It is not a once-only activity but something that happens right from the start of any engagement with a supplier and continues throughout the relationship. The need for conditioning is greater for value-claiming scenarios, whereas in longer-term collaborative relationships it is replaced by a more open and transparent engagement between parties.

In a negotiation supplier conditioning happens before and during the event. Pre-event conditioning can be highly effective in shaping supplier LDO setting. If, for example, they believe they are turning up to negotiate with a cash-rich oil and gas company, they will arrive with high expectations and an over-ambitious MDO and LDO and thus it will be harder to shift their position. However, preconditioning can completely change this. Remember, the process of negotiation is not confined to the event but starts the moment we engage with the supplier. With each interaction there is an opportunity for conditioning within what is said and any documents that pass to them.

Sending an agenda or outline of topics to be discussed ahead of a supplier negotiation presents a great opportunity to influence the supplier's thinking, and how this is written can make all the difference. Consider these two extracts from 'topics for discussion' e-mails to the supplier ahead of a value-claiming negotiation:

Example 1

Proposed topics for discussion at our meeting:

1 Review of current business situation.

2 Performance review.

3 Pricing for next year.

4 Future plans.

Example 2

Proposed topics for discussion at our meeting:

1 Discussion around increasing business challenges.

2 Review of quality issues over recent months.

3 Agree reduced pricing for next year.

4 Future opportunities and potential for higher volumes.

In the first example, each topic is no more than a theme that can be interpreted by the supplier in many ways. However, in the second example, implied in each topic is an indication of the current situation and expectations for change. The second example also hints at great opportunities for the supplier and begins to condition that there might be a trade of reduced pricing in return for future volumes. This would leave the supplier in no doubt as to outcomes being sought, thus forcing them to consider their approach carefully.

In the second example 'Discussion around increasing business challenges' sets the scene that things are not easy and there are pressures that will impact the negotiation. This type of 'prevailing situation conditioning' can be very powerful to frame the negotiation. Both positive and negative conditioning can be used here, individually or together, and suggests either that there are forces at work in the negotiation that are apparently beyond the influence of either party or that there is great potential for the other party if, of course, they agree to what we want. Examples of positive and negative conditioning are given in Table 10.2 and both should be used carefully.

A smart supplier will attempt to condition first or counter-condition in response to things we do, perhaps by a response in writing to the example above or during the opening introductions during the event. Where possible this 'buyer conditioning' should be countered to ensure the supplier understands our position cannot easily be shifted. There is little purpose in getting into multiple conditioning exchanges. Instead, once the pre-negotiation position has been outlined defer all other discussions until the event itself.

Supplier conditioning is not an activity that should be confined to purchasing people. For it to be effective, stakeholders must play their part using a single, aligned message. In fact it can often be more powerful for suppliers to be conditioned by stakeholders, as they are more likely to believe what they hear. The elevator speech described above can play a key role in doing this.

The power of the event

A negotiation should not be treated as just another business meeting. Where the event is held, how parties arrive, where they sit and what happens in the room; all present opportunities to project power, and if we can control or influence these things then we have an advantage.

Location, location, location

Greene (2002) suggests: 'when you force the other person to act, you are the one in control. It is always better to make your opponent come to you, abandoning his own plans in the process. Lure him with fabulous gains – then attack. You hold the cards'. The location is important; if we can get them to come to us then the negotiation will be on our familiar territory and this gives us power over them. Not only do we get to control the event, but also psychologically; the 'visiting party' may feel slightly subservient, just like when the boss asks you to come to his or her office or why sports teams feel they have a greater chance on home turf.

Practicalities might mean this is not possible and so we may end up having to negotiate on their territory. This is part of negotiating but might require the use of a few tactics to retain control that I'll cover shortly. Alternatively, negotiation on neutral territory takes away the issues with either party having control or advantage and many negotiators will insist on this, especially if the negotiation is delicate. For this reason political negotiations between countries on the verge of unrest often take place in a different, neutral location.

Consider also the setting for the location; should it be a formal business meeting or a more relaxed affair? Cultural norms have an influence on this and where the relationship is important, negotiations will often be structured with this in mind. As an example, in Ireland it is commonplace for the bulk of a negotiation to happen in relaxed neutral territory such as the pub but this would be a very unlikely location for a negotiation in Japan. Research into cultural expectations is therefore important in determining where to meet.

The power of room layout

Having someone sit in a chair facing a bank of spotlights hearing only the voice of the other person somewhere else in the room is an approach unlikely to work in a business negotiation. However, it does raise the question: if we are organizing the event is it appropriate to deliberately make them uncomfortable to throw them off course? I ask this same question each time I teach negotiation. Consistently around one-fifth of delegates seem to believe this is appropriate and there is an advantage to be gained by creating some discomfort for the other party. Those asked usually admit that recreating a Hollywood interrogation scene would be a bit extreme but support, and some even admit having tried, deliberate tactics such as having the other party face the window so the morning sun is in their eyes or turning up the heating. These tactics might have some limited effect in a value-claiming negotiation, but generally, if we are negotiating with someone who is experienced they will have a response in their repertoire to deal with such situations. Most likely they will stop proceedings until they are comfortable. Alternatively they might resist making an agreement and want to go away to reflect. Discomfort tactics rarely work and taking the time to ensure the other party is comfortable tends to be a more productive approach. Furthermore, choosing to extend good hospitality and human kindness naturally places us in a position of strength and power.

If we have control over the event then it is worth taking time to think about the location, the room and, if possible, how we might lay out the room and where people will sit. Negotiations by both individuals or teams conducted in the same room across a table have been common place around the world for eternity. The 2020 pandemic drove in long-lasting change to the way negotiations take place. The need for face-to-face dramatically dropped, more in some cultures than others, and the need for distancing suddenly applied to any in person meetings. Irrespective of how close people can be to each other, the same principles apply. Factors to consider here are:

- The nature of the negotiation – value objectives, relationship objectives and target outcomes.
- Where will the negotiation take place?
- What are the cultural implications – do certain individuals need to be seated in certain places?
- Where will everybody sit – should we sit across a table or have a less formal layout in more comfortable seating and surroundings to encourage collaborative discussions?
- Comfort level – how comfortable should we make them?
- Barriers on the table? Any object between us and them is a barrier; remove these to stimulate a more open dialogue.
- Arrangements for refreshments.

Every room has a natural power spot, the focal point of the room where the most powerful person would be expected to be found. In Western culture this is not something we pay too much attention to, but in Eastern culture it is a science all of its own. The Chinese call this the 'power position' or 'dragon's seat' and is part of the ancient practice of Feng Shui. The person sitting in this position can see all entrances to the room and they are seated against a wall or other structure so that no activity occurs behind them. This makes them the focus of attention for all persons present. Power positions

Figure 10.2 Power positions

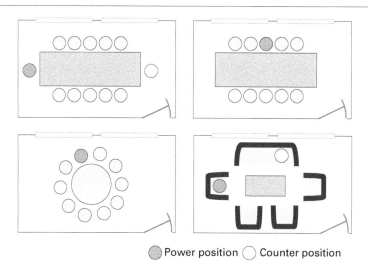

Power position ⬤ Counter position ◯

come from some innate self-preservation force that evolved in our fore-fathers to protect us from enemy attack. Figure 10.2 shows typical power positions and their counterposition, ie where you or the other party would naturally sit to oppose the power position (assuming no social distancing).

Most negotiations tend to favour a 'face off' configuration with one side facing across the table from the other. There is good reason for this as it is the layout that enables both sides to see each other while creating a degree of adversarial tension. However, in value-creating negotiations it is entirely possible that a more relaxed arrangement would work better; perhaps sitting in a couple of comfortable arm chairs placed at 90 degrees to each other.

If we control the event then it is beneficial to determine the seating arrangements so they work in our favour. It is possible to control how to usher the other party into the room and direct them to where we would like them to sit. Ultimately they may make their own minds up about where in the room they sit, but if the only remaining chairs are the ones we want them to sit in, their choices are limited. If an empty chair is left beside us on our side of the table, it is possible one of their team could sit there. Such a move on their part would create a collaborative bridge from them to us as well as affording them the opportunity to see our notes. Therefore, manage carefully what seating options they are left with.

For team negotiations consider where people should be placed. Clearly the team leader should occupy the power position with Mr Data in the next seat so facts and supporting details are to hand. The Sweeper should be in

Figure 10.3   Typical seating layout

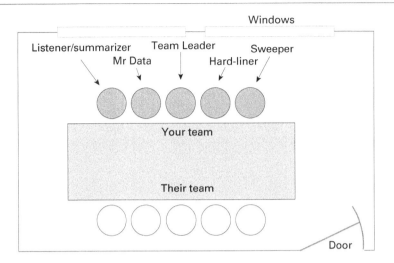

one corner so they can see all of the other team. Figure 10.3 gives a typical seating layout (again assuming no social distancing).

In some cultures there are strict protocols for room layout and indeed where people must sit. Ignore these and it could jeopardize the negotiation. For example, in a negotiation with the Chinese, seating is arranged by rank. The host is required to escort the most senior of guests to his or her seat, which should be opposite the room's doors and directly across the table from the hosts. On a sofa, or where there is no table, the most senior guest sits to the right of the host. Prior research of any cultural norms or expectations is essential.

Meeting and greeting

The power we project starts from the moment we meet the other party so this should be planned carefully. If they are visiting our company and guests need to check in at reception, then it is likely there will be some checking-in formalities, after which they would be escorted to the location of the negotiation. Decide at what point during the arrival process to engage with them for the first time. If there is a strong pre-existing relationship it will usually be appropriate to go and collect them once they have arrived. This, however, may be inappropriate for a value-claiming negotiation with a supplier being met for the first time. Instead it might be preferable to have someone meet them and bring them to the meeting room where the team are all assembled and then all that remains is to manage introductions and seating them.

The process of making introductions must be considered too. A room of people clumsily attempting to greet and introduce each other and perhaps exchange business cards is not a great start but worse, it is easy to overlook cultural norms or expectations if unprepared. Remember, the order in which people enter the room and introduce each other is important in some Eastern cultures. Furthermore, the ritual of exchanging business cards must happen as if each party is giving up something of the utmost beauty and fragility, holding the card with both hands and presenting it 'right way up' for the other party to receive in the same way and study with great respect. Despite the 'new normal' after Covid-19 some cultures may still kiss or expect a firm handshake, others less so – and a welcome speech is a must-do with the Chinese. Therefore, once again, it is essential to understand what is culturally expected and plan the process of meeting and greeting accordingly.

When they control the event

A negotiation is a bit like a stage performance; to give your best you need to feel comfortable and in control. However, if the other party are in control of the event then they may want to make us feel a bit uncomfortable and should this happen it is easy for an inexperienced negotiator to respond by muddling through, as if they were being interrogated by the police.

If things are not right then take control and ask to change things. If you feel as if you are seated too far from the action or squinting because the sun is in your eyes, or if you are desperately thirsty, your performance will be sub-optimum and you may well feel inferior in that setting. As any performer will tell you, if you feel inferior then your performance will lack confidence. This can be damaging in a negotiation and may even be exactly what the other party is counting on.

Taking control of things not only addresses specific issues, but it is also a show of power. 'Powerful people' will always find something to change or request something different as a way of marking some sort of territory. In practice, to make such intervention follow simple steps: pause, name, ask and act:

1 **Pause** proceedings: 'Sorry, could we stop a moment...'

2 **Name** the problem or create a good reason for needing to change something: making this personal is hugely powerful as others cannot easily challenge how you feel but are likely to naturally show some empathy: '... I'm feeling like I'm sitting in the wrong place...'

3 Ask: frame the desired change by asking permission: '… do you mind if I come and sit there?'

4 Act: don't wait for them to give permission or give them the opportunity to say no, just do it. Stand up and gather your papers before you have finished asking the question.

The need to visit the restroom provides a great opportunity for a short time-out to reflect on something and don't be afraid to ask for them to bring you water or to fulfil other reasonable requests. All these things can create a vital break in proceedings to marshal your thoughts.

Building the negotiation event plan

We now come to planning what happens during the negotiation event itself. We have reached the point were all the research and planning work we have done thus far can converge to create our negotiation plan for the event. Here we use step 12 of the Red Sheet to define our event plan and timeline and this becomes the key output of the entire planning process; our game plan and that which provides the means to go into a negotiation fully equipped to manage and be in full control of proceedings. Figure 10.4 gives a worked example of the first part of step 12 and Figure 10.5 gives the second part.

Negotiation event management would be straightforward if we could be confident about how the event would unfold. Even if we sit in a powerful position we cannot entirely control the event; instead the best we can hope for is to control only certain aspects of the event.

If we are negotiating the release of a hostage there might seem little point in planning how the discussions will proceed and an agenda will be of little use. Furthermore, the perpetrators are unlikely to follow it should one get sent across to where they are holed up! Negotiation events are unpredictable and proceedings will ebb and flow as each party asserts different positions and deploys various tactics. It can be like sailing into unchartered waters while the storm clouds gather. It is not possible for the sailor to stop the winds raging or the waves crashing over the bow; instead they can only react to what is happening around them, all the while maintaining a heading and using their skill to steer a course away from danger and towards their goal. Just as in the case of any good sailor planning a course before setting sail, we should plan how we hope to conduct our negotiation but while keeping in mind that we may also be blown off course or have to alter our course in order to reach our goal as we sail into the tempest.

Table 10.2 Prevailing situation conditioning messages

Type	Theme	Message this sends
Negative conditioning	**Difficult times**	We're in difficult times, business is tough, financials are poor, our competitors are beating us, or we're struggling and need help through this. *Use sparingly and only when plausible. Will not work repeatedly. Consider using alongside a positive message.*
	Major changes	Impact of acquisition process, restructuring or closures. New people at the top with new ideas threatening the status quo.
	Landscape change	The market has changed, supply or demand has shifted, what was good before is now out of line and needs to be revised. *This can be challenged so ensure good facts and data.*
Positive conditioning	**Growth ahead**	New projects or services, or entry into new markets; driving growth and expanding future volumes/size of business with the chance for the supplier to be part of this.
	Pole position	'You are the number 1 choice... it all hangs on this negotiation.' Everything to win yet everything to lose. *Only use when the removal of the competitive tension will not be detrimental. Have a good BATNA.*

Start and end times

Does the negotiation have a fixed start and end time? It is important to understand what these are and how much time there is available for the negotiation itself. A prompt start is usually expected, important with monochronic cultures and even some that would be regarded as polychronic, so some research into cultural expectations can help with this.

If we set the end time, then this could work against us. If the other party knows we have a flight to catch or we have a long journey home then they will also know we are likely to be anxious to strike a deal in the last five minutes. All they need to do is hold their position and bide their time.

Figure 10.4 Red Sheet step 12 (Part 1) Event management and timeline (worked example)

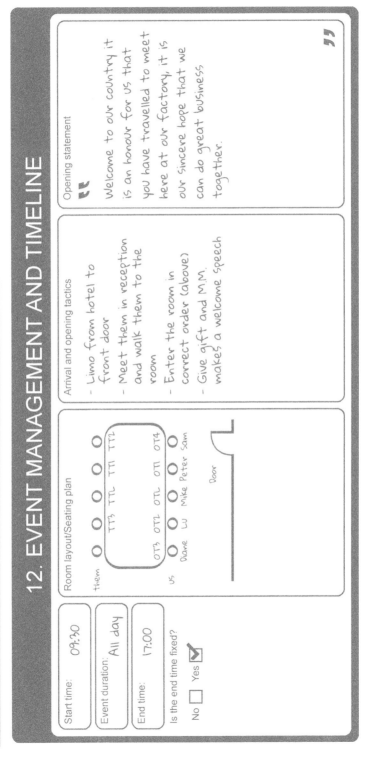

12. EVENT MANAGEMENT AND TIMELINE

Start time: 09:30

Event duration: All day

End time: 17:00

Is the end time fixed?

No ☐ Yes ☑

Room layout/Seating plan

them

OT3 OT2 OT1 OT4

OT3 OTL OT1 OT2

TT3 TTL TT1 TTL

us

Diane LU Mike Peter Sam

Door

Arrival and opening tactics

- Limo from hotel to front door
- Meet them in reception and walk them to the room
- Enter the room in correct order (above)
- Give gift and M.M. makes a welcome speech

Opening statement

Welcome to our country it is an honour for us that you have travelled to meet here at our factory, it is our sincere hope that we can do great business together.

Therefore consider carefully whether or not to tell them about any time constraints and, if possible, leave all options open in terms of finish time or have an alternative lined up. I know of one negotiator who will book two flights home for important meetings so if discussions need to overrun he has an alternative; however, he keeps quiet about his alternative and allows the other side to assume he is on a deadline. This often works to his advantage and serves to make the other side believe he is serious about his position and, when the concessions they are expecting don't come, creating a sense of confusion and panic that turns the tables.

Opening the negotiation

First impressions count! How we open a negotiation can determine how the other side perceives us. Open with some hesitant, ill-prepared words and we have already shown weakness. The power lies with the person who opens a meeting, as this gesture tends to be universally associated with authority. There are some cultural protocols around opening that should be observed; for example, when negotiating with the Chinese the host should always start with a welcoming speech. Unless culture dictates otherwise it helps to be the one who opens proceedings and this also provides a great opportunity to include a piece of conditioning.

The pressure of the moment can make opening a very stressful thing to do; all eyes are on us and snap judgements about us and our stature will be made within the first few seconds. Therefore opening should not be left to chance; instead a well-prepared opening statement should be used. As a former broadcaster I can share that the hardest part about live radio broadcasting is the first 10 words to any show. 'Going live' is possibly one of the scariest moments imaginable and one that seems to make even the simplest of introductions fall apart. So early on in my broadcasting career I learnt to script my opening 'hello and welcome' lines and to perfect them on paper so when the red light came on I had it all worked out. This same technique is highly effective for opening negotiations; develop a simple welcoming, scene-setting and perhaps conditioning message and script it. An example might look like this:

> Thank you for taking the time to come here today and it's great to meet you all. We have a lot to discuss and I hope that we can find a mutually agreeable outcome from today. As you know there is a great opportunity here but we also have a number of challenges and obstacles to overcome. I'd like to begin by...

A smart supplier will try to open too, for the same reasons we try this. This is OK and to be expected, and here there are two choices:

1 Let them open, then counter open – counter conditioning and effectively trumping their opening.

2 Cut them off to take control, perhaps saying something such as, 'Sorry, before you begin, I'd just like to start by thanking you…'.

Using an agenda

If negotiation is unpredictable, how could an agenda possibly help? The answer is it can help because it serves to define the ideal course through the negotiation if things pan out as anticipated. It also helps to regain our bearings as the discussions pull us in different directions. A good negotiation agenda is much more than a list of topics; it is the melding of all the planning so far into a practical route map and does many things, specifically:

• defines the list of topics to be covered – informed by the negotiation requirements;

• sets the ideal sequence for these discussions – informed by the concession strategy and pain factors;

• allows approximate timings to be assigned;

• enables pre-planning of the process and tactics to be used through the event including any triggers to use a specific tactic or take a pre-defined course of action;

• helps be clear about the purpose and pay-off for each element.

The overall sequence of the agenda should be designed with the four stages of open, explore, bargain and deal (see Figure 9.7) in mind and within this, referring back to the thinking around requirements, concession strategy and pain factors. The sequence needs to be considered strategically according to the outcome needed. It doesn't follow that the requirements with high pain should go first; in fact it might be better strategically to cover several small items first. In creating an agenda we are effectively defining the timeline for the entire negotiation strategy. There is no formula or model that can determine what to do here; instead it needs good old-fashioned brainpower. However, by this point in the planning there should be good clarity regarding our position, our strengths and weaknesses and the best way to move forward should by now be emerging from the mélange of information and insight.

Figure 10.5 Red Sheet step 12 (Part 2) – Event management and timeline (worked example)

12. EVENT MANAGEMENT AND TIMELINE

Event Agenda & Timing

Time	Negotiation Phase & Topics	Purpose	Process	Pay-Off	Tactics to be used	Trigger
09.30	Meet, greet & walk	Build relationship & observe cultural protocols	M.M. to wait in reception in order to meet and collect their team. He will then bring them to the room and then show them their seats in correct order. P.W. to do the introductions, exchange cards.	Formalities complete and the negotiation may start	Santa Claus	Welcome speech.
09.40	Introduction and exchange business cards and gift.					
09.45	Opening statement and welcome speech.					
09.50	Test negotiationality;	…to understand how much their proposal might be negotiable	Initial conditioning & invite them to make suggestions for improvement for U.K, questioning to find the cracks.	We will know whether or not we have reached their L.O.O	Find the cracks and Lines in the sand	When welcome is complete
10.30	Create a basis to give an easy concession later.	To create a decoy	Use the topic of minimum production runs to suggest this is a big issue. It will be a big deal to them due to set-up we will concede later.	Score set for future concession.	The Decoy	When we have established if there is movement
11.00	Price discussion	To secure agreement individually and then as a complete package	Work on: 1. Main Assembly Price 2. Mem. Boards 3. Big Picture 4. Transition Time 5. Use Decoy	Agreement for parts of negotiation in place.	Facts & Data Big Picture Big Picture Salami Slicing	When the decoy is secured
12.00	Payment terms.	To secure just one more thing	To secure just one more thing re: lead times, see if we can agree today	Negotiation complete.	Columbo For a deal today	When the rest of the deal is agreed

The recommended way of developing an agenda is to use the 3P format, so named as for each topic we consider the 'Purpose, Process and Pay-off' for that subject. While this might seem over the top, developing a 3P agenda drives the discipline of considering why each session is important, what outcomes we hope for and the way each session will run. Adding potential tactics and triggers makes this a comprehensive piece of negotiation planning. Figure 10.5 gives an example.

When sending an agenda to the supplier, consider carefully what gets shared. Clearly sharing tactics, the actual 'purpose' or 'pay-off' would give away our position to the supplier. Therefore agendas for transmission to the supplier should be prepared separately. As we saw earlier, sending the supplier an agenda can provide a great opportunity for conditioning, especially if the 3P format is used where 'purpose' and 'pay-off' can be written to set expectations. Furthermore, if the sequence is important, then the agenda can claim this in advance.

Keep in mind the fact that we are not only forming an agenda but defining our approach to how we will manage and remain in control of the negotiation event.

Closing the negotiation

When agreement is reached close the negotiation. The longer discussions are permitted to roll on the greater the likelihood of revisiting points where there is already agreement or at least no disagreement. The aim here is therefore to attempt to close as soon as agreement is reached. Plan how to close in advance including how to summarize and agree actions and next steps. In Chapter 12 we will explore how to spot when to close when negotiating. A summary of key pre-event techniques is given in Figure 10.6.

Actually doing it

Red Sheet steps 11 and 12 – Preparation, event management and timeline

Purpose of these steps

Steps 11 and 12 are concerned with planning and executing the negotiation event itself, incorporating any cultural changes we need to make (from step 4B), to provide the route map for the event. Figure 10.1 gives an example of

▶

pre-event planning and Figures 10.4 and 10.5 provide examples of the plan, agenda and timeline for negotiation event management. The templates can be found in the Appendix.

Completing step 11

1 Start by listing all the event-planning actions and assign individuals and deadlines to these actions. Ensure the individuals accept their actions.

2 Complete the communications plan by listing the various key messages and identifying the stakeholders or groups of stakeholders who need to be engaged with. Identify the media or means by which each message will be communicated.

3 Determine supplier pre-conditioning messages and publish internally and with the supplier as needed.

4 Determine the internal elevator speech and communicate to key stakeholders.

Completing step 12 (parts 1 and 2)

1 Determine the event start and finish times, and duration.

2 Determine the room layout and seating plan (assuming there is control over this).

3 Determine the event and opening tactics.

4 Determine the opening statement.

5 List the topics for discussion in the desired sequence and assign estimated timing. For each, complete the agenda 3Ps and determine any tactics to be used and any triggers to use each tactic.

Figure 10.6   Winning techniques – Pre-event

Winning Techniques – Pre-event

11 On your turf

If you can control the event, have them come to you. A negotiation on your 'home turf' gives you a natural psychological advantage. If you can't control the location, try and incorporate something that negotiates on your terms eg to your timing, on the day of your choosing etc.

12 Pre-condition

Work to pre-condition them in advance so as to set expectations in their minds around the outcomes you are seeking, and factors that might be driving things (eg organizational changes, times are tough etc). Ensure everyone in your organization is aligned and on message.

13 Role play in advance

Practice the negotiation beforehand, especially if negotiating as part of a group. Take time to think how they will approach it, what things they might say. Agree how you will respond, practise and role play in advance. If possible, sit in the chair they will sit in and imagine you are them.

14 Manage the meeting and great

If you can, manage the meeting and greeting of your opponent. If they are coming to you, manage their first impressions and how they are greeted. use initial interaction to calibrate their body language. If not on your turf, plan how you will first engage on them.

15 Control the room

If you have control over the venue, control the room and plan in advance where you will sit, and how you want them to be seated. Don't leave it to chance or allow a situation where they can decide. Instead organize it so they are seated where you want them. Consider any cultural requirements.

Winning event tactics and techniques   11

Negotiation is about process, personality and repertoire and this chapter explores what repertoire is, why it is important and how to develop and deploy a strong repertoire of winning tactics and techniques for any negotiation and any stage of a negotiation.

Pathway questions addressed in this chapter

19 What tactics and techniques will help me be successful?

Red Sheet steps covered in this chapter

11 and 12

Build your repertoire

A repertoire is a stock of items that a performer knows or is prepared to perform; it is a supply of skills or behaviours that a person habitually uses.

The UK comedian and game show host Bob Monkhouse famously had a joke for every situation. When he died in 2003, at the end of more than four decades of appearing on British TV, he had come to be regarded as a comedy legend. However, those who knew him tell of a man who felt he lacked the same natural comedic ability as other comedians of the time. Bob Monkhouse gained his advantage by developing a huge repertoire of jokes and comedic ideas that he catalogued and indexed in a series of hard-backed volumes. The compilation came to represent a life's work and accompanied him everywhere he went, constantly being added to, learnt and re-learnt. The result on stage or in front of the camera was the ability to recall and deliver a joke about any topic on demand. When the books were stolen in 1995 the loss was so great that Mr Monkhouse immediately offered a £10,000 reward. They were returned safely 18 months later.

Repertoires become pivotal tools that enable performers to do what they do with confidence, as they know they have something to call on to get them out of any situation. Committing things to writing is a great discipline because it helps deepen our repertoire and provides something we can revise to aid recall. However, it is the repertoire we carry in our minds that is important and any written document can only ever be an 'aide-memoire' to help learn and remember. It would be somewhat unusual during a negotiation to ask for a moment to consult a notebook for a suitable tactic to use. Developing a negotiation repertoire is therefore about building a mental library of tactics, techniques, behaviours, styles, gestures, learnings, powerful phrases, things to say and things to do. All these things should be selected according to what works and also determined by experience, observation or research, and stored in a way so as to enable future recall. Keeping a notebook or file can help; however, some of the best negotiators would say they have never done this, but rather will describe ways they simply remember the various approaches they use or put it all down to 'experience'.

Our personal repertoire defines our negotiation style but there is no magic reference book for such a thing; instead repertoire building is a personal journey. Cohen (1997) describes negotiation style as a 'family of possibilities rather than a rigid and invariant pre-selection', suggesting that repertoire is more than a mental library – it is also about learning what to use when and so making us more effective in different situations. Therefore as a repertoire develops so too does negotiation capability. Within this book a range of tactics and techniques are provided; these are in no way definitive but rather a launching-off point for personal repertoire development. The rest is down to you.

Choosing the right tactic or technique

Neither this, nor any other book, can truly do justice to what exactly we should do in the eye of the storm, in the midst of a tough negotiation. As a negotiation plays out, each party will deploy tactics and techniques among the exchanges and interactions designed to win or realize desired outcomes. Familiarization with the use of common tactics and the ability to spot and counter these when used by the other party is essential.

This chapter provides the 50 individual tactics (including 15 counter-measure tactics). A further 50 winning techniques are also included in this and other chapters. Together, the 100 tactics and techniques provide every-thing a negotiator could ever need. However, bear in mind that it is not about how many tactics can be squeezed in, it is about deploying the right tactic at the right time.

50 winning tactics

I will cover each of the 50 tactics over the following sections. They are organized according to the four phases of negotiation (Figure 11.1).

Figure 11.1   Complete list of negotiation tactics and countermeasures

Opening tactics

In the last chapter we explored the opening statement to kick things off and after that the negotiation begins; but how, with what? If you go to an auction then things start once the auctioneer invites people to agree to an open-ing bid level. In a negotiation, however, there may be a reluctance to make the first move. If they lead then we can follow. If we need to lead then the starting point is always our negotiation 3P agenda based upon the conces-sion strategy and therefore should reflect how we want to approach the discussions, eg small things first or go straight for the big thing and so on.

There are some specific opening tactics that can help when used in conjunction with the concession strategy and these are given in Table 11.1.

Tactics to explore positions

Once things get moving, the early stages involve each party attempting to understand each other's LDOs. Our LDOs represent a vital intelligence for the other party. They will have attempted to anticipate what our LDOs might be before the negotiation; however, once the negotiation commences they will want to 'smoke out our LDO'. If they can do this then all they need to do is maintain a hard position designed to make us believe our LDO is unachievable in the hope it will force us to reconsider our position and perhaps even go beyond the LDO we had set (Figure 11.2).

Figure 11.2 Tactic – Smoking out the LDO

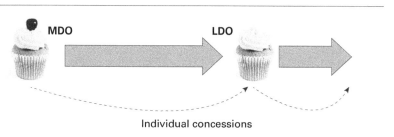

Individual concessions

There are many tactics that they might use to try and discover our LDO, and these are the same tactics we can use to attempt to ascertain their LDO. Hypothetical questions test what might be possible, apparently mishearing what was said in favour of a position a step closer, or testing for cracks in their positions all help. Table 11.2 outlines some tactics for exploring positions. Exploring is about testing positions and it is the reactions that are provoked that often reveal more than what is said. Later I will cover body language, but, for now the most important thing to bear in mind during the explore phase is to seek to prevent giving the game away by non-verbal reaction, but to watch theirs carefully.

Table 11.1 Tactics and techniques: tactics to open

Tactic	How it works and how to deploy	Countermeasures if used against you
 1 Santa claus Use to soften them at the outset	One party opens by giving a gift to the other, the principle being that any gift creates a sense of obligation in the other. This can take two forms: **1** A real gift – in some countries there are cultural reasons why gift giving is expected. Many companies also have rules preventing gifts above a certain value so prior research is needed. Giving a gift makes it difficult for them to then start being hard with you. Make it something of low intrinsic value that is relevant to you and your visit. When I negotiate overseas I often take some British tea or perhaps some fudge from Cornwall, where I was born. Always ask permission to give the gift 'would you mind if I give a gift from where I come from?' **2** The gift of a concession – same principle as giving a real gift applies but here you are offering an upfront concession with no conditions. Choose something you know they want and is easy to give: 'First, I know that you have requested a price increase on this item due to rising costs, and I want to start by saying that we are happy to agree to this.' However, ensure your gift doesn't jeopardize the rest of your negotiation. Note: real gifts tend to be received personally while concessions benefit the organization. This can change the impact of the gift. **Watch out for:** Gifts of value that would fall outside of any corporate rules on what can be accepted. Don't be offended if they say they cannot accept.	• First decide if it is appropriate to you to accept the gift (within any corporate policy on such matters). If not, then either politely thank them but explain you are unable to accept or follow any corporate rules for such occurrences, eg many companies pool such gifts and then raffle them for charity. • If you are able to accept the gift then decide if you want to. It is usually polite to accept and so you should thank them, ask them a question or two about the item and then remove it from the table, putting it 'out of sight and mind' and get down to business as usual. • If you decide not to accept the gift, perhaps because it is not appropriate as you are about to conduct a hard value-claiming negotiation, then politely decline, finding an appropriate reason for doing so.

Table 11.1 *continued*

Tactic	How it works and how to deploy	Countermeasures if used against you
START 2 Easy start Use to start with something that will bring both parties together	Here the difficult items are kept back and instead, one party leads by opening discussions regarding a point where the other party is expected to agree and where there can be collaborative discussions about the outcome. This will engender trust and break the ice before moving onto the bigger, more difficult topics. **Watch out for:** Them 'setting it aside' as they want to talk about the bigger topics first in which case you're off and running.	Unless you have a time pressure, go with it.
3 Full reveal Use when under time pressure or to win someone over and initiate relationship building by a display of upfront honesty and transparency	This is a high-risk opener and one that I used to believe belonged to inexperienced negotiators; however, having had this done to me successfully several times I now think it has its place if you intend to build a relationship. One party opens by laying out what they are able to offer in its entirety or perhaps keeping only one thing back. It is offered with some conditioning such as, 'Let me just cut to the chase and give you my best offer.' The other side will of course believe this is just an opening shot and will push for more. Here, if one thing was kept back it can be given. Then the first party just holds firm to 'This is the best I can offer.' Soon the other party will catch on and once the surprise has subsided the full reveal will have the same effect as a gift. **Watch out for:** Them refusing to accept that this is your final position, in which case suggest that they can go away and think about it or set a deadline for them to decide.	Test if this is really a full reveal or just a tactic by looking for cracks that suggest there is more, in which case keep negotiating. If it is real then accept it.

Tactic	How it works and how to deploy	Countermeasures if used against you

4 It's non-negotiable

Use to take a hard line from the outset that suggests you are not prepared to give any concessions | One party opens by making it clear the position is non-negotiable and the meeting is a courtesy only.

The tactic works by seeking to remove the basis for any negotiation in the first place. If there is no negotiation then there are no concessions. Remember, when parties normally agree to come to the table they are in effect signalling they are ready to give some sort of concession.

This tactic can be deployed to maintain a non-negotiable position or as an opening gambit to assert an initial position. Either way it is a hard-line position, and with it comes the risk that the other party walks away. However, it can have its place, and can be a very powerful tactic to secure your MDO if used carefully for certain scenarios. This tactic is frequently used by lawyers and retailers.

It's non-negotiable can work when

1   The party holds all the power and the other has no or little choice.
2   The other has already signalled some sort of keen willingness to agree (eg emotional attachment to an outcome).
3   When there is a policy or the terms are set by a *higher authority* and cannot be challenged (eg buying something in a shop).

When using non-negotiable as an initial position to assert some power, apply it carefully in a way that leaves a crack for the other to prise open. Use language such as 'I'm happy to talk about this but I don't see that we can give anything further on this' – such language doesn't completely close the door and provides hope on the other.

Watch out for:
Them walking away or damaging a relationship if this is important. | • Ask 'so why are you here?' – the fact that they have 'come to the table' suggests they might be prepared to negotiate after all.
• Try to establish why it is non-negotiable and attempt to remove obstacles.
• Look for cracks in their position (see *find the cracks* tactic).
• Call their bluff and play your BATNA. |

Bargaining tactics

The process of bargaining happens when parties have a feel for what each other might want, although in practice this is never fully understood and good negotiators can always hold back a surprise or two. During the bargain phase parties have shifted into testing what it would take to reach agreement, either for individual requirements or for the entire negotiation. They may even have begun to agree on certain things. During the bargain stage parties also continue to explore each other's positions.

There are many bargaining tactics, and all work in the same way: to get the other party to a point where they agree in full. How bargaining tactics are used can make all the difference to the outcome. These tactics can also work against us if we don't spot and counter them. For example, it might seem harmless and even helpful to agree to a seemingly small concession, and then perhaps another one, but if the other party is using a tactic called 'salami slicing' then their aim is to secure our agreement to a series of small concessions (slices) and when these dry up go after the big stuff. It is easy to believe that the small trades are the main event, but they are not (Figure 11.3).

Figure 11.3   Tactic – Salami slicing

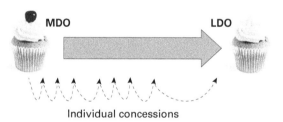

Individual concessions

Another common bargaining tactic is 'you're hurting me'. Here one party creates the illusion of an LDO some way away from their actual LDO designed to make us believe there is little room for negotiation. By keeping concessions tight and diminishing, and showing pain when conceding, a good bit of acting can make the other party believe they have reached the bottom. It seems this is the tactic most used by the domestic plumbers and builders I've encountered who will negotiate using deliberate displays of suffering at having to concede, finishing with a sharp intake of breath as if to say, 'OK... this is my final price but you're hurting me here' (Figure 11.4). Table 11.3 defines these and other common tactics and techniques used for concessions.

Table 11.2 Tactics and techniques: tactics to explore positions

Tactic	How it works and how to deploy	Countermeasures if used against you
5 Smoke out their LDO Use to try to maximize your outcomes Typically used early on within the 'explore' phase	One party attempts to find out where the other's LDO might lie. This tactic works by making the other party believe they have misjudged their position, making them question their LDO and be forced to reveal 'they can go no further'. **How to use this tactic:** **1** Get them to reveal what they want. **2** Display incredulity at the prosperousness of their position (making them question their LDO). **3** Secure agreement that there is room for manoeuvre. **4** Encourage them to make 'more sensible' proposals so you can begin discussions. **5** Eventually, make an absurd proposal (likely to be beyond their LDO). **6** Move, only very slowly, from this point towards them. **Watch out for:** False LDO reveals by the other: 'I can go no further', keep pushing to test this until you see their pain is real.	• Carefully manage what you reveal, avoid leading if possible but when you do remember you are drawing a 'line in the sand' which will anchor future discussions from this point. • Remember absurd proposals and displays of incredulity are all part of the act. Don't be fooled. • Stay calm, maintain your position, hold fast to your LDO and keep reinforcing your arguments or difficulties in moving. • Don't doubt yourself! • Create a 'false LDO' for them to find but make them work for it and make it appear painful for you to go that far.

Table 11.2 *continued*

Tactic	How it works and how to deploy	Countermeasures if used against you
6 "IF..." **Hypothetically speaking** Use to leverage movement when the other side is being intransigent and help smoke out their LDO Used in explore and bargain phases to test potential points of agreement	One party asks a hypothetical question to test if the other party might agree to something. Because it is just a hypothetical question there is no commitment and so it is easier for the other party to answer. For example, 'If I could find a way to accommodate some of your price increase request would you bring forward the timescales here?' **How to use this tactic:** 1 Determine the potential trade you are prepared to make and what you want from them. 2 Ask them as a hypothetical question, 'If I do this, would you do that?' The response you get will determine if this is a real possibility or not. 3 Keep asking hypothetical questions to test different scenarios. 4 Use the intelligence you gain to bargain further and help shape the deal. 5 Use a summary of the hypothetical points of agreement to move towards a deal. **Watch out for:** Giving your position away. Despite not committing, hypothetical questions mean you are still revealing your position; be cautious.	• Decide whether to play along or deflect. • If you play along remember that the question is designed to get you to reveal your position; manage responses carefully in line with your concession strategy and the message you want to give. • Alternatively deflect the question by not answering but changing the subject and/ or asking your own hypothetical question.

Tactic	How it works and how to deploy	Countermeasures if used against you
7 Lines in the sand Use to establish the region within which their LDO lies	One party is encouraged, or even voluntarily, states what they want as if 'putting a line in the sand'. Often questions like 'Will you make me an offer? What price will you accept?' or 'What are you prepared to pay?' are used here. Once a line in the sand is made, this then anchors all future discussions around that point. For example, consider the sale of a bicycle: Buyer: 'How much do you want for it?' Seller: 'Make me an offer...' Buyer: 'OK, I'm prepared to pay £50.' Seller: [Guffaws] 'That's a low offer; it cost £150 new and I've kept it in good condition. It has to be worth £80.' Buyer: 'The most I can offer is £70.' Seller: 'OK, let's split the difference at £75?' Buyer: 'Done' In this example the buyer walks away feeling he has struck a good deal and negotiated well. However, what if the seller had started believing he would do well to get £40 for the bicycle? By getting the other party to lay out their position, imagine his pleasant surprise when they started with a price of £50. He would have known that if they started with this offer then they would likely go much higher; all he had to do was get them there. Once a line in the sand is made it hands power to the other party. Sometimes it is necessary or unavoidable to make the first line; however, provided this is done recognizing future discussions will be anchored to this point, then it can be used to an advantage. **Watch out for:** Very high or very low offers and cultural differences. In Europe and the United States the first offer is often only 10–20 per cent away from where it ends up. In Russia and parts of the Middle East the first line is often less than 10–20 per cent of where it ends up.	• Resist if possible being the first to put a line in the sand but instead encourage them to do this first. • If you do need to lead then understand the cultural 'distance' between the first offer and the expected final position. • If they insist you 'make an offer' then make an outrageous high or low offer. When they flinch blame them for inviting you to make the offer and use humour if appropriate. Work back slowly from your outrageous offer, encouraging them to tell you what they want.

Table 11.2 *continued*

Tactic	How it works and how to deploy	Countermeasures if used against you
8 Find the cracks Use to test where a position might be prised open further	When a party is holding firm to a particular position on a requirement, the other party tests to see exactly how real this position is or where there is a 'crack' that can be prised open. The tactic works by removing the other party's position from the immediate context of the negotiation and placing it in a new hypothetical context, with either a new hypothetical benefit available or current problem solved if they conceded further. A test question then asks if they would agree to a further concession in these new circumstances. Because the question is hypothetical it is easy to answer and difficult to deflect but in doing so they reveal a crack and the fact that there is room to move. For example: Supplier: 'It is impossible to improve on my offer any further; as it is we are anticipating increases in overhead costs at our overseas facilities and currently we can't predict the scale of these.' Buyer: 'So imagine we had a different contract with a mechanism to provide for genuine cost increases so you don't need to build risk protection into the price, then an improved position would be possible right?' **Watch out for:** Them taking your hypothetical suggestion and making it a real offer. Remember, it's just a test question at this point so don't commit yet.	• Recognize what they are doing and decide if you want to play along; if so then when you reveal a crack make it conditional upon them hypothetically giving you something in return. • If you don't want to show a crack then deflect the question by either refusing to answer, answering with another 'find the crack' question or noting it to come back to later.

Tactic	How it works and how to deploy	Countermeasures if used against you
9 Instant replay Use to check where you've got to and what has been agreed or decided so far	One party asks to pause and proceeds to recap or replay their understanding of where the discussions have led to so far. Crucially, however, this should be done as if you are replaying events from their standpoint, as if them. This allows testing of understanding and provides the opportunity to check assumptions about their position. **How to use this tactic:** 1 At key points ask to pause proceedings and suggest you would like to summarize where you think the discussions have got to. 2 Summarize the key points of discussion 'as if them', eg, 'You stated that... you expressed concern about...' and so on. 3 Don't be afraid to embellish some statement with suggestions of their motives to see if they agree or correct you. 4 Ask them to confirm they agree with your recap. If they agree, it is harder for them to change their story later on. **Watch out for:** Their body language... do they agree or are there any signs of discomfort?	• Let them do this but watch your body language carefully. Show visible agreement where they have summarized as you want them to see things. • If their replay is not accurate then correct them. • If they add or adapt what was discussed more in their favour they are testing you; ensure you correct them. • Show visible signs of puzzlement if they are replaying incorrectly.

Table 11.2 *continued*

Tactic	How it works and how to deploy	Countermeasures if used against you
10 The mishear Use to test their comfort, acceptance or otherwise for a particular position and drive one step further towards their LDO	This is a variant of 'instant replay' except one fact is deliberately changed to an outcome that is more favourable to you. Crucially only one fact is changed and the degree of change would equate to what you believe would be an acceptable concession on their part. Rounding up or down figures can work nicely here too. The other party will either correct you or, if the new point is still within their range, may let it slide or they may not notice. If you are challenged then you can apologize for 'mishearing'; otherwise all future discussions proceed from this new point and it is difficult for them to challenge later as you can then remind them or 'cry foul'. For example, if the proposed price has already been discussed at £110, then your recap might say '… and in terms of price we are at or around the £100 mark…' **How to use this tactic:** 1 Use the instant replay technique but change one fact in your favour by a reasonable step. 2 Ensure you recap without drawing any special attention to the bit that has changed. 3 If they call it out, apologize and correct yourself; if not use this figure from now on. 4 Ask them to confirm they agree with your recap. **Watch out for:** Them returning to their original position and claiming they had not agreed to it.	• Correct them immediately; don't allow your position to slide unless you are in control.

Tactic	How it works and how to deploy	Countermeasures if used against you
11 Cherry picking Use to devalue their offer, unbundle any 'value adds' they might have and establish what is important to them	One party attempts to pick out or 'cherry-pick' only certain aspects of the negotiation for discussion, the remainder appearing to be of little interest (even if this is not the true position). This forces the supplier to either agree to go along with the reduced scope or to resist and question. If they resist, they might reveal other elements that are important to them or perhaps the complete bundle gives them an advantage, locking you in to them in some way. **How to use this tactic:** 1 Signal your interest in specific elements and disinterest in others. Do not rule them out, just leave as a suggestion for now. 2 Watch their reaction and how they respond. 3 If the excluded items are important to you come back to them later, possibly even making them believe you are helping them out. **Watch out for:** Them calling your bluff and removing them from the discussion. Don't react; come back to it later when you can suggest 'things have changed'.	• Suggest that you are entirely open to remove certain components from the discussion but suggest this has an impact on the remainder and so it changes your position. • If they have removed something important from the discussion, don't react (they may be watching for you to do this). Remember instead that you can come back to it and ask for it to be brought back onto the table as a condition of a later trade. You don't need to agree to anything until you are happy with the entire deal.

Figure 11.4   Tactic – You're hurting me

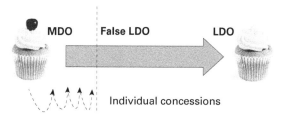

Deal-closing tactics

Closing the deal is a crucial part of negotiation and a phase that is frequently underestimated. Knowing how to close, but more importantly when to close, is a skill. The right moment is determined by many factors and most people inadvertently reveal when they are ready though their body language and their eyes. I will come back to how this works later. However, inexperienced negotiators tend to keep going beyond this point as if waiting for the other party to make a move. The longer this goes on the more power passes to the other party as they will get an increasing sense that they are in control and they will have too much time to think about arguments and alternatives.

In the early days of the life insurance industry, before financial regulation, salesmen had a well-developed technique: first, be likable and win trust; second, engender feelings of fear and guilt at the prospect of leaving loved ones unprovided for, should the worst happen; and third, give them a way out by handing them a form to sign and a pen. Most would sign there and then, but those who chose to think about it instead were much less likely to sign.

Deal-closing tactics are tactics designed to tip the balance towards agreement and these work when the other side is close to being ready to agree. If they are used too early, they will fail; however, all is not lost as the use of a deal-closing tactic simply serves to continue the exploration process. Table 11.4 provides tactics for deal closing.

Dirty tactics

This section would be incomplete without some dirty tactics, and there are plenty; the only question is whether or not to use them. Whether a tactic is dirty or not is a matter of personal and cultural judgement and what would

Table 11.3 Tactics and techniques: bargaining tactics

Tactic	How it works and how to deploy	Countermeasures if used against you
12 Big picture Use to avoid getting stuck in lots of points of detail Used mainly in the bargain and deal phases	One party suggests that rather than focus on all the different points of detail (the negotiation requirements) discussions should focus on agreeing the 'big picture', ie one single agreement that covers everything. **How to use this tactic:** 1 Name the problem: 'We're getting stuck in the points of detail.' 2 Secure agreement to go 'big picture'. 3 Move proposals to discuss respective positions; it is likely that the party suggesting 'big picture' will need to lead on making a proposal. 4 Be prepared to give the other side time to check their position. **Watch out for:** Not being informed. You can only do 'big picture' if you truly understand your big picture MDO and LDO.	• Unless you have planned for this scenario (ie have MDO and LDO worked out) then ask for a time-out to consider your position. • Get them to make the first proposal. • Don't be afraid to move away from 'big picture' to covering detailed points of negotiation if you are not getting what you want. • Don't be afraid to ask for one more thing once you have reached agreement on the big picture.

Table 11.3 *continued*

Tactic	How it works and how to deploy	Countermeasures if used against you
13 You're Hurting Me *Use to create the impression to the other side that they are asking too much and you are at, near to or beyond your LDO.* Used in bargain and deal phases to secure better outcomes	Create a 'false LDO' and project the impression there is no more to give, to compel them to concede more or stop seeking concessions. To escalate the position, make it appear like their demands hurt you and they are pushing too far, maybe show signs of physical discomfort. **How to use this tactic:** 1 Determine a false bottom LDO that is much closer to our MDO than our real LDO, which must remain hidden. 2 Allow the other side to smoke out our false LDO, but don't make it too easy; it needs to be believable and we have to make them work to reach it for this tactic to work. 3 Once there, hold our position firm, appearing visibly distressed by how hard this concession is for us. 4 Continue to show distress and discomfort at the deal, showing them you can go no further. **Watch out for:** • Them having BATNAs we hadn't anticipated. • Taking things too far and making them walk away. • Watch our body language carefully, using it to project what we want it to say.	• Confirm that this is what they are doing by pushing a bit further and watching their reactions. • Watch for them acting distressed. • When they make their 'painful concession', thank them, but don't be afraid to keep negotiating, or to make a deal-closing offer of our own. • If all else fails, give them an ultimatum or use a BATNA.

Tactic	How it works and how to deploy	Countermeasures if used against you
14 Take it or leave it *Use to try and make the other side close on your terms by appearing to remove the opportunity to negotiate.* Used in 'bargain' and 'deal" phases to drive agreement to conclusion.	Either from the outset or after allowing some concessions, take a firm position and be clear you will concede no further so they have to either 'Take it or Leave it.' Hold firm, don't give any hint of weakness and be prepared for them to walk away. **How to use this tactic:** 1 Use to take a hard position, either from the beginning, or after a few concessions have been made. 2 Ensure we have a good BATNA before deploying this tactic. 3 Take a firm position, making it clear that you aren't willing to give anything else. 4 Be patient, and hold firm. 5 Be prepared to walk away if necessary. **Watch out for:** • Them having BATNAs you hadn't anticipated. • Taking things too far and making them walk away. • Watch their body language carefully.	• Confirm that this is what they are doing by arguing our position; watch for them simply restating their position. • Introduce a time pressure or other reason to move forward. • Suggest that we aren't getting what we need here, so we may as well adjourn if we can't move forward. • Don't appear desperate to reach an agreement; this is the sign they are watching for. Stay calm and act like we have the best BATNA in the world. • If all else fails, give them an ultimatum or use a BATNA.

Table 11.3 *continued*

Tactic	How it works and how to deploy	Countermeasures if used against you
15 It means little to me Use to try and encourage the other side to give a concession Used in bargain phase to make individual agreements	One party proposes a trade, perhaps using a hypothetical question to test first, and in doing so offers something in return for something. What is being offered is easy to give and perhaps of little value to that party but could be highly valued by the other party. For example, a buyer could offer contractual provision for the seller to be permitted to publish they are a 'preferred supplier to...' and have access to the brand to use on promotional material. **How to use this tactic:** 1 Consider their potential requirements for the negotiation and what would be attractive to them. Determine what would be easy for you to give. 2 Propose this as your offer for a specific thing in return. Remember to 'sell' the benefits of what you are offering and make it believable! **Watch out for:** Offering something that really has no value in return for something of incredible value as this could damage any trust you have built up.	• Decide if the thing that is being offered is of value to you and if so, is it worth the trade. • If it is not then propose a different trade. • Return to the thing they offered at the end and 'sweep it up' into the final deal. After all it is of little value to them so they will most likely be happy to throw it in.

Tactic	How it works and how to deploy	Countermeasures if used against you
16 The nibble Use to secure a small concession from the other	One party asks for a small concession that is easy for the other party to give away and secures agreement for that concession. The nibble works when the concession in question is something that the other party is unlikely to question, can and will easily give, and for which they might not necessarily require something in return. The request should be framed as if by giving the concession it will move things closer to a deal. Key to the success of this is that agreement is secured for the nibble, making it difficult for the other party to renege later as the 'nibble has been banked'. Successive use of nibbling becomes the *Salami Slicing* tactic. Other related tactics include *The Columbo* which is an end-of-negotiation nibble. **Watch out for:** Them placing a value on the nibble that doesn't match yours and asking for a trade in return. If this happens, backing away from the nibble might be the best course of action.	• Avoid making a firm agreement to a nibble, but instead agree in principle and leave room to reverse. • Ask for something in return. • Agree in principle subject to getting everything on the table.

Table 11.3 *continued*

Tactic	How it works and how to deploy	Countermeasures if used against you
 17 Salami slicing Use to secure an overall advantage by driving a series of apparently small individual agreements; however, all the little things add up to a much bigger shift in position Used in bargain phase to make individual agreements	This is a step on from The Nibble and combines multiple nibbles. One party encourages the other to give a series of apparently small concessions but secures agreement on each along the way. The other party might be fooled into believing each small gift is influencing the outcome. Slowly all the little 'slices' build but then the real negotiation starts and the first party tackles the big things. The other party suddenly realizes they have already given too much away but it is too late as they have already agreed to these and so end up closer to their LDO than planned. **How to use this tactic:** 1 Put off discussing the main topics but find a series of small demands and ask the other to agree to them. Position the discussions as if you are helping them and the process by 'removing obstacles', eg 'Before we get to that, it would help if we are aligned on some things; can we just agree that...' 2 Keep finding new small points of agreement as if you are just remembering them. 'Oh... and there is just one more thing, can we just...' 3 Secure agreement from them for each point. 4 When this ceases to work move on to the main negotiation points. 5 Prevent the other party from revisiting what has been agreed. 'But we have agreed these things already. I would have a problem if you were going back on this.' **Watch out for:** Conditional agreement; if the other party leaves any way out this, the tactic becomes little more than an exploration of what is possible.	• Avoid giving any sort of signal of agreement along the way; reserve this until the end so you can make the deal on your terms considering the big picture. • Give non-committal responses that leave you with a way out, eg 'That is possible, let's talk about the other things and we can come back to that.'

Tactic	How it works and how to deploy	Countermeasures if used against you
18 Higher authority Use to make arguments irrelevant and create artificial boundaries	One party creates a constraint or reason why a certain action is necessary because it is policy, beyond their authority or mandated by a higher authority who is of course too important to participate in the negotiation and cannot be questioned. Call centres use this tactic when you ask for compensation: 'The most I am authorized to offer is £50 otherwise you would need to put the complaint in writing to my manager'. **How to use this tactic:** 1 Create a plausible immovable obstacle that is 'above your authority' or has apparently been set by a 'higher authority'. This could be a budgetary limit, company policy or edict, a safety consideration or an approval limit. **Watch out for:** Using a higher authority that the other party could challenge directly or has a relationship with or suggesting a problem that they could volunteer to solve.	• Prevent this at the outset of the negotiation by asking if the other party has the authority to act and make an agreement. If they say 'yes' then it is hard for them to use this against you later on. If they say 'no' then you could opt to suggest there is little point in continuing until all the right people are present. • Try to establish if the claim is genuine by watching their body language. • Challenge the higher authority or refuse to accept its validity. • Give the other party an ultimatum that they either need to find a way to overcome the obstacle or there is little point in continuing. • Be prepared to use your BATNA.

Table 11.3 *continued*

Tactic	How it works and how to deploy	Countermeasures if used against you
19 The Decoy Use to avoid giving too much away	One party creates a decoy by pretending to give great importance to an issue or requirement that is actually of little or no consequence. By maintaining the illusion, the issue can later be traded for a major concession from them but in reality little has been lost and the other side will believe they have traded equally. **How to use this tactic:** 1 Pick a requirement that is of little importance. 2 Develop a series of plausible arguments to make it seem important. 3 Deploy these, holding firm to your position and insisting the matter is important. Do not concede at this point but move on and return to this later and then offer a concession in return for a trade. **Watch out for:** Unbelievable arguments.	• If they are suggesting that something that you believe is trivial is very important, then don't challenge them but try to get behind what they are saying by asking questions around what is driving the importance here to see if their posturing is genuine. • Call their bluff by asking them to rank the importance of the requirement against another item that has already been discussed, eg 'Clearly we can only compromise so far, so is this more or less important to you than this other thing'. Implied here is the suggestion that you can accommodate their request but it will mean undoing what has been agreed.

Tactic	How it works and how to deploy	Countermeasures if used against you
20 Facts and data Use to give credibility to your arguments, strengthen your position, weaken theirs and compel the other to concede	One party makes arguments that are informed by pre-prepared facts and data. The arguments are deliberately thought out so as to disarm them and establish a position that is difficult to dispute. For example, a demand for a price reduction might be supported by commodity data that show raw material prices or labour rates have fallen recently or quality or performance data suggesting the supplier has been underperforming. Use facts and data to establish the general state of the marketplace that also give power. If they say you are misinformed then ask them to explain their understanding. **How to use this tactic:** 1 Do your research and develop your arguments. 2 Determine what outcome you want based upon facts and data but ensure you do the maths correctly. Remember if input costs change (eg raw material prices fall) then the degree of impact this could be expected to have depends upon how much of the finished goods or service price this represents. 3 Deploy your arguments and hold your position firm; if they contest what you are saying ask them to back it up with their data. Either they are bluffing or they have real data in which case understand their position and take a time-out to reconsider yours. **Watch out for:** Inaccurate data and falling into a data trap. If they are better informed, you have nowhere to go as you have already established the use of facts and data as a basis to agree an outcome.	• Be prepared and don't get taken by surprise; do your own data gathering and understand your position. • Anticipate what arguments they might use. • Develop counter arguments that allow you to acknowledge their position but trump it, eg 'You are correct, some raw material prices have decreased, however these account for less than 10 per cent of the selling price and despite this, oil and energy prices have increased by much more.' • Once you have established your counter arguments push hard for an agreement on your terms, as it will be hard for them to argue.

Table 11.3 *continued*

Tactic	How it works and how to deploy	Countermeasures if used against you
21 You need me Use to draw attention to their dependency on you	One party draws attention to factors that mean the other party is dependent in some way. At the heart of this is creating a fear, specifically of loss of something or missing out on something. A variant of this tactic is often used by sales people who might say things like 'This is a good opportunity for you right now' or 'Imagine how terrible things would be if something happened to you and you hadn't taken out this life insurance policy.' **How to use this tactic:** If possible, identify what the other party might need or value beyond the deal itself or identify if any particular loss could impact the other party and make the deal such that it takes away the risk of this loss. For example: 'Can you afford to risk not doing this with us and risk starting again with someone new when we know your business so well?' 'No one ever got fired for hiring [*enter big consultancy company name here*].' 'Remember, we are the only company who have this unique technology that you need.' **Watch out for:** Be aware who has the power in the situation before attempting this tactic. If you don't, then there may not be a dependency or this tactic may be used against you.	• Consider the dependency that is being conveyed; decide if it is real. If it is, then either: 1 Decide how much you value it and determine what you could do to remove or reduce this dependency (create an alternative). 2 Attempt to make the other side believe it is not so important to you after all. 3 Ensure the dependency is provided for within the deal.

be unthinkable for one person, or one situation, would be fair game for another. Furthermore, many would not hesitate to condemn you for choosing such tactics when they would happily do likewise. There are also degrees here and the tactic 'good cop/bad cop' can be played in a variety of ways ranging from 'gently' to 'interrogation standard'.

Dirty tactics reside in the domain of value-claiming negotiations, as, by their nature, they would be at odds with value creation. They tend to be used across both explore and bargain phases and often it is impossible to predict when someone might use them. The only help here is to ask ourselves: 'is there a solid reason why a dirty tactic would not be used?' If there isn't a good answer then trust no one. True relationships generally tend to prevent dirty tactics being used. Paradoxically when business is transacted in polychronic and collective cultures, the relationship facilitates agreement, but if the relationship is not firm or genuine then anything goes and ruthless dirty tactics can be fair game for those outside the favoured group.

The appropriateness of using dirty tactics is a personal choice as many necessitate lying or being aggressive, rude or ruthless. Care should also be given to whether such a tactic will help or hinder a negotiation. I once witnessed the lead negotiator play his BATNA early on when a dirty tactic was used against him. He simply got up and said, 'I'm sorry but I am no longer prepared to discuss this with you as you are behaving unethically, so this meeting ends here' and promptly walked out never to return. The other party, the rest of his team, and I, were left in the room to use the uncomfortable silence to gather our things. Use dirty tactics cautiously and only with full understanding of the risk. Table 11.5 provides some dirty tactics that could be used.

Don't forget the small things

Don't forget the small things; every point of engagement is an opportunity to project power and gather information. It is often the little things that can help here so when planning a negotiation take a moment to consider the details. Things to think about for face-to-face negotiations include:

- *What is visible?* Good negotiators can read upside down! It is a skill that can be learnt easily with practice and so it is likely they will attempt to read anything we place in front of us or write down. As a rule of thumb, assume everything that is on show can be read so conceal anything that they shouldn't see and shield it when referring to it. This also presents the opportunity to feed them misinformation and fool them into believing

Table 11.4 Tactics and techniques: deal-closing tactics

Tactic	How it works and how to deploy	Countermeasures if used against you
ONE MORE THING 22 *The Columbo* Use to secure one final small concession from the other side	Just at the point when the other party is ready to close and there appear to be no remaining obstacles and they are just waiting for you to signal your agreement, you simply say, 'Oh... just one more thing...' (the line made famous by the bumbling TV detective Columbo) and then you ask for one more final, but relatively insignificant concession. For this to work your request must be something that is easy for the other party to 'throw in' and it must appear that the entire deal might be lost if they don't comply. For example, if you are buying a car, once the deal is done and the salesman thinks you're about to sign you say, 'One more thing... will you throw in a tank of gas?' **How to use this tactic:** 1 As the negotiation unfolds, identify a small concession you would like and keep it out of the discussions until the end. 2 When you and the other party are apparently ready to agree and close, say, as if an afterthought, 'Oh... there is just one more thing...' and then ask for your concession. 3 If they say no then recommence negotiations and argue firmly for this last point. **Watch out for:** Them doing brinkmanship and adopting a 'take it or leave it' stance on you.	• Decide if the request is something easy for you to give and worth doing to close the deal. • If you do decide to go with it then make it conditional: 'OK, so I'll give you that but on the basis that that concludes our discussions and we now proceed.... Do you agree?' • If you are not prepared to give this final concession then take a firm line as if you are quite prepared to reopen discussion or even walk away. 'I'm sorry but we've reached the end of what I can give here, this is the best deal I am able to do'. Hold fast to this position.

Tactic	How it works and how to deploy	Countermeasures if used against you
23 Split the difference Use to bring an end to a negotiation by driving an apparent mutual concession Typically used when people are uncomfortable with negotiation	When parties are maintaining separate positions and continuing to bargain but not reaching agreement one party suggests they 'split the difference', in other words agree at a point midway between the two positions. For example, party 'A' says, 'The price is €150', 'B' says 'I'm only prepared to pay €100', so 'A' says, 'Let's split the difference and call it €125'. **How to use this tactic:** **1** At the point where you believe the other side is near to closing, and the mid-point between both positions would be acceptable to you, offer to 'split the difference'. **2** Ask as if you are suggesting a good idea to a friend, 'Why don't we split the difference?' or 'Let's split the difference.' **3** Sometimes it helps to follow the proposal with something that reinforces closure is near such as extending a hand ready to shake hands or suggesting 'And we can get you a purchase order today.' **Watch out for:** Your proposal revealing a new, lower LDO to them, giving them the chance to take you lower still. Either plan to hold fast to the new position or plan for further concessions past this point.	• If this is used early on in the negotiation chances are the other party is inexperienced and this may be their only tactic. Politely explain why that would be inappropriate with a reason to support it, but do use it as an opportunity to make a trade, eg 'It's not appropriate to get into common bartering but focus on the realities of our position. I'm prepared to…' • If used towards the end then decide if the proposed concession is acceptable in return for closure. If so, first try to offer a smaller concession instead by suggesting a new position close to the split point but slightly in your favour. If this fails then agree to split the difference as they have suggested.

Table 11.4 continued

Tactic	How it works and how to deploy	Countermeasures if used against you
24 The ogre Use to create a compelling reason for the other party to concede or agree	At the point where a party is being intransigent and holding firm to their position, the other party suggests that unless they are able to reach a satisfactory conclusion then 'the Ogre' will want to step in. 'The Ogre' is a real or imaginary individual who has an interest in the outcome and whose intervention would be catastrophic for the other side as he/she will be ruthless, unpredictable and would carry with him/her the real possibility of stopping proceedings dead in favour of an alternative. For this to work, the second party needs to progressively build up the notion that there is an ogre 'waiting in the wings' and that 'it is in both our interests not to get to that point where he comes in as it could stop everything dead.' **How to use this tactic:** 1 Determine who will be 'the Ogre'. Ideally, this is a real person – someone more senior and scary who needs to be fully briefed and prepared if you actually want to follow through. There must be a plausible reason for this person to potentially intervene, perhaps because he/she is a senior stakeholder. They must also have the apparent power to call a halt and do something different. 2 Throughout the negotiation signal the existence of this individual, why they are interested in what is happening and the possibility that this individual may want to intervene, but how it would be preferable for all if this didn't happen.	• Validate their claims – ask questions regarding the identity and interest of this other party and why he/she is not present in the negotiation. • If you know the individual and their claims are real, consider playing along to keep him/her out. • If you think it is a bluff then hold your position firm, appearing unfazed by their threats. • Turn the tables on them. 'It sounds like this individual is a key decision maker so I really think he/she should be brought in to hear what we have to say.'

Tactic	How it works and how to deploy	Countermeasures if used against you
	3 If you reach a deadlock suggest that you cannot report back with what is proposed and you will either need to bring 'the Ogre' in or reconvene another day with him/her present.	
	4 Follow through or just keep going as if you are 'on the verge' of bringing him/her in.	
	Watch out for:	
	Them knowing, or having a relationship with the individual who is 'the Ogre', who they know is nothing like you are portraying him/her.	

Table 11.4 *continued*

Tactic	How it works and how to deploy	Countermeasures if used against you
JAM **25** Jam tomorrow Use to provide a potential benefit to the other side if they agree	At the point when the other party is close to agreeing, a potential incentive is offered in the form of something that might happen in the future if they agree. This is a variant on the 'Trust' game, as the suggestion is not formalized as part of the negotiation but rather a personal commitment. For example, 'Look, if we can agree on this then I think it will put you in a good place later in the year when we negotiate the bigger thing.' **How to use this tactic:** 1 Identify a potential future benefit that you can suggest they receive. 2 Suggest this, being careful not to make any firm commitment but rather a hint of what might happen. 3 Decide if you will follow through later or if 'things will change'. **Watch out for:** Them asking you to commit to your suggestion; here you must prepare a deflection that suggests there can be no commitment but they need to take their chances.	• Quantify what they are suggesting. • Decide if the relationship is such that you wish to proceed based upon this suggestion; after all, implied with it is a sense of obligation to follow through. • If you are not comfortable then bring the suggestion into the negotiation as something to be formalized as part of the deal. If they resist then suggest their suggestion appears somewhat empty so they are not really offering anything. Continue to negotiate.

Tactic	How it works and how to deploy	Countermeasures if used against you

Tactic

26 For a deal today

Use to compel the other side to make a decision or close

Used towards the end of a negotiation in the 'deal' phase

How it works and how to deploy

One party creates some sort of deadline designed to compel the other into closing or making a decision. This is a classic tactic used by car salesmen who will offer you a special discount 'for a deal today' that is apparently only available today, designed to prevent you walking away to think about it. Negotiators will often use personal factors to trigger empathy in the other, eg 'Look, I'm under pressure from my boss to agree on this....'

How to use this tactic:

1 Create a plausible deadline and an incentive within the current deal if agreement can be reached by the deadline.

2 Make the offer; ensure they understand it is conditional on reaching agreement in time.

Watch out for:

The other side encouraging you to play this tactic as part of their smoking out your LDO.

Countermeasures if used against you

- Let them make the offer; it will give you vital intelligence regarding their lowest offer so far.
- Keep your options open; either:
  - Suggest you are not prepared or unable to agree now. They will most likely reiterate the fact that this is a time-bound offer; in response, suggest you will take your chances on that.

OR

  - If you are in a position to proceed then turn the tables and make a counter offer more in your favour 'for a deal today'.

Table 11.4 *continued*

Tactic	How it works and how to deploy	Countermeasures if used against you
 27 I'm leaving Use to create an ultimatum to act or not	If the negotiation is not making progress in the required direction, one party announces that they are not getting what they want and are therefore leaving. This could be accompanied by a build-up of displays of discomfort and some sort of emotional outburst. Once the party announces they are leaving they must immediately pack up and prepare to go and be prepared to then follow through. The premise of this tactic is that either they will stop you or you must be prepared to keep walking. You cannot easily return if they let you leave. **How to use this tactic:** 1 Decide the trigger point for trying this tactic. 2 Decide what you will do next if you actually end up walking out. 3 Build up shows of discomfort and perhaps some emotion before making your announcement, but keep calm and retain composure. 4 Use your 'packing-up time' to keep making a point about your position. 5 Apologize for the fact that you couldn't reach agreement then walk out. 6 If they stop you or come after you then recommence negotiation. **Watch out for:** 1 Them letting you leave. If so, keep going. 2 Playing this more than once; it is less likely to succeed the second time.	• Show no surprise but stay calm and seated, perhaps help them to pack up. • Give them one opportunity to stay but don't appear in any way needy. Say something like, 'We are of course disappointed that you feel the need to give up and leave. If you would like to stay, we would like to keep the discussions going as it felt like we were starting to make progress.' If they don't bite then respond with 'OK... well thank you for coming' and move to show them out. • Be prepared to reconvene if they change their mind.

Tactic	How it works and how to deploy	Countermeasures if used against you
28 Carried away by the moment Use to create a euphoric environment where hasty decisions are made	This is the same dynamic as you get in an auction situation where the pressure and exhilaration of the moment compels people to make rapid and perhaps ill-considered decisions. It is possible to create the same scenario in a negotiation. As discussions progress, one party starts getting excited about how the two parties will be working together and shares all sorts of ambitious end points that, together, they can achieve. As the enthusiasm is mirrored, the first party then makes a series of fast, excited suggestions of all the things that could happen, which include a series of things the other party will contribute to realizing the dream. If done well, the other party will get carried away by the moment and signal agreement to all sorts of things. **How to use this tactic:** 1 Pre-plan how you will build excitement and the requirements that will be slipped into the euphoria of the moment. 2 Determine who will do this and practise. Get the rest of the team on-board and briefed to help build enthusiasm too. 3 Deploy. **Watch out for:** Them qualifying their responses or back-tracking later.	• Join in, but keep your answers 'hypothetical' or as 'possible' courses of action and qualify them. Say things like, 'Well it could be possible' or 'If we can agree the right commercials then anything is possible' and so on.

Table 11.4 *continued*

Tactic	How it works and how to deploy	Countermeasures if used against you
29 'Yes… in principle' Use to signal broad or conditional agreement	One party lays out a position and asks the direct question 'Can you agree to this?' The other party answers 'Yes, in principle; however, there are some points of detail that would need to be worked out.' This prevents full agreement and keeps the door open to keep negotiating on all the other points. This should only be used when you are close to agreement and is powerful because it avoids saying 'no' but also doesn't fully say 'yes'. **How to use this tactic:** 1 When given an ultimatum that is nearly how you want it, signal conditional agreement. 2 Move to negotiate the other points on your terms and come back to full agreement only when you are ready. **Watch out for:** Them asking you to define precisely what is preventing full agreement. Have an answer prepared.	• Ask them to quantify what is preventing full agreement. 'Please tell me what needs to happen for you to agree unconditionally.' • Work on these points and keep returning to test agreement.

Tactic	How it works and how to deploy	Countermeasures if used against you
30 So we have a deal! Use to pre-emptively close the deal	When a negotiation reaches an advanced point, close to a deal, as final concessions are traded one party acts as though the deal has been done. This tactic needs to be accompanied by firm and decisive gestures that suggest closure. The tactic works by attempting to disarm the other side and prevent them from objecting in the hope they will be swept along by the moment and just agree. The gestures here are important. This tactic used to be used with shaking hands where people would rarely resist if you offer your hand to them. After Covid-19 this is less so. Instead consider actions that get them to signal agreement such as nodding at the right moment to get them to nod with agreement.	• Allow them to do this but at the point where they get you to either shake their hand or nod with them say something like 'It is great you want to close the deal but you're a little premature... I haven't agreed yet.' Then counter it with what you want: 'What I want to shake hands properly on is....'

How to use this tactic:

1 Identify the point where the deal is nearly finished but the other party may still want you to make some final concessions.

2 Smile, and (depending on the degree of physical contact that is appropriate) either reach out and shake the other party's hand or nod enthusiastically to encourage them to nod with you and say something like, 'OK... so we're agreed at one hundred euros... thank you. It's great we are going to work together.'

Watch out for:

Using the tactic too early. It only works when they are close.

Table 11.4 *continued*

Tactic	How it works and how to deploy	Countermeasures if used against you
31 Sign here! Use to make the deal irresistible by having the goods on the table	This tactic works by having a pre-determined offer ready there in the room to go so the other side can realize immediate benefit. **How to use this tactic:** 1 Prepare an offer in advance of the meeting. Set the deal at a point where you are closer to your MDO than theirs but not so far that they won't be tempted. 2 Confidently make an offer such as, 'I like this car but I'm not paying that price, I have £10,000 in cash in a bag here…. If you will do the deal at this price the cash is yours now.' Or say, 'If you can agree to this, here is the contract and I'll sign it now.' **Watch out for:** Whether the apparent benefit you are being told you are about to get actually exists or if there are further obstacles.	• Decide if the offer is too good to resist or not. If it is a good deal take it, otherwise push for a bit more (even if they say this is not possible) and then settle or walk away.

our LDO is at a certain point as per a figure deliberately written on the pad in front of us and the new figures we keep adding to it. It also helps to learn to read what their papers say and so this is a skill worth developing and can be practised in any business meeting to relieve the boredom.

- *Competitor's props?* Having something from a competitor visible (but not making it too obvious) can suggest we are talking to other suppliers also, even if this is not the case. This might be a report, document or something that bears a competitor's logo, but be ready for a challenge question and have an answer prepared. Such a tactic only really fits in value-claiming situations.

- *Visitors' book.* Most companies require suppliers to 'sign in'. Some companies still employ a traditional paper-based visitors' book with the history of prior visitors on display. Where this is the case it is fair game for any supplier to look back and see who else has been visiting. Data protection rules and modern electronic systems have resigned the visitors book to a place in history for many. However, a supplier visiting for a negotiation may not know this. Consider using the tactic of instigating a visitors, book left on display just for one day with receiving staff briefed about the need to have people attending the negotiation sign in.

- *Taxis and transfers.* A gesture of hospitality to organize taxis or transfers from an airport or train station can provide valuable intelligence. Negotiators frequently assume the negotiation has ended and they are safe once they have left the meeting and are on their way home in the taxi. They are likely to openly discuss how it went with one another or they will phone their boss. It doesn't take much to have a special relationship with the taxi company so their driver is briefed to listen and report back.

Using a secret code

Team-based negotiations can be chaos, especially when we have a team of enthusiastic negotiators each trying to make their mark and have their questions answered. Add to this misalignment in the team and it is all too easy to give our position away. For any team-based negotiation, agree who is leading and agree roles, rules and how each individual must act and behave in the room. However, things don't always go to plan. Team members can talk too much or start giving something away or miss vital clues within what is said. In addition, discussions might take an unexpected turn or a team member could spot a problem he or she must raise with the team leader. Teams need some sort of secret code system.

Table 11.5 Tactics and techniques: dirty tactics

Tactic	How it works and how to deploy	Countermeasures if used against you
32 KGB Use to get your way no matter what Typically used in hard value-claiming negotiations where lying and deceit are acceptable, where no future relationship is needed and the other party cannot easily walk away This is regarded as an unethical negotiation approach	This is a tactic used widely by the KGB. You negotiate hard with your opponent and you secure and signal clear agreement. Just as your opponent begins to relax, believing it is all over, you stage some sort of interruption prior to concluding the meeting. For example, pretend that your boss has asked you to step out for a moment, and when you return announce that the situation has changed and you begin negotiating all over again; however, this time you want much more. When the KGB used this tactic they would repeat it more than once with the sole intention of wearing down their opponent. **Warning** – this tactic involves lying and deceit; many would regard this tactic as somewhat unethical. It's good to understand it but be careful if you choose to use it. **How to use this tactic** 1 Negotiate to a conclusion. 2 Stage an intervention such as leaving the room to secure approval. 3 Suggest you need to revisit things, eg 'I'm really sorry but it seems I have been a bit hasty...' or 'It seems we have a problem....' 4 Recommence negotiations but now for increased demands. **Watch out for:** The other party walking away or using their BATNA.	• Resist fiercely the revisiting of what was agreed. • Use moral arguments to attempt to make them see they are acting unethically. • Resist giving any indication that your previous final position could be revised; hold your ground. • Attempt to take control of the event by calling a time-out. • If forced to revisit your position then trade hard and get something in return. • Remember this tactic is designed to 'wear you down' to your lowest point. Don't be afraid to use ultimatums. • Use your BATNA or walk away.

Tactic	How it works and how to deploy	Countermeasures if used against you
33 Good cop, bad cop Use to win trust while wearing the other party down so they just want to agree and get to the end	This classic police interrogation technique works well in negotiation if used carefully. One party plays the part of the 'bad cop' and is unpleasant, aggressive and perhaps even angry with the other party, attempting to wear them down with a succession of condemning arguments. The 'bad cop' then either leaves the room or is asked to back off by the leader and then the 'good cop' takes over, smiling, showing empathy and apologizing for the previous outburst. As the 'good cop' attempts to win over the opponent he/she then gently suggests considering agreeing to the 'bad cop's' demands but this time with new arguments, one of which is the implied threat that the bad cop will keep going. **How to use this tactic:** 1 Agree in advance who will play the good and bad cop roles. Agree arguments and trigger points. Agree how the bad cop will deliberately be 'stopped'. 2 Let it play out but watch body language carefully to gauge discomfort and thus how close to agreeing the opponent is. 3 Keep going until you get what you want. **Watch out for:** Them playing their BATNA or walking away.	• Remember this is a tactic; learn to spot it and don't be thrown off course by it. • Be deliberately calm and empathic towards the bad cop while maintaining a firm position. Use phrases such as, 'I'm sorry you feel that way but I'm afraid it doesn't change anything' and so on. • Use facts and data. • If things get too tough then call it out and suggest that you are not prepared to continue unless they start being more professional and abandon the cheap tactics.

Table 11.5 *continued*

Tactic	How it works and how to deploy	Countermeasures if used against you
34 Norman Bates Use to unsettle the other party with a show of discomfort designed to make them believe they have pushed too far	Named after the character in the movie *Psycho* who would be calm and collected one moment and suddenly flip into a knife-wielding psychopathic killer. This is perhaps a bit too strong for most negotiations, and so this tactic is about a deliberate and sudden change of behaviour by one individual, perhaps becoming more emotional or even a bit aggressive. This serves to make the other party believe they have pushed too far, thus unsettling them by creating a few seconds of shock, or perhaps even triggering the other party to become submissive or get aggressive back. **How to use this tactic:** **1** Agree in advance who will play Norman Bates, what the trigger will be and how you will close the charade out (eg time-out, someone calms him down etc). **2** Let it play out as agreed. **3** Immediately after, act like things have changed and demand the other side 'sees sense'. **Watch out for:** Poor and unconvincing acting. If you play Norman Bates, they must believe they have really made you angry. Leave out the knife, though.	• Sit back, watch, learn, and then calmly keep going as if nothing happened.

Tactic	How it works and how to deploy	Countermeasures if used against you
35 Brinkmanship Use to aggressively pursue a particular requirement to the point where the other party must either agree or walk away	One party outlines their demands and maintains this position, perhaps aggressively, without compromise, effectively pushing the other party to the 'brink' or edge of what that party is willing to accommodate. Brinksmanship is about convincing the other party they have no choice but to accept the offer and there is no acceptable alternative to the proposed agreement unless they are prepared to walk away. **How to use this tactic:** 1 Determine the position and the outcome you require. 2 Lay out your demands to the other side. It is efficient to signal that your position is strictly non-negotiable. Hold fast to your position. 3 Determine if you wish to spend time engaging in their various arguments (which maintains a human dimension and might prevent them walking away) or just keep reiterating that your position will not shift. **Watch out for:** Them being able to walk away.	• Test to see if they are doing brinkmanship by using an assortment of tactics to see if you can secure any sort of concessions. • Unless you have no choice but to accept the offer, use a BATNA or walk away.

It is not inappropriate to pass an occasional message to another team member in a negotiation; while this would be considered rude in many meetings it seems to be something that is often accepted in a negotiation providing it is not done too often. A more subtle approach is to use an object to communicate a pre-agreed code. One technique some negotiators use is the position of their mobile phone. The team arrive and, as is accepted practice today, place their mobile phone on the desk in front of them. Turning it 90 degrees might be a signal from the team leader to stop talking, turning it towards another team member might indicate who should speak next and any team member turning their phone over could mean there is a problem, signalling the team leader to do something. It doesn't matter what the code is or what prop is used, if any, but it does matter that there is a system and everyone understands it. The same applies for negotiations conducted remotely using technology, except here teams can message each other using a separate messaging app. Always use a separate system to the web conference tool you are negotiating with to avoid the risk of accidentally posting a private message to your opponent. These and other key winning event tactics are summarized in Figure 11.5.

Facts, data and experts

You can never have enough facts, data and expertise. A good negotiation strategy will be informed by thorough research to understand the balance of power; however, facts, data and expertise may also be needed during the event itself. The problem is it could be impossible to predict exactly what might be needed to defend or strengthen a particular position and impractical to refer to detailed analysis. Things that can help here include:

- *Do your homework.* Get familiar with the key facts ahead of the event; if you can't learn everything then learn some key facts. If they believe you know your position and are well informed they will regard you as a powerful force.
- *Agree roles.* Avoid trying both to lead the negotiation and to be agile with a complex set of supporting data at the same time; instead appoint a Mr Data or someone with the role of looking after the facts and data in concert with you leading.
- *Bring an expert.* Make sure they are properly briefed and know how far to go and what not to say.

Figure 11.5 Winning techniques – The event

Winning Techniques – Event

16 Solve problems & remove obstacles

Focus on solving problems and removing obstacles preventing moving forward rather than trading and concessions. Put yourself in their shoes or ask 'what is holding you back here?' then focus negotiations on how you might be able to solve this problem. Negotiate from there.

17 Give yourself room to negotiate

Watch you don't negotiate near to your LDO or give too much too soon. Leave room for them to work to shift you. Be alert to tactics they might use to get you to your LDO quickly.

18 Secret code

For a group negotiation, agree a secret code to communicate with your team during the event eg when someone should speak, stop speaking or a time-out is needed. Consider using a mobile phone placed on the table top and turning it one way or the other to give signals to your team.

19 Find some personal theatre

Find a bit of personal theatre that you can use to break state or signal a change from one state to another. Eg, if you wear glasses, the act of removing them and placing them on the table buys thinking time and allows you to switch to 'get tough' mode until the glasses are replaced.

20 Time out

If things take an unexpected turn, or if you need to realign (perhaps with fellow negotiators or colleagues) then take a time-out. Ask or politely inform the other that you need to take a quick 'time-out,' then leave the room and collect your thoughts or realign as needed.

- *Don't bluff.* If you are unsure of your position, avoid bluffing as they are likely to be more informed than you; instead defer to another team member or seek a time-out to go and do your research.

Get the maths right

If the entire negotiation strategy centres around a single piece of data then this must be correct. If they can discredit our data or indeed any maths supporting it then the entire argument is lost and this could be irrecoverable. Check the data, check the maths and develop a BATNA in case they provide some unexpected piece of evidence. If all else fails then use the 'I'm sorry, I must be misinformed' line and buy some time to go and investigate further.

One common mistake made when negotiating cost decreases or increases with suppliers is a failure to correctly quantify the actual impact of a particular cost driver. For example, in the United Kingdom the cost of the famous English 'fish and chips' has increased significantly in recent times, largely due to environmental issues associated with over-fishing, making certain fish types scarce or unpopular, and rising costs of potatoes. Recently, I saw a sign in one outlet that read: 'Customers please note; we apologize but we have had to increase our prices 10 per cent. This is due to the fact that potato prices have risen by 10 per cent recently.' I asked if any customers had raised objection. The shop owner replied, 'Nearly everyone has been very understanding.' However, in this case the potato cost represents only a fraction of the total cost of a portion of fish and chips. Once the cost of the fish, oil, packaging, energy, staff and overheads is added the potato represents only about 20 per cent of the final selling price, meaning a 10 per cent increase in potatoes should be reflected as a 2 per cent increase in the selling price to the consumer. This is a common tactic used by many suppliers to justify cost increases accompanied with some compelling data. Ideally, if the supplier has signalled such a discussion in advance, then get them to provide the data ahead of the event so it can be analysed properly. Otherwise don't get taken by surprise but seek time to properly review what they provide and do the maths.

Round numbers

Generally round numbers mean they are not calculated and are 'in the region' rather than precise. Round numbers have their place though, especially when talking about a 'big picture' agreement or in value-creation negotiations. However, in other situations they might be something to be aware of and the basis for the numbers should be established as far as possible. Questions such as 'Please tell me how you arrived at that number?' or 'Can you break down that number so I can understand what makes it up?' can help here.

When it goes wrong

Negotiations can go wrong. They can crash and burn, people can walk out, discussions can get tense and, in security negotiations, people can die. Sometimes failure is unavoidable and no one can ever win them all. However, there are some things that can help when the meeting gets difficult.

Dealing with deadlock

Conflict is a necessary part of negotiation, due to the different positions parties take. If neither party is prepared to back down then this conflict can end up in deadlock. Consider this exchange:

Husband: 'I don't want to go to the party.'
Wife: 'But we've said we will be there.'
Husband: 'They won't notice if we don't turn up.'
Wife: 'If we say we are going to be there we should.'
Husband: 'Why don't you go on your own?'
Wife: 'Then everyone will think we've had an argument.'
Husband: 'But I don't want to go.'
Wife: 'But I want to go.'

Fisher and Ury (2012) state that conflict in negotiation can be avoided by focusing on interests rather than position. Focusing on position drives parties to simply keep restating their position and hold firmer. Problems usually do not lie in conflicting positions but in the unspoken conflict between the needs, desires, concerns and fears on each side. It is our interests that motivate us and if we can look behind the position and see these we can begin to find ways to accommodate them. Let's revisit our example:

Husband: 'I don't want to go because just lately I'm finding I'm struggling in crowds and starting to feel a bit claustrophobic.'
Wife: 'I feel afraid to let others down.'
Husband: 'Perhaps we go for a short while and slip away early?'

The most powerful interests are human needs, and most things will come down to fear, money, sex, control or power somewhere along the way. In a supplier negotiation context fear (of failure or embarrassment), and money (personal bonus and likelihood of promotion) tend to be the main personal interests. By understanding them it is possible to switch tactics or propose trades that satisfy an interest while stepping closer to what we want. If their interest is personal they may even sacrifice going further than their LDO so they get what they want. Interests can be established in four ways:

- *The 'five whys' technique.* Ask 'why' and keep asking 'why' up to five times until the real reason emerges. Note however that resistant 'whys' can be annoying or a bit childlike, so consider replacing 'why' questions with alternatives such as '...and how does it do that?' or '...in what way does that help?' and so on. Use carefully and be ready to stop if the tactic is being counterproductive.

- *Hypothetical choices.* Suggest hypothetical choices to test what the problem is: 'So is it the party or not wanting to go out that is the problem?'

- *How do you feel?* Interests often get expressed as feelings. Individuals may not always be aware of their interests but they will understand their feelings so questions such as 'How do you feel about what is happening here?' can provoke revealing answers.

- *Build on what they say.* Respond to their stating their position by using questioning to get them to build on their answer. Similar to the 'five whys' above, use questions such as 'And how does it do that?' 'And what effect does that have?' 'And why is that a difficulty?'

Resolving conflict

Conflict doesn't always end up in deadlock, but instead it can be counterproductive in other ways, causing outcomes to be sub-optimum by removing the appetite for cooperation and collaboration. In a value-claiming negotiation where we hold the power this may be entirely acceptable. However, if a value-creation outcome is sought then conflict needs to be defused.

Ury (1991) suggests the barriers to cooperation include how we react, the other party's ability or otherwise to control their emotions, their position, their dissatisfaction and their power. Of these the one we can influence is the way we react. To do this we first need to know what our natural conflict style is and this is part of negotionality explored in Chapter 6. If we have a natural propensity to collaborate then this will help in negotiation conflict; however, if we tend to compete or accommodate then managing our reactions is essential if we are to handle conflict effectively. In addition, focusing on interests will help but there are also a couple of approaches that, with practice, can do great things.

Reflect, rewind then react

Ury (1991) suggests we have a tendency either to strike back, give in or break off when faced with a conflict situation. However, each of these responses is destructive for different reasons. A more useful response is to take a moment to reflect on what was said, to rewind it in the silence of our mind and to consider what interests might lie behind the words. Playing back what they have said as if we are clarifying understanding helps: 'So you're suggesting that...' or 'Just so I understand, you feel that...'. All of this buys precious time to form the right response so when we do finally react we are able to do this more collaboratively.

Feel, felt, found

Arguing fuels more arguments. However, when we acknowledge someone's argument then they have no reason to keep arguing with us, and at the heart of every argument lie interests and feelings. 'Feel, felt, found' is a great technique to convert arguments into agreements and works by responding to an argument with three statements that acknowledge their position and suggest rather than impose a solution. For example: 'I understand how you feel about a further price reduction', 'I also felt it was a step too far when it was first suggested', 'However, I found that when I reviewed the market data it is actually in line with how the market is moving.'

Countermeasure tactics

But what can we do when they use clever tactics on us? Building repertoire includes having a response for every conceivable scenario we might find ourselves in. While the tactics explored so far that we could use have also included countermeasures in case these get used against us, there are further countermeasures that a good negotiator should have ready to go and these are listed in Table 11.6. Generally these tactics are defensive or reactive to a particular ploy. We can of course use these ploys on them also; however, I have not presented these in that way as many of the ploys in question tend to be either ineffective, are used by inexperienced negotiators or are simply responses to something the other side is doing without realizing it.

If all else fails

If things go wrong then buy some time to reconsider your position, either by taking a 'time-out' from the negotiation or asking to reconvene. If you find yourself boxed into a corner, you have made a mistake or things are tense then use humour to make light of the situation and retract or reframe your position. However, if all else fails then play your BATNA or ultimately walk away, regroup, consider your options and note what you have learnt from the experience.

Table 11.6   Tactics and techniques: countermeasure tactics

Tactic and how it is used	What you can do
36 Set aside A tactic for when things stall through multiple issues and demands Often used as a deliberate delaying tactic or by inexperienced negotiators	You simply ask to 'set aside' or park all the additional or new issues or demands being thrown in and focus on the main point first, perhaps with the promise of coming back to these later. In practice you may not need to come back to these detailed points (unless they are important to you) as securing the main agreement may actually be what the other party seeks, so even if you commit to revisit it is often good not to prompt this unless the other side prompts you. **Things to say:** **_Collaborative_**: 'Yes, we need to discuss that too but I suggest first we conclude this...' **_Firm_**: 'Let's come back to that once we have agreement on this main point.' **_Assertive_**: 'I've noted that and I'm prepared to discuss that but only after we have concluded this.'
KEEP CALM **37** Keep calm and carry on When they get aggressive, angry or upset	When the other side gets angry and aggressive, perhaps with displays of either genuine or staged rage then sit back, pause and calmly respond. Anger is a power tactic; if you respond in the same way you are showing weakness and then it is the party who shouts loudest that will win but typically such exchanges tend to be counterproductive. Keep calm and carry on will give you the upper hand and will quickly disperse any anger. Simply sit back in your chair, talk gently, show palms and don't argue but rather use 'feel, felt, found' or similar techniques. If it continues then name the problem. **Things to say:** **_Collaborative_**: 'I understand how you feel... I felt the same when... I found that...' **_Firm_**: 'Let's just calm this down because I'm not going to continue until you are engaging with me in a more appropriate manner.' **_Assertive_**: 'Have you finished? If so let's continue.'

Table 11.6 *continued*

Tactic and how it is used	What you can do
  38 That's outrageous! For when they make an outrageous demand	Outrageous demands that will often be rejected are used as a precursor to the real demand. The initial demand is designed to throw you off your guard so you will more readily agree to a lesser second that you might otherwise not agree to. For example, if a boss says, 'I want you to work every weekend for the next year' a suitably outraged response might be, 'There is just no way!' But if the boss then says 'OK... you're right, but will you work this weekend?' then you are more likely to agree because it feels like the boss is compromising. Beware what follows the outrageous demand and treat each in isolation.
  39 Hands off my salami A tactic to use when they try to get you to make a series of apparently small concessions, but one slice leads to another	Negotiators who use salami slicing often have a sense of 'I'm trying my luck' when they slice salami and it is easy to make them feel cheap for doing so, which helps deflect the slicing tactic. Don't give in, as a persistent salami slicer will come back for slice after if they get what they want the first time. Be clear about what is and is not part of your discussion; avoid giving anything away but trade instead if you need to. Use 'set aside' to park it for a later discussion if you need, or elect to reserve agreement until you know everything they are asking. **Things to say:** ***Collaborative***: 'I'm sorry I can't agree to that, we have not provided for that in our calculations; it is not part of what we are discussing,' or 'in principle, I may be able to agree that but I want to understand all the things you are asking for first.' ***Firm***: 'I cannot agree to that; you are asking for something new and that has a cost,' or 'I need to understand all your requirements before we discuss where we may or may not be able to agree something.' ***Assertive***: 'No I cannot agree to that.'

Table 11.6 *continued*

Tactic and how it is used	What you can do
40 Deadlock deflector A tactic to deal with 'take it or leave it' or 'it's non-negotiable'	'Take it or leave it' and 'it's non-negotiable' are powerful tactics that are intended to signal to the other that the end of the line has been reached and there is nowhere further to go. It can stop a negotiation dead and many do not know how to handle it. It is also a tactic that will leave the other feeling cheated. However, everything is negotiable somehow! First you should test their stance by looking for small cracks: 'So if it was impossible for us to meet your price point because of the way our internal approval system works, are you happy to lose this on that basis?' Once you have established they are not going to budge, there is little point in continuing to argue. Instead, there are a few things you can do but bear in mind that you need to give the other side a way out so they don't lose face if you are negotiating with a polychronic or collective culture: 1 Act like you didn't hear it and carry on regardless. 2 Acknowledge the position and use the 'set aside' to attempt to discuss other requirements. 3 Attempt to secure something in return if you agree to their position. When you sign a new contract for a cell phone the package is usually non-negotiable but you can often secure a month free or a car charger. 4 Try to establish what is making it non-negotiable; perhaps a higher authority. You may be able to help with a creative solution. 5 Show them the consequences and make it collaborative. 'If we have to end up doing X then we need to understand that we will have to deal with Y.' 6 Walk away; again if it is just a tactic they won't let you. If you do this, however, you must be prepared to see this one through and keep walking just in case they don't call you back.

Table 11.6 *continued*

Tactic and how it is used	What you can do

41 Bomb defusal

A tactic to deal with threats

Making a threat is like dropping a bomb into the negotiation. A threat is a projection of power, and something that belongs with bullies, but it may be real or just bravado aimed at forcing you to concede. However, a threat is only as powerful as the willingness or ability of the other party to follow through and implement it. If they are making threats then there is some reason why they are anxious to secure your agreement so first reassess your position and check you haven't missed anything. Then there are three possible responses to threats:

1 Ignore them and keep going as if it was never said.

2 Expose the threat and ask them to clarify precisely what they are saying; either they will or they will back down.

3 Call their bluff with a BATNA and suggest that if they want to go ahead with their threatened course of action then the game changes.

For example:

Supplier: Unless you agree, we will need to put this matter in the hands of our lawyers.

Buyer: OK, well if we are now into legal territory then I'm afraid I won't be able to continue to discuss this matter and your lawyers will now need to speak directly with our lawyers... Are you certain that is what you want to do?

WHY

?

42 But...why?

A tactic for when things have stalled because they keep responding with 'but...' and a series of different arguments

Used either as a deliberately delaying tactic or because they feel unsure or unable to proceed

Respond to each 'but...' statement they make by acknowledging their concern and asking questions about what is driving their concern. For example: 'I can see you're reluctant to commit on this but please tell me exactly what is preventing you here.'

If they persist with 'buts...' then use the 'Five Whys' technique: respond to each 'but...' statement by asking them 'Why?' This will force them to explain differently or give you some more insight into what is behind their 'but...'. Do this five times and they will most likely give you the real reason. This is a powerful technique that comes naturally to children but gets lost into adulthood.

Table 11.6 *continued*

Tactic and how it is used	What you can do
43 Same old argument A tactic for when they keep repeating the same argument as a reason not to move forward	This happens for two reasons: first it may be a deliberate tactic and second it may be the manifestation of a deeper concern or fear. You need to identify which it is and then respond appropriately. For example, if the supplier keeps saying, 'We just cannot agree to 60 days' payment terms as our standard terms are 30 days and that is that.' If this is being used as a tactic then the supplier needs a reason to trade or concede, so test this. 'Is there room for manoeuvre if we can make it attractive elsewhere?' If they agree then it is a tactic and proceed to negotiate it; if they don't agree then it is hiding something deeper. Perhaps they have cash flow issues; perhaps the salesperson has been given strict orders. Here you should focus on trying to understand what is behind this either by using some test questions, eg 'Please tell me what would need happen to agree new terms' or suggest what you think the problem is together with a solution and watch their reaction. 'If this is about cash flow then can we look at a different approach to help here?' Once again the Five Whys technique can help here.
44 Hot potato When they try to make their problem your problem For example, 'I'm under pressure to get this work included as part of this financial year which means I need to close on this today'	Their problem is not your problem, so throw the hot potato back, eg 'I'm sorry but our timing is not driven by the internal matters within your organization.' The hot potato can, however, provide an opportunity to trade as you can offer to help them solve their problem, but this of course comes at a price!

Table 11.6 *continued*

Tactic and how it is used	What you can do
45 Are you sure? A tactic to deal with misinformation When they plant misinformation in among genuine information to suggest they have more power than they actually have, eg 'I have two other buyers who want this but neither have confirmed yet so "for a deal today" I can give you priority'	Remember misinformation is an attempt to project power so you should be on your guard for this and expect dialogue to be peppered with some misinformation, which you simply ignore. However, should something they say be significant and represent a real threat then there are several possible responses: 1 Write it down as if their words are of great importance. Suggest, 'OK, let's come back to that later.' The threat of their lies being challenged after may well be enough to stop them implanting further misinformation. 2 Challenge it with, 'I am surprised by that, tell me more...' and keep asking questions of detail forcing them to explain. Watch for signs of discomfort as they reply. 3 Call their bluff by suggesting, 'Well if you really are that busy then I have concerns about continuing with the negotiation as I'm worried you may not have sufficient capacity to meet our needs.'
46 Defector realignment When they manage to divide and conquer your team When the other party wins allies in your camp before or during a negotiation and uses this to their advantage	This can take two forms: 1 Using an established relationship with someone senior in your organization as leverage. Reaffirm your authority for this negotiation on behalf of the entire business and suggest you will talk directly to the individual following the event. 2 Creating disagreement among your team during the event. Ideally prevent this in the first place by agreeing ground rules; however, if it should happen call a time-out and get your team in line.

Table 11.6   *continued*

Tactic and how it is used	What you can do
 47 I'm no expert A tactic to deal with their expert who overwhelms us with information Usually used in the hope we will not understand or it will devalue our position in some way	If you are able to establish in advance who they are bringing, then you have the chance to bring your own experts who should be briefed to ask them lots of searching questions but defer to you on your cue. If you find yourself exposed to their expert then there are a few things you can do: 1 Avoid being interrogated or allowing their technical knowledge to give them the upper hand. Answer only if you want to and are confident to do so, otherwise: 2 Play dumb and sideline them. 'I'm sorry but I'm not an expert – my role here is to agree the commercial terms.' 3 Ask them to explain; get them to show you the technical reports they cite and so on. 4 Make their expert the obstacle. Agree to note any questions they have so you can take it back to your own expert for a response later. This of course will signal a delayed outcome if they insist their technical questions are really that important. 5 Flatter them. Chances are their expert is not a core member of their team and probably not fully briefed on his or her role. You may be able to win an ally on the other side of the table with a smile and some words of praise. This might make their expert less provocative.
 48 But we agreed... A tactic for when the other party attempts to undo what has previously been agreed	Negotiators will have all sorts of arguments why it is suddenly appropriate to revisit something that was either agreed for sure or there was a sense of an agreement. They may say things like, 'Things have moved on' or 'Yes, but that was based upon how things looked back then.' No matter, don't let them do this but instead call foul and use the moral arguments around the fact that rescinding an agreement is a dirty trick and it would be difficult for you to continue to have any trust in them if they are not prepared to honour what was agreed. Don't let them suggest 'things have changed' but instead rebuff this with comments like 'Things have not changed, this is a negotiation. We all knew how things might progress when we came here.'

Table 11.6 *continued*

Tactic and how it is used	What you can do
49 Silence is golden A tactic to make them uncomfortable when they lay out a position	Silence is a very powerful weapon and one that can help reveal how serious they are about their position and buy you valuable thinking time. Once they have made a demand or suggested a certain concession, simply stay silent and make no reaction at all. This creates a very uncomfortable tension for them, and one they may even feel the need to fill by saying something further. Often this is their downfall as this new 'something' may be unguarded, with a suggestion of retraction or a hint that they know their demand is unrealistic. For example, if they say, 'We need to achieve £10 per unit', and you stay silent and show no reaction, eventually they are likely to say 'or something very close to it'.
Diversion **50** Break state Use when you need to completely disorient your opponent and then regain control of the situation	This is used to snap your opponents out of their current mindset and allows you to regain control of the situation. It involves doing something so completely unexpected that it forces the other person to stop dead in their tracks, after which you can create a new 'state' for the negotiation and work from there. For example, if the discussion is getting quite heated and the other party is trying to intimidate you with a Norman Bates display, suddenly look out the window and say, 'Hey, look at that cloud shaped like Homer Simpson!' It could even be as simple as suggesting a coffee break. The key is to change the current state of the situation, allowing a shift in control.

More winning techniques for great outcomes

We covered some pre-event techniques in Chapter 10. A summary of the key winning techniques for the event itself is given in Figure 11.5. In addition there are a range of techniques that can give us power both in the negotiation and around the event itself. For example one of the most powerful negotiation techniques we can sometimes play is simply to decline to go the negotiation table. If we agree to negotiate we are effectively signalling we are ready to make concessions. Maintaining radio silence between events and engagements can help make the other side feel we are not interested and heighten our projected power. Using the social proof of 'Everyone else is doing this – why aren't you?' frequently tips the other side towards making a deal. Ten of these winning techniques are given in Figure 11.6.

Figure 11.6 Winning techniques – Power play

Winning Techniques – Power plays 1

21 Divide and conquer

Work on picking off their team one by one individually, ideally before the negotiation and during it, finding ways to win over each person in turn according to their different interests, perhaps using several different approaches to do so.

22 Don't go to the table

When we engage and 'go to the table' we are signaling that we are ready to negotiate and therefore likely to be prepared to give concessions. Delaying or even avoiding going to the table (if you can and have the strength of position) is very powerful and can disarm an opponent.

23 Maintain radio silence

For remote negotiations or repeat engagements, maintain some 'radio silence' when the other is waiting a response or answer on something. Take time to respond or don't take calls. Buy time, make them sweat and this will put you in a more powerful position.

20 imperative to act

Create an imperative to act and close, either with a time constraint, scarcity or other factor.

25 Powerless posturing

If you don't have the power, act like you do! Work to make them believe that they need you more than you need them. Project power – be less interested, appear to have alternatives they don't know about, be confident and even a bit bolshie.

Figure 11.6 *continued*

Winning Techniques – Power plays 2

26 Don't you know who I am

Use position or assigned role to assert authority eg 'I'm leading this project' or 'I've been tasked by the CEO to head this up' etc. If there is not senior authority, use the authority of the team. 'I'll need to get the team to agree they want to do this' and so on.

27 Create reciprocity

Find ways to create a sense of obligation in them by giving something. This could be a full tactic such as Santa Clause or simply kind hospitality, making the engagement or visit enjoyable for them or thoughtful social engagement that takes an interest in them.

28 Use social proof

Social proof is a powerful reason to act – 'If others are doing it then so should you' or 'don't get left behind' etc. Throughout the negotiation find ways to show or describe what others are doing and try to create compelling reasons to do the same.

29 Find their motivation

Everyone is motivated by different things. Look beyond the negotiation to the individual and try to figure out what motivates them eg winning, career progression, doing the right thing, being the expert etc. Try to weave this into discussions and illustrate how the outcome will satisfy their motivators.

30 Appeal to their ego

Find ways to compliment them and make them feel good. Avoid making this too obvious or personal. For example find reasons to weave in comments that suggest how effective their negotiation is, or how good they are at this, how well structured and planned the engagement is etc.

Body language   12

This chapter explores the unspoken forms of communication through our gestures, reactions and body language and what these say and give away.

Pathway questions addressed in this chapter

19 What tactics and techniques will help me be successful?

20 How can I stay in control of my body language and read that of my opponent?

Red Sheet steps covered in this chapter

12 and every interaction with the supplier

Non-verbal communication

When we engage in face-to-face discussion with someone, believe it or not, only around 7 per cent of the message they receive is based upon the actual words that are said; paralanguage accounts for 38 per cent. Paralanguage is what is implied by the sound of our voice: our pitch, tone and speed. The remaining 55 per cent of our message is delivered through our body language (Borg, 2010). For this reason face-to-face negotiations work differently from those conducted remotely. However, negotiation is increasingly being conducted by remote means, some with, some without the means to see the other party and their non-verbal communication.

Why we need to understand body language

Body language is our demeanour, what our bodies do and how part or all of our bodies move and react to what is happening around us. To the trained eye our bodies can tell more about what we are thinking than we may even be aware of ourselves. It might seem crazy to think that we could reveal so much. Surely we can manage how we act? However, it is almost impossible to completely suppress involuntary bodily reactions. The reason for this is that we have evolved with incredibly powerful brains that take care of everything, constantly monitoring what is going on all around us and reacting instantly without conscious thought. If you need proof of this then throw a tennis ball at someone who is not expecting it and watch them effect a lightning catch.

In critical situations where truth is needed, but there is a likelihood that what people actually say cannot be relied upon, then body language and non-verbal cues come to the fore. Police, security services, customs and immigration officers receive training on such matters. In some cases specialist psychologists may sit in on an interrogation to observe. Salespeople often receive the same training to help gain an advantage. Those in the purchasing community rarely receive such training, putting us at an immediate disadvantage.

In a negotiation body language is our best friend and worst enemy. Each party knows the words the other speaks are unlikely to reflect the true position, as, by the very nature of negotiation, it is fair game to bluff, mislead, lie, manipulate, misrepresent and so on to maximize outcomes. If we can successfully read their body language then we can gain vital clues as to where their LDO is or if we are close to agreement. The problem however is they will most likely be watching us closely for similar clues. Effective use of body language in a negotiation is therefore about reading them but not letting them read us, and that is quite a challenge. In this book I can only scratch the surface of this subject and so further reading is recommended (see References and Further Reading).

The health warning

So if we learn what each body language signal and gesture means then we can read people? Sadly, no! If it were that simple the world might be a different place. Reading body language accurately is immensely difficult and even the professionals have margins of error. There are several reasons for this:

- *People differ.* A common belief, reinforced by some books on body language, suggests that every time someone folds their arms they are being closed to us. However, it might just mean they are cold or, as often is the case for women, they might just feel more comfortable sitting like this.

- *Cross-wired*. It is often said that if people look up to the right they are lying. Perhaps this is true, but perhaps not. Sometimes people seem to do the complete opposite, as if they are cross-wired, and whether they are left- or right-handed changes things too.

- *People respond to the environment*. Body language changes according to their environment. Put someone in a stress situation and you may well see a different set of reactions and behaviours.

- *People could deliberately mislead*. Experienced practitioners who have learnt to manage their own body language may well be able to deliberately mislead us through gestures and actions.

Steps to reading them

Despite the health warning it is possible to have a good degree of success in reading others' body language but this success comes by building up a picture of a specific individual over time. Here we use the 'Cues, Clusters, Changes' model for reading body language (Figure 12.1).

Figure 12.1   Reading body language – Cues, clusters and changes

Watching for visible cues

I slowed the car and stopped beside the customs officer who had waved me down ahead of boarding a cross-channel ferry. He peered into the car then looked straight at me and started being surprisingly friendly. He asked a series of seemingly irrelevant questions and joked about my children, seeming to be completely and independently consumed by their electronic games. We chuckled with him for a moment or two, then, still making direct eye contact with me he said, 'OK, so is there anything you have on board that might cause you to break out into a sweat when you arrive at customs on the other side?' Without moving or breaking eye contact I replied simply, 'No, no such thing'. He wished us a good holiday and waved us on. Anyone who travels can tell similar stories but few ever stop to think why a customs officer would want to make time for small talk. However, the friendly exchange was deliberate to quickly establish a baseline of my body language in a friendly and non-threatening situation. Once complete, he switched to ask a difficult question and watched carefully to see if my reaction changed. This is a classic technique used by security forces the world over.

In a negotiation, reading body language starts the moment we meet someone and continues through every engagement. Visible cues indicate what they are thinking and how they feel: the signals or gestures they use; how they move, sit or respond to certain things; what their hands do; what their eyes are saying; the position of their head; where their feet or shoulders are pointing, and so on. Spotting the visible cues is something that takes practice and involves keeping deliberate, constant observation on every part of them that is visible. For the sake of good manners this should be done covertly and so learning to use peripheral vision while maintaining as much eye contact as possible is essential. Interestingly, women are, more often than not, naturally better able than men at discerning these factors as they have better peripheral vision and tend to be more attuned to body language than many men.

Baselining is important too and the friendly exchanges and small talk at the start of a meeting provide an opportunity to watch them when they will feel unthreatened. Through observation it is possible to build up a picture of what they do in certain situations. I will cover some of the most common body language signals later; however, when reading body language there are two things we are looking for: an indication of how they are feeling now and their reactions either when things change or to things we do. It is impossible to describe precisely what to watch for; however, with practice, and observation, it is possible to identify things of significance no matter how small. For example, if we ask them a question and then note by their shoulders that they shift in their seat slightly when they answer, this is significant and could suggest they are uncomfortable answering that question, perhaps because they are lying. It may of course be unconnected, which is why it is dangerous to make judgements based upon observation of a single response or action.

Body language can be observed in any public space and so the opportunity to practise is all around us. Engaging in the art of people-watching on trains, buses and at airports can be great negotiation training.

Looking for clusters

It is the clusters of certain gestures, actions or responses, matched against what is happening and what is being said that help understand body language. Clusters allow us to differentiate random bodily movements or deliberate misleads from the actions that truly reveal something.

If the other person repeatedly makes a certain action when they say some things, but not others, then this is a cluster, perhaps suggesting these specific things they say are not as correct as the others.

By becoming familiar with, and learning to read a certain individual, it is possible to further verify what you see by testing and triangulation; for example, asking questions we already know the answer to helps to establish response patterns.

Spotting the changes

Once we can read an individual's body language the aim is to be able to spot when things change, say as an indicator that they have shifted from one state to another. It is the changes that can help us identify when we have reached their LDO or when they are ready to make a deal. Poker players use the same principle; if the opponent looks at his cards and there is suddenly a glimmer of excitement somewhere in his body then this might be just enough intelligence to know to fold early.

Relevant changes might include becoming more excited, animated, impatient, uncomfortable or even aggressive. We will cover what might be observed for each of these later. It may be straightforward to make a correlation between the change and events within the negotiation but sometimes unexpected changes in body language can happen for no obvious reason. This can signal that things are not what they might seem and so if this happens, rewind and check what just happened and go from there.

Comfort and discomfort

Former FBI counterintelligence Special Agent Joe Navarro (2008) suggests that a more reliable approach than watching for specific actions is to look for signs of comfort and discomfort and individuals switching from one state to the other. If we feel in control of our situation we will appear comfortable. However, Navarro suggests that when someone is put in a stress situation, say because they are being interrogated and they are shown some evidence that might convict them, then they experience discomfort and this is often visible through a variety of bodily actions. Therefore by studying body language and specifically looking for switches between comfort and discomfort we can gain vital intelligence in our negotiation. Later, I will explore how discomfort manifests itself and what to look for as well as how to deliberately show discomfort to suggest a certain position.

Capturing the intelligence

Write it down! Few people ever do this and rely on some mental recall when they next engage with the person, but if you have worked out someone's body language and you plan future engagements with them, capturing what you know to help with future planning is advised.

What everybody is saying

Of course I'm lying

> I did not have sexual relations with that woman.
> Bill Clinton, 1998

He blinked a bit more than he normally does, his tone of voice got ever so slightly more gentle and he over-emphasized a head shake to coincide with 'did not', but at least he didn't rub his nose or look up to the right. All in all a convincing performance and one many politicians pull off with ease. I, and millions of others, believed him at the time. The problem with lying is that it is a very difficult thing to detect in others. Navarro (2008) suggests our chances of detecting when someone is lying are at best 50:50. It is worse for men, who are less able to detect lies than women (Pease and Pease, 2004). Women tend to pay more attention to body language and look for congruence between what is said and body language.

We learn to lie early on. Children soon discover that a lie is an easy thing to pull off and can bring great benefits or avoid punishment. Ask the kid with the chocolate-covered face if she has been eating the chocolates and she may well be able to shake her head, look you in the eye and give you a convincing 'no'. Some children will lie, others will confess. For some the risk of a disappointed parent is enough to prevent them from lying, for others the risk is worth taking. In adulthood we understand better the difficulties and consequences associated with lying and so we decide what our personal boundaries are; never to lie, only to lie when it's really necessary or to certain people, or that lying is acceptable providing we don't get caught. Things are different in a negotiation: it is an artificial environment, like being on stage or acting, and so people who might choose not to lie in everyday life can be quite happy to lie in a negotiation and would see it as part of the charade. However, here it tends to be given more gentle labels such as bluffing or creating a position and so on. Novice or junior negotiators tend to lie more, possibly because a common misconception is that this is how negotiation is done or because a strategy based upon lying appears, on the surface, an easier approach. This means that when we negotiate we can expect the other party to lie and we need to be prepared for that and work to detect it as best as possible.

Despite how accomplished some may be at lying, as humans we are programmed not to lie. Lying has consistently being regarded as socially unacceptable throughout the ages and at certain times in our evolution, and also in certain cultures, the consequences of lying were, and still are, dire. Lying is therefore something the average person finds difficult to do. This is because our brains tell us it is wrong and then react instinctively, and without conscious thought, to try and stop it happening. It is through this reaction that we can detect when someone is lying. One of the most common instincts is to put a hand over the mouth as if trying to stop the lie. What might be witnessed in them is an arm raising or even just a slight twitch, or a touch of the mouth or somewhere nearby. Pease and Pease (2004) suggest some of these involuntary reactions include:

- covering the mouth;
- touching the nose;
- itching something;
- rubbing the eyes;
- grabbing the ear;
- scratching the neck;
- pulling the collar;
- putting a finger in the mouth.

The problem with watching for bodily movement alone is that all these actions can be used deliberately to create misinformation.

As I mentioned previously, another widely used detection method is to watch for eye movement, the theory being that if our eyes look up to our left we are accessing facts from our left brain and so what we say is correct, but if they look up to the right we are accessing our right, creative hemisphere and so constructing a lie. Eye movement is still used by many professions as a test of lying, but what if they are cross-wired and we have no baseline? What if they trying to create misinformation? Moreover, an accomplished liar will be able to look us directly in the eyes and keep theirs still. Once again, watching for individual actions alone is not an infallible test.

Navarro (2008) suggests that as well as looking for changes in body language we should listen for shifts in the voice too. When we lie, our voice changes, the brain tries to stop the lie and the tone, steadiness and degree of inflection of our voice changes. Many will lie with a slightly quieter tone and with less inflection, in others it is the opposite; the point is that there is a change. But this is not all; lying triggers a mini-stress reaction and under stress a tremor can often be heard in the person's voice. This is frequently detectible when someone nervous has to make a speech in front of lots of people. In everyday life the voice tremor is not so discernable to the human ear, but it is still there. Increasingly, in line with technology advancement, professionals are favouring detection methods associated with voice changes as the most reliable. Modern Voice Stress Analysis (VSA) equipment looks for changes in patterns and micro-tremors. It is used widely by police, intelligence and security forces and would be one of the first pieces of equipment a hostage negotiator would hook up to the phone to get real-time 'truth' or 'lie' readings in any exchanges. This technology is already in use by some insurance companies when claims interviews are conducted by phone. We are just a small leap away from VSA being an effective smartphone app or standard equipment for call centres and telephone sales teams. It may even have its place for remote negotiations in the future.

It is possible to negotiate and never lie, but we need to have our arguments prepared. Deciding whether or not to lie is a personal choice and what we choose to do in one scenario might be different to another. In any case, for any lie, bluff or mislead there are some basic rules to follow because if you get found out it can damage your future credibility in this relationship, should this be important to you. The common rules to follow include:

- Never lie 'on the spot': always plan your misinformation.
- Do your research and pick something they can't know.
- Avoid something that will create the need to maintain the lie.
- Have your answers prepared should you get challenged.
- Always have an exit route in case you do get found out.
- Deliver it so you don't give the game away.
- Pepper truths with lies. The most convincing lies are those where real facts are combined with the lie to create a believable and semi-verifiable position, and one that is easy to deliver.

Experienced negotiators tend not to lie or to be very selective about the lies they use. For example, in a hostage negotiation establishing an apparent 'honest' exchange with the perpetrator is essential as the negotiator is their only friend; any suggestion the exchange is anything other than honest could get a hostage killed. However, it is also true that in any hostage situation it will at some point be necessary to lie if the situation is to be brought under control. In my own experience I have found there is a certain power that comes from taking a consistently honest line, especially for value creation, and one that the other side seems to pick up on. It removes all concern about being caught out but also means the arguments need to be more robust.

It's all in the eyes

So the eyes can help identify lies, but we can tell a lot more from the eyes in a negotiation. They are possibly the most revealing part of our body. You don't need a crystal ball and a colourful shawl to read someone; you just need to know what to look for. Specifically, there are four things to watch for: where they are looking, blink rate, attempts to cover the eyes and what their pupils are doing.

Many people will momentarily glance up, down and sideways as we talk to them, often without realizing it. Maintaining constant eye contact can be uncomfortable so glancing away is our brain's way of taking the pressure off, but where we glance is significant. Pease and Pease (2004) and Knight (2009) suggest the direction of our glance reveals what our brain is focusing on according to how we think and remember things (Figure 12.2). It typically follows that people who look up and either left or right tend think visually. Those who look sideways use auditory recall. When we look left we are accessing facts or things that are real and when we look to the right we are creating new facts; this is sometimes reversed in left-handed people. Looking down and to the left is about internal dialogue and to look down to the right is about feeling and emotions. Understanding if someone thinks in a visual, auditory or feelings-based way enables us to construct the approach to resonate with their style of thinking.

Watch their pupils carefully. Our pupils dilate when we're aroused, happy or comfortable and narrow when we are uncomfortable (Figure 12.3). This is very significant in a negotiation and can signal reaching important points. First, it can reveal they have shifted from a place of comfort to a place of discomfort, perhaps because they have reached their LDO and have a poor BATNA. Discomfort would appear as constricted pupils but there is more. When we encounter a sudden threat our eyes will dilate so they take in as

Figure 12.2   What eye movement can mean

'I'm remembering what I heard or "let me listen"'

'I'm considering how this is going to sound in my head'

'Let me get my thoughts clear in my mind'

'Perhaps I'm telling the truth or recalling something by visualizing in my head'

'Either I'm lying or visualizing a new idea something'

'I'm thinking about how I felt then and how I'm feeling now'

Figure 12.3   Watching the pupils can tell us much about how they feel

Dilated pupils – 'I'm comfortable and I'm ready to make a deal'

Narrowed pupils – 'I'm uncomfortable and not happy about what is happening'

much light as possible and give our brain all the information it needs to decide what to do about the threat. In a negotiation, once our brain realizes that there is no need to freeze, run or fight, dilation is no longer required and so then our pupils narrow to shut out what we don't like. This change happens very quickly, within a second. Navarro (2008) calls this the 'flashbulb effect' and it is a solid indicator that something we have just said has caused discomfort. When we want to test something, lay out a proposal or reveal something that we think might get them concerned, watch their pupils. If a fast dilation then contraction is seen then we have probably got to them. Lines that sometimes induce this with suppliers include, 'We don't feel this offer is competitive enough so unless we can improve it we need to run a competitive market exercise' or 'I'd like you to give me a breakdown of your figures.' Pupils also show when they are ready to move to agreement, as they will dilate slightly, showing something has changed and they are now more comfortable.

Our eyes and eyebrows show when we are happy or excited but they also show when we are uncomfortable or unhappy. When we are in the midst of things we don't like, our brains instinctively want to shut these things out. This appears as more rapid blinking or the eyelids staying closed a bit longer. It may also manifest itself as squinting, a deliberate closing of the eyes or a hand over the eyes (Figure 12.4).

Figure 12.4   How the eyes show how we feel

'I'm ready to make a deal!'

'Oh no! I really don't like that so I'm shutting it out'

'Are you sure?'

'I am still not convinced'

'It looks like I'm taking a moment to think, but really I'm blocking something out'

'Full discomfort, eye block and pacifying rub'

Assuming cultural norms don't suggest otherwise, making and maintaining eye contact is important throughout the negotiation, using peripheral vision to watch their body language while other team members work the paperwork around facts and data or note taking. How we make eye contact depends upon the type of negotiation. At close range, eye contact tends to be made by switching our gaze on them progressively from one eye to the other and to other points on the face that are slightly above or below the eye line. This is significant, as a gaze slightly below the eye line tends to be an intimate form of eye contact and something that people do when they are friendly with the other person. Gaze from eye to eye and to their forehead and you are projecting an air of superiority or aloofness. Although inappropriate for a negotiation, this superiority effect is further emphasized when no direct eye contact is made at all but instead a spot above the eye line is focused on. If you want to experience this then next time you walk down a busy street, avoid making eye contact with people coming towards you but instead look slightly above them and you may well find that people instinctively yield for you. How eye contact should be made depends upon the type of negotiation as per Figure 12.5.

Figure 12.5   Eye contact for value-claiming and value-creating negotiations

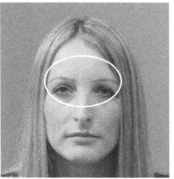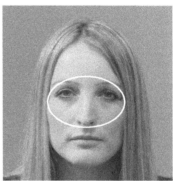

Eye contact region for hard
value-claiming negotiations

Eye contact region for
value-creating negotiations

If our counterparts are experienced then they will be watching our eyes carefully too, so be careful where you look or deliberately avert your eyes in a certain direction to mislead them. Watch your blink rate and don't cover your eyes. We cannot control what our pupils do and this puts us at risk. It is rumoured that the KGB would use eye drops to dilate their pupils and agents would have a drawing pin in the shoe that they could push their toe against when they needed to narrow their pupils. This may be a bit extreme; instead, when you encounter moments where you know your eyes will give you away simply decide it's time to look down at your notes or write something down. Accessorizing can help too; if you wear spectacles then these make it difficult to see your pupils. If you don't wear spectacles then think about getting some as they make props for negotiations. Most online retailers will supply zero-correction spectacles and the act of taking them off and putting them on through the negotiation can buy precious moments to gather thoughts.

Turn away from that which is bad

We tend to turn away from that which we don't like and turn towards that which we do, but we often don't realize it. Next time you engage in people-watching look at couples sitting together or groups interacting and observe how their bodies, and especially their feet, either turn towards or away from something or someone. You may need to watch carefully as the signs could be quite subtle but very revealing as often one part of a couple might seem to be more interested in someone other than the person he or she is with.

Once again this is our brain acting on our behalf without conscious thought and it is a reaction that is hard to suppress because something somewhere turns. The feet are usually most telling as they act as big pointers. When you see people standing and talking, look where their feet point. If they are interested in the person they are talking to or what they are saying the feet point towards that person; if not, or they are ready to part company or they would prefer to be talking to someone else, then one foot or even both will point away towards where they would rather be. The same happens when we are sitting down.

If we are sitting at a table in a negotiation chances are we won't see their feet, but 'turning away' is visible in the torso too. While sitting, try turning a foot and you'll find you can't help but turn your head slightly. People will also turn their entire body away or lean to one side, perhaps shifting weight onto one arm of the chair but in doing so leaning away from the person beside them.

We also turn away with our shoulders. One or both shoulders will rise as if to shield us. When we are trying to escape something that is all around us, then both our shoulders tend to go up and our head goes down. We may even clasp our hands together. Navarro (2008) calls this the 'turtle' and describes it as 'hiding in the open' and cites the example of what a losing team does when they leave the pitch. Figure 12.6 shows examples of turning away.

In a negotiation, observing what the other party is turning towards or away from is significant as this gives vital indicators of comfort or discomfort levels. Where our team are seated in the room is relevant as your opponent may try to turn away from one particular team member, perhaps the person who is being the most challenging. If you choose to use the tactic 'good cop/bad cop', it is important that those on your team who are deploying

Figure 12.6   Ways we turn away

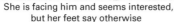

She is facing him and seems interested,   Defensive backing away
but her feet say otherwise

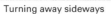

Turning away sideways   'The Turtle'

He wants to go, she wants him to stay (right)

the tactic are seated some way apart so you can see how your opponent turns, and if the bad cop is succeeding in making them sweat.

Watch those hands and arms

Our hands and arms are possibly the second most dangerous part of our body in a negotiation. Left to do their own thing our limbic responses can tell the other party all sorts of things about how we are feeling. There are certain hand and arm actions that are associated with specific feelings in an individual (Figure 12.7). They are often, but not always, accurate and there is scope for misleading with deliberate gestures. Once again, it is more useful to watch for clusters and changes, especially changes that suggest someone is shifted from comfort to discomfort.

The position of our arms and hands can encourage or discourage dialogue. Crossing arms creates a barrier, something between us and them that suggests to their subconscious that things stand in the way of an open exchange. If you are one of those people who like to cross arms to be comfortable then learn not to do this in a negotiation.

As we have already seen, our brain is a powerful force, acting reflexively and instinctively to protect us. There is great tendency to touch part of our

Figure 12.7 What those arms and hands are saying

'Am I cold, nervous or closed to you?'

'I'm not cold, but I do want a barrier between us'

Using an object to create a barrier

Clenched fists mean I'm not happy about something

'I'm really excited about this'

'I can't hold back on this one'

'So there you go; that's everything I have to give you'

'Woah! Stop right there, lets just calm down'

Steepled hands – 'I'm confident about this'

Rubbing cheek – 'I'm evaluating'

'I'm listening and contemplating'

Hand wringing – 'I'm a bit nervous'

'Good job, I'm positive about this'. Be careful where you use this one

'D'oh! How could I be so stupid'

face as if to shield us from something bad or stop us from lying. But it doesn't stop there. Our hands and arms will want to say something for everything that is happening around us. In Western culture many people will, without thinking, point one or both thumbs upwards to show they are positive about something. This doesn't need to be the full thumbs-up sign, but can happen when sitting with our arms on the desk in front of us. When people, most often men, stand with their hands in their pockets but with their thumbs sticking out and up, it is a display of confidence. Nervousness can make us wring our hands as we speak and making a steeple with our fingers tends to suggest confidence. Many people like to talk with their hands and move hands and arms to illustrate particular points. Mostly this is harmless; the problem is our hands are also telling a story so it is important to be certain they say only what we want them to. Experienced negotiators tend to avoid using any hand gestures during a negotiation.

Talking with our palms facing down is a show of authority. Showing one's palms is a pacifying action that tells the other's subconscious we are not a threat and we are not carrying any weapons. When things get tense, outstretched arms showing palms (Figure 12.7) can help defuse the situation.

Face up to the problem

Our faces have a lot to say. As we have seen, the eyes tell much, but so do our eyebrows, our mouths, foreheads, cheeks and indeed our entire face and head. We have on average 43 muscles in our face and by using different combinations of these we are able to show happiness, sadness, fear, anger, disgust and surprise. Once again instinctive brain reflexes make it difficult to prevent displaying our emotions in our faces. It is easier to see this in some people and this has a lot to do with facial muscle tone, making younger people easier to read than those who are older. This is perhaps one reason why more mature, senior people, manage to create an impression of being more self-controlled and collected.

Our mouths do all sorts of things (Figure 12.8). They can suggest we are really happy or just politely happy to keep it professional; they can say we don't agree or don't like something or that we're hiding something. Add a hand to the mouth too and then we really do have something to hide. It is possible to learn to control what our mouths do, but it is hard to suppress a smile. If we've just tried for what we thought was a ridiculous outcome from the other party and they have agreed, it can be hard to resist the instinctive

Figure 12.8　Reading the head and face

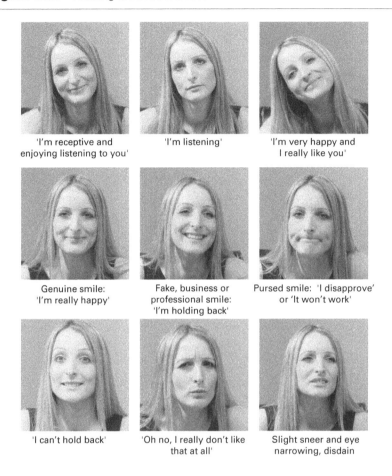

'I'm receptive and enjoying listening to you'

'I'm listening'

'I'm very happy and I really like you'

Genuine smile: 'I'm really happy'

Fake, business or professional smile: 'I'm holding back'

Pursed smile: 'I disapprove' or 'It won't work'

'I can't hold back'

'Oh no, I really don't like that at all'

Slight sneer and eye narrowing, disdain

desire to punch the air and smile. Even if our mouths don't move, the muscles around our eyes will and this could give the game away. At those moments when a smile is raging to get out, convert it into a 'polite smile' by clamping the mouth together tightly and squinting slightly. This should mask true feelings.

The eyebrows are great reaction tools, used to great effect by Roger Moore during his tenure as James Bond. Eyebrows are less of a risk area for involuntary responses but very useful to project power and elicit deeper responses. Using the tactic 'silence' together with a slight tilt of the head and raised eyebrows might just be enough to make them think again. Finally, how we hold our head is significant: looking down suggests discomfort and a tilt of the head to one side suggests listening and being receptive.

Make yourself comfortable, but not too comfortable

Whether seated in comfortable sofas or at a table, how we sit says a lot about us, how professional we are and how we feel right now. When out with family or friends it would not be out of place to sit back in a chair, perhaps cross your legs with your arms behind your head or even sit with an arm outstretched across the back of the chair beside you (Figure 12.9). In a negotiation, adopting such a relaxed and comfortable position would normally be out of place or seen to be unprofessional. Pease and Pease (2004) suggest women in particular take a dislike to men who sit this way during meetings. In a hard value-claiming negotiation, using a power position or territorial display might be appropriate, but generally it is not advised and is counterproductive.

Figure 12.9   How you sit can make all the difference

'I'm open and receptive'   Claiming territory: Relaxed, comfortable
                            'I own this place'   and open

'I'm ready to make a deal'   'I'm looking at you   'I need a barrier between
                              but I'm closed'   me and you'

Body language and culture

Some cultures use more bodily movement than others. Certain actions or gestures have different meanings in different countries and ignorance about this can easily cause offence. However, Pease and Pease (2004) suggest that despite the many differences the basic body language signals are the same everywhere. Research into what you should or should not do is always essential.

Vital signs

Once we know what to look for and we have established the specific responses an individual makes, we are looking for changes that tell us something and indicate we have reached a key point in our negotiation. Discomfort might tell us we've hit their LDO or the vital signs that give us the 'green light' to close the deal.

What discomfort looks like

As Navarro (2008) suggests, it is the shift from comfort to discomfort that is most revealing. Navarro's experience is based upon criminal interrogations and situations that are arguably more stressful than your average supplier negotiation where the signs will be less extreme. An experienced salesperson is unlikely to break into a sweat at the suggestion we want a lower price, so discomfort can be difficult to spot in everyday negotiations, although it is still there. In multimillion-pound supplier negotiations, where parties have planned for months and the salesperson's future career and bonus is dependent upon a successful outcome, discomfort is often clearly apparent.

So far we have considered some of the responses our brains drive during discomfort and these are associated with trying to shield ourselves, hide from something or stop ourselves doing something. However, Navarro (2008) suggests that as humans, when we feel discomfort, we tend to try to pacify ourselves and so it is this pacifying behaviour that can be most revealing. Pacifying behaviour can be seen at work in animals. Dogs muzzle, nudge, paw or lower their tails to reassure they are not a threat to adult dogs or other dogs that could hurt them if they are perceived as a threat. When a school of dolphins encounters a stress situation, perhaps with predators, then once out of the trouble the dolphins will swim close to one another as they flee and gently rub fins together to pacify each other. Pacifying behaviour is equally part of being human and starts when a parent or carer picks up and gently rubs a crying child to calm him down. As children get older the pain of a grazed knee seems to subside with a parent's magic rub. These are not simply nice things to do; Gray (2008) cites research that suggests that the act of rubbing stimulates pleasure nerves beneath the skin which offset the sensation of pain from other nerves thus making the pain go away. As we get older the chances of a knee rub from someone else get fewer and so we shift to self-pacification and this is exactly what to watch for in a negotiation. A rub of the forehead, rubbing hands together, stroking the chin, cheek or a beard or rubbing hands up and down the top of the legs suggests pacifying behaviour. Other signs include neck covering, pulling the collar as if 'venting' and licking the lips (Figure 12.10).

Watch for the green light

The body language behind the 'green light' is taught to salespeople and it plays an important part in negotiation. There is little point in trying to close the deal until the other party is ready; similarly, failing to close when the other party is ready could result in a missed opportunity.

People will give away how they feel much more when they are ready to proceed. Even experienced negotiators will let their guard down. When the right deal is on the table then the stress of the situation has passed; the threat has gone and there is little more to worry about. Moreover the other party may well be very excited and happy about the outcome they appear to have secured. The 'green light' is therefore a wave of emotion and a clear shift in body language and is the cue for the other side to close the deal. Signs of the 'green light' include:

- dilated pupils;
- turning toward the deal – perhaps sitting more forward or leaning towards the person whom they are negotiating with;
- visible or suppressed smile;
- face appears to 'light up' with excitement or happiness;
- any arguments or points of discussion are detail only;
- they become impatient.

Figure 12.10 Signs of discomfort and pacifying behaviour

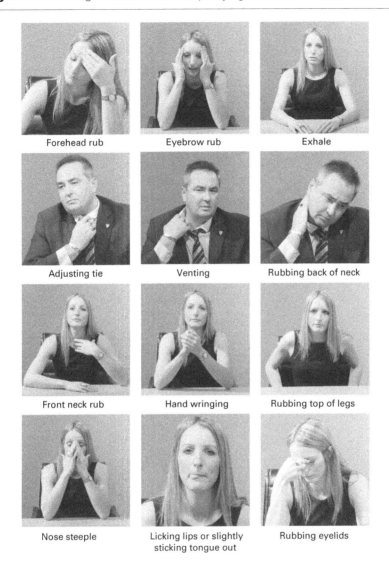

Forehead rub	Eyebrow rub	Exhale
Adjusting tie	Venting	Rubbing back of neck
Front neck rub	Hand wringing	Rubbing top of legs
Nose steeple	Licking lips or slightly sticking tongue out	Rubbing eyelids

Using body language to our advantage

Body language is something to be mastered and with well-practised observation and self-control it is possible to gain great advantage in negotiation, business, and life in general. It can even improve your love life and there are not too many negotiation books that can make that claim. Getting good is about learning to read people. This is a remarkably easy thing to do and opportunities to people-watch happen every day, but next time look harder and ask what their bodies are saying. Mastering body language requires self-awareness. You can try to put into practice what you have learnt but chances are you will not be aware of all the things you do. Asking colleagues to give feedback or even setting up role-plays and videoing yourself can provide good insight. Masking body language will help face-to-face negotiations and also those conducted by remote means where we can see our opponent (eg web conferencing tools).

Things to avoid

There are some actions that should be avoided in a negotiation. First check for any cultural taboos, but aside from these, certain actions are universally inappropriate or counterproductive and the most significant is pointing. Pointing is authoritative, condemning and aggressive; the gesture often provokes a negative response in the other and should be avoided. However, if by squeezing the thumb and forefinger together the point becomes all the less threatening and if you are a natural pointer then this is a great way to temper this gesture.

Running fingers through hair, cleaning our ears, nail biting and any other sort of preening or bodily habit should be avoided. All such actions suggest we are either not listening or we are nervous and show the other side they have achieved discomfort. Even the action of removing a small piece of fluff from a jacket lapel suggests we are not completely tuned in. Figure 12.11 shows some things to avoid.

Assume the position

There is an optimum way to sit in a negotiation (see Figure 12.12): it is sitting upright towards the edge of the chair, leaning slightly forward and with our body facing them. Hold your head up and either rest your hands palm down on the desk in front of you or, if you are prone to hand and arm movement, clasp them together in front of you. Your feet should be firmly planted on the floor either together or with one foot slightly in front of the other (which is usually more comfortable). Make eye contact and smile.

It would be somewhat impractical and odd to sit motionless during a negotiation; however, this optimum position is the 'base position'. Only let yourself break it when you want to make a deliberate move or shift, perhaps to make a certain gesture or sit back to appear relaxed for a moment, but always return to base position. It helps to imagine you are magnetically fixed into that position and if you move away then you will be drawn back.

Figure 12.11   Things to avoid in a negotiation

Pointing: 'You will do as I tell you!'

Less aggressive 'finger and thumb' pointing

Nail biting: 'I'm a bit nervous'

Preening or playing with hair; suggests you're uninterested

Removing fluff from clothing

Checking yourself

Figure 12.12   The optimum 'base position' for negotiation

The optimum 'base position' for negotiation

The optimum 'base position' if you need to keep your hands still

Mirroring

Mirroring is the art of using synchronous behaviour to build rapport. By watching what they do and doing the same (as if they are looking in a mirror) it has the effect of endearing us to them. If they put a hand on their chin then do this too. But mirroring must be subtle as, if they realize we are copying their behaviour, it will have the opposite effect. There are three ways to mirror body language:

- **Posture and movement.** Mirror how they hold their head, what they do, where they place their limbs and the speed of movement.
- **Expression and gaze.** If they look somewhere, look there too.
- **Breathing rate.** This is one of the most powerful things you can do; mirroring someone's breathing pattern establishes a strong connection. As you talk, using your peripheral vision watch when they inhale and exhale by looking at the rise or fall of their shoulders and chest.

The flinch

'The flinch' is a deliberate visual display of discomfort in response to something the other party says or does. It is designed to make the other side believe we are suffering, perhaps to create the illusion that they have pushed too far or we are at our LDO and to make them believe their proposal or suggestion is absurd. Common examples of flinching include a sudden gasp or intake of breath, a shocked expression or moving back or away from the other person. The flinch is particular powerful because watching a physical reaction registers more than someone saying 'I'm shocked'. Furthermore, seeing someone hurting triggers an empathic response and desire to help relieve the suffering. The flinch forms part of the tactic 'you're hurting me'.

While the other party may use flinching to suggest discomfort to us, equally this is a technique that can be used on them to help shore up our LDO.

Don't forget to smile and be enthusiastic

Displaying positive emotion (eg happiness, being enthusiastic, getting excited about the discussion) has a powerful effect on the other party, especially if they are inexperienced in negotiation. Such displays engender trust in the other and this in turn precipitates communication, discussion about interests and priorities and can convert a value-claiming stance by the other into value creation.

From the outset of any engagement, and at every interaction, adopt a positive persona; smile, make eye contact and demonstrate enthusiasm towards the other party.

Winning techniques for rapport building and managing body language

So as we have seen there are many things we can do to manage our body language and look for signs in others. Body language is also a key component in rapport building with our opponent. Rapport building is a key enabler within a negotiation. If we can build rapport with our opponent then we can win trust and they are more likely to do what we want. Rapport building is a key technique in life, one sales people rely on, and is an approach that can enable you to get what you want. Rapport building is not only about projecting the impression that we are genuinely interested in the other, but it is supported by some specific body language techniques. Five winning techniques for rapport building are given in Figure 12.13, along with five winning techniques for body language in Figure 12.14.

Top 10 tips for managing body language

1 Assume the perfect negotiation 'base position'; hold it and always return to it.

2 Learn to be aware of and suppress your instinctive bodily responses.

3 Smile and be enthusiastic.

4 Make good eye contact.

5 Watch their body language; use your peripheral vision to observe as much of their body as you can see. Look for clusters and changes.

6 Mirror them.

7 Accessorize… consider using glasses to hide those pupils.

8 Laugh, but only when it is appropriate. Laugher is contagious; it heals, releases endorphins and makes others laugh with you. It also helps you out when things get tricky.

9 Feel positive; be positive. If you feel good about what you are doing your entire body will reflect how you feel. It is far easier to not need to act but let your body show your true feelings. Work on getting yourself into the right frame of mind. Your body will do the rest.

10 Practise, practise, practise! Getting good at body language is within the reach of us all. Practise observation at any and every opportunity and work to become more self aware of your own body language so you can better manage it.

Figure 12.13 Winning techniques – Rapport building

Winning Techniques – Rapport

31 Build rapport

Rapport building is about building relationships quickly to gain trust and confidence of the other. It lies at the heart of selling and can help with even the most value-claiming negotiations (we are always selling some sort of outcome!) Use body and verbal language to be interested in the other.

32 Smile and make them like you

There is always room for a smile in a negotiation! Smiling, being friendly and amiable is part of rapport building and helps to win the trust and confidence of the other. It also makes them like you more and it is often possible to secure greater outcomes in a negotiation if your opponent likes you.

33 Use their name

Find ways to use the name(s) of your opponent in discussions. Using someone's name helps connect with them and show you are interested in, and value them. We love to hear our own name used so finding ways to use their name(s) helps build rapport.

34 Mirror them

Subtly mirror their body language. Adopt a similar posture and position and gently change with them, but be careful not to make it obvious. Mirroring gives the other a subconscious reassurance that you are 'just like them' so they are more likely to like and trust you.

35 Make eye contact watch theirs

Make good eye contact throughout the negotiation (aim for 70-80% of discussions). Eye contact is part of rapport building, but also allows us to watch eye movement and watch for changes that could indicate something. Keep your eye movement in check throughout.

Figure 12.14 Winning techniques – Body language

Winning Techniques – Body language

36 Good base position

Adopt a good base position to manage body language. Feet together, pointing forward, sat up straight with hands together on the desk, or apart. Move and use gestures as you need, but manage your movement so you always return to the base position. This will give you greater overall control.

37 Cues, clusters and changes

Watch them and their body language. If you can, calibrate them in a social situation. Watch for cues (movements, actions, eye direction and the things they do), look for clusters (eg same eye movement when they are recalling) and then watch for changes. Changes signal something different is happening.

38 Control yourself

Be mindful of your body language. If they are experienced, everything you do will be watched. Be alert to eye movement, how your hands move, how you sit or lean and your posture. Manage your actions and movement carefully. Always use the base position to return to.

39 Say what you want them to see

Use body language to your advantage by deliberately giving them different cues when you want them to believe something eg switch eye direction to make them think you are bluffing or fake discomfort to make them believe you are struggling and so close to your LDO.

40 And breath

Negotiations can be intense and we can get carried away by the moment. Take control of the pace, buy yourself time to consider responses and slow things down to suit you. Controlling your breathing and taking deeper, slower breaths, not only keeps you calm but puts you in control.

Managing what you say and how you say it 13

This chapter builds on the importance of body language to consider how our spoken language can also influence outcomes. It considers how we speak, ways to be more effective in our choice of language, what to avoid and how to ask and respond to questions.

Pathway questions addressed in this chapter

19 What tactics and techniques will help me be successful?

21 How can I tune into what is hidden 'behind the words' of my opponent and how can I manage what I say and how I say it to be most effective?

Red Sheet steps covered in this chapter

12 and every interaction with the supplier

Connecting with them

If only 7 per cent of received communication is based upon the actual words we use (Borg, 2010), we had better make sure we choose the ones that work as effectively as possible. If 38 per cent is based upon how we say the words, we had better make sure we are in control how we deliver the message. The problem is that our choice of language and how we use it is influenced by how we think and the way we see the world. If the person we are talking to thinks and sees the world in the same way as we do then we are all set for a meaningful exchange and good understanding. Otherwise it can be as if each is speaking a different language. Perhaps you've experienced this. It is easy to assume that everyone 'thinks' just like us. They do not. In order to negotiate effectively we need to understand and overcome what prevents us from communicating effectively and adopt some simple techniques in our spoken word.

Do you see how I feel?

Knight (2009) suggests there are three ways we represent information in our minds. I touched on these when I explored eye movement, but here they are in more detail:

- *Visual.* Thinking and seeing things in pictures. Complex concepts will be arranged visually in the mind as a pattern of elements. Recall is by seeing it in the mind. Words and numbers appear in the mind so when a visual person is remembering how to spell they are doing it by seeing the word. Visual people might say, 'I can see your point of view' or 'Looking at our current situation...'
- *Auditory.* Thinking in sounds. Concepts are considered, evaluated and remembered by hearing the words in the mind. Auditory people might say, 'I hear what you say' or 'It sounds like you've made up your mind'.
- *Feeling* (kinaesthetic). Thinking is based upon emotion and how something feels. Recall is based upon how something felt inside or recall of physical stimuli (touch, taste or smell). Feeling people might say, 'I feel we are close to agreement' or 'This outcome could leave a bad taste in my mouth'.

If a visual person gets up and attempts to illustrate a concept on a flip chart to an auditory person, the auditory person may well sit there looking overwhelmed because of the need to translate what they are seeing into a way they can process. This can sometimes be seen happening as an auditory person may well read out each drawn component, as if talking to him- or herself so as to make sense of what is seen. By understanding how our opponent thinks we can tailor our interaction with them so our words don't need to be translated by them. Drawing a concept out for a visual person goes straight into their mind. The clues to whether they understand are there in what the other person says. If you are unsure, then throw out some test questions like, 'How do you see this?' or 'Tell me how you feel about this' to see how readily or not they respond and, of course, watch where their eyes go when they are recalling something.

Listen up

> There's a saying among negotiators that whoever talks the most during a
> negotiation loses.
> Covic (2004)

The word 'listen' contains the same letters as the word 'silent', which is a
happy coincidence as learning to stay silent and not talk too much is a pre-
requisite if we are to hear what is really said and unsaid. In doing so, we
increase the chances of figuring out what they want and how we can go
about moving towards an agreement. Not only do we need to fully and accurately understand the other's position 'as spoken' but buried in the words
we are hearing our opponent say may be golden nuggets of information,
implication or inference that can reveal much more than the actual words
intended. We will only spot these if we truly listen.

Covey (2004) said 'most people do not listen with the intent to understand; they listen with the intent to reply'. We all think we are great listeners,
myself included, until I did some listening skills training and found out that
what I was actually good at was the art of waiting for a gap in the conversation to say what I wanted to say, which apparently doesn't count. I later
recounted my epiphany to those close to me who were less surprised than I
had hoped. The problem is when we listen we tend to hear only some of
what the other party says and the rest we miss because:

- we relate what we hear to how we think and see the world;
- we add in new detail based upon our experiences;
- we are too busy thinking about what we will say when it's our turn;
- we drift off and think about what we are going to have for dinner tonight.

Body language that gives the impression of being 'receptive and interested'
is important to show we are listening, but despite this any lack of interest
can still be apparent. Eyes glaze over or facial expressions can betray. The
only true way to listen is to actually listen – intently, blocking out all other
thoughts, and concentrating only on the other party. Head-nodding helps to
show affirmation and interestingly this originates from the act of bowing to
show being subordinate to the other party, which of course is exactly what
happens when we listen.

It is worth some further reading on listening skills as it is a topic all of its
own. However, there are some simple techniques that can be used to develop
listening skills, outlined below.

Learning to listen

A technique to develop your skills

Find a quiet space and willing colleague or someone you trust to help you. Sit together facing each other with no table between you. Ask your colleague or friend to think of something in their life that is concerning them that they are prepared to talk about. You should agree that this discussion will remain between the two of you.

Have this person talk to you for a full seven minutes about their concern. During this time you must face your opponent and work to give all the signs you are listening (eg make eye contact, nod etc). However, you must remain silent, speaking only to ask for clarification if needed but not making any comment on what is being said. You cannot make notes and you have to remember what is being said, creating themes or groupings in your mind to make sense of what you hear. You will need to concentrate hard not to relate what you hear to your own experiences or to add anything of your own.

At the end of the seven minutes play back to your colleague or friend a summary of what you think you heard and ask them to tell you how accurate you were and if you added, changed or missed anything. If you like you can swap and do the same in reverse. The secret of listening is what you do in your mind and the way you theme, group and resist embellishment to what you hear. This is a skill you can develop and by repeating this exercise and applying listening skills in everyday life you will soon develop your technique.

Paralanguage and metalanguage

There are two components that sit behind the words we say that can convey deeper meaning: 'paralanguage' and 'metalanguage'. Both provide a useful ally in a negotiation if we can code what we say and decode what we hear but if we are not aware of our actions, both can leave us vulnerable to revealing too much.

Paralanguage means the non-verbal elements to spoken communication including the pitch, volume, rate, inflection and intonation of our speech. Through paralanguage we convey emotion and expression. Once again, the brain is managing what we do in response to our situation or what we are trying to convey and so typically we might express emotion despite not intending to do so or inadvertently try to hide emotions that seem out of place. All this means that changes in the voice can reveal deeper feelings and emotions if the listener knows what to listen for.

Metalanguage, as described at length by Pease and Garner (1992), means the encoding of ideas other than the one of the spoken language, in other words saying something more than, or different to, what the words alone say. The result is what we say has a 'surface' meaning and 'deeper' meaning (Chomsky, 1975). Job interviews, and the resumés that precede them, are breeding grounds for metalanguage; 'I have extensive practical experience across a wide range of industries' really means 'I've no qualifications and don't stick in a job for very long.' Metalanguage includes a range of language techniques used deliberately, habitually or without intention. Deeper meaning is conveyed through embellishments, emphasizing, hidden meaning, generalizations, the way sentences are distorted, or by what is left out. I will explore some of these over the next few sections.

Mirror paralanguage

In the last chapter we explored the concept of body language mirroring with similar gestures and matching their breathing. Mirroring paralanguage is another powerful component in building rapport and winning their trust. If one individual is speaking frantically fast and then receiving a reply from another speaking in a slow considered fashion then the mismatch is obvious and the exchange appears more about tolerance than real listening.

If someone speaks slowly in a quiet tone then mirror this; if they like to get excited and animated then mirror this and a natural empathy will develop. However, don't mirror when their paralanguage escalates and becomes negative or aggressive, as this will fuel the escalation. Instead do the opposite and the resultant mismatch will draw attention to their changed behaviour and should trigger them to reconsider their approach. Don't get too carried away with mirroring as it is easy to inadvertently imitate accents and that can be interpreted as a form of ridicule. Be careful not to make it obvious that they are being copied.

Reading between the lines

Ahead of the Olympics in 2012 the New York Bakery Company published a 'Guide to British', a translator for New Yorkers, used to brash and direct exchanges, who were travelling to the United Kingdom for the Games, as an aid to integrate (Ward, 2012). The guide proposed that we British generally tend to avoid being confrontational or saying how we feel and that we will use more words than necessary for the sake of politeness. It is true that when asked how we are, we might answer, 'I'm fine' even when we are not, even in the most dire of situations, and in a crowd we prefer to say, 'I'm sorry' rather than 'Watch where you're going.' Within British culture there is a universal understanding of what we actually mean when we don't say it directly, but observe us from outside and the indirectness might seem strange and unnecessary.

Saying something that is different, or even opposite to what is meant is not just a curious British thing but is something that happens to a greater or lesser extent in many cultures, so prior cultural research around how direct a culture can be expected to be is important. Furthermore, negotiation presents greater scope for hidden meaning because, by the very nature of negotiation, parties will tend to dress things up to mislead or lay out a position and will reveal cautiously.

Reading between the lines is the ability to understand the true meaning behind what is spoken. It is simply a case of considering the subtext to their spoken words and perhaps testing what they say. It is a skill that develops with practice. Combine this with body language observation and we have a wealth of different cues to tell us what they are actually thinking. Consider these examples:

- 'To consider further reduction in price we would need to have some guarantee of volumes' means 'You're not at my LDO yet but I'm trading.' Test with: 'If we could guarantee volumes then what price point can you offer?' If they answer, then irrespective of whether you can guarantee volumes you now know more about their LDO.

- 'We would need a commitment before the last day of this month in order to qualify for the old pricing' means 'I need this sale to get my bonus' or 'We need cash.'

- 'We'll put our best team and project manager on it' means 'We don't really know who will do this yet.'

- 'I don't wish to start haggling on this but...' means 'I'm about to start haggling with you on this.'

- 'I'm not sure exactly' means 'I know but don't want to say.'

Emphasizing words

By emphasizing certain words the entire meaning of what we say can change. This type of metalanguage is often used to communicate a hidden intent where it is inappropriate to state something directly. For example: 'I must tell you that we have no budget to do this *this* year' might be the correct statement in line with a corporate position but the emphasized *this* also tells a valued supplier you are hopeful for next year. Consider the statement, 'I don't feel your proposal is quite good enough for me to agree to it.' The meaning is changed completely by emphasizing certain words:

- '*I* don't feel your proposal is quite good enough for me to agree to it' means I don't like it but suggests others might.

- 'I don't feel *your* proposal is quite good enough for me to agree to it' suggests there are other proposals and they are better.

- 'I don't feel your proposal is *quite* good enough for me to agree to it' suggests it is very close and there is only a small gap to bridge.

- 'I don't feel your proposal is quite good enough for *me* to agree to it' suggests it might be agreed but by someone else.

Embellishments

Additional words designed to boost the meaning behind a simple statement are typically added in order to disguise misinformation. Ask a child what she is doing in a place she is not supposed to be and the reply might be '*I'm just* looking for something I lost' as if adding '*I'm just...*' will de-emphasize and minimize the impact of the stated reason. Embellishments that de-emphasize tend to be used when the speaker is uncomfortable with what they have to say, perhaps because it is not entirely true. Other examples include: 'I *absolutely* did not say that...' or 'I *especially* want to...' with the addition of 'absolutely' and 'especially' augmenting the rest of the sentence. Others are 'to be honest with you' and 'I won't lie to you'. These are not reliable indicators of whether someone is lying or providing misinformation because the need to add embellishments becomes habitual in some people, possibly reflecting an insecurity or lack of confidence. However, in a negotiation embellishments should be avoided as they can have the effect of suggesting we are not being entirely honest or our statements alone are not enough.

Questions and answers

Questioning helps to project power, and Pease and Garner (1992) suggest that when we ask the questions we control, to a large extent, the topics that are discussed. In a negotiation, questioning helps develop understanding, gathers intelligence about their position, and buys time to think while they do all the talking.

Clarifying questions

The deeper meaning behind our words is neither expressed, nor known consciously (Chomsky, 1975). Is it easy to assume that because we have a clear understanding of something then our words will communicate this in full. This is rarely the case.

Knight (2009) suggests our use of language is based upon the filters our minds use to help us make sense of the world and filter out what our brains think is not relevant to us. Our perspective then drives what we say. Knight suggests this manifests itself in three different ways depending upon how we filter: deleting some of the experience in what we say, distorting what we say, or by generalizing. In a negotiation, statements that have deletions, are distorted or which use generalizations are unhelpful and deny us access to the intelligence we need to advance our position. Therefore we need to be attuned to what is not being said or communicated and use questioning to fill in the missing details. Knight (2009) calls these 'precision questions'. It is this technique that the police and those investigating incidents are taught to use. An eyewitness account of a crime is only of value if the witness's observation skills are reliable (and without training most of us will fall short here) and if it is possible to extract an accurate account from him or her. When the witness says, 'I saw the burglar leave the house and head quickly up the road. I thought there was something odd about him', then the interviewer might respond with a series of clarifying questions to gain a more precise account. For example, to clarify they might ask: 'Where did you observe this from? How did you know it was the burglar? Which way is "up" the road? How did he head up the road – on foot, running or by other means? Quickly, compared to what? What suggested there was something odd? How do you know it was a man?' and so on.

In a negotiation, the use of clarifying questions is an important skill needed in order to collect a precise understanding. Such questions also serve to reconnect the speaker with their own internal understanding. This triggers them to revaluate their words and even their thoughts and then to restate, but in doing so they are required to provide more information. Examples include:

- *Being vague.* 'They don't let us discount our products.' Who is they? Why are 'they' not in the room?

- *Personal opinions presented as facts.* 'It is wrong to keep asking us to reduce our prices.' Says who? Why would this be unreasonable if the market is shifting?

- *An abstract situation.* 'We're in a changing market situation.' Changing how?

- *Unsubstantiated comparisons.* 'Our service is second to none.' Compared with whose? How and when was this measured?

- *Telling you how you feel.* 'I know you'll not like what we are about to offer, but...' How can you know that?

- *Judgements.* 'Your company is difficult to do business with.' What makes you say that? What makes it difficult?

- *Using feelings to blame.* 'You are making me feel threatened.' How can I be doing that?

- *Interpretations.* 'Volumes have declined in recent months. Obviously you have a problem?'

- *Generalizations.* 'I never haggle in a negotiation.' Never? How do you win any sales? Why are you here?

- *Imperatives.* 'I must close this deal by the end of the month.' Or what? Why do you need this so much?

- *Unsubstantiated dead stops.* 'I can't agree to that.' Why not? Where do we go from here?

Building on what they say

Use of questioning that builds on what they say means finding the question to ask is easy as they have already given us the prompt and this approach serves to boost their ego, convey interest, buys us time to think, to watch their body language and assess. Knight (2009) describes this as a highly effective technique and suggests such questions should be asked as if naïve, not knowing, fascinated, selfless and eager to learn. Questions that build work by mirroring and repeating part of what the other party says, and then asking them to tell us more. This type of question will also often elicit more information than they set out to give. For example:

Supplier: '... and of course we are working on some exciting new innovations that could help your business as we move forward.'

Buyer: 'Innovations that could help in what way?'

Supplier: 'We could help you enhance your brand by improving your customers' experience.'

Buyer: 'Improve it... how could you do that?'

Supplier: 'We are developing a new interactive client portal that could be fully branded so it looks like it is an extension of your business.'

Buyer: 'What would our customers do in this extension of our business?' And so on.

Avoiding answering

It would be great if we got to ask all the questions and they got to provide all the answers. However, in reality questions and answers is a two-way exchange but it is possible to gain an advantage here.

A significant risk is being asked a loaded question. These are questions where whichever way we answer might weaken our position or give away information. For example, 'Is there any room for movement here?' is a loaded question. Answer 'no' and we have entered into an unproductive game of brinkmanship; answer 'yes' and we have signalled that they haven't reached our LDO after all. There are several lines of defence here:

- *Answer with a question.* 'Do you really think there could be any room for improvement, given where we are at with this?'

- *Question the question.* 'Why are you asking that of me, I've already outlined my position?'

- *Duck the question.* 'I'm not going to enter into that sort of "street trader" exchange with you.'

- *Defer the question.* 'Let's come back to that later once we've discussed everything else.'

However, when we ask them a question that gets evaded by deflecting discussions elsewhere, they can be brought back by answering the question for them, giving the answer we would like to hear and waiting for them to either confirm or deny.

If we end up fielding question after question from the other party, as if being interrogated, then this can shift the balance of power more in their favour because the individual asking is accumulating lots of information on his terms while we can only answer and give over information. Clearly answering their questions may well be a necessary part of the exchange, but if this becomes imbalanced then change the game. Simply start deferring and switching the subject to start asking them the questions, for example, 'Okay, let's come back to that, but first I'd like to understand…'.

Open and closed questions

Open questions are those that elicit an explanatory response such as 'Tell me about your proposal' or 'Can you explain how you arrived at this figure?' Closed questions require a definitive single word response such as 'Is this your final offer?' or 'Will you agree to my offer?'

Both open and closed questions have their place in negotiation but use the right type of question for the right scenario. Open questions are great to get them talking, but if our questions are too open-ended then it can have the reverse effect. Asking a question such as 'How is business right now?' might seem a good test of how much they need a good outcome, but this question is unlikely to yield a meaningful response. First, the supplier will recognize why it is being asked; second, the scope is too broad so it is easy for them to answer with a vague response that tells us little such as, 'Oh we're fairly busy, a few challenges here and there but nothing we're not used to.' A more revealing question might be, 'If we can reach an agreement, how fast can you resource this?' Similarly, using a closed question can be self-defeating if they give the unwanted response and cut off valuable options. After all it is unlikely any supplier would ever answer 'No' to 'Is that your final offer?'

Leading and manipulative questions

Leading questions are highly manipulative and are questions that are designed to lead the respondent to give only the desired response. The question is phrased in such a way that the expected answer is included within the question. An example would be, 'We're both in agreement here aren't we?' Leading questions are often used by salespeople to close a deal as a way of removing obstacles to buying; if there is a glimmer of truth in what they ask then it is difficult not to give the desired answer. An example in this instance might be, 'Don't you think that this is exactly the right model for what you want?'

Winning approaches

Influence and persuasion

Mastering the art of influence and persuasion can unlock all sorts of outcomes in business and in life generally. It is the subject of many sales and personal effectiveness books with a host of approaches and winning ways. Influencing *people* is just that; it is about individuals not companies. In business negotiations parties will be acting on behalf of a company but it is individuals who will ultimately make the decision to agree or not agree, acting within the remit they have been assigned. Therefore influencing individuals secures outcomes.

Cialdini (2001) suggests there are six principles of influence that persuade people and these can be used to structure negotiation approaches and arguments. Note that some of the tactics previously outlined use one or more of these:

- *Reciprocity*. If we give a gift or favour people tend to return the favour.
- *Commitment and consistency*. People tend to be consistent and if they commit to an outcome, goal, idea or to doing something then they are more likely to honour that commitment, even if the original motivation is removed. People who decide to leave a job will often want to 'see things through' before they leave. (This is the basis for the countermeasure tactic 'but we agreed'.)
- *Social proof*. People do things they see others doing and follow the lead of others 'just like them'.
- *Authority*. People tend to obey those in apparent authority.
- *Liking*. People are more easily persuaded if they like the other person.
- *Scarcity*. Perceived scarcity creates demand; people tend to act more readily if they think time is running out or only a few remain. (This is the basis for the tactics 'for a deal today…' and 'carried away by the moment'.)

Weaving one or more of these six principles into our discussions can improve our power. Reciprocity sits at the heart of the 'Trust' game and is the basis for the 'Santa Claus' tactic. Authority and liking come from how we present and conduct ourselves and we have explored this at length already.

If we can secure commitment to an outcome then we may well have already won the negotiation, even if discussions are not concluded. Double-glazed windows are standard in most of northern Europe and North

America, but the salesmen who call at people's homes to try to sell replacements often use hard sales tactics. At the heart of their approach is the notion of getting commitment. If they can convince the homeowner to invite them in to 'discuss the possibility' then they are already committed to the idea of buying new windows. If the customer allows them to start measuring up then they are almost certainly committed and likely to follow through; from there on in it is just a discussion about price. In a negotiation getting them committed to the outcome means from that point on the discussions need to focus on closing the deal. This works in practice by encouraging them to focus on how things will be if the negotiation is concluded successfully, as if the rest of the negotiation is just a formality. At the point when they start talking enthusiastically about how things will work and use language such as '... and we will do X' or 'we can do Y...' rather than 'if we are successful here...'.

Social proof can frighten people into action if they feel they are letting their company lag behind. Very few companies really understand how they compare to their peers. Even those that spend large sums of money for consultancy companies to benchmark them in some way can only gain access to information according to the companies the consultancy has had exposure to or those who have agreed to participate. Social proof is therefore a powerful weapon in negotiation and using it puts us in an authoritative position. Examples of this could be, 'You should know that your competitors are already offering this feature as standard' or 'All of our other suppliers have agreed to the new terms.' If you elect to bluff here, be careful that you can handle a subsequent challenge either immediately or later.

Finally, scarcity drives agreement based upon creating a fear of missing an opportunity. Scarcity can be a limited time offer, infrequent opportunities such as being selected for inclusion on a master or framework agreement, or to be one of a very few number of selected suppliers. Selling the benefits of the outcome, and then introducing the factors that suggest the opportunity is rare or limited, creates scarcity. This in turn compels the other party to make a rapid decision with the risk of loss if they don't agree to our offer.

Say their name

Including the other party's name within some of our sentences will make them pay more attention. If we can include something complimentary and unique to them the effect is highly potent. Pease and Garner (1992) suggest that people consider their name to be the most beautiful sound in the world and will pay more attention to sentences in which it appears. 'Sascha, I've reviewed your extremely thorough and well-presented spreadsheet and I have some questions' would likely result in a positive response from Sascha.

Glass is half-full

Instead of suggesting the glass is half-empty, tell them it's half-full and see how well they respond. Negative statements can cut like a knife, stop things dead and dash all hope. Talking in the positive is more likely to provoke a similar positive response. For example, if you say to a supplier that you want to work with, 'You haven't been working closely enough with us on this', it will most likely provoke a defensive response, some retaliation and shifting some blame back to us. However, a more positive phrasing is likely to release the desired outcome and more importantly ownership by them: 'Moving forward, there is much greater opportunity for us to work together, and we will both benefit if you could get closer to what we are doing.' Chances are they will come up with some suggestions to do just this.

And now for something completely different

And is such a small word but can convey great power by building on what they say or adding a further incentive. For example, if they say, 'We could put one of our staff into your team to help mobilize the project' a reply might be, '*And* we will train them up in how we work.' Alternatively 'and' can extend the attractiveness of an offer: 'I can agree to X, *and* I can throw in Y as well.' 'And' can also help to make hypothetical questions more appealing by building on what they say: '*And* if we did agree to these terms, describe the increased value that this new arrangement will bring our business.'

Watch what you say

Oral contracts

It may be necessary or intentional in some negotiations to give a verbal instruction and make a clear commitment to the supplier. If I buy a car I might negotiate, agree a price and then shake hands to confirm the agreement, concluding the deal there and then. However, many business negotiations are a prelude to crystallizing the points of agreement in a robust legal document. The deal is therefore not finalized in the negotiation itself.

An oral contract is where a contract is agreed by verbal exchanges between two or more parties. It is easy to inadvertently enter into an oral contract within a negotiation. In most countries oral contracts are legally binding and there are remedies in law for breach. However, the practicalities of enforcing an oral contract mean it often comes down to our word against theirs. In my experience, accounts of what was agreed can change post-negotiation if someone believes they signed up to something they later regretted. In a team-based negotiation where there are witnesses to what is said on both sides the risk of an inadvertent oral contract becoming enforceable is heightened. Understanding how oral contracts get made and how to avoid doing this is therefore essential for any negotiator.

Under English Law, for any contract (including oral contracts) to be formed four components need to be in place:

- *An offer.* An expression of willingness by one party to buy or sell something at a stated price or on stated terms. Note that if the supplier presents a proposal, price list or defines fees in some way this is not an offer but an 'invitation to treat'. The offer is the subsequent act of offering to buy the stated goods or service.
- *Acceptance of the offer.* The other party signals that they accept the offer as stated. If acceptance is conditional then this becomes a counter offer.
- *Consideration.* The exchange of something of value between parties for such a sum of money.
- *Intent.* By both parties to enter into, and be capable of entering into, a legally binding agreement and to be bound by that agreement.

When something is purchased from a shop it is clear how these components come together, so it is hard to buy something accidently in WalMart. Within the exchanges that happen in a negotiation it can be less obvious and that presents risk. Essentially, if we agree to do something, sell something or buy something and someone else acts on our statement then an oral contract may be formed. The difficulty here is that negotiation is all about exploring positions and individual points of agreement in order to unlock a larger-scale agreement. Consider this example:

The oral contract for consultancy support

A consultancy company offered a discount on the consultant day rates they have set out in a proposal based upon the client's buying 200 consultant days to support the project over the next year. No minimum commitment was subsequently formalized as, during the negotiation, the buyer had suggested the project would more than exceed that number of days, but for budgetary reasons the consultancy company would need to bill monthly based upon days worked each month. During the negotiation it was agreed the consultancy company would start the engagement immediately on this basis. However, after just two months, the client announced a reorganization and promptly cancelled the project. The consultancy company was told to 'stand down'. The consultancy company claimed there was an oral contract for 200 days and because the client had accepted the reduced rate (the first invoice billed for days at the lower rate when compared to the original proposal and this invoice had been paid without question), that they were in breach of contract. The buyer claimed there was never any firm commitment on number of days. The dispute could not be resolved and after considering legal action the consultancy company decided its best option was to walk away.

In this case the buyer may well have been acting with good intentions or just testing positions to see where the consultancy company's LDO was, believing the 200 days to be no more than a basis for trading. The consultancy company didn't secure any formal agreement and so had engaged at a risk anyway. So who was right? Only a court of law could have ultimately decided if there was an oral contract, if indeed there was a breach and what a suitable remedy might be. However, what this case shows is that getting into a dispute is almost always damaging to one and usually both parties. Pursuing remedies through the courts is expensive, time-consuming and stressful. Disputes should be avoided and so to do this, the risk of a scenario where a party could allege an oral contract had been made must be avoided too. The risk comes from the way offer and acceptance happens but we can mitigate this risk some by:

- *Making offers conditional.* Treitel (2007) defines the offer as an 'an expression of willingness to contract on certain terms without further negotiations', suggesting that if we are clear that the negotiations are incomplete when we are exploring possible positions or points of agreement they cannot comprise an offer. For example consider this exchange:

> Supplier: 'So if we reduce the fee structure in our proposal by 20 per cent as you have suggested will that be acceptable?'
>
> Buyer: 'Yes, in principle, subject to us agreeing terms and the final contract.'

- *Signposting non-acceptance.* Acceptance could be accidently signalled at any point within the process of exploring and bargaining. Even a nod of the head at the wrong time could count. This risk can be reduced by clear signposting of our responses when needed: 'To be clear, I am not signalling any sort of acceptance here, we are just exploring positions at this stage...'.

The games of 'Trust' and 'Prisoner's Dilemma' carry risk of oral contracts if a suggested agreement is defaulted on. The way these games are played needs careful consideration to avoid any risk of oral contract being made.

Use 'No' sparingly

No means 'No'! When we say 'no' we close a door and we are providing a strong signal to the other party that we are not prepared to re-open this door. There are points in a negotiation where saying 'no' to an offer provides a heavy piece of conditioning to prevent revealing our LDO too early. The key here is to be aware how absolute using 'no' is in a negotiation; either we are clear we are saying 'no' because we won't accept what is offered or we are confident it is a tactic that won't jeopardize future discussions. There are many alternatives to 'no' which often work better and keep our options more open: instead of rejecting a proposal, provide an alternative ('as an alternative I suggest...'); or if the other party makes an unreasonable request, instead of simply saying 'no', respond with a counter proposal that makes an equally unreasonable request back.

Bluffing

A bluff is a lie! Therefore every bluff carries with it all the trappings of lying so bluffs should be used with great care. Bluffing does have its place in negotiation but the problem is that if we get found out then we lose credibility with our opponent for this, and all future engagements with them. It is a dangerous game. However, if you choose to bluff then think about the following:

- *Make it real.* Do your homework and check out the facts. Determine a bluff that is plausible but more importantly one that they won't be able to verify. Remember they are probably better informed than you so you should only bluff with something they can't have checked out in advance.

- *Be certain your stakeholders are fully on board.* There is no point bluffing about the risk of the supplier losing business if they don't win the negotiation if a senior stakeholder has already given them commitment elsewhere.

- *Always leave yourself an exit route.* Be prepared to be found out and then have a countermeasure you will deploy should this happen. The best is to act dumb and misinformed, saying something such as, 'Oh, I'm sorry, perhaps I'm misinformed or perhaps you know more than I so I need to go and check this out some more.'

Things to avoid

Some verbal or language practices can be counterproductive to negotiation or the process of building rapport. Here are the top 10 things to avoid, including those proposed by Hazeldine (2011):

Top 10 things to avoid

- **Sarcasm.** It rarely translates across geographical boundaries, can offend and can suggest a lack of confidence.

- **Clichés.** Clichés are overused phrases or sayings that people copy and adopt when they are unable to create their own words. Examples include: 'at the end of the day', 'incidentally' or clichés to illustrate a position such as 'any port in a storm' or 'let's not beat around the bush here'. Clichés can be annoying, often don't translate across geographical boundaries and some can offend. More importantly clichés don't help project power. People who seem to have a certain air of authority or are compelling in some way will rarely use clichés but will make the effort to use original forms of words and be direct about what they mean and want.

- **Talking too much.** If you're talking you're not listening and they gain the power of space to reflect.

- **Interrupting too much**. Interrupting suggests you are not listening and that you are determining meaning from your own experiences and so you will miss vital metalanguage.

- **Blaming**. Creates conflict and puts them in a defensive position and rarely serves any meaningful purpose.

- **Threats**. Could make them play their BATNA but in any case will reduce scope for collaboration.

- **'But'**. The moment you end a sentence with 'but' you are reversing and contradicting everything you or they just said. For example, 'you have given a good presentation but...'

- **Personal insults**. Insults are unnecessary and unprofessional and making it personal suggests a lack of control that puts you in a lower power position.

- **Reacting to provocation**. Puts them in the power position and you become subordinate. Suggests they are getting to you and could create a downward spiral of conflict.

- **Swearing**. Swearing can offend but more importantly powerful, respected people will rarely find the need to swear but will leave that to those who feel they need to add something more to get their point across.

Cultural norms might also dictate certain practices that should be avoided and so prior research should identify and plan for these as appropriate.

Winning verbal techniques

The key techniques for how we use language and the way we speak during a negotiation are summarized in Figure 13.1.

Figure 13.1   Winning techniques – Verbal

Winning Techniques – Verbal 1

41 Mirror paralanguage

Match the tone, speed and perhaps even inflection of their voice as they talk. This will make you 'just like them', will connect on a subconscious level with them and build rapport. Don't match when they get confrontational, instead do the opposite and use your paralanguage to calm things down.

42 Match language to their mindset

Figure out how they think and represent the world in their minds – are they mostly visual, auditory or kinesthetic (based on feeling). Do this by listening for clues in the language they use (eg 'do you see what I mean?') and eye movement. Match your language to their mindset to build rapport (eg 'yes I get the picture').

43 Be positive

Be positive and enthusiastic. If you act positive you will feel positive and your entire body language will reflect this. Positive outward behaviour is contagious and very likeable, and so builds rapport with the other. It also makes you someone who appears to achieve things and so brings a deal closer.

44 Use clarifying questions

As they lay out negotiation positions, use clarifying questions to gain the advantage. Distil things down to pure fact and remove generalizations, opinions, feelings, interpretations and anything that is unsubstantiated. Eg 'we are very competitive on this', 'competitive compared to whom?'

45 Read between the lines

Listen to what is being said 'between the lines'. The language people use often betrays true thoughts and feelings. Listen for embellishments, quantifiers and vague statements. For example 'We simply cannot go any lower, the price has to be around £100 per unit' means there is more to be had.

Figure 13.1 *continued*

Winning Techniques – Verbal 2

46 Build on what they say

Building on what they say builds rapport and serves to boost their ego by conveying interest. Use questions that repeat part of what they say then ask them to tell more to elicit more information from them. Eg 'Our service could help improve your business.' 'You could improve our business – how would you do that?'

47 And now for something different

The word 'and' is a very powerful rapport, building tool and helps with the 'build on what they say' technique and adds a further incentive. Eg 'and if we did agree to that' or 'and if you did agree to X we could provide Y to' or 'and of course we both want to make a deal here' and so on.

48 We not I

Using 'I' when negotiating can project an egotistical position and makes you the single obstacle to be won over. It makes the negotiation personal. Instead 'we' makes you more collaborative and likeable but also serves to create the illusion of a higher authority – ie others will need to be convinced also.

49 Use no sparingly

There is a place for 'no' in some negotiations, but use it sparingly. No means 'no' and closes a door. It is a strong signal that can sometimes establish a strong position, but might also jeopardize future discussions. Watch you don't use 'no' and change your mind too often or you will lose credibility.

50 Don't make an oral contract

Choose you language carefully so you don't enter into an oral contract. Avoid making firm commitment until you are ready. Make offers and discussions 'conditional on agreeing the final contract' and signpost you are 'not agreeing or accepting but exploring positions.

Post-negotiation 14 activities a success

This chapter explores how post-negotiation activities are provided for, including a 'lessons learnt review'. We cover exactly what we must do in order to ensure the agreement we made during the event gets realized.

Pathway questions addressed in this chapter

22 How do I ensure what we agreed during the negotiation is followed through and realized?

Red Sheet steps covered in this chapter

13, 14 and 15

It ain't over till...

'It ain't over until the fat lady sings' said Dan Cook in 1978 after the basketball game between the San Antonio Spurs and the Washington Bullets, to suggest that while Spurs had won, the series was not over yet.

When we walk away from a successful negotiation it can often be as if walking off a battlefield, victorious but bearing battle scars and tending to wounds. The desire to leave it all behind and go and celebrate over a beer or two can be overwhelming. Celebrating success is important, especially for team-based negotiations, in order to reward hard work and keep the team motivated for the next negotiation. But the negotiation may not yet be complete and chances are there is still work to do. Parties may have agreed the deal but until all the formalities are in place and new arrangements are fully implemented, the deal is not yet done.

It is not uncommon for a 'firm deal' made in the room to suddenly evaporate after the event, perhaps following reflection on the part of the other party or perhaps they reported back only to be told the deal is unacceptable when they believed they had the remit to make such an agreement. Perhaps it is a deliberate tactic (as in the tactic 'KGB'). I have experienced a supplier make a clear agreement during a negotiation and subsequently deny he ever said anything of the sort. When I pushed him about what he thought we had discussed and agreed during three hours we were together, his recollection was a bit hazy and confused. So in concluding a negotiation be aware that there is always a chance that things change after you walk away. This risk is reduced if:

1 You previously established that your opponent has the necessary authority.

2 Before you leave the negotiation, you ensure that there is clear alignment of understanding of what was agreed.

3 The negotiation tactics are constructed so they walk away happy, feeling as if they have achieved a win, even if this is not the case. If they walk away feeling duped or disadvantaged too much, they may well decide to renege on what was agreed.

The aim and focus of post-negotiation activities is therefore to finalize the deal and make what was agreed in a meeting a reality as fast as possible so the risk of things changing is reduced. All actions, whether agreed during the negotiation or identified post-negotiation should be planned and carried out so an action plan (what, by when and who) is essential with clear accountabilities and timescales for each. Step 13 is where we record and action plan all post-event actions. A completed example is given in Figure 14.1 and the template is provided in the Appendix.

The legal contract

The negotiation may not be complete when we leave the room. While agreement may have been reached, and even effected, say with a handshake or an instruction, many negotiations in business will require that the points

Figure 14.1 Red Sheet step 13 – Post-event actions (worked example)

13. POST-EVENT ACTIONS

Post-Event Actions

	Who	when
- Have a legal develop the contract	M.M.	May 15th
- Organize factory visit	M.M.	End of May
- Appoint transition project manager	M.M.	End of May

To carry forward to the next negotiation

- Operations Manager's body language reveals his thinking... watch his arms

- We think there is more to be gained in overhead structures

- Their costs reduce as the factory reaches capacity... scope for future negotiations of agreement are subsequently formalized with a contractually binding arrangement, perhaps in the form of a purchase order, master or framework agreement or a full written contract.

The final legal framework, wrapped around the specific negotiation outcomes, should provide clarification to parties about how the arrangement will work and can provide protection if the unexpected happens. This might typically include the terms and conditions expected to be present in most contracts including aspects such as termination, limits of liabilities should things go wrong, and provision for unforeseen events or things outside of the control of the parties. Unless these have been specifically agreed prior to or during the negotiation, then further negotiation may be required to agree these finer points. Exchanges between parties around terms and conditions can drag on or even stop proceedings dead if parties cannot agree. Furthermore, if the process of finalizing the legal framework is handed off to separate legal teams, who may have had little or no involvement in the discussions up to that point, then the risk of last-minute complications is heightened. Sometimes the stated need for the legal team to get involved can be a deliberate tactic to reopen negotiations and secure further concessions, using the veil of corporate policy and so on to hide the real intention.

The successful negotiation that failed

Following an RFP (Request for Proposal) exercise, a buyer acting on behalf of a global corporation with a presence in most countries worldwide secured a favourable agreement for global audio and web conferencing services with a single provider based in the United States. Following the negotiation the buyer formalized what had been agreed into a master agreement supported by standard terms and conditions. The provider's legal team rejected this and stated it was policy that only their terms and conditions could be used. Eventually it was agreed that terms would need to be negotiated and the seller's terms would be used as the starting point. A series of lengthy discussions and exchanges between the legal functions in both companies ensued and while agreement was reached for most of the points under discussion, there were two issues that could not be agreed upon: appropriate levels of insurance provision and limits of liability, with both parties claiming that this was a matter of policy. In the end discussions stalled and an alternative supplier who had made a proposal needed to be re-engaged.

A contract completes the negotiation process. It is then down to parties to do what they have agreed or the other will have legal remedies should breach occur. However, a contract does many things and at some point in time a contract will be required – or the absence of a contract will become detrimental. Contracts provide:

- formal definition of what was agreed by each party during the negotiation;
- the legal framework to bring all aspects of the agreement together and contextualize it within the prevailing laws of the specified country;
- formal definition of the detail regarding what is to be provided and the way in which it will be provided, as well as how the relationship will work;
- definition of what happens when things change or go wrong;
- a vehicle for parties to signal formal agreement, eg by signing.

The role of purchasing in the contractual process varies from organization to organization. Some companies, especially US ones, place all aspects of contract development and execution within a legal function. Others place this role within the purchasing function. Some combine both, with purchasing developing an outline of the contractual elements before they are passed over to a legal function to complete the process and make it legally watertight. Whatever the arrangements are, it is important to remember that most purchasing people are not lawyers and therefore the degree of responsibility purchasing assumes with respect to establishing and managing appropriate legal arrangements should be considered carefully and should be balanced according to capability, experience and training.

Negotiation and the business of defining and agreeing a suitable contract should not be considered as separate activities; they are part of the same process. Negotiation planning should be approached with this in mind so ideally there are no surprises or unexpected hurdles once the parties leave the room. In practice this means:

- getting legal functions involved early on in the planning process;
- developing terms and conditions ahead of the negotiation, providing them to suppliers, and pre-qualifying them so only those who have confirmed they can accept the proposed terms and conditions, or have advised reasonable areas where alternative or modified terms are needed are invited to submit proposals;
- incorporating areas where discussion over terms is required into the negotiation;

- structuring the final contract post-negotiation around the business requirements and the points of agreement from the negotiation.

Pre-contract summaries – the problem

An e-mail by one party summarizing what they believed was agreed can sometimes follow a negotiation, having been sent to the other party with the hope that they will reply to signal confirmation. These serve to crystallize the agreement and to check alignment, but more importantly to get something down in writing so it would be more difficult for the other party to renege on the agreement. Suppliers are often keen to use summarizing e-mails so they can book the sale against their internal sales targets.

Summarizing e-mails can be problematic. Despite what was discussed, if the e-mail provides commitments around something such as pricing or minimum volumes/scale of business and the second party replies to agree with the summary, this could be enough to form a binding contract. This might seem acceptable if the e-mail contract reflects what was discussed and agreed; however, the problem is that the e-mail exists in isolation without the wider contractual framework, terms and conditions that would provide important provision and protection. This could cause difficulty later should one party want to exit the arrangement or in the event of dispute or unforeseen circumstances.

Phrases such as 'subject to contract' or 'without prejudice' are often included in such e-mails in the belief that these eliminate the risk of an unintended contract, but this is not necessarily the case. 'Subject to contract' tends to be appropriate when parties are still negotiating and are not yet ready to be bound by a contract. Clearly this is not the case in a post-successful negotiation summarizing e-mail where there is clear intent on the side of both parties to be bound by a contract. This fact could potentially render 'subject to contract' meaningless (Jirehouse Capital & Ors v Beller & Anor, 2009 at judgemental.org.uk). Furthermore, it seems widely understood that documents marked 'without prejudice' cannot be submitted as evidence in a court of law and so too can often be found in summarizing e-mails. However, this phrase may also be inappropriate; for it to be effective, it must be used within correspondence relating to a dispute and genuine attempts to resolve the dispute. A post-successful negotiation summarizing e-mail is not such a thing. Therefore, while e-mail summaries following a negotiation can be useful to keep momentum and help cement a relationship, it is advisable to keep them brief, focusing only on non-contractual aspects such as expressions of gratitude or thanks, eg for hospitality extended, and next steps or agreed actions to move forward and conclude the negotiation or formalize a legal contract. If in any doubt then seek legal advice beforehand.

Letters of Intent/Heads of Agreement

Other ways to secure agreement and commitment ahead of the final contract include Letters of Intent (LOI) and Heads of Agreement (HOA), sometimes called Heads of Terms (HOTs) in the United Kingdom. Again suppliers are often very keen to agree such documents in order to secure the deal. For lengthy negotiations the use of LOIs or HOAs may be unavoidable, necessary or even desirable in order to secure an early claim over something. However, there are potential pitfalls to beware of with both.

Heads of Agreement

The HOA is a document that both parties agree that summarizes the main points of agreement reached between the parties but recognizes that the rest of the agreement is yet to be negotiated. HOAs are therefore subject to the final contract being agreed. However, in signing the Heads of Agreement, both parties are then committing to reach a final agreement and move to a signed contract. HOAs should be non-binding and should only become enforceable when incorporated into the final contract and subsequently agreed. However, if an HOA too closely resembles a legal agreement it can become binding.

Letter of Intent

An LOI is similar to an HOA and is used to outline or clarify key points of agreement or to agree specific safeguards or provision should the negotiation fail. LOIs are sometimes also used to declare that certain parties are in negotiations (eg in the case of a merger or acquisition). LOIs should not be binding in their entirety but may contain certain provisions that become binding. As with the HOA, if the overall LOI too closely resembles a legal agreement then it can become binding.

Both of these documents are developed ahead of, and subject to, the final contract and in both cases, if the document is written in a way that, for example, provides commitments then it can potentially become binding. Most lawyers I have engaged with on these matters suggest that ideally these interim steps should be avoided if at all possible as they are fraught with risk should they become binding and will consume effort and energy to put in place. Instead, if at all possible, it is better to direct efforts into moving straight to developing the final contract. Once again, a qualified lawyer should advise on the best course of action here.

Post-event implementation

When the deal is done it's time to make it happen. Depending upon what was agreed implementation could be a major undertaking. Agreeing a price for the purchase of a single item or area of supply might simply require the transaction to be completed and the goods (or service) provided. In contrast, a new deal involving switching suppliers for a managed service across multiple sites could require a large-scale project. Any supplier-related implementation will demand resources and support on the buyer side if the new arrangements are to be successfully realized. Resistance to change, poor communication, lack of visible executive support, poor buy-in are just some of the reasons why projects in organizations fail and so good change management of the transition is essential. So too is effective project management, supported by sufficient resources to make the project a reality.

Finally there is the matter of compliance. The corporate world is littered with examples of great deals done by procurement functions that have failed to have been realized because the internal customers out in the wider business have chosen to, or been able to, revert to other suppliers they favour more. Compliance is essential and if this cannot be mandated then it needs to be won by close stakeholder management and by selling hard why the new deal is right for the business and the benefits it will bring.

If implementation of what was agreed is straightforward then a simple implementation plan should be developed, perhaps using a Gantt chart format and this forms Red Sheet step 14. A worked examples is given in Figure 14.2.

Planning the next negotiation

The planning and experience from this negotiation is vital intelligence for the next. If this negotiation is one of many within a relationship then now is the time to do some outline planning for the next negotiation while things are still forefront in the mind. This is a simple piece of thought or group brainstorming with outputs noted down ready for next time. It should include:

Figure 14.2 Red Sheet step 14 – Implementation plan (worked example)

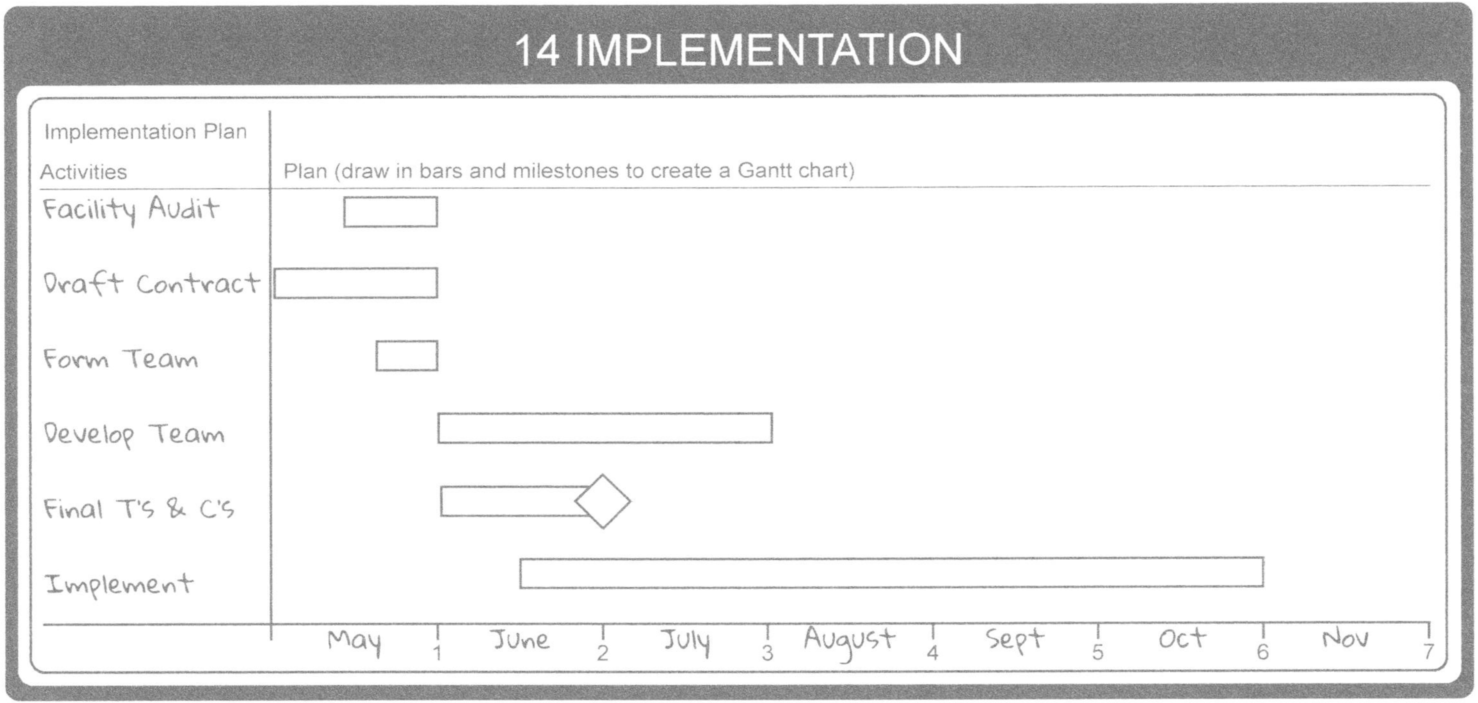

14 IMPLEMENTATION

Implementation Plan								
Activities	Plan (draw in bars and milestones to create a Gantt chart)							
Facility Audit								
Draft Contract								
Form Team								
Develop Team								
Final T's & C's								
Implement								
	May	June	July	August	Sept	Oct	Nov	
	1	2	3	4	5	6	7	

- any concessions sought during this negotiation, but yet were not secured, to which you should return;
- known changes (eg market or technology shifts) that will present a future opportunity;
- notes about their team and how they operate;
- when to schedule the next negotiation;
- topics for discussion;
- any factors that might boost or dilute our future power.

Actually doing it

Red Sheet Steps 13 and 14 – Post-event actions and implementation plan

Purpose of this step

Steps 13 and 14 are concerned with capturing the actions arising from the negotiation and planning the implementation activities as well as noting any key intelligence or insight to be carried forward to a future negotiation. Figures 14.1 and 14.2 give worked examples and the templates can be found in the Appendix.

Completing this step

1 Identify the post-event actions in step 13, assign an owner and timescale for each and record them.

2 Identify what is required to implement what was agreed in the negotiation and develop a simple implementation plan. Use Gantt chart format with bars and milestones to represent each activity and deadlines respectively.

3 Identify and record things to carry forward to the next negotiation.

Lessons learnt review

From the moment the negotiation finishes the lessons learnt review begins. Once the other party have left or the negotiation has ended, it is natural and expected that the team will start to discuss what happened and what they saw: who said what, moments where they gave the game away, unexpected surprises, how they reacted, what was missed and so on. Such interaction is likely to continue for some time in the room and then later on if the team decide to go and celebrate somewhere. This is a fantastically powerful part of personal and team development and allows the team and individuals to build a shared understanding of how negotiation theory works in practice. To capture learning, this precious exchange should be given some structure and insights noted. Red Sheet step 15 provides this structure and a worked example is provided in Figure 14.3. Whether a formal review meeting is convened immediately after the negotiation is concluded or whether this happens in a bar or pub doesn't matter. Either way, provoke the discussion by asking people to talk about what they heard and saw, and ideally make some notes regarding:

- What did they give away and how did we spot this?
- Where was their LDO and what tactics did they use to hide this?
- What games were played?
- What tactics were used?
- What things did we do that made a difference?
- What did we miss?
- What did we give away?
- How did we stick to our assigned roles and planned agenda?
- What did we learn about each of their team and how they negotiate?

Finally, summarize the review and what was learnt so the knowledge can be captured. This could well be a separate meeting a day or two later but using the notes captured immediately post-negotiation. Encourage the team to reflect on the experience and agree a written summary. Determine:

- what went well;
- what could be improved – 'even more effective if…';
- what was achieved;
- what are the key learnings.

Knowledge sharing within organizations provides the potential to increase organizational capability. Proactively sharing what was learnt with others who would benefit can make a difference to future negotiations elsewhere in the organization. In doing so it is important to be confident that sharing

Figure 14.3 Red Sheet step 15 – Outcomes and learnings (worked example)

15 OUTCOMES AND LEARNING

What went well?

- Relationship building
- Culture protocols followed
- Opening
- Body language of whole team
- Use of smiles and eye contact
- Playing 'stag hunt' changed the game...literally!

What did we achieve?

- 15% price reduction across all products
- Transition plan by 1st November
- 5 000 units minimum commitment

Even more effective if

- We have better planned what to do when things got difficult
- We had a code to communicate between each other on the team during the negotiation
- We had researched more on their team

Key learnings

It is essential the team fully agree rules for who speaks when and we have a way of communicating & deferring to the Team Leader when unexpected events take place during the negotiation.

information could not compromise you later; for example, if the supplier somehow got to see what you have recorded. The nature of what is appropriate to share and the audience for such knowledge depends upon the circumstances. Suggestions for knowledge sharing include:

- Circulate a brief summary of the negotiation to others it would help.
- Organize a short presentation to 'tell the story' and share experiences.
- Maintain a shared resource so people can access historical negotiation reviews.
- The 'key learnings' represent the summary of the entire journey and the most valuable insights gained. Consider making up small cards for the team listing these for people to carry or pin up somewhere.

Actually doing it

Red Sheet step 15 – Outcomes and Learnings

Purpose of this step

Step 15 is concerned with capturing knowledge and recording a summary of the negotiation that can serve to help future negotiations. Figure 14.3 gives an example and the template can be found in the Appendix.

Completing this step

1 Capture as many insights from the negotiation team post-negotiation as possible. Ideally convene a meeting with the team to review the negotiation and agree a summary of what was learnt.

2 Identify the most significant things that went well and record in the 'What went well?' box.

3 Identify the key areas where outcomes could have been improved if things had been done differently and record in the 'Even more effective if?' box.

4 Summarize the key achievements (personal, team and negotiation outcomes) and record in the 'What did we achieve?' box.

5 Identify the key learnings from the entire negotiation (around five is recommended) and enter into the 'Key learnings' box.

6 Share the knowledge as appropriate to those who would benefit from the insights you have gained.

Negotiation as a 15 key enabler for success

This concluding chapter explores what organizations and individuals must do to become highly successful at negotiation and embed negotiation as a key enabler of business success. We explore the current and changing role of negotiation within procurement and the supply chain and where we need different negotiation approaches including when negotiating remotely or with multiple opponents concurrently. Finally, reflecting on the journey through this book concludes the chapter, together with some suggestions for ongoing development.

Pathway questions addressed in this chapter

23 How do I negotiate effectively with multiple opponents or when I am not face-to-face with my opponent?

24 What must organizations do to improve negotiation capability overall?

25 What can I do to develop my skills to become really good at negotiation?

Red Sheet steps covered in this chapter

All steps and every interaction

As we are near the end of our journey which has explored, in detail, the art of negotiation, the planning process for securing great negotiation outcomes and how we can deliver a winning performance every time, we will turn our attention to making negotiation a key enabler for success at an individual level and organization-wide. Good negotiation capability offers the potential to bring real advantage to an organization; however, this doesn't happen by chance but rather requires the organization to consider and plan for the role negotiation can play and what needs to be put in place to realize this.

So far, we have generally considered negotiation in the traditional way it gets viewed: as two parties meeting to negotiate. Prior to the Covid-19 pandemic more and more negotiations were being conducted remotely, but this devastating event drove in a sea change in how individuals and companies would negotiate from that point on towards requiring those who negotiate to learn to master negotiating remotely. Sometimes the 'rules' for what can or cannot happen in a negotiation change, especially in the public sector, and sometimes there can be more than two parties. Add to this the changing role of procurement and supply chain functions and the incredible change that digital and data will bring in the near term and we see that negotiation can exist in a number of different and changing contexts. Whilst the underlying principles of negotiation don't change, how we apply them does, so we must know how we can adapt our skills accordingly. We will begin to explore negotiations conducted remotely.

Negotiating remotely

Today most negotiations, or parts of a negotiation, are being conducted remotely, without a physical face-to-face engagement or using technology to help leverage a favourable outcome. The principles of negotiation remain the same; however, the approach needed to secure the right result varies.

Effective remote negotiation

The technology to enable remote negotiation has been with us for several decades now but adoption has been slow, as the different style of personal interaction did not, at first, come naturally to many. Despite global companies equipping offices around the world with state-of-the-art web and video teleconferencing suites, people would for many years, if permitted, still opt to hop onto a plane and fly somewhere for a meeting face-to-face. However, things have changed. Covid-19 forced companies the world over to find new ways to operate effectively without the need for travel. Employees who previously resisted it became masters of Zoom, Skype, Microsoft Teams or other web-conferencing tools. Even with the possibility for travel returning many companies decided not to return to what was before, restricting travel, reducing or removing travel budgets and pursuing a new means of working and engaging with suppliers, claiming the added bonus of a smaller carbon footprint. Not only has technology advanced to become more user-friendly but crucially people, and not only those from the texting generations, can use it effectively and have even come to prefer it. Remote methods of engagement are here to stay and will continue to develop to be more and more mainstream.

Remote negotiations fall into four broad categories: written word, audio, video, or via an intermediary, or a combination of these effected by:

- phone;
- e-mail;
- social networking;
- SMS text message;
- traditional video teleconferencing;
- telepresence suites (full-size video teleconferencing as if in the same room);
- desktop or mobile video phone software (eg FaceTime);
- webconference (Skype, Zoom, Webex, GoTo Meeting, Microsoft Teams etc used for presentation, words, audio and perhaps video);
- intermediary.

Irrespective of the technology or means used for exchanges and interaction, the rules and principles of negotiation remain the same, it is just the means by which it is conducted that changes. Depending upon the technology deployed, the difficulty with the interaction is the absence or reduction in body language and paralanguage cues to help understand what lies behind the words. This can make it very difficult to read the other party, but it also means they can't read us and so heightening the reliance upon the words spoken or written. Further, Anderson and Thompson (2004) suggest that in face-to-face negotiations powerful negotiators use positive affect (a positive outward demeanour, empathy and friendliness) to the other party, to invoke similar states in the other party leading to increased trust, cooperation and better outcomes. This is possibly to the advantage of the buyer as it reduces the influence of the experienced salesperson's 'nice manner'.

Eye contact is either removed or reduced significantly and this dehumanizes the interaction. In hostage situations, experienced hostage takers will put a bag over the victim's head to prevent eye contact. Contrary to how Hollywood portrays such situations this is not just to prevent identification; it is to dehumanize the interaction. The moment eye contact is made it is difficult not to empathize with the other party. This is called the Stockholm syndrome, named after a six-day hostage situation in Norrmalmstorg in 1973 during which the victims became emotionally attached to their captors and even defended them after they were freed. As a result, remote negotiation can be cold, lack empathy, prevent winning trust and collaboration and rely much more just on the words used. However, these types of negotiation represent the future of how many deals will be done. Getting good at the new skill set needed is essential for today's negotiators. Each technology demands different approaches in order to be effective. Table 15.1 provides guidance for each type.

Remote negotiation only appears a compromise in the context of traditional face-to-face negotiation. It is an opportunity if we master the media. I conduct almost all my meetings and training via web meeting today but I always enable my video feed, use a separate microphone or headset and ensure good lighting so they can see me and I then make direct eye contact into my webcam when I'm talking rather than looking somewhere else on my desktop. I exaggerate signs of affirmation such as nodding, hand gestures and showing interest. This seems to help create a more empathic rapport. I also make a point of regularly switching between 'face communication'

Table 15.1   Tips for remote negotiation

Type of remote negotiation	Tips for success
Written word e-mail, SMS text message, social networking, web messaging, traditional written letter	Written word is asynchronous; there will always be a gap between sending and receiving. No body language or paralanguage means words alone must convey the full and precise meaning and there is increased scope for misunderstanding without any audio or visual cues to check mood or intended meaning. It is harder to convey meaning in writing words. **Negotiating effectively:** • Agree timescales for responses within the mail, message etc. • If you don't understand a communication or it annoys or makes you angry then seek clarification. • Never respond when angry. Instead sleep on it and consider your response carefully in the morning. • Allow time for the negotiation to progress. • Summarize regularly but be careful not to inadvertently signal acceptance unless this is your intent. • Consider wording carefully.

Table 15.1 *continued*

Type of remote negotiation	Tips for success
Audio Phone, teleconference, call	No body language makes reaching agreement much harder. Furthermore, speech by phone or web phone is not reproduced as spoken, instead only a small part of the frequency spectrum actually makes it to the other end in order to minimize the transmission bandwidth. We hear enough of the voice to understand it but not nearly enough to fully hear paralanguage. **Negotiating effectively:** • More effective if there has been a prior meeting. • Prepare thoroughly so you can concentrate on listening during the negotiation. • Listen actively to everything they say and how they say it. • Recognize key points. • It is easy to get carried away with the immediacy of the call as if it were a normal phone call. • Use silence, taking breaks, summarizing. • Use secret messaging within your team to align on key points during the call and be aware they might be doing the same.
Video Web meeting tools, video call, video conference or telepresence	As technology and connectivity develop so do the quality, realism and accessibility of video interaction, making this a developing area. Today we all have access to the latest generation web meeting tools on our desktops and organizations are now enabling and encouraging their use. With modern telepresence suites built in a dedicated room where participants see the entire room and their opponent across a table full size as if in the room, then negotiation becomes as if face-to-face. However, with older video suite technology using cameras and TV screens limitations in what can be seen mean some of the visual stimuli in a group negotiation will be lost. **Negotiating effectively:** • Let them see you – include a webcam video feed for web conferencing and talk to the camera. Insist that they switch theirs on too (eg by establishing ground rules for the negotiation or stressing 'It is essential we can see each other').

Table 15.1 *continued*

Type of remote negotiation	Tips for success
	• Treat the interaction as if face-to-face.
	• If using professional video conferencing facilities then make the most of the technology – watch as much of them as you can and let them see you, cutting between room-wide and close-up views.
	• Smile and overemphasize gestures.
	• If possible check in advance that the technology works at both ends.
	• Secret messaging within your team is still possible, sometimes as a closed message within the technology or separately via your phone.
Intermediary Negotiation by proxy	The problem with negotiation through an intermediary is you can't be there. Furthermore, unless you know and trust the intermediary it is hard to be certain they are really acting in your favour with the zeal you would wish. However, intermediaries are necessary in certain situations, usually when there is a reason to keep a degree of separation between parties or because local presence or knowledge is needed.
	Negotiating effectively:
	• Know your intermediary; if they are new then follow up references and check their track record.
	• If possible, incentivize them to maximize your outcome so they have something to win by pushing hard.
	• Recognize the risk that they may have relationships with the other party that could act against you. Ask them about this beforehand and watch for signs but assume the worst and manage them closely. Actively involve them in the planning process and ensure they contribute to the development of an agreed concession strategy using their knowledge and experience to shape this.
	• Avoid giving them a free hand, but require them to follow the agreed concession strategy and to check in with you at certain points to seek your agreement to move further.
	• Agree the tactics they will use.
	• Depending upon the circumstances, it is sometimes advisable not to reveal your full LDO to the intermediary but leave yourself a margin that you can give later if needed. This can compel them to push harder.

where they are looking at me and something I am showing them. Modern telepresence suites mean the interaction is almost face-to-face and it is possible to build an effective relationship with someone we have never met by phone over time. Through repeated interaction we build up a mental picture of them and who they are and this seems to enable rapport building. A businessman I know who imports fruit juice built a very successful business by establishing relationships with producers and processors around the world and his entire business was built through telephone negotiations and never once did he meet his suppliers. Yet he established some very strong working relationships and negotiated highly competitive deals.

Multi-party negotiations

So far we have considered negotiation as that between two parties and in this section we will turn our attention to multi-party negotiations. Multi-party negotiation is where there are three or more parties, each with its own interests and each trying or needing to reach agreement. Whilst the basic principles and process for negotiation we have explored throughout this book still apply, the context of how they apply is quite different. In fact, multi-party negotiations are a world apart from negotiations between two parties and so warrant an exploration if we are to master these also.

Know when you're in one

Multi-party negotiations might seem like an exceptional activity and something only found in play by trade unions or where many countries come together to agree a treaty. However, they are more common than we might think. Consider a family agreeing something so all are happy, a group of friends on vacation together trying to decide on what to do or a senior individual in a company attempting to put in place new arrangements such as agreeing a budget with many departments, each trying to realize its goals to help achieve corporate targets yet with only a fixed amount of investment possible. Scenarios such as these don't typically get regarded as multi-party negotiations, yet they are and what makes them so is the fact that agreement has to be reached with all parties separately and collectively. This is a key test that can be applied to determine whether or not we have ended up in a multi-party negotiation – 'Is my agreement, and that of others, required here to proceed?' If yes, we have power in the negotiation, perhaps more than we realize. Good outcomes to multi-party negotiations can often be claimed simply because parties don't realize the power they have, a factor that smart negotiators will seize and use to their advantage. As a parent of now-teenage children I know that reaching 'agreement' by all can be a challenge and there have been times when I attempted to go down the 'this is how it is going to be' route rather than seeking 'agreement', expecting to be ignored and overruled but being pleasantly surprised that they went along with what I asked. What I knew to be a multi-party negotiation, requiring agreement, was something my teenage children had not realized and so they missed the fact that they had power and could have elected to not agree and I would have had to figure out a different way through. I didn't reveal my surprise but made the most of the fact that I had held on to some parental authority.

If other parties don't realize they have power, inviting them to negotiate can draw their attention to their power when they would have otherwise been ready to agree to a particular request. For this reason multi-party negotiations often don't start as such but rather may be some sort of request to a number of parties to agree to something, perhaps with an incentive. For example, a drug company with a product that has developed nasty side effects in some patients might attempt to shut down any risk of a class action by writing to affected patients with an apology and offer of compensation. When viewed in isolation, the offer might appear very attractive and acceptance would avert the need to get into a multi-party agreement.

The power of coalitions

Another significant source of power in multi-party negotiations, and one that can either completely decimate the entire negotiation or can be the key to success is the power of coalitions. In any multi-party negotiation coalitions form easily and quickly, driven by the degree to which individuals feel threatened or eager for what they stand to lose or win. Coalitions may be unorganized and simply emerge as those with likeminded interests talk, share thoughts and stories and seize the power of uniting together against what is being proposed. Coalitions may equally be deliberately initiated, organized and managed. Unorganized coalitions can be the most dangerous as they can grow and become unpredictable and emerge with power out of nowhere, especially if someone steps up and seeks to bring some organization and a purpose to the coalition. Similarly, a disorganized coalition that is against us can be converted to support us with the right intervention.

In a company I worked for, I, and the rest of the workforce, were called into an 'all hands' meeting where the HR Director announced to all that the company was seeking to introduce changes to the company pension scheme.

The changes offered some new tax advantages to the company and potential upsides to employees. In theory it would have been a win/win for all. However, the company could only introduce the changes if there was universal agreement. It failed in its attempts to introduce the changes. Different coalitions soon formed, many fuelled by misinformation about hidden agendas on the part of the company which perpetuated a 'them and us' stance. The HR Director came under attack from all sides and eventually the scheme was abandoned. This is not an uncommon result when companies attempt to introduce changes that require agreement. Failure to realize these are multi-party negotiations and treat them as corporate briefings can be disastrous simply because the power of the coalitions that form is ignored.

Possibly the biggest factor that makes coalitions such a threat to us is their unstable and often unpredictable nature. To see this in action watch any reality 'play off' gameshow show such as *Big Brother*, *I'm a Celebrity*, *Love Island*, *Survivor* etc, where participants are placed in a situation they cannot easily exit, each with their own interests, each trying to win but each knowing they can only do this with a degree of social cooperation in order to do so. In all of these shows, coalitions form, break up, re-form with new allegiances and so on. Often, those who win such shows are the ones that manage to successfully build relationships across all participants and then manage coalitions that form and their part within them in order to move group consensus in their direction. It is this same dynamic that we need to manage in a multi-party negotiation.

Types of coalition and approaches we can use to manage them are as follows:

- *Prevented coalition* – Remove the ability for coalitions to form in the first place; where this is possible, it is the most effective means to guarantee a good outcome. Especially when those involved don't realize the power they hold. Sometimes this can be as simple as preventing those involved from talking to each other or getting to them before others can.

- *Offensive coalitions* – Well ahead of the negotiation and ideally before parties even contemplate that they are about to be part of a negotiation, work to build a winning coalition. This is a coalition that is behind and championing our cause. If well executed, sometimes parties can perceive the negotiation itself as a response to deal with an issue they are concerned about rather than the thing we are working towards. Winning coalitions are formed through conditioning and gaining support for an outcome. In the case of our HR Director, a more successful outcome might have occurred if he had engaged with people across the business to socialize the idea and 'gauge appetite' one-on-one, worked to get other managers on board or made sure people got to know what other companies were doing and benefitting their employees. These actions might have stimulated an offensive coalition that supported a review of the pension arrangements. The corporate briefing would then be supported from the outset.

- *Defensive coalitions* – These are coalitions deliberately formed to protect our position or block aggressive actions from other parties. If our HR Director had met with managers first, secured their support, and had them brief out the potential changes at team meetings, asking for feedback through them outside the meeting then this would have created a blocking coalition that would diffuse any aggressive concerns and certainly keep them isolated from the wider population, removing the likelihood of a mass revolt.

- *Unformed coalition* – Coalitions where parties share the same interest but have not yet got together with others to form a coalition. Whilst these are not true coalitions (as they have not yet formed so lack any collective power), they are worthy of note as seizing on these shared interests in a way that resonates or offers a solution is a quick an easy way to initiate a coalition supportive to our position.

- *Opportunistic coalitions* – Coalitions require organization and planning in order to succeed, therefore parties only invest time in organizing a coalition if they stand to gain from it. Sometimes a coalition can be formed through the opportunity of gain from the difference in interests of parties. For example, consider a legal firm that sets out to initiate a class action against the drug company and invests time in doing so with the aim of gaining from the potential of ensuring all parties understand the extent of their power and brokering an agreement.

We manage coalitions by anticipating them, putting in measures to deal with them or proactively forming them. We do this by using a stakeholder map as we explored in Chapter 4 and identifying all the parties and more importantly what we know about them, then considering their interests (more on that shortly) and where like-minded coalitions are likely to form. From here we can determine what we will do for each stakeholder group.

How to work towards agreement

A family discussing a family holiday and where to go might agree in a single event with all gathered around the kitchen negotiating table, or potentially via discussions over a few days. Here agreement will be reached by all being present or part of the discussion. However, multi-party negotiations rarely have all involved gathered 'around a table', on the same Skype call or even involved in all the discussions, but rather take the form of a series of negotiations and interactions with different parties, each achieving a small step towards a bigger unified agreement. Consider the example of a company merger or acquisition where the degree to which a small group of owners of the respective businesses stand to gain depends upon various parameters of the deal and what stake and involvement they may have in the new company. Here negotiations may be one-on-one with each individual. Parties may never meet or if they do so it may only be at the very end, either in person or via web conference and then to sign documents (whether physical documents or via digital signing).

On a bigger scale, some multi-party negotiations will take place with everyone together, whether in person or online, yet the process of reaching agreement with all requires a different approach. Some of the biggest and arguably some of the most critical multi-party negotiations that we have seen in recent years are those on climate change. In 1997 15 EU member states agreed the Kyoto Protocol; the Paris Agreement on Climate Change of 2015 was made by representatives of 196 state parties and in 2019 COP25 in Madrid saw 200 countries coming together and participating in a negotiation attempting to agree how to ensure the Paris Climate Agreement could be implemented more effectively so targets would be achieved. Securing agreement from 200 parties is no small task and we get a clue for how this happened by watching the TV coverage of how the events were organized. It is true that representatives from all 200 (and more) gathered in the same room during the negotiations. The room was a vast arena with countries' representatives seated at fixed desks with microphones and translated audio, arranged in concentric circles around a central small table where the four or five senior individuals leading the negotiation were sat. Looking back at these global events gives us an insight into how big-scale multi-party negotiations are managed. Here we don't see the typical debate between parties over positions or playing tactics but instead the negotiation proceeds by the leaders coordinating a series of activities, each set up to explore positions for a single negotiable, to consider options, test for potential agreement and then share progress with the bigger group. This 'sub team' approach repeats for individual negotiables or points of discussion until the group signals there is a sufficient groundswell of potential agreement to enable an actual universal agreement. For large-number multi-party negotiations the majority of the negotiation therefore does not take place within the room, but rather prior to the event or in smaller groups tasked with working on individual points and then bringing back proposed courses of action that might be agreeable to the wider group.

The big group does not negotiate as such, but instead agrees or rejects a series of possible ways forward presented to it until there is sufficient widespread agreement to reach a deal all will support. The key enabler to success here is therefore determining the topics that will be worked on outside the room and establishing up front how the big group will make decisions eg by consensus, by vote or is universal agreement required? This may take some selling to all those involved who may firmly believe they must retain the power of veto in any circumstances. Working on changing this mindset early on can help accelerate progress. Tactics that can help this include:

- Begin ahead of the event – Don't wait until everyone is in the room to begin the negotiation, instead engage with parties in advance to understand their interests, and therefore their negotiables, and to inform and pre-condition them around how the negotiation will run and encourage a 'mindset of making agreement happen'.

- Create an imperative to act – Work to sell 'the size of the prize', what parties collectively stand to gain if agreement can be reached or lose otherwise.

- Establish a 'spirit of the negotiation' – This is something that can be articulated in an evangelical way to describe the imperative to prioritize universal agreement over individual positions.

- Open with gusto – A key note opening by someone highly respected who can lay out the imperative to act and emphasize that the 'spirit of the negotiation' can go a long way.

Understanding interests

Until now, I have described negotiation as a process where we determine the negotiables then put in place a concession strategy determined to work toward, or more often than not, prevent working away from the outcomes we seek for each and all of our negotiables. For this reason we start with our MDO and establish our LDO before we engage. This is sound practice for one-on-one negotiations built upon establishing just the right degree of carefully choreographed compromise to suit our situation. However, for multi-party negotiations we need to shift our thinking slightly away from managing concessions steps back from our ideal outcome and towards the degree to which individual interests can be met. It is hard to manage multiple parties from 'where they want to be' to a point of global compromise and what would otherwise be a normal tactics of knocking down the others' position rarely works in a multi-party negotiation. Instead we need to focus on the degree to which interests can be satisfied whilst achieving the overall outcome of universal agreement. Each party will have their own interests and each will have its own priority for them so understanding these early on is key to beginning to manage our way through the negotiation.

The biggest interest of all is usually to do a deal, otherwise why would parties have engaged? This is a source of great power and risk that helps to temper parties' expectations as no one gets what they want unless everyone agrees. For example, for those countries negotiating action to tackle climate change in recent years there has been a clear and stark imperative to agree a deal; to ensure the survival of future generations. Interests were not typically around whether or not countries should act, but rather focused on the degree to which certain countries should take a greater burden considering factors such as those countries that most contributed to the problem, who could most afford it and how quickly should it happen.

A further component to understanding interest is to understand BATNAs. As for one-on-one negotiations, having, and attempting to anticipate the other's, BATNAs is essential. In multi-party negotiations, however, anticipating all the individual BATNAs for all the interests and negotiables across every party may prove impractical. Instead here we should focus on general BATNAs that parties and coalitions may hold and be ready for BATNAs to shift as negotiations progress.

10 steps for managing multi-party negotiations

The Red Sheet negotiation planning process will support multi-party negotiations and should be applied at a high level to support planning. Where many parties are involved, the full process could become too unwieldy as we would, in effect, need to work through the process separately with each party and that would be impractical. Instead utilize the general principles of Red Sheet planning and adopt a more holistic approach to managing multiple parties, switching away from developing a concession strategy to one where we manage interests of parties and track how our negotiation satisfies these interests. The 10 steps for managing multi-party negotiations are as follows:

Ahead of the negotiation

1 **What do we want?** – Begin, as for any negotiation, by clarifying our position, what we want to get out of the negotiation, our negotiables and our respective MDOs and LDOs for each as well as our BATNAs (for each negotiable or overall).

2 **Multi-party negotiation check** – Confirm we are in a multi-party negotiation – Check what power we have and that our agreement is required and also that of other parties. Check if other parties realize they have negotiation power or not. If not, consider if we can move forward without a negotiation.

3 **Anticipate coalitions and prepare for them** – Map stakeholders and determine who, where and how coalitions might form. Build relationships with each party but don't allow these to undermine our relationships with other parties. Determine and build our own offensive, defensive or opportunistic coalitions.

Managing the multi-party event

4 **Pre-condition parties** – Emphasize the importance of reaching agreement, what is at stake if agreement can or cannot be reached and attempt to establish a 'spirit of the negotiation' around this. Encourage people to think about the bigger picture and focus on their 'next best' option if all their requirements cannot be met, so they are ready to compromise.

5 **Create an imperative to act** – Determine what outcome we are looking for – What good looks like and the reasons it is important to achieve this (or the risk to all involved if we do not achieve this). Work to make it crucially important to all that agreement is reached.

6 **Determine how decisions will be made** – Attempt to secure agreement with all parties at the outset around the negotiation process and how decisions will be made, ground rules and how problems will be solved.

7 **Understand negotiables, interests and priorities of parties** – Work to understand all the interests of all parties and/or coalitions and from these determine the negotiables and therefore points for discussion. If possible, draw up a table of interests for each party and/or coalition. Determine the common interests eg 'we must fix climate change' and those where parties have conflicting or opposing interests eg 'every

country must pay the same to clean up the mess of a few countries.' Start with securing agreement where there is common interest. Track payoffs against respective interests for each negotiable. Use this to structure and prioritize the flow of the individual negotiations and also to gauge when there is sufficient payoff against parties, interests to push for closure on points of agreement.

8 **Determine BATNAs** – Determine our BATNAs and anticipate the potential BATNAs for key negotiables for each party or at coalition level.

9 **Break it down** –Work on the negotiables one by one, focusing on where there is conflicting or opposing interests. For large multi-party negotiations consider breaking into sub-groups, each tasked with working on a specific negotiable, considering the various interests, considering ideas and hypothetical positions, exploring options to test what will gain support and identifying potential ways through then bringing proposals back to the bigger group for consideration. Where there are powerful coalitions care should be taken to ensure each coalition is represented on the sub-group.

10 **Propose-Gauge-Refine-Agree** – Manage the negotiation one negotiable at a time by applying a process of propose-gauge-refine-agree – Propose an option or way through (eg by the sub team proposing to the full group). Gauge appetite for agreement (eg by a vote or other means), where agreement is not in sight identify factors that stand in the way. Refine the proposal accordingly (eg the sub team goes away and works on new solutions) and repeat the process until agreement can be reached on each point. Secure agreement point-by-point or by negotiable, avoid returning to them if at all possible, then finally summarize and secure final agreement overall, sign, go home.

Negotiating throughout the supply chain

This edition of this book focuses on negotiation for both procurement and supply chain professionals, and for good reason. The general convergence of procurement and supply chain functions in recent years demands new skills and new approaches in order to realize the true potential possible from a supply base. What happens beyond our immediate suppliers matters if we are to truly be effective.

Supply chain professionals are well versed with considering the steps that exist prior to, and often onward from, our organization and how these are understood and managed to ensure the optimum and most effective unhindered flow of value from original source right up to the end user or customer. Exemplars such as modern big retailers do this well and secure significant competitive advantage through having exactly what the customer seeks, at that time, at the required place and at the right price no matter what. These companies make managing an entire supply chain nothing short of an artform with advance systems to manage the flow of goods and services from the original factory or plantation towards the end customer and also to manage how information about demand flows back, often anticipating what the customer will want before they know it so as to minimize costly inventories. These highly agile supply chains highlight one payoff that is possible with effective supply chain management. However, there are many more and how the goods got here and where they came from has become equally important. Key drivers that make supply chain management something we must attend to alongside procurement include:

- The global marketplace drives global supply chains and distribution networks.

- Global distribution drives fewer 'super-sized' production facilities and fewer 'super-sized' inventories providing economies of scale over many regional factories.

- Corporate Social Responsibility means we are now interested in what happens in a global supply chain, but first-hand knowledge and understanding is more difficult to secure.

- Increased demand for traceability and transparency.

- Consumer demands for personalization are now being met through clever production technology and good logistics.

- Regional variations and localization can similarly be catered for so one product facility can produce a range of different products for different markets on the same production line in real time.

The supply chain presents implications for how we negotiate. Indeed, negotiation is often considered as something that takes place with another party or parties whom we have or are seeking a direct relationship with such as an immediate supplier. That has been the focus of this book this far. However, the supply chain means we need new approaches to negotiation that go beyond our immediate supplier and here we end up drawing on what we have just explored for multi-party negotiations.

The challenge with supply chain negotiations

The challenge with supply chain negotiations is we typically have no contractual relationship with those suppliers beyond our immediate supplier, yet we may find ourselves needing to interact with, and secure favourable outcomes or points of agreement from, entities many contractual steps removed from us. We could impose a requirement on our supplier that obliges them to negotiate and agree specific requirements with their supplier and so on. However, and depending upon the complexity of the supply chain and how much power we and other entities hold, attempts to push obligations back up the supply chain typically fail. For example, if our corporate CSR policy demands compliance to anti-slavery legislation or that our supply chains must be free from child labour, we could impose this as a contractual requirement on our supplier. Maybe our supplier would be happy to agree to such a requirement, especially if they have control over, or understand, their supply chains. Yet for most, where the supply chain is complex, perhaps spanning multiple geographies and cultures, having sufficient confidence to agree such a contractual requirement would be a challenge. The brutal reality here is that unless our immediate supplier is the original source, we are negotiating with the wrong entity if we want to influence what happens many steps removed from them up the supply chain. Here we stumble upon one of the biggest challenges facing businesses attempting to drive in CSR – that of making it happen back up the supply chain with success. In order to do this we need a slightly different approach to negotiation.

Achieving CSR is not the only consideration demanding negotiation back up the supply chain, it is also how information flows. Without intervention, information about demand flows from the end customer back up the supply chain. Typically, this information only flows so far, meaning parties further back up the supply chain become either overly reactive or take steps to anticipate demand eg by holding more inventory, impacting speed of flow, responsiveness and cost.

Whether we are working to implement a CSR policy or we need a more agile supply chain with better information flow, the solution is the same – we have to engage with, and negotiate arrangements with, the parties back up, and possibly further on, in the supply chain. These may be parties we have no contractual relationship with, with whom there may not be an appetite at first to engage with us or we may lack the knowledge of how to engage with them. Yet we can unlock great potential if we can figure out how to negotiate arrangements with multiple parties within a supply chain and possibly outside of the chain of contractual relationships.

Figure 15.1 Negotiating in a typical supply chain (or network)

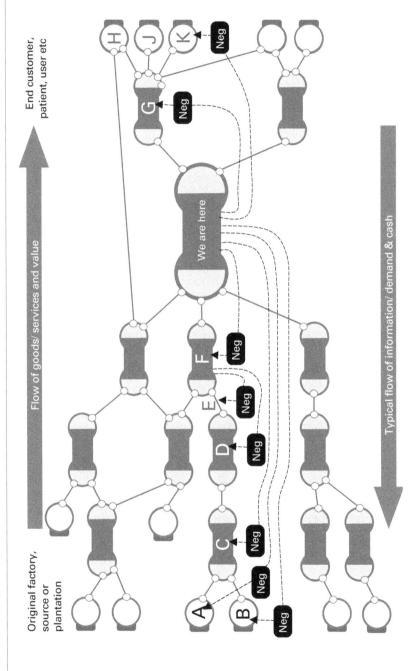

End customer, patient, user etc

Flow of goods/ services and value

Typical flow of information/ demand & cash

Original factory, source or plantation

Figure 15.1 illustrates now a multi-party supply chain negotiation might take place. Whilst we talk of 'supply chains', they are, in fact, more 'networks' as Figure 15.1 shows. Supplier 'F' is our immediate supplier with whom we would negotiate and agree a contractual relationship. We might oblige supplier F to agree specific arrangements with their supplier (supplier D) and perhaps a logistics provider (E). However, in order to realize our objectives, it might be necessary to also 'go around' our immediate supplier, ideally with their approval, and negotiate what happens at the original sources, factories or plantations (A and B) and what the parties further up the supply chain do (C). We may also negotiate with our customer (G) and the end customer or users (H, J and K) around how we can secure more advance information around demand.

Negotiation in the supply chain therefore requires that we treat the negotiation as a multi-party negotiation, conducting individual negotiations with parties throughout the supply chain with the aim of putting some sort or arrangement in place. Success is about focusing on the interests of parties and creating an imperative to act so as to agree new arrangements that will benefit all players in the supply chain eg by reducing their cost exposure. Agreement becomes possible because as well as maintaining their contractual relationship with immediate suppliers and customers in the supply chain, parties typically enter into an additional, perhaps voluntary, 'side arrangement' agreed with all parties for how certain things will work.

Making tea sustainable

A major buyer of tea sought to establish its range of products as sustainable so plantation workers would receive fair recompense and growers would be able to invest in the future of their operations. The tea was sourced through an importer who would buy from approved plantations to a particular grade in government commodity trading rooms. However, the trading process hindered sourcing sustainably, especially where there was an oversupply and prices were forced low. Recent issues at some plantations who could not invest in plant and equipment suggested a different approach was needed. Initial discussions with the immediate supplier, the importer, confirmed they held little ability to influence things as all growers were required to trade their tea through the official trading process.

With the agreement of the importer, the company therefore entered into negotiations with the plantations they wanted to buy from around levels of

▶

investment needed and certain arrangements that would be put in place to ensure fair wage and good working conditions for workers. With this agreed, the only challenge was how to get the money for the investment to the plantations whilst maintaining trading within the commodity trading process. In the end the company tasked the importer to over bid for tea in the trading rooms from the specific named plantations by a pre-determined amount so the additional funds would flow to the plantations with a separate agreement with the plantations regarding how these would be utilized.

Negotiation in the public sector

Public sector procurement can require a different negotiation approach to that in the commercial sector. This is because in a public sector organization the strategic imperatives are different. First there are different objectives – organizations are guided by such needs as being able to demonstrate value for taxpayers' money, transparency of spend or improving outcomes for the resident, patient, passenger etc. Second, procurement approaches are required to operate within a regulated framework that invokes strict rules around how contracts are awarded, designed to demonstrate transparency in all engagement and negotiations with suppliers, to minimize corruption and to drive fairness to suppliers. Demonstrating fairness to suppliers can restrict our ability to negotiate freely with one or more suppliers at the same time as we might in the commercial sector. Furthermore, sometimes governmental legislation will even demand positive discrimination towards suppliers in certain minority groups or supplier selection based upon promoting the well-being of a given area – 'Supplier Diversity' in the US, targets for business with SMEs (small to medium-sized enterprises) or minority-owned businesses in the EU and the UK, the Social Value Act (2012) being some examples. All this can completely change the way we might approach a negotiation or indeed whether there is any negotiation at all. What we are negotiating might be more around service levels and assurance of supply, perhaps even with positive support to get a supplier compliant with core requirements. Different regulation for public organizations exists the world over and each is an entire specialism of its own, so further reading is recommended. In Europe, the legislation that defines the requirements for procurement in public bodies is collectively known as EU Procurement Legislation and is founded upon the four pillars of European Union Law. These are:

- subsidiarity (the principle of needs and problems being dealt with at the most immediate or local country level, typically through local supporting, not subservient, bodies that are part of the whole);
- transparency;
- equal treatment; and
- proportionality (ensuring the correct balance of the different but related needs that must be satisfied).

At the same time it seeks to ensure that the public sector is pursuing simplification, value for money, sustainability, innovation, efficiency, opportunities for SMEs and growth, whilst maintaining the single market and complying with World Trade Organization rules. EU Procurement Legislation regulates any governmental or public purchasing entity for expenditure above certain, published thresholds. In this case the opportunity must be advertised in the Official Journal of the European Union (OJEU). Prospective suppliers can then register their interest and potentially be invited to participate in some form of competitive bidding exercise according to one of a number of set procedures. There are strict rules for these procedures and these have implications for any negotiation. Whilst hard 'dog eat dog' negotiations with multiple suppliers can be standard practice for many commercial companies, such an approach can fall foul of EU public sector procurement legislation because of the conflict with the underpinning pillars of equal treatment, transparency and proportionality. Indeed, until recently, there was very little scope for negotiation, but in 2015 changes in EU Procurement Legislation moved some way forward with the introduction of new negotiated procedures and some increased flexibility for buyers. Negotiation in the public sector might mean we have to change our approach or adopt practices to demonstrate fairness with all suppliers involved. It means that the negotiation itself can be less about refining and agreeing the make-up of what we are buying or building on a basic idea of need, but rather that our overall requirements must be precisely defined from the outset and cannot change along the way so all who end up in some form of negotiation have had the opportunity to compete to supply the very same thing. Negotiations will typically be part of a competitive bid or tender process, following strict procedures, and must be rigorously documented. They cannot be isolated events. Generally, where there are multiple bidders, any dialogue with suppliers and therefore negotiations must be fair and transparent to all, with no scope to favour a supplier. An engagement with one supplier must be replicated identically with all other suppliers under consideration, as if all were in their own swim lanes progressing forward individually, but identically in terms of discussion and engagement. Further reading is recommended to better understand the rules and opportunities for negotiation within EU procurement legislation if this applies. It might seem that public sector procurement legislation places an unnecessary burden on procurement teams, restricting our ability to negotiate freely with suppliers, and driving down cost works against the public interest. But advocates of EU procurement legislation would counter that it has a much bigger agenda than the needs of an individual entity and seeks to balance good procurement with a wider social and country progression. In other words, it is a necessary part of the bigger picture. It is in fact possible to balance both here and deliver highly effective procurement whilst complying with public procurement legislation. However, an advanced level of capability is required to ensure compliance. It also means those leading public sector buying functions need to guide teams to think more about the most effective.

How negotiation fits into the organization

Negotiation is not an island. However, it frequently seems to be regarded as one within the wider context of the purchasing or supply chain function. It is as if negotiation is considered a separate activity that certain individuals go and do from time to time. Regarding negotiation as separate to the wider activities of the procurement or supply chain function will drive suboptimum results. Instead, negotiation should be regarded as an integral part of everything the procurement or supply chain function does, especially each and every interaction with a supplier or throughout the supply chain in whatever form. Negotiation skills therefore underpin and enable everything within procurement and so should not be considered a specialist capability for the few in senior positions but a skill that every team member should have to a greater or lesser degree depending upon their role. Investment in negotiation capability development at a team-wide level is essential and all interactions with suppliers should be regarded as part of the overall negotiation process.

Strategic sourcing

Negotiation underpins the strategic sourcing approaches that drive value, reduce risk, reduce cost and secure supply chain innovation for today's leading organizations. Within Category Management negotiation is a key phase in implementing new sourcing strategies. Collaborative value-creating negotiations, held with the critical few suppliers who can make a dramatic difference to an organization, are an integral part of Supplier Relationship Management. Sustainable procurement requires specialist negotiation to drive in supply chain improvements, often many contractual steps removed from the organization. In each case these strategic sourcing approaches provide a rich wealth of facts and data, insights and analysis that can be invaluable in negotiation planning. The development of business requirements within a Category Management project provides the basis to determine the individual points to be negotiated or the *negotiables* as well as many of the analytical tools helping to determine the balance of power. Negotiation should therefore be regarded as integral to, and enabled by, the wider strategic methodologies within procurement. You can read more about this and how negotiation enables strategic sourcing in my books *Category Management in Purchasing* and *Supplier Relationship Management* (both published by Kogan Page).

Negotiation and e-sourcing

E-sourcing is a toolkit that forms part of modern purchasing, and it should not be regarded as separate. Rather e-sourcing, in all its forms, is another part or variant of the negotiation process. Therefore use of such tools should not be in isolation to any wider negotiation planning.

E-sourcing covers the various tools, available from a plethora of suppliers, that use online platforms for the solicitation of information from suppliers in a structured way. This includes RFx (eRFx) – Request for either Information, Proposal or Quotation. The RFx is typically part of the procurement toolkit for running competitive bid processes and can be a highly effective means of negotiation or pre-negotiaton if well executed. It also covers e-auctions – the platforms that allow online reverse auctions to be carried out where multiple suppliers will bid in real time against competitors for the contract to supply specified goods or services. Suppliers progressively improve their offer until there is a winner at the end of the auction, often the supplier who bid the lowest price. These tools gained huge popularity in the nineties and naughties. They continue to be used by many industries and remain relevant for certain areas of spend if well executed. E-auctions remove the problems associated with face-to-face negotiation and prevent suppliers from gaining advantage through their personality and as a result of the extensive training they have received. However, an e-auction is only suitable in certain circumstances.

The e-sourcing tools are exactly that: they are tools. As with any tool, the tool alone will do nothing, but if used skilfully can help leverage great benefit. Table 15.2 provides some guidance on how to do this and how to integrate use of these tools within a wider negotiation process. E-sourcing is a separate topic all of its own and so further reading is recommended if you are not already familiar with such tools.

Table 15.2   E-sourcing and negotiation

Type of e-sourcing approach	Tips for success
RFI Request For Information A request for a supplier to provide information by giving answers to a structured set of pre-determined questions using an online platform Usually used to precede a tender or competitive exercise and typically sent to many suppliers	An RFI may precede negotiation planning activity so it may not be possible to know exactly what you need to ask. However, there are some questions that will enable you to collect information that could prove useful later when you are attempting to assess the balance of power and who their team are. **Using eRFIs to support the negotiation process:** • Use to condition the supplier that something is about to change • Gather information about their position in the marketplace (which marketplace do they believe they are in?) so you can use this information to gauge the power they might hold later. • Ask them to describe their differentiators. This will help you determine power balance later but will also give you insight into how they might approach a subsequent negotiation. • Gather details of their organizational structure and possibly details of key individuals to help you understand who their negotiation team might be in a subsequent negotiation.

Table 15.2 *continued*

Type of e-sourcing approach	Tips for success
RFP or RFQ Request For Proposal or Quotation A request for a supplier to provide either a proposal or a firm quotation for the supply of certain goods or services Forms the main component of a tender or competitive exercise and is typically sent to a small number of suppliers who have been pre-qualified	The RFP or RFQ replaces or precedes the negotiation event. A favourable RFQ might be enough to proceed to contract. However, typically a subsequent negotiation event or e-auction would take place to finalize the deal. **Using RFPs and RFQs to support the negotiation process:** • Include the terms and conditions that will form part of any subsequent contract within these documents and ask the supplier to either confirm they are acceptable or to outline any issues. This will prevent unexpected obstacles later. • Determine the structure using the business requirements, asking for proposals and, for the RFQ, proposed pricing for each. • If possible ask for a breakdown of proposed pricing to help you determine LDOs. They may decline to provide this or have a good reason to avoid doing so. • Ask questions that test what is important to them, eg 'Could you offer further discount on proposed pricing and what would need to happen to do this?' • Ask for alternative proposals; it may help develop BATNAs.

Table 15.2 *continued*

Type of e-sourcing approach	Tips for success
e-auction Electronic auction An electronic reverse auction run using an online platform where suppliers bid in real time against each other for the supply of specified goods or services. At the end of the auction, the supplier with the winning bid (often the lowest) wins. Depending upon the rules of the auction they either win the contract or there may be a further negotiation e-auctions are only suitable for certain areas of supply where competition exists	The e-auction is an alternative means of conducting the negotiation event. E-auctions have three phases: initial pre-qualification of and engagement with the suppliers who will participate; the e-auction itself, run at a pre-determined time with all suppliers participating; and the post-auction activities that might include a subsequent negotiation for the supplier or suppliers with the lowest bids. **Using e-auctions to support the negotiation process:** • Avoid using for value-creation negotiations where a long-term relationship is required unless you are certain it won't damage the relationship. • Define precisely what the auction is for and the requirements that need to be satisfied including any terms and conditions. • Keep as many options open as possible. Clearly define the rules of engagement, specifically rules for winning and if there will be further negotiation. • Ensure any lotting strategy (dividing up the area for supply into multiple lots or mini-auctions) will not compromise your desired outcomes, for example, if different suppliers are able to bid for different lots. • Pre-qualify suppliers and sell the benefits in participation, to ensure they fully understand the process and agree to any terms and conditions in advance.

The future of negotiation

It might seem odd to include a section on the future of negotiation. After all, the general principles of negotiation are part of human nature and how we have evolved to exist in this world. Whilst the basic principles of negotiation principles are not set to change, the context within which they will exist within the future, more integrated procurement and the supply chain function is set to change dramatically, demanding some re-framing of how we approach negotiation.

Core to what will happen here is data and the emergence of new intelligent ways of accessing and utilizing vast data sets to drive what we do. Data and our future ability to exploit it is set to become central to the procurement and supply chain functions of the future and offers the potential to create unprecedented competitive advantage driven by four shifts that are nothing short of tectonic compared to what has been before:

- There is likely to be a shift towards the wholesale automation of routine spend, driven by data and the emergence of new supersized 'Amazon. com' type marketplaces for the generic and non-differentiated spend where we can be confident market forces are presenting the best value. Such marketplaces will eliminate much of what is core business in procurement today such as tactical buying, conducting RFPs and everyday negotiating with suppliers for these areas of spend.

- We will see an increased focus on the strategic sourcing areas and suppliers for the unique, complex or areas that hold the potential to bring competitive advantage. Many of these will be with new, supersized suppliers or networks of talent, perhaps not operating under a single roof but connected in real time around the world.

- Procurement and supply chain functions will need to become architects of a new generation of digital systems that will revolutionize how we work and enable us to maximize the potential from the data revolution.

- We will see new levels of responsiveness and connection of suppliers and supply base possibilities to end user or customer needs and aspirations (even those they don't know about yet) driven by an agile data-driven approach operating in real time.

The implications for negotiation into the future suggest we will be doing less 'value claiming' negotiations around the everyday spend, but rather the negotiation that will have the greatest impact will be the 'value creating' negotiations with fewer, larger suppliers, which are of strategic importance or hold the potential to bring competitive advantage to what we do. Future negotiables will be less around price and cost but more around how we can secure advantage our competitors cannot access and protect what we do. Arguably negotiation for the future is more advanced and quite different from that which many in procurement and supply chain know today and will demand a new generation of highly skilled negotiators.

Perfecting the art of negotiation

If you have got this far in this book then well done on having the staying power to work though some complex concepts that bring together theory, experience and wisdom from the many areas that explain negotiation. In order to perfect the art of negotiation we need to combine personality, process and repertoire in a way that makes negotiation as familiar and routine to us as organizing a dinner party or planning a vacation.

Building personal capability

Developing negotiation capability is not a once-only activity but rather part of ongoing personal and organizational development. Unlike some professions where opportunities for development rely on access to a specific environment (eg a helicopter pilot needs a helicopter or at least a simulator to learn), opportunities to develop negotiation skills are all around us. You just need to spot them and seize them and there is always something new to be learnt. Once the fundamentals are understood, training and studying the wealth of published literature out there can help to continue learning, but real capability comes from learning by doing. Every personal interaction is an opportunity to practise something, whether it is the use of questioning or to watch body language. Every significant thing we purchase presents the opportunity to try some negotiation tactics. When we ask the boss for a raise and he promises 'jam tomorrow' then can we change the game to Stag Hunt? I know someone who found himself in this very predicament and proposed an innovative payment-by-results scheme to his employers that subsequently benefitted both parties by doubling pay and profits. Attending a business meeting, whether in person or online, is a great chance to practise mirroring, spot body language and perhaps learn to read upside down.

Building organizational capability

When was the last time someone gave you feedback about your negotiation style? I sometimes ask this question to delegates attending training. The response is usually a thoughtful expression followed by something like 'I don't think I've ever...' or 'I can't remember...' and so on. The problem is that negotiation is more than a personal capability: it is an organizational capability too. If the organization is to achieve the results and outcomes needed from the supply base then the capability of individuals who manage and negotiate with suppliers to deliver these is crucial, yet organizations rarely consider negotiation skills as something to continually invest in developing. While many organizations elect to organize some form of negotiation training for key procurement or supply chain individuals, the expectation is often that once they have done the course they have 'earned their wings' and that is enough. Furthermore, by the very nature of negotiation it is impossible to know how much money is being left on the table and every dollar left is a dollar less on our bottom line.

If a company with sales of US $1bn could improve negotiation capability to get just 1 per cent more from deals with suppliers, the benefit would be around US$3.6m (assuming US$450m third-party spend of which 80 per cent would be negotiated in some way). This increases to US $18m if an additional 5 per cent could be negotiated. Clearly the benefit possible depends upon many factors including how much margin there is within the sector, how much spend can be negotiated and how much work has already been done. However, what is certain is that increased negotiation capability at an organizational level means increased value to the organization.

Building organizational capability in negotiation requires a paradigm shift away from the traditional view of negotiation as a skill people arrive with when they join the company or go on a course to learn. Instead it should be considered an essential enabling skill that will yield significantly higher benefits if those involved are operating at the peak of their performance. People who play competitive team sports don't learn their sport and then stop learning when they join a team to play for real; instead they continue to train and develop, individually and as a team. A soccer team manager will organize strict regimes of training ongoing to get and keep everyone at peak performance. Furthermore, these days teams not only train physically but receive psychological training to equip them with certain techniques to cope with the pressure of the moment when they have to perform to the world. This model used by sports coaches is the same model organizations need to adopt with purchasing teams, and indeed wider stakeholders, to ensure peak negotiation performance. There are several things that can help achieve this:

- *Don't leave it to chance.* Organizational development doesn't happen organically; instead it needs to be organized and structured with assigned roles and responsibilities to make this happen. Many organizations choose to incorporate this within the HR domain; however, in my experience, if this role is detached from the procurement function then traction will be limited. Organizations that do this well have someone dedicated to the role of developing the purchasing function, either part- or full-time, who is actively involved in this day to day.

- *Training*. Negotiation training is essential but it must align with organizational aims and it must equip individuals with practical skills gained by doing it for real. There are many poor negotiation courses out there and there is little point in teaching the team lots of theory if they cannot make the leap to implementing it. Choose training carefully.

- *Observation and feedback*. Every negotiation is an opportunity for someone to sit in and observe in order to learn and to give feedback (providing that being discussed is not too sensitive). They will need to be briefed and perhaps even assigned a passive role.

- *Role-play*. For those in purchasing, some of the best negotiation training comes from learning how salespeople work and what they have to say. In most organizations there are sales teams negotiating with customers and purchasing teams negotiating with suppliers. Despite both having the shared interest in negotiation these functions might as well exist on different planets as, in the case of many companies I have worked with, knowledge sharing between these two functions is typically poor or non-existent. Often teams use entirely different methodologies. It doesn't take much to organize a meeting of minds to swap stories and techniques. Staging negotiation role-plays is also within reach and just takes a simple scenario and a video camera or two or a Zoom call..

- *Show and tell*. As described previously, share the learnings from a specific negotiation by organizing a 'show and tell' session with colleagues and talking them through the story and insights gained.

- *Personal development plans*. Agree individual personal development plans for ongoing learning. This might include self-study reading or e-learning, exposure to specific learning opportunities and so on.

- *Establish a common language, planning process and ways of working*. This is where the Red Sheet methodology supports organization capability by helping create a single, reviewable, approach for negotiation planning.

Negotiation for life

This book began by considering negotiation as a skill for life, something that we have evolved to use to advance ourselves and provide for those close to us who we love and value. It is much more than an event or something people go and do but rather it forms part of our personal and working lives. The line between negotiation, selling and the way individuals interact and influence each other is indistinct.

Suppliers do a remarkably good job at making us believe there is little scope for improving our position but effective negotiation can unlock benefits that don't appear possible. Negotiation capability in purchasing teams is typically not as well developed as our sales counterparts who are better resourced and better supported. This means we need to work harder to secure the results we need.

Every negotiation is different and to succeed we must make personality, process and repertoire work for us within the context of the specific negotiation. How we approach the entire negotiation depends upon what sort of outcome we need from it; is it to claim or create value and do we need a future relationship?

Our personalities can work for or against us in a negotiation so self-awareness and the ability to compensate for, or enhance, specific behaviours and personality traits according to the type of negotiation we are conducting is essential. We must know our opponent and understand everything possible about them and where their interests lie: who they are, their culture, whether they think individualistically or collectively and the nature of their personality. We must understand the true balance of power, distinct from power they might be projecting, and make use of that which gives us leverage, and we must be able to select and play the right game to secure our desired outcomes.

Where or how the negotiation takes place needs consideration and what is expected or likely to create the right conditions changes with culture. Culture may even suggest that our first engagement may need to be entirely about relationship development and rapport building. Intense team preparation is a pre-requisite so everyone is prepared, aligned and clear about the roles they are playing. What signals will the team use to communicate once the event is started?

Once the negotiation is under way we are at 'all at sea', attempting to sail through unfamiliar and complex waters but with a clear end point in sight. We will need to tack and adjust our course along the way as winds blow us in all directions, and reaching our end point, and not a lesser destination, is all down to how well we navigate. If our shore-based preparations were done well then we will know every point along the way we need to reach and every obstacle that could impede us. Our map is the concession strategy that covers all our negotiation requirements as well as defining our MDO, LDO, BATNAs for each.

We should, of course, avoid giving the thumbs-up when negotiation with an Egyptian and pay attention to cultural norms around gestures and body language. We must sit tight, adopt the optimum base position for negotiation and avoid inadvertently touching our mouth or face at the wrong time.

Once we've smoked out their LDO maybe we'll use a decoy, or salami slicing, perhaps rounding things off with a carefully planned Columbo. Maybe we'll even come back and do a KGB on them, but only if we are doing hard value-claiming. If the negotiation is part of a broader relationship then we would, instead, want to find ways and resource to collaborate in pursuit of the bigger prize.

I hope this book equips you with a comprehensive roadmap for highly effective negotiation that will net great benefits. The rest is down to you.

Negotiation is about personality, process and repertoire and there are no limits to how good you can get at it. Getting there depends on how good you want to be and how much effort you put into taking forward what I hope you have learnt from this book.

Watch their eyes. Listen intently, hear what is said and unsaid, choose questions well and know when to close. You won't win them all but embrace the experience no matter what. Be certain of your LDO, always have a BATNA and never settle before the third offer.

APPENDIX

A STEP* by step process for negotiation
*Situation, Target, Event, Post-event

Use of Red Sheet template

This appendix contains the full Red Sheet template reproduced over a series of pages. The Red Sheet supports negotiation planning and execution; it is also designed to be used collaboratively. If you have purchased this book you may make copies and use these templates for your own personal use. These templates may not be copied, distributed or published for any other purpose and may not be modified (other than to complete them) or used commercially.

To use the Red Sheet follow the sequence of steps laid out in this section.

How to obtain Red Sheets and access the online app

Copies of the full Red Sheet in poster form, the Red Sheet Lite and Red Sheet Nano can be obtained from our store at positivepurchasing.com and at redsheetnegotiation.com

Access the Red Sheet digital planning tool (plan, collaborate and build your negotiation plan online) together with the full suite of Red Sheet negotiation planning resources and the digital learning library at redsheetonline. com. Purchase a subscription at redsheetnegotiation.com

Red Sheet is copyright Positive Purchasing Ltd 2006–2020, all rights reserved.

Red Sheet ® is a registered trademark of Positive Purchasing Ltd.

NEGOTIATION PLANNING TOOL

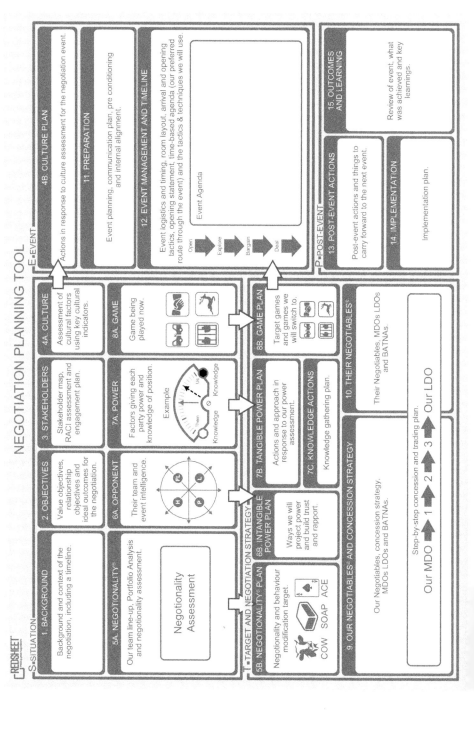

REDSHEET

S - SITUATION

1. BACKGROUND
Background and context of the negotiation, including a timeline.

2. OBJECTIVES
Value objectives, relationship objectives and ideal outcomes for the negotiation.

3. STAKEHOLDERS
Stakeholder map, RACI assessment and engagement plan.

4A. CULTURE
Assessment of cultural factors using key cultural indicators.

4B. CULTURE PLAN
Actions in response to culture assessment for the negotiation event.

11. PREPARATION
Event planning, communication plan, pre conditioning and internal alignment.

5A. NEGOTIONALITY®
Our team line-up, Portfolio Analysis and negotionality assessment.

Negotionality Assessment

6A. OPPONENT
Their team and event intelligence.

7A. POWER
Factors giving each party power and knowledge of position.

Example

Knowledge   Knowledge

8A. GAME
Game being played now.

12. EVENT MANAGEMENT AND TIMELINE
Event logistics and timing, room layout, arrival and opening tactics, opening statement, time-based agenda (our preferred route through the event) and the tactics & techniques we will use.

Event Agenda

Open → Explore → Bargain → Deal

T - TARGET AND NEGOTIATION STRATEGY

5B. NEGOTIONALITY® PLAN
Negotionality and behaviour modification target.

COW   SOAP   ACE

6B. INTANGIBLE POWER PLAN
Ways we will project power and build trust and rapport.

7B. TANGIBLE POWER PLAN
Actions and approach in response to our power assessment.

7C. KNOWLEDGE ACTIONS
Knowledge gathering plan.

8B. GAME PLAN
Target games and games we will switch to.

9. OUR NEGOTIABLES® AND CONCESSION STRATEGY
Our Negotiables, concession strategy, MDOs LDOs and BATNAs.

Step-by-step concession and trading plan.
Our MDO ← 1 2 3 → Our LDO

10. THEIR NEGOTIABLES®
Their Negotiables, MDOs LDOs and BATNAs.

P - POST-EVENT

13. POST-EVENT ACTIONS
Post-event actions and things to carry forward to the next event.

14. IMPLEMENTATION
Implementation plan.

15. OUTCOMES AND LEARNING
Review of event, what was achieved and key learnings.

1. BACKGROUND

Who are we negotiating with?

What are we negotiating?

Why are we negotiating?

Known issues or risks

This negotiation event

☐ One-off   ☐ Part of a journey   ☐ First engagement   ☐ Repeat

How will we negotiate?

☐ F2F   ☐ Email   ☐ Phone   ☐ VTC   ☐ Web   ☐ Other

Date

Location

Key events or milestones

Timeline (enter dates)

Desired outcomes over time

2. OBJECTIVES

Value objective		Relationship objective	
☐	☐	☐	☐
Claim	Create	None	Some/med-term	Close/long-term

Long-term ambition for this relationship

Objectives and ideal outcomes for this negotiation

1.

2.

3.

4.

5.

6.

3. STAKEHOLDERS

Who	R	A	C	I	Action required?

4A. CULTURE

Us

Countries

- [ ] Monochronic / [ ] Polychronic
- [ ] Individualistic / [ ] Collective
- [ ] Short Term / [ ] Long Term
- [ ] Egalitarian / [ ] Authoritative

Notes about assessment of culture

Them

Countries

- [ ] Monochronic / [ ] Polychronic
- [ ] Individualistic / [ ] Collective
- [ ] Short Term / [ ] Long Term
- [ ] Egalitarian / [ ] Authoritative

4B. CULTURE PLAN

Plan to build rapport

What to say

What not to say

How the meeting must run

How to act

Gestures to avoid

5A. NEGOTIONALITY®

Our team

No.	Name	Role in the negotiation
OTL		
OT1		
OT2		
OT3		
OT4		

Portfolio Analysis

Determine the quadrant for the category being negotiated (mark with a 'X')

	Critical	Strategic
	Acquisition	Leverage

Market difficulty (buyer)
Strength in market (seller)

→ Spread/Potential to impact our profit
Spread/Potential to impact the Buyer's profit

Personality assessment for our team. Insert 'H, M or L' (High, Medium or Low) for all except assertiveness and conflict style where the possible responses are given below in brackets

			OT1	OT2	OT3	OT4
C	CONSCIENTIOUS	Hardworking, organized and self-disciplined with attention to detail. High-scoring individuals are typically very reliable and will persevere to get things right				
O	OUTGOING	Socially confident and easily met in conversation, comfortable speaking about their ideas and making new social connections quickly				
W	WILL TO WIN	Competitive and highly ambitious. The need to achieve goals that are important to the individual is more important than personal relationships to the individuals scoring highly here				
S	SOLUTION FOCUSED	Can assimilate new information accurately and rapidly and identify effective solutions. Collects and analyses data and makes data-based decisions				
O	OPEN MINDED	Ability to work well in the absence of structure. Creative, imaginative and often curious. Is comfortable working in vague, fluid or rapidly changing environments				
A	AGREEABLE	Good natured and helpful with a strong desire to place the needs of others in front of one's own needs. Acts selflessly (tries to nurture and meet the emotional needs of others				
P	PERSONAL CALM	Relaxed, at ease and secure. Controls own emotions and individuals scoring high are often patient and even tempered				
A	ASSERTIVENESS	Comfortable in asserting one's own ideas, views or needs and to remain insistent about these in the face of disagreement, criticism or adversely in order to satisfy one's own concerns (High, Low or Choice)				
C	CONFLICT STYLE	The individual's behaviour in conflict situations. Compete (Cpt), Collaborate (Col), Compromise (Cm), Avoid (Av) or Accommodate (Acc)				
E	EMOTIONAL COMPETENCE	The ability to identify, evaluate and manage the emotions of oneself, others and of groups.				

5B. NEGOTIONALITY® PLAN

Negotionality required for this negotiation:

Determine the culture of the other party (section 4A) and the Portfolio Analysis quadrant for this negotiation (section 5A) and tick the relevant box here; then identify the required negotionality from the matrix below. Enter into the 'Required' column on the right of this section and then determine the negotionality behaviour modifiers for each team member.

Critical

Personality		Mono		Poly	
Conscientious		High		High	
Outgoing		High		High	
Will to win		Low		Low	
Solution focused		High		Med	
Open minded		High		High	
Agreeable		High		High	
Personal calm		High		High	
Style	Assertiveness		Off		Off
	Conflict style		Acc		Acc
	Emotional competence		Essential		Essential

Strategic

Personality		Mono		Poly	
Conscientious		High		High	
Outgoing		High		High	
Will to win		Med		Low	
Solution focused		Med		Low	
Open minded		High		High	
Agreeable		High		High	
Personal calm		High		High	
Style	Assertiveness		Moderate		Off
	Conflict style		Col		Col
	Emotional competence		Essential		Essential

Acquisition

Personality		Mono		Poly	
Conscientious		Med		Med	
Outgoing		Low		Med	
Will to win		Med		Low	
Solution focused		High		Med	
Open minded		Med		Med	
Agreeable		Low		High	
Personal calm		High		Med	
Style	Assertiveness		On		Off
	Conflict style		Cpt		Col
	Emotional competence		Desirable		Desirable

Leverage

Personality		Mono		Poly	
Conscientious		Med		Med	
Outgoing		Med		Med	
Will to win		High		Med	
Solution focused		Med		Low	
Open minded		Low		Med	
Agreeable		Low		Med	
Personal calm		Low		Med	
Style	Assertiveness		On		Off
	Conflict style		Cpt		Col
	Emotional competence		Desirable		Essential

Market difficulty (buyer) - Strength in market (seller)

Spread/Potential to impact our profit
Spread/Potential to impact the Buyer's profit

Negotionality Behaviour Modifiers

Enter the required behaviours from the relevant column in the matrix on the left. Then, for each team member, enter the actions to change behaviour and compensate for personality traits:

	Required?	OTL	OT1	OT2	OT3	OT4
C						
O						
W						
S						
O						
A						
P						
A						
C						
E						

(enter 'A' - avoid, 'S' - sustain, 'R' - reinforce)

(enter 'On', 'Off' or 'Moderate')

(enter 'Cpt', 'Col', 'Cmr', 'Av' or 'Acc')

(enter ✓ or ✗)

6A. OPPONENT

Our team
No.	Name	Role in the negotiation
OT1		
OT1		
OT2		
OT3		
OT4		

Their negotiation personality (our best assessment)

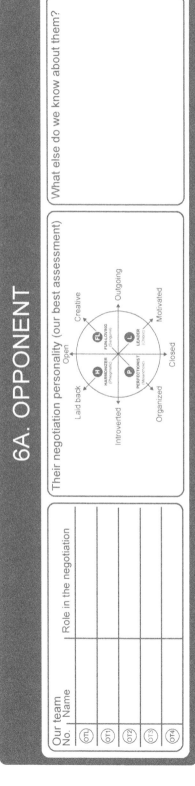

Open — Laid back — Introverted — Creative — Outgoing — Organized — Closed — Motivated

FL FUN-LOVING (Sanguine)
L LEADER (Choleric)
H HARMONIZER (Phlegmatic)
P PERFECTIONIST (Melancholic)

What else do we know about them?

6B. INTANGIBLE POWER PLAN

Plan for 'our style' and demeanour to project power and how we will build trust and rapport.

7A. POWER

For each power gauge, draw a pointer according to the actual balance of power between them and us. If the actual power differs from the projected power, draw a second dotted arrow to indicate the projected power position. Colour in the knowledge indicators if we have, or believe they have, knowledge of the power position. If our knowledge is lacking identify knowledge or data gathering actions in section 7C below.

Example

Dependency

Them   Ø   Us

Knowledge   Ø   Knowledge

Degree of importance. Reliance upon you or the other party and the impact of failing to reach a favourable outcome. Speed and ease with which an alternative could be secured. Rationale:

Market

Them   Ø   Us

Knowledge   Ø   Knowledge

Strength of position in the market place. Changes in market dynamics and availability of alternatives. Rationale:

Relationships

Them   Ø   Us

Knowledge   Ø   Knowledge

Longevity of relationship, extent and influence of relationships and business arrangements between the two parties, degree of stakeholder support across the wider business. Rationale:

Time

Them   Ø   Us

Knowledge   Ø   Knowledge

Time available before a deal needs to be concluded. Rationale:

Future Opportunities

Them   Ø   Us

Knowledge   Ø   Knowledge

Potential for one party to benefit and support the other's future plans. Rationale:

7C. KNOWLEDGE ACTIONS

Actions to improve or prove knowledge

Knowledge or data required	Source	Who	By when

7B. TANGIBLE POWER PLAN

What we will do to utilize or improve our power position

8A. GAME

Determine the game that has been or is currently being played and which game we anticipate they will play at the event.

 Chicken   Trust   Prisoner's Dilemma   Stag Hunt

Current game
The game that has been played previously or the current game being played

| | Us ☐ | Us ☐ | Us ☐ |
| Them ☐ | Them ☐ | Them ☐ | Them ☐ |

The game they will play
The game we anticipate them playing at the event

Them ☐   Them ☐   Them ☐   Them ☐

Rationale for our assumptions:

Chicken
A game in which two players engage that will result in significant loss to both sides unless one of them backs down. It is commonly applied to a game where two motor vehicles are driven towards each other at speed; the first to swerve loses and is humiliated as the 'chicken'.

Stag Hunt
Two individuals go on a hunt. Each of them can choose to hunt a stag or hunt a hare. Each must choose an action without knowing the choice of the other. If either individual hunts stag, they must have the co-operation of the other in order to succeed. Either party can hunt for hare alone, but a hare is worth less than a stag

Trust
One party offers a gift, benefit or concession to the other on the basis that the other party will give back something in return, however the allocation or size of benefit given back in return is determined by the other party. The initial party 'trusts' the other party to make an appropriately sized return gesture.

Prisoner's Dilemma
Two parties make a trade off, the outcome of which is unknown to both parties until the trade off is complete. Parties might have an understanding of what will be traded, however each can chose to honour this or defect. If both co-operate and honour what was agreed both win, however if one defects he wins much whilst the other loses much. If both defect, both lose

---

8B. GAME PLAN

 Chicken   Trust   Prisoner's Dilemma   Stag Hunt

Game 1
☐   ☐   ☐   ☐

How we will play

Trigger to switch game

Game 2
☐   ☐   ☐   ☐

How we will play

Trigger to switch game

Game 3
☐   ☐   ☐   ☐

How we will play

Trigger to switch game

9. Our Negotiables® and Concession Strategy

Our Negotiables® (our requirements)	Pain Factor (High, Medium or Low)	Our M.D.O. (1st position)	2nd Step	3rd Step	4th Step	Our L.D.O. (final position)	ZoMA?
							☐
							☐
							☐
							☐
							☐
							☐
							☐
							☐
							☐
							☐

Big picture – all requirements combined in one

Our BATNAs:

Our strategy for concessions and trading:

10. Their Negotiables®

Their L.D.O. (our best guess)	Their M.D.O. (our best guess)	Their Negotiables® or outcomes (o.ir best guess):

Their BATNA (our best guess)

11. PREPARATION

Event-Planning Actions

What	Who	When

Communications Plan

Message	To	Media/Means

Pre-conditioning message for the other party

Internal elevator speech

12. EVENT MANAGEMENT AND TIMELINE

Opening statement

Arrival and opening tactics

Room layout/Seating plan

Start time:

Event duration:

End time:

Is the end time fixed?

No ☐   Yes ☐

12. EVENT MANAGEMENT AND TIMELINE

Event Agenda & Timing

Time	Negotiation Phase & Topics	Purpose	Process	Pay-Off	Tactics to be used	Trigger

13. POST-EVENT ACTIONS

Post-Event Actions

Who	when

To carry forward to the next negotiation

14 IMPLEMENTATION

Implementation Plan

Activities	Plan (draw in bars and milestones to create a Gantt chart)						
	1	2	3	4	5	6	7

15 OUTCOMES AND LEARNING

What went well?

Even more effective if

What did we achieve?

Key learnings

GLOSSARY

BATNA   Best Alternative To a Negotiated Agreement – alternatives to the deal or specific requirement if an acceptable agreement is not reached.

Body language   A form of human mental and physical non-verbal communication, which consists of body posture, gestures, facial expressions and eye movements. Humans send and interpret such signals almost entirely subconsciously.

Category management   A strategic procurement approach that can add significant value. It works by segmenting third-party spend into discrete categories according to their market-facing nature and developing new sourcing strategies for each that reduce cost and risk and increase value and innovation from the supply chain.

Declarative knowledge   Also called declarative memory, this is 'knowing what' and is memory or knowledge of facts and events, and refers to those memories that can be consciously recalled.

Framework agreement   Another name for master agreement.

LDO   Least Desirable Outcome; the least you are prepared to accept in a negotiation.

Master agreement   A procurement agreement made with a supplier that defines the overarching terms, conditions and arrangements for the relationship that will apply to individual purchase orders between parties. Such an agreement is usually non-contractual and becomes part of a contract when invoked and referenced with a purchase order. However, if the agreement makes commitments, say around volumes, then it can become contractual.

MDO   Most Desirable Outcome; our ideal desired outcome from a negotiation.

NLP   Neuro-linguistic programming (NLP) is an approach for personal development, communication and self-development. The title refers to a stated connection between the neurological processes, language and behavioural patterns that have been learnt through experience and can be organized to achieve specific goals in life.

Plain sailing   An easy uncomplicated course.

Pocket money   UK term for an allowance, regular money given to children.

Procedural skills   Also known as procedural memory, this is 'knowing how' and is the unconscious memory of skills and how to do things, particularly the use of objects or movements of the body, such as playing a guitar or riding a bike.

Supplier relationship management A strategic procurement approach for identifying and managing those suppliers who are important and those who are critical or have the potential to add significant value. The process approach identifies ways to manage these suppliers and develop the right relationship that will secure the, often mutual, value and benefits.

Sustainable purchasing A strategic procurement approach to understand potential risk areas in the supply chain around detrimental human, environmental and good neighbour practices and develop improvement programmes to reduce risk and better manage the suppliers concerned.

ZoMA Zone of Mutual Agreement; the overlap between the lowest you will accept and the most the other party will go to.

REFERENCES AND FURTHER READING

References

Adair, J (1987) *Effective Teambuilding*, Pan Books, London

Allport, GW and Odbert, HS (1936) *Trait-names: A psycho-lexical study*, Psychological Monographs, 47(211)

Anderson, C and Thompson, LL (2004) *Management in Teams and Groups*, Vol 7, Elsevier Science Press, Greenwich, CT

Astley, WG and Zajac, EJ (1991) Intra-organizational power and organizational design: reconciling rational and coalitional models of organization, *Organization Science*, 2(4), pp 399–411

Bazerman, MH and Neale, MA (1992) *Negotiating rationally*, Free Press, New York

Berkowitz, L (1969) The frustration-aggression hypothesis revisited, in: *Roots of Aggression*, ed L Berokowitz, Atherton Press, New York

Blair, SC (2011) *Lessons of the Financial Crisis – The dangers of short-termism*, Harvard Law School Forum on Corporate Governance and Financial Regulation, http://blogs.law.harvard.edu (archived at https://perma.cc/8AAM-YM8K), posted 4 July

Bolton, R and Bolton, D (1984) *Social Style/Management Style*, American Marketing Association, Chicago

Borg, J (2010) *Body Language: 7 easy lessons to master the silent language*, FT Press, Upper Saddle River, New Jersey

Brett, J (2001) *Negotiating Globally*, Jossey-Bass, San Francisco

Camp, JR (2002) *Start With No*, Crown Business, New York

Caniëls, MCJ and Gelderman, CJ (accessed 31 December 2008) *Power and interdependence in Kraljic's purchasing portfolio matrix*, Open University of the Netherlands, competitive paper presented at IPSERA conference 20–24 March 2005, Archamps, France

Carnevale, PJD and Isen, AM (1986) The influence of positive affect and visual access on the discovery of integrative solutions in bilateral negotiation, *Organizational Behavior and Human Decision Processes*, 37, pp 1–13

Chen, Y, Brockner, J and Greenberg, J (2003) When is it 'a pleasure to do business with you'? The effects of relative status, outcome favorability, and procedural fairness, *Organizational Behavior and Human Decision Processes*, 92, pp 1–15

Chomsky, N (1975) *Reflections on Language*, Pantheon, New York

Cialdini, RB (2001) *Influence: Science and practice* (4th edn), Allyn and Bacon, Boston, MA

Clark, JDR (2006a) *The Magic of Influence*, CD Book, Club Rhino Inc

Clark, JDR (2006b) *The Magic of Colours*, CD Book, Club Rhino Inc

Cohen, R (1997) *Negotiating Across Cultures: International communication in an interdependent world* (rev edn), United States Institute of Peace, Washington, DC

Conroy, DE, Willow, JP and Metzler, JN (2002) Multidimensional fear of failure measurement: The performance failure appraisal inventory, *Journal of Applied Sport Psychology*, 14(2), pp 76–90

Costa, PT Jr and McCrae, RR (1992) Revised NEO Personality Inventory (NEO-PI-R) and NEO Five-Factor Inventory (NEO-FFI) manual, Psychological Assessment Resources, Odessa, FL

Covey, SR (2004) *7 Habits of Highly Effective People*, Simon and Schuster, London

Covic, B (2004) *Everything's Negotiable*, Pendulum Publishing, Incline Village, NV

Deutsch, F and Madle, R (1975) Empathy: Historic and current conceptualizations, measurement, and a cognitive theoretical perspective, *Human Development*, 18, pp 267–87

Dichter, E (1964) *The Handbook of Consumer Motivations*, McGraw-Hill, New York

Dilts, RB and DeLozier, JA (2000) *Encyclopedia of Systemic Neuro-Linguistic Programming and NLP New Coding*, NLP University Press, Scotts Valley, CA

Donaldson, MC (2007) *Negotiating for Dummies*, Wiley Publishing Inc, Indianapolis, IN

Dorland's Illustrated Medical Dictionary (currently in its 32nd edition)

Ellis, B and Raymond, MA (1993) Sales Force Quality: A framework for improvement, *Journal of Business and Industrial Marketing*, 8(3)

Eysenck, HJ (1992) Four ways five factors are not basic, *Personality and Individual Differences*, 13, pp 667–73

Fisher, R and Ury, W (1991) *Getting to Yes: Negotiating agreement without giving in*, Houghton Mifflin, Boston, MA

Fisher, R and Ury, W (2012) *Getting to Yes* (Kindle edn), Cornerstone Digital

Frank, RH (1988) *Passions within Reason*, WW Norton, New York

Franken, RE and Brown, DJ (1995) The Need to Win is Not Adaptive: The need to win, coping strategies and self-esteem, University of Calgary paper published by Elsevier Science Press, Greenwich, CT

French, JRP, Raven, B (1959) The bases of social power, in: *Group Dynamics*, eds D Cartwright and A Zander, Harper and Row, New York

Freud, S (various) *The Standard Edition of the Complete Psychological Works of Sigmund Freud*, translated from the German under the General Editorship of James Strachey, in collaboration with Anna Freud, assisted by Alix Strachey and Alan Tyson, 24 volumes, Vintage, 1999

Fridlund, AJ (1994) *Human Facial Expression: An evolutionary view*, Academic Press, San Diego, CA

Gates, S (2011) *The Negotiation Book*, Wiley, London

Gelderman, CJ (2000) *Rethinking Kraljic – Towards a purchasing portfolio model, based on mutual buyer–supplier dependence*, Open University of the Netherlands, Rotterdam

Gelderman, CJ and Weele, AJV (2005) *Purchasing Portfolio Usage and Purchasing Sophistication*, Open University of the Netherlands, Rotterdam

Gelfand, MJ and Brette, JM (2004) *The Handbook of Negotiation and Culture*, Stanford University Press, CA

Goleman, D (1996) *Emotional Intelligence*, Bloomsbury Publishing, London

Goodman, B (2007) The Art of Negotiation, *Psychology Today*, updated 8 February, 2012

Gorelick, C (1993) *Performance through Learning: Knowledge management in practice*, Elsevier Butterworth-Heinemann, Oxford

Graham, JL, and Lam, NM (2003) The Chinese Negotiation, *Harvard Business Review*, October 2003, downloaded from www.hbr.org (archived at https://perma.cc/7ESY-SUTM) (product 5100)

Gray, R (2008) Why rubbing it better makes the pain go away, *The Telegraph* online, 10 September

Greene, R (2002) *48 Laws of Power*, Profile Books, London

Hagenmayer, SJ (1995) Albert W Tucker, 89, Famed Mathematician, *The Philadelphia Inquirer*, 2 February, p B7

Hall, ET (1983) *The Dance of Life: The other dimension of time*, Anchor Press/ Doubleday, Garden City, NY

Hall, ET (1990a) *The Silent Language*, Anchor Books, New York

Hall, ET (1990b) *The Hidden Dimension*, Anchor Books, New York

Hansen, J (2010) You don't get what you deserve, you get what you negotiate! *Procurement Insights*, blog article, August http://procureinsights.wordpress.com (archived at https://perma.cc/9NWR-DRFK)

Harvard Business School (2003) *Negotiation*, Harvard Business School Press, Boston, MA

Hazeldine, S (2011) *Bare Knuckle Negotiating*, Bookshaker, Great Yarmouth, UK

Hindle, T (1998) *Negotiating Skills*, Dorling Kindersley, London

Hofstede, G (1980) *Culture's Consequences*, Sage, Beverly Hills, CA

Hofstede, G, Hofstede, GJ and Minkov, M (2010) *Cultures and Organizations: Software of the mind*, McGraw-Hill, Beverly Hills, CA

House, RJ *et al* (2004) *Culture, Leadership and Organizations: The GLOBE study of 62 societies*, Sage, Beverly Hills, CA

Jung, CG ([1921] 1971) *Psychological Types*, Collected Works, 6, Princeton, NJ, Princeton University Press, Princeton, NJ

Kagan, J (1998) *Galen's Prophecy: Temperament in human nature*, Basic Books, New York

Karras, Dr CL (1996) *In Business as in Life – You don't get what you deserve, you get what you negotiate*, Stanford Street Press, Stanford, CA

Karrass, Dr CL (2003) *Effective Negotiating*, Karrass Ltd, Beverly Hills, CA

Kaufmann-Scarborough, C and Jay, DL (1999) The Polychronic Attitude Index: Refinement and preliminary consumer marketplace behavior applications, *Marketing Theory and Applications*, American Marketing Association Winter Educators, 10, pp 151–57

Kennedy, G (1998) *The New Negotiating Edge*, Nicholas Brealey Publishing, London

Knight, S (2009) *NLP at Work*, Nicholas Brealey Publishing, Boston, MA

Knutson, B (1996) Facial expressions of emotion influence interpersonal trait inferences, *Journal of Nonverbal Behavior*, 20, pp 165–82

Kolb, DA and Fry, R (1975) Toward an applied theory of experiential learning, in: *Theory of Group Processes*, ed C Cooper, John Wiley and Sons, New York

Kolb, DM and Williams, J (2001) Breakthrough bargaining, *Harvard Business Review*, OnPoint enhanced edn, Harvard Business School Publishing, Boston

Kraljic, P (1983) Purchasing must become supply management, *Harvard Business Review*, 61(5) pp 109–117

Kramer, RM and Tyler, TR (1996) *Trust in Organizations*, Sage, Beverly Hills, CA

Lewicki, RJ, Minton, J and Saunders, D (1999) *Zone of Potential Agreement in Negotiation*, 3rd edn, Irwin/McGraw-Hill, Burr Ridge, IL

Lewis, E St E (1903) Catch-Line and Argument, *The Book-Keeper*, 15, February, p 124

Littauer, F (1992) *Personality Plus*, Flemming H Revell/Baker Publishing Group, Michigan

Littauer, F and Sweet, R (2011) *Personality Plus at Work* (e-book edn), Revell, Grand Rapids, MI

Luecke, R (2003) *Negotiation*, Harvard Business School, Boston, MA

McBane, D (1995) Empathy and the salesperson: A multidimensional perspective, *Psychological Marketing*, 12(4), pp 349–70

McCrae, RR and Costa, PT (1997) Personality trait structure as a human universal, *American Psychologist*, 52, pp 509–516

McCain, RA (2004) *Game Theory – A non-technical introduction to the analysis of strategy*, Thomson South-Western, Mason, OH

McKnight, DH, Cummings, LL and Chervany, NL (1995) *Trust Formation in New Organizational Relationships*, University of Minnesota

McKnight, DH, Cummings, LL and Chervany, NL (1998) Initial trust formation in new organizational relationships, *Academy of Management Review*, University of Minnesota, Minneapolis, MN, 23(3), pp 473–90

Malim, T and Birch, A (1998) *Introductory Psychology*, Macmillan, London

Mannix, EA (1993) The influence of power, distribution norms and task meeting structure on resource allocation in small group negotiation, *International Journal of Conflict Management*, 4, pp 5–23

Marfleet, B and Gregory, J (2000) The operational cost of John F Kennedy during the Cuban Missile Crisis: A comparison of public and private rhetoric, *Political Psychology*, 21(3), pp 545–58

Maslow, AH (1943) A theory of human motivation, *Psychological Review*, 50(4), pp 370–96

Mayer, J and Salovey, P (1997) What is emotional intelligence?, in: *Emotional Development and Emotional Intelligence*, eds P Salovey and DJ Sluyter, Basic Books, New York

Mead, GH (1934) *Mind, Self and Society*, University of Chicago Press, Chicago

Mick, DG, DeMoss, M and Faber, RJ (1992) A projective study of motivation and meanings of self-gifts: implications for retail management, *Journal of Retailing*, 68(2), pp 122–44

Miller, RB and Williams, GA (2004) *5 Paths to Persuasion: The art of selling your message*, Kogan Page, London

Miller, SM, Brody, DS and Summerton, J (1988) Styles of coping with threat: implications for health, *Journal of Personality and Social Psychology*, 54(1), pp 142–48

Moulden, D (2007) *NLP Business Masterclass*, Prentice Hall, London

Navarro, J with Karlins, M (2008) *What Every Body Is Saying*, HarperCollins, New York

O'Brien, J (2018) *Category Management in Purchasing*, 24th edn, Kogan Page, London

O'Brien, J (2017), *Supplier Relationship Management*, 2nd edn, Kogan Page, London

O'Hara, MW, Schlechte, JA, Lewis, DA and Varner, MW (1991) Controlled prospective study of postpartum mood disorders: psychological, environmental, and hormonal variables, *Journal of Abnormal Psychology*, 100, pp 63–73

Oechsli, M (1993) Making success a habit, *Sales and Marketing Management*, 145(4), pp 24–26

Pease, A and Pease, B (2004) *The Definitive Book Of Body Language*, Orion Books, London

Pease, A and Garner, A (1992) *Talk Language*, Simon and Schuster, London

Potter, JP (2008) *The Expert Negotiator*, John Potter

Potter, JP *et al* (1997) *Negotiating Tactics*, Wyvern Crest Publications, Cambridge, UK

Randall, G (1993) *Principles of Marketing*, Routledge, London

Red Sheet Negotiation Tool (2013), Positive Purchasing Ltd, Portsmouth, UK

Saarni, C (1999) *The Development of Emotional Competence*, The Guilford Press, New York

Saxe, R and Weitz, BA (1982) A measure of the customer orientation of salespeople, *Journal of Marketing Research*, 19(3), August, pp 343–51

Schwartz, SH (1994) Beyond individualism/collectivism – new cultural dimensions of values, in: *Individualism and Collectivism: Theory, method and applications*, eds U Kim, HC Triandis, C Kagitcibasi, SC Choi and G Yoon, Thousand Oaks, CA

Schwartz, SH, Siegel, JI and Licht, AN (2012) Egalitarianism, cultural distance and FDI: a new approach, *Organization Science*, http://ssrn.com/abstract=957306

(archived at https://perma.cc/SF2T-VNLU) or http://dx.doi.org/10.2139/ssrn.957306 (archived at https://perma.cc/A7GD-AG6H)

Skyrms (2004) *The Stag Hunt and the Evolution of Social Structure*, Cambridge University Press, Cambridge, UK

Slocombe, TE and Bluedorn, AC (1997) Organizational behavior implications of the congruence between preferred polychronicity and experienced work-unit polychronicity, *Journal of Organizational Behavior*, 18

Spiro, R, Stanton, W and Rich, G W (2007) *Management of a Sales Force*, 12th edn, Irwin/McGraw-Hill, New York

Spiro, RL and Weitz, BA (1990) Adaptive selling: conceptualization, measurement, and nomological validity, *Journal of Marketing Research*, 27 (February), pp 61–69

Stiff, JB, Dillard, JP, Somera, L, Kim, H and Sleight, C (1988) Empathy communication and prosocial behavior, *Communication Mongraphs*, 55, pp 198–213

Sullivan, HS (1953) *The Interpersonal Theory of Psychiatry*, Norton, New York

Sun, Tzu (1981) *The Art of War*, Hodder and Stoughton, London

Sweet, C (2010) *Change your life with CBT*, Pearson, Harlow, UK

Szalay, LB (1981) Intercultural communication: a process model, *International Journal of Intercultural Relations*, 5, pp 133–46

Thompson, JB (1990) *Critical Social Theory in the Era of Mass Communication*, Stanford University Press, CA

Treitel, GH (2007) *The Law of Contract*, 10th edn, p 8, Sweet & Maxwell, London

Tyler, T and Degoey, P (1996) Collective restraint in social dilemmas: procedural justice and social identification effects on support for authorities, *Journal of Personality and Social Psychology*, 69, pp 482–97

Ury, W (1991) *Getting Past No*, Business Books, London

Vaknin, S (2010) *The Big Book of NLP Expanded*, Inner Patch Publishing, USA

Van den Bos, K, Wilke, HAM and Lind, EA (1998) When do we need procedural fairness? The role of trust in authority, *Journal of Personality and Social Psychology*, 75, pp 1449–58

Vermeiren, J and Verdonck, B (2011) *How to REALLY Use LinkedIn*, 2nd edn, www.how-to-really-use-linkedin.com (archived at https://perma.cc/VA69-Q5WF)

Von Bergen, CW and Shealy, RE (1982) How's your empathy?, *Training and Development Journal*, 36, pp 22–28

Von Neumann, J and Morgenstern, O (1944) *Theory of Games and Economic Behaviour*, Princeton University Press, Princeton, NJ

Ward, Alex (2012) What we say and what we really mean, *Mail Online*, 17 July, article 2174269

Webster Universal Dictionary (1968) Harver Publishing Ltd, New York

Weitz, BA, Sujan, H and Sujan, M (1986) Knowledge motivation and adaptive behavior: a framework for improving selling effectiveness, *Journal of Marketing*, 45 (Winter), pp 85–103

Wells, LE and Sweeney, PD (1986) A test of three models of bias in self-assessment, *Social Psychology Quarterly*, 49(1), pp 1–10

Wolfe, R and McGinn, KL (2005) Perceived, relative power and its influence on negotiations, *Group Decision and Negotiation*, 14(1) January, pp 3–20

Wolff, SB (2005) *Emotional Competence Inventory (ECI)*, Hay Group, McClelland Center for Research and Innovation

World Values Survey (current), www.worldvaluessurvey.org (archived at https://perma.cc/L6YX-ZX6B)

Zartman, IW and Berman, MR (1982) *Practical Negotiator*, Yale University Press, New Haven, CT

Recommended further reading

Of all the books I could recommend here, a handful stick out as particularly relevant, well written and practical for those learning to negotiate.

On negotiation

There are many in this space, few are any good. *Getting to Yes* by Fisher and Ury is a must have. Harvard Business School publishes many good books and leading-edge articles in this field. *Negotiation* compiled by Michael Watkins for Harvard is worth a read and Chester Karrass who is one of the founders of theory in this space has many publications worth reading including *In Business As In Life – You Don't Get What You Deserve, You Get What You Negotiate*.

On personality

Personality Plus by Florence Littauer is a powerful book based around the four temperaments that helps to understand both self and others.

For body language

The various books by Allan Pease are recommended. *The Definitive Book of Body Language* by Allan and Barbara Pease is highly recommended. So too is to *What Every Body is Saying* by ex-FBI agent Joe Navarro.

On NLP

NLP at work by Sue Knight provides practical guidance for effective interaction and seems to give the most useful summary of how this complex topic can help in everyday situations. Also consider *The Big Book of NLP Expanded* by Shlomo Vaknin

On culture

The Handbook of Negotiation and Culture by Gelfand and Brette. Any of the works by Geert Hofstede including *Cultures and Organizations*.

On strategic procurement

Category Management in Purchasing and *Supplier Relationship Management*, my other books, provide practical guidance on using a range of strategic procurement tools that can help prepare for a negotiation.

Websites

General

http://en.wikipedia.org (archived at https://perma.cc/J47B-Z6F9)

http://www.britannica.com (archived at https://perma.cc/YEG5-QJYM)

http://www.inhouselawyer.co.uk (archived at https://perma.cc/54NC-J55A)

http://www.charlesrussell.co.uk (archived at https://perma.cc/3KKZ-MC32)

http://www.defense.gov/transcripts/transcript.aspx?transcriptid=2636 (archived at https://perma.cc/T5S6-U6XR)

http://judgmental.org.uk/judgments/EWHC-Ch/2009/[2009]_EWHC_2538_(Ch).html (archived at https://perma.cc/QVN2-4WJ5) – Jirehouse Capital and Ors v Beller and Anor (2009)

Culture

http://www.kwintessential.co.uk (archived at https://perma.cc/SHQ8-PTY6) – online guides for cultural etiquette

http://www.clearlycultural.com (archived at https://perma.cc/EA2V-KCSE) – cultural guides

http://www.geerthofstede.nl (archived at https://perma.cc/6S4J-FTYK) – the site of Geert Hofstede

http://business.uni.edu/buscomm (archived at https://perma.cc/Z9AY-ULYG) – University of Iowa

http://chineseculture.about.com (archived at https://perma.cc/FS3A-9J78) – Chinese culture

Psychology

http://www.psychologytoday.com (archived at https://perma.cc/JYG3-CUXE)

http://eqi.org (archived at https://perma.cc/PY7T-EX73) – a site containing a wealth of emotional intelligence-related articles and information

www.myskillsprofile.com (archived at https://perma.cc/YZX7-MA9W) – online emotional intelligence assessment

www.kilmanndiagnostics.com (archived at https://perma.cc/9YSQ-2L9G) – website of Thomas–Kilmann Conflict Style Instrument

INDEX

Printed in the USA
CPSIA information can be obtained
at www.ICGtesting.com
JSHW041914160424
61276JS00009B/274

9 781789 662258